HONG KONG TAXATION

AUSTRALIA
The Law Book Company Ltd.
Sydney: Melbourne: Brisbane

CANADA AND U.S.A.
The Carswell Company Ltd.
Agincourt, Ontario

INDIA
N. M. Tripathi Private Ltd.
Bombay
and
Eastern Law House Private Ltd.
Calcutta
M.P.P. House
Bangalore

ISRAEL
Steimatzky's Agency Ltd.
Jerusalem: Tel Aviv: Haifa

NEW ZEALAND
Sweet & Maxwell (N. Z.) Ltd.
Auckland

PAKISTAN
Pakistan Law House
Karachi

Hong Kong Taxation:
Law and Practice

David Flux

THE CHINESE UNIVERSITY PRESS
Hong Kong

SWEET & MAXWELL
LONDON
1982

ISBN: 0-421-30910-5, D2-091-LL

Printing by Ngai Kwong Printing Co., Ltd., Hong Kong

TABLE OF CONTENTS

PREFACE

This book has been prepared in a style which it is hoped all will find easy to understand and, because it is liberally illustrated with practical examples and cross-referred to relevant tax cases both in Hong Kong and elsewhere, should appeal not only to students of the basic principles of Hong Kong taxation but also to businessmen and practicing tax advisors who require a comprehensive but practical guide to Hong Kong taxation and who are also faced with more complex problems. To complete its all round usefulness, the text is also cross referred to the more important Board of Review decisions and to the relevant sections of the Inland Revenue Ordinance.

Major changes took place in 1974 in the law governing the basis of assessment of Profits Tax and this book deals only with the law as it stands following those changes and no detailed consideration has been given to the old law or the transitional provisions other than to briefly refer to them where this clarifies the understanding of the present law.

Inevitably, tax law contains areas of contention and opinion and in relevant places I have expressed my personal opinion on doubtful issues. This is clear from the context but the reader should accept that these are indeed personal opinions and not categorical statements of the law.

Finally, I would like to give credit to my late partner in Hong Kong, now sadly deceased, Brian Osborne, for his assistance in reading and commenting upon the manuscript.

David Flux

May 1981, Hong Kong

Since writing the first edition, I have been most gratified to receive so many kind and constructive comments and this revised edition incorporates most if not all of those constructive suggestions plus all of the change in the law and practice in Hong Kong up to date as well as further ideas that have occurred to me in the past year.

David Flux

May 1982, Hong Kong

ABBREVIATIONS

The following abbreviations have been used in the text:—

AITR   Australian Income Tax Reports

ATC   Annotated Tax Cases (UK)

ATD   Australian Tax Decisions

CIR   Commissioner of Inland Revenue

FC of T Federal Commissioner of Taxation (Australia)

HKTC   Hong Kong Tax Cases

IRD   Inland Revenue Department

IRO   Inland Revenue Ordinance

IRR   Inland Revenue Rules

NZ   New Zealand

SATC   South African Tax Cases

Sec(s) Section(s) (of the IRO unless otherwise specified)

TC   U.K. Tax Cases

WDV   Written Down Value

y/e   Year Ended

TABLE OF CASES

The following cases are referred to in the text:

PUBLISHED BOARD OF REVIEW DECISIONS

The following cases are referred to in the text:

INLAND REVENUE ORDINANCE

Reference to the relevant Sections of the IRO and the IRR will be found as follows:

Chapter 1
GENERAL SCHEME OF TAXATION IN HONG KONG

1. Law and Policy

The law governing the imposition of taxation in Hong Kong is contained in the Inland Revenue Ordinance (IRO) and its subsidiary legislation, the Inland Revenue Rules (IRR). The IRO which was enacted in 1947 to bring income taxes to Hong Kong is based on the U.K. Commonwealth "tax package". Precisely the same package was the basis of the taxation systems in many of the U.K. Commonwealth countries although those countries have now modified their package to such an extent that it is no longer recognisable in its original form.

Consequently the IRO contains similar, and in some cases, identical wording to taxation legislation currently in use in the U.K. and in Australia and South Africa, which is why interpretation of the IRO relies to some extent upon legal decisions in those countries. The IRO has in fact been changed very little from its original form and the reasons for this can be easily understood by researching into the policies of successive Government administrations as regards taxation of income in Hong Kong. The following terms of reference given to the Third Inland Revenue Ordinance Review Committee in 1976 speak for themselves:—

> "Having regard to the economic circumstances of Hong Kong which dictate —
> (a) a comparatively low level of direct taxation;
> (b) that the system at given tax rates should be as productive of revenue as possible; and
> (c) that the relevant legislation should be simple and inexpensive to administer;
> To consider the present system of taxation of profits and other forms of income contained in the Inland Revenue Ordinance ...."

All laws including amendments to the IRO and IRR are enacted by the Legislative Council and the practice is increasing, in respect of important proposed changes, to give advanced notice and invite comments and representations from the public and furthermore to have some regard to legitimate and reasoned views in formulating the final form of the changes. It is important to appreciate that, despite their collective title, the Inland Revenue Rules are not unilateral rules formulated by the Inland Revenue Department but are effectively additional sections to the IRO which are subject to exactly the same legislative process as the IRO itself. Nevertheless the Inland Revenue Department (IRD) has a number of extra-statutory practices and concessions both published and unpublished and these are mentioned in their appropriate context.

As indicated, the IRO is from time to time subjected to review by a committee appointed for the purpose whose brief is to report to the Governor on various specific and general aspects of the IRO and to recommend appropriate changes. This is not a standing committee but is separately constituted on each occasion. The first such committee, the Inland Revenue Ordinance Committee reported in 1954, the Second Inland Revenue Ordinance Review Committee reported in 1967 and also in 1968 and the Third Inland Revenue Ordinance Review Committee reported in 1976. The Committee solicits comment and representations from the public including in particular the professional bodies, major companies and trade associations. In addition, representations are invited from individuals. The Committee's report and recommendations are published and the recommendations considered by a Government committee for rejection or ultimate incorporation into the IRO. Most of the Third Inland Revenue Ordinance Review Committee's recommendations have been rejected although one has been partially adopted and certain others are still under consideration at the time of writing. These are mentioned in the appropriate context.

2. The Taxes in General

There is no total income tax in Hong Kong which has four separate and distinct taxes on income:

Property Tax	Interest Tax
Salaries Tax	Profits Tax

The IRO and IRR cover the whole of the law for the four taxes which has separate parts for each of the taxes and parts common to all of the taxes such as the law relating to assessment, collection and administration.

Certain fundamental principles are common to all four taxes and an understanding of these assists greatly in understanding the taxes, their context and relationship with each other. These are:–

(1)   There is no total income concept, each of the taxes is assessed without regard for what the individual's or company's income may be under other headings. There are however exceptions to this rule in that an individual may, in appropriate circumstances, elect for Personal Assessment (see Chapter 7) which has the effect of bringing all of his sources of

income into a single assessment for which he must make a separate total income return. In the case of companies there is an effective merging of most heads of taxation into a single assessment.

Accordingly, unless an individual elects for Personal Assessment, he does not make a return of total income, he makes separate returns and declarations for each of the four taxes under which he has sources of income. His total sources of income are therefore not immediately brought to the attention of any single officer of the Inland Revenue Department. That Department therefore has considerable practical difficulties in checking returns, particularly where checking into the adequacy and accuracy of returns is required by the Investigation Unit although the department does maintain a central index of files so that assessors have access to files other than the one under immediate examination. Furthermore, the existence of separate rates of tax and deductions for each of the taxes gives rise to some interesting anomalies, particularly in respect of individuals in receipt of income subject to Salaries Tax where there is an automatic right to personal allowances and progressive rates of tax and income subject to Profits Tax where there is no such automatic right.

These anomalies are illustrated as follows:—

Example 1

		Taxpayer A	Taxpayer B
1)	Salary from Employment	$ 55,000	
2)	Profits from business	145,000	$200,000
		$200,000	$200,000
	Profits Tax (A) $145,000 @ 15%	$ 21,750	
	Profits Tax (B) $200,000 @ 15%		$ 30,000
	Salaries Tax (A) $55,000		
	Allowances $56,000	Nil	
		$ 21,750	$ 30,000

Notes

(a) Despite having the same total income B pays 38% more tax than A. If B claims allowances by way of Personal Assessment (see Chapter 7) such are the rates of progressive tax that his liability would be $31,000 (assuming married allowance only) and the election would not therefore apply.

(b) The anomaly arises because income subject to Salaries Tax attracts personal allowances whatever the individual's other sources of income whereas to obtain those allowances B must elect Personal Assessment and thereby bring in all his sources of income.

(c) For rates of tax and allowances, see relevant chapters.

Example 2

		Taxpayer A	Taxpayer B
1) Salary from Employment		$ 95,000	–
2) Interest income		20,000	$ 20,000
3) Profits from Business		–	95,000
		$115,000	$115,000

Salaries Tax (A)	$95,000			
Allowance (married)	56,000			
Tax on	$39,000	=	$4,800	
Interest Tax (A) and (B)	20,000 @ 10%	=	2,000	2,000
Profits Tax (B)	95,000 @ 15%	=		14,250
			$6,800	$16,250

If B elects Personal Assessment: –

Total income	$115,000		
Allowance (married)	56,000		
	$ 59,000	=	$ 9,750

Notes

(a) Although B can reduce his liability by electing Personal Assessment he still pays more than 43% more tax than A on the same total income.

(b) The reason for the anomaly is that B must elect Personal Assessment to obtain the personal allowance which A obtains automatically in his Salaries Tax Assessment and by so doing he subjects his interest income to a marginal progressive rate of 25% whereas A is satisfied with Interest Tax at 10%.

(c) For rates of tax and allowances see relevant chapters.

For these and other reasons, the Third Inland Revenue Ordinance Review Committee recommended that total income returns should be introduced for all taxpayers and total income assessments should be mandatory. This would involve radical changes and is still under consideration by the Government.

(2)   Except in the limited circumstances already illustrated i.e. Salaries Tax and Personal Assessment, tax is levied at a fixed standard rate and is not progressive.

(3)   The extent of exposure to tax is not governed by residence status, either of individuals or companies, which is a familiar fundamental principle of many other tax administrations. Residence status has a limited application in certain specific instances which are mentioned in their context. Otherwise, the extent of liability under each of the taxes is limited to income which "arises in or is derived from" Hong Kong and

certain other sources which are deemed by the IRO to arise in Hong Kong. Such income is charged on residents and non residents alike. Accordingly, determination of source of income is probably the single most important factor in determining liability to tax in Hong Kong.

(4)   There is no provision in the IRO which brings into tax all items of income not specifically charged elsewhere in the IRO. The logical feature of the four tax system is that any item of income which does not fall within one of the charging heads is not subject to tax at all. Furthermore, certain other sources of income are specifically exempted from tax in circumstances where they would otherwise fall under one of the heads. The most important is the exemption from Profits Tax of dividends received from Hong Kong companies. (Sec. 26(a))

(5)   There is no tax on capital gains. Profits Tax may be charged on the profits of speculative transactions if they can be shown to constitute an adventure in the nature of trade. (See Chapter 5.)

(6)   Because of the necessity to satisfy the requirement of simplicity in administration there is very little strict anti-avoidance legislation. Section 61 of the IRO provides that transactions which can be regarded as artificial or fictitious are to be disregarded for tax purposes. The apparently wide nature of this provision has however been limited by legal interpretation. For an examination of the principles involved see Kum Hing Land Investment Co., Ltd. v CIR (HKTC 301), CIR v Rico Internationale Ltd. (HKTC 246) and CIR v Douglas Henry Howe (HKTC 936).

(7)   The income of a wife who is not living apart from her husband is regarded as her husband's income for the purposes of Salaries Tax, Profits Tax and Personal Assessment. Accordingly the husband must pay the tax even though he may not receive the income. There are however provisions whereby, in default of payment by a husband, that part of the tax bill which relates to a wife's earnings chargeable to Salaries Tax on her husband or which relates to the wife's income included in an assessment on her husband under Personal Assessment, may be collected from her. (Sec. 75A)

(8)   Except for Interest Tax (see Chapter 4), there are no withholding taxes either on dividends or on any other source of income, whether paid to residents or non residents. There are instances however where an assessment on a non resident may be made on or through an agent in Hong Kong who is entitled to retain the tax out of payments due to the non resident. (See Chapter 5.)

Brief summaries of the taxes follow and a summary chart appears at the end of the chapter.

3.   Year of Assessment (Sec. 2)

Every assessment and deduction is related to a year of assessment. The year of assessment is the year to 31st March, e.g. the year ended 31st March 1978 is known as the year of assessment 1977/78. Each tax has its own rules as to what income and deductions form the basis for a given year of assessment.

4.   Property Tax (Part II IRO)

Property Tax is a tax based on a notional income. It is levied at the standard rate of 15% on the owner of land and/or buildings on the net assessable value of land and/or buildings situated in Hong Kong other than certain properties in the New Territories.

The charge is levied for a year of assessment throughout which the property is owned or proportionately where it is only owned for part of the year. The assessable value is broadly equivalent to the estimated annual rental obtainable and a statutory deduction of 20% for repairs and outgoings is made in arriving at net assessable value. Accordingly an individual owning and leasing out a property pays a fixed Property Tax and his rental receipts are not taxed.

Example 3

Mr. B. Wong owns a block of 6 flats from which he receives total annual rents of $216,000. At the last valuation the assessable value of each flat was valued at $30,000.

1)	Assessable Value of Block 6 x $30,000	=	$180,000
	Less 20%		36,000
2)	Net Assessable Value		$144,000
	Annual Property Tax $144,000 @ 15%		$ 21,600

Notes
(a)   He pays tax of $21,600 per annum and his rents of $216,000 and actual outgoings are ignored.
(b)   In practice a separate assessment is raised on each rateable unit and therefore each flat would be assessed separately.

Exemptions are available for properties owned and occupied by individuals for residential purposes and to companies owning and using the property in their business when any rents are brought into their Profits Tax return instead. (See Chapter 5.)

The person who pays the rates on the property is responsible for the payment of Property Tax. If that person is not the owner there is a right of recovery from the owner. If no rates are levied, the owner is responsible for payment of Property Tax. (See Chapter 2.)

5. Salaries Tax (Part III IRO)

Salaries Tax is imposed on income arising in or derived from Hong Kong from any office or employment of profit and pensions. The income arises in or derives from Hong Kong if the fundamental source of the employment is in Hong Kong, in which case remuneration for services both rendered in and outside Hong Kong is liable. If the source of the employment is outside Hong Kong, only remuneration for services rendered in Hong Kong is liable. If however a person derives income from an employment and renders services during a visit or visits to Hong Kong which do not exceed in total 60 days during the year of assessment, that income will be exempt whether or not the employment has a source in Hong Kong.

Income from any office or employment includes wages, salary, leave pay, fee, commission, bonus, gratuity, perquisite and allowances whether derived from the employer or others. Certain types of remuneration and cash benefits are exempt from the charge while certain other benefits are specifically taxable. In general however, benefits in kind are not taxable unless convertible into cash or representing an employee's personal liability assumed by the employer.

Tax is levied for a year of assessment on income earned in the year although it cannot be assessed until it is actually received. The earnings accruing to a person and his wife living with him less expenses wholly, exclusively and necessarily incurred in the production of assessable income, depreciation allowances on plant and machinery used for the production of assessable income and allowable charitable donations are charged to tax. The tax charged is the lower of 15% of net chargeable income or net chargeable income less personal allowances charged at progressive rates (see pages 20-21).

There are no provisions for deduction at source and tax is paid direct by the taxpayer to the Inland Revenue Department on or before the due date specified on the notice of assessment. The charging of Salaries Tax incorporates a system of prepaid tax known as Provisional Salaries Tax. The provisional assessment is an estimate, normally based on the previous year's agreed assessment and is payable in two instalments, one of 75% in the final quarter of the year of assessment and the remaining 25% three months later, just after the end of the year of assessment. When the actual income for the year of assessment is known, an assessment is issued based on the actual income and crediting the Provisional Salaries Tax already paid. At the same time, Provisional Salaries Tax is levied for the following year of assessment. Any excess/deficit of Provisional Salaries Tax over the actual finally determined liability is offset against/added to the Provisional Salaries Tax payable for the following year of assessment. There are provisions to enable collection of Salaries Tax and Provisional Salaries Tax to be held over in appropriate circumstances. See Chapter 3.

6. Interest Tax (Part V IRO)

Interest tax is in effect a withholding tax on interest or certain deemed interest which has a source in Hong Kong, deducted by the payer of the interest. It is deductible at 15% although a reduced rate of 10% applies to Hong Kong dollar deposits with financial institutions. Any person who pays or credits such interest is required to deduct the tax and account to the Government within 30 days. Failure to deduct results in action to recover the tax either from the payer or, in appropriate circumstances, by direct assessment upon the recipient.

There are however numerous exemptions from Interest Tax depending upon the status of the payer, the rate of interest, the status of the recipient etc. In particular, companies carrying on business in Hong Kong are not subject to Interest Tax but bring interest receipts into their Profits Tax computation.

Interest includes the interest element of a purchased annuity and the profit on maturity on a Bill of Exchange. See Chapter 4.

7. Profits Tax (Part IV IRO)

Profits tax is chargeable at the standard rate on every person who is carrying on a trade, profession or business in Hong Kong in respect of his assessable profits arising in or derived from Hong Kong from such trade, profession or business. There is no distinction between resident and non resident persons, it is merely necessary to determine whether a person, which includes a company, a partnership or a body of persons, is carrying on a trade, profession or business in Hong Kong and, if so, whether he has a Hong Kong source of profits in connection therewith. In addition, certain sources of income are deemed to be from a business carried on in Hong Kong and are therefore subject to Profits Tax automatically even if that is the recipient's only source of income in Hong Kong and he has no presence there at all.

Other than the deemed Hong Kong sources of income, the IRO gives no guidance in ascertaining the source of income or profits. It is of course not necessarily important to ascertain exactly where the geographical source is but merely to determine whether or not it is in Hong Kong. The determination of source requires a consideration of several factors and the applicable case law precedent of general and specific application. There have been some important decisions by the Hong Kong Courts which are dealt with in Chapter 5 and, where relevant, legal decisions in other countries also provide guidance. Subject to the qualification that each case must be considered on its individual merits, a good general rule for determining the source of profits is to ascertain "where in substance the operations which gave rise to the profits took place" after having isolated each step in the series of transactions involved in the particular trade or business.

Assessable profits are profits arrived at in accordance with normally accepted accounting principles as adjusted to comply with the requirements of the IRO, e.g. a difference between depreciation for accounting purposes and statutory rates of depreciation allowances for taxation purposes, the exclusion of non Hong Kong source profits, and adjustments where accounting principles and taxation principles conflict as to what constitutes capital and revenue expenditure and profits. Where part of the profits is taxable and part is not it is of course necessary to disallow an appropriate proportion of expenditure and the IRR provide the various rules governing this. Similarly the IRR provide rules for determining assessable branch profits of companies having their head office elsewhere.

Profits Tax assessments are raised for a year of assessment and the IRO provides the rules for determining the basis period for a year of assessment with special rules for commencement, cessation and change of accounting date. The standard rate is presently 15% for individuals and 16½% for corporations. Partnerships are assessed as a single unit and to the extent that the profits are shared by individuals are assessed at 15% and at 16½% in respect of that part of the profits owned by corporate partners.

The charging of Profits Tax incorporates a system of tax paid on account during the year of assessment known as Provisional Profits Tax. An estimate is made of assessable profits for the year of assessment and Provisional Profits Tax is levied on this estimate. In the case of a continuing business, the estimate is based on the actual assessable profits for the preceeding year of assessment. When the actual assessable profits for the year of assessment are ascertained, a final assessment is issued and credit is given for the Provisional Profits Tax paid. Any excess/deficit of Provisional Profits Tax paid over the final liability is offset against/added to the Provisional Profits Tax payable for the following year of assessment. In the event that there is available any balance of Provisional Profits Tax, it is refunded to the taxpayer. There are provisions to enable collection of Profits Tax and Provisional Profits Tax to be held over in appropriate circumstances.

Because of the relative simplicity of the legislation, it is not necessarily adequate to cope with the taxation of special types of business and the IRO therefore includes specific provisions relating to special types of business as follows:—

Life Insurance	Shipping (including aircraft)
Other Insurance	Clubs/Trade Associations

(See Chapter 5.)

8. Depreciation Allowances (Part VI IRO)

The IRO lays down statutory depreciation allowances in respect of appropriate expenditure on capital assets. These are granted for Profits Tax and, in limited circumstances for Salaries Tax, where capital assets are used wholly or partly to produce assessable profits. Allowances are granted for:—

Industrial Buildings	Commercial Buildings

Plant & Machinery

The general scheme of depreciation allowances is to grant an initial allowance in the year in which the expenditure is incurred and annual allowances thereafter. Upon disposal of the asset or upon other specified occasions a balancing allowance or charge may be made although as a general rule no such charge or allowance arises in the case of plant & machinery. In the case of commercial buildings, only a fixed annual allowance of ¾% is given.

The rates of initial allowance are fixed at 20% for industrial buildings and 55% for plant & machinery. The annual allowance is 4% for industrial buildings (or varying rates in respect of inherited expenditure) and at rates of 10%, 20% and 30% for plant & machinery.
(See Chapter 6.)

9. Rates of Tax (2nd Schedule IRO)

The Second Schedule to the IRO sets out the progressive rates of tax which are applicable, after deducting personal allowances, for Salaries Tax and, where an election has been made for a total income assessment, under Personal Assessment. The Second Schedule gives all of the rates since 1947/48, the rates applicable since 1978/79 have been:—

Upon the first	$10,000	5%
Upon the next	$10,000	10%
– do –		15%
– do –		20%
Upon the remainder		25%

In the case of Salaries Tax, the total tax payable is not to exceed tax at the standard rate of 15% on net assessable income before personal allowances. Accordingly there is a break-even point, depending upon personal circumstances, above which the standard rate applies. (See Chapter 3.)

In the case of Personal Assessment, the tax payable is also not to exceed tax at the standard rate on total income less charitable contributions and losses but not personal allowances. (See Chapter 7.)

Example 4

This example illustrates the relationship between the standard rate and the progressive rates for Salaries Tax.

Salary, bonus and taxable benefits			$206,000
Less: Expenses and Depreciation Allowances	$3,000		
Charitable Donations	250		3,250
Net Assessable Income			$202,750
Less: Personal Allowance and additional allowance			56,000
Net Chargeable Income			$146,750

$ 10,000	@ 5%	=	$ 500	
10,000	@ 10%		1,000	
10,000	@ 15%		1,500	
10,000	@ 20%		2,000	
106,750	@ 25%		26,687	
$146,750			$31,687	. . . . (1)

15% on Net Assessable Income = 15% x 202,750
= $30,412 . . . . (2)

Accordingly the progressive rates are not applicable in this case.

10.   Personal Allowances (Sec. 42B IRO)

Personal allowances are deductible for Salaries Tax, below the break-even point (see Chapter 3) and for Personal Assessment (see Chapter 7). The following are the current allowances:—

Personal Allowance		$20,500
Wife Allowance		$20,500
Additional Allowance —	Single	$ 7,500 (Note (a))
	— Married	$15,000 (Note (b))
Child Allowance —	1st Child	$ 8,000
	2nd Child	$ 5,500
	3rd Child	$ 3,000
	4th Child	$ 2,000
	5th Child	$ 2,000
	6th Child	$ 2,000
	Each Subsequent Child	$ 1,000 (Note (c))
Dependent Relative		$ 8,000 (Note (d))

Notes:
(a) Prior to 1979/80 the allowance was reduced by a percentage of the amount by which income, as follows, exceeded $12,500. The percentage was 15% for 1976/77 and 1977/78 and 10% for 1978/79.

  Salaries Tax cases — Assessable income less expenses, depreciation allowances, charitable contributions and losses (under Salaries Tax rules).

  Personal Assessment cases — Total income less charitable contributions and losses.

(b) Prior to 1979/80 the allowance was reduced by a percentage of the amount by which the income as in (a) exceeded $25,000. The percentage was 15% for 1976/77 and 1977/78 and 10% for 1978/79.

(c) The maximum aggregate child allowances is $25,500.

(d) First introduced for 1978/79.

For full details of personal allowances, see Chapter 7.

11. Personal Assessment (Part VII IRO)

Although there is no total income concept in Hong Kong taxation, the IRO recognises the situation that a total income assessment would, in appropriate circumstances, result in a smaller total tax liability of an individual than the sum of his liabilities under the separate income taxes so long as the personal allowances and progressive tax rates, that only apply automatically to Salaries Tax, extended to his total income.

The IRO therefore provides for an individual to elect for personal assessment of his total income which means that against his income assessable under the various heads, subject to the various rules contained in Part VII of the IRO, he can deduct the personal allowances and have the net chargeable income charged at progressive rates.

The ability to elect is only open to an individual who is a permanent resident of Hong Kong or who falls within the definition of temporary resident.

An individual will elect, for example, in the following circumstances:—

(1) He has losses for Profits Tax purposes and chargeable income under one or more of the other heads; or

(2) He has sources of income which do not automatically attract the personal allowances and progressive tax rates and his total income is below the "break-even" point (see Chapter 3 for break-even point); or

(3) His marginal rate of Salaries Tax is lower than the standard rate and he has another source of taxable income; or

(4) He has incurred certain interest charges which are otherwise not deductible.

See Chapter 7.

Example 5

An illustration of (1) above.

Mr. X had an adjusted loss in his business of $10,500 for 1981/82 and his wife had earnings from employment for 1981/82 of $202,000 on which he has been assessed Salaries Tax at 15% = $30,300. He claims no allowance except for self and wife.

1)	Salary		$202,000	
2)	Less Losses		10,500	
			$191,500	
3)	Allowances — Self & Wife	$41,000		
	— Additional	15,000	56,000	
	Net Chargeable Income		$135,000	
	10,000 @ 5%		500	
	10,000 @ 10%		1,000	
	10,000 @ 15%		1,500	
	10,000 @ 20%		2,000	
	95,500 @ 25%		23,875	
			$ 28,875	limited to $28,725
	Tax paid			30,300
	Refund			$ 1,575

Note that the liability is limited to tax at the standard rate on total income less losses and therefore the refund is effectively the loss at standard rate. The refund could never be less than this and would be greater if the total income less losses was below the "break-even" point (see Chapter 3).

An example of circumstances in which it would not be advantageous to claim personal assessment follows:—

Example 6

Mr. Y is married with 3 children for whom allowances are given and has the following sources of assessable income for 1981/82:—
(1) Interest of $20,000 from which Interest Tax of $2,000 has been deducted.
(2) He owns a flat which has an assessable value of $25,000. He has received a net rental income of $27,500 and has paid Property Tax of $3,000.
(3) His wife owns a business for which the assessable profits are $200,000 and on which Profits Tax of $30,000 has been assessed.

Personal Assessment would give the following liability:—

1)	Interest		$ 20,000
2)	Property ($25,000 less 20% statutory deduction)		20,000
3)	Wife's Business Profits		200,000
	Total Income		$240,000
4)	Allowances – Personal	$20,500	
	– Wife	20,500	
	– Additional	15,000	
	– Children	16,500	
		$72,500	72,500
	Net Chargeable Income		$167,500
	Tax thereon at progressive rates		36,875

Liability without Personal Assessment:—		
	Interest Tax	$ 2,000
	Property Tax	3,000
	Profits Tax	30,000
		$ 35,000

Note that if Y paid mortgage interest on the property, although it would not be deductible for Property Tax purposes it would be deductible under Personal Assessment and therefore any such interest in excess of $7,500 would make the claim worthwhile in the above example.

12. Returns and Information (Part IX IRO)

The IRO gives the Inland Revenue Department wide powers to obtain not only standard returns of income from taxpayers but also all kinds of information from a wide variety of persons including information which does not touch upon their own tax liability. In cases of fraud and wilful default the Inland Revenue Department's powers are even wider including, in appropriate circumstances, the power of entry and search.

The Board of Inland Revenue has the power to specify any forms which are necessary for the administration of the IRO and is charged with the obligation of laying down the form and content of any return such that any return not made in the specified form is treated as invalid and therefore not made.

There are extensive penalty provisions for failure to make returns or provide information statutorily requested within the statutory time limits although there are provisions whereby the time limits can be extended at the Commissioner's discretion which, in practice, is delegated to officers of the Inland Revenue Department.

Where returns are submitted late, the Commissioner has power to compound the penalty and in practice this power is also delegated and it is usual for a modest fine to be imposed. However, the Commissioner prosecutes where circumstances dictate. (See Chapter 8.)

13.   Assessments and Payment of Tax (Part X, XA, XB and XII IRO)

The Assessor is empowered to make assessments and provisional tax (Profit Tax and Salaries Tax only) assessments and has wide powers to raise estimated assessments in specified circumstances. Normally he will make an assessment on an agreed figure and, at the same time, a provisional assessment for the following year in the same amount. In the absence of a valid return or where he cannot accept the amount shown in the return, he may estimate. Similarly, where accounts of a business have not been kept in a satisfactory form, he may make an assessment based on the usual rate of profit applied to the actual turnover and the Board of Inland Revenue is empowered to prescribe the usual rates of profit although it is believed that this power has never been exercised.

The time limit for making additional assessments is within 6 years after the end of the year of assessment but in the case of fraud or wilful evasion, the time limit is extended to 10 years. An assessment becomes final and conclusive when either there has been no valid objection or, where an objection has been given, the objection has been determined by the Commissioner and no appeal given or the assessment has been adjusted as agreed between the taxpayer and the Assessor. Where an appeal has been given, the assessment becomes final and conclusive when determined by the Board of Review or High Court and no higher appeal is made. There are only limited circumstances in which a final assessment can be re-opened, the main ones being where the IRO specifically permits it in election cases or in the case of an "error or omission" claim. (See Chapter 10.)

Upon making an assessment, the dates of payment of the tax are fixed by the Commissioner and are then specified in the notice. The provisional tax may be payable in two instalments and this is always the case for Provisional Salaries Tax but only the case for Provisional Profits Tax where the first instalment normally falls due within the currency of the accounting period which forms the basis period for the year of assessment.

Even where a valid notice of objection or appeal has been submitted, there is no statutory entitlement of the taxpayer to a holdover of the tax payable, this is entirely at the Commissioner's discretion and there is no appeal against his decision. In the case of Provisional Profits Tax and Provisional Salaries Tax there are specific circumstances in which applications can be made for a holdover but the decision is again at the discretion of the Commissioner.

Where tax is not paid on or before the due date, the Commissioner can, and normally does, impose a 5% surcharge. Where tax is in default for 6 months or more, a further 10% surcharge will normally be added.

The Inland Revenue Department has wide powers to enforce collection including preventing defaulters from leaving Hong Kong. (See Chapter 9.)

14. Objections and Appeals (Part XI)

Any person in receipt of an assessment may, within the appropriate time limit submit an objection subject to the rules as to the form of an objection. This is determined by agreement, or failing agreement, determined unilaterally by the Commissioner.

Where a taxpayer is dissatisfied with the Commissioner's determination, again within the allowed time limit and subject to the correct form, an appeal can be made. In the first instance the appeal is to the Board of Review which is an informal hearing by an independent panel drawn from a panel of laymen, although the chairman is always a person of legal experience and qualification. From the Board of Review's decision the taxpayer or the Commissioner can appeal to the High Court on a point of law and then subsequently, given leave, to a higher court and ultimately to the Privy Council in the U.K. There are provisions whereby, with the agreement of both parties an appeal from the Commissioner's determination may proceed direct to the High Court and an appeal from the Board of Review's decision may proceed direct to the Court of Appeal.

Because of the informality and nominal or nil costs involved, numerous cases proceed to the Board of Review, sometimes with the taxpayer conducting his own case but the material cost and formality of taking a case to the High Court means that relatively few cases are heard at that level. (See Chapter 10.)

15. Board of Inland Revenue (Sec. 3)

The Board of Inland Revenue has a limited although important administrative function. It comprises the Financial Secretary and four other members, appointed by the Governor, presently the Commissioner of Inland Revenue, a practising accountant, a practising solicitor and a banker. They hold office until they resign or are removed by the Governor. There must not be more than one Government employee among the members, apart from the Financial Secretary.

The Board's function is primarily to prescribe the form and content of Inland Revenue forms as required by Sec. 86 and it meets at least once annually for this purpose. It is also empowered to prescribe any matter or procedure where the IRO so requires and particularly to make the Inland Revenue Rules although these are subject to the approval of the Legislative Council. (See Chapter 11.)

16. Inland Revenue Department

The Commissioner of Inland Revenue is charged with the responsibility of administering the IRO and for this purpose heads the Inland Revenue Department which is divided into five operating divisions or "Units". The division of these functions is indicated on the organisational chart on page 19.

The Commissioner is assisted by a Deputy Commissioner, five Assistant Commissioners and numerous Assessors and other officers of varying grades with a total complement of clerical and non-clerical staff of over 2,500 persons. Where the IRO permits, various statutory functions are delegated by the Commissioner to other officers (Sec. 3A) but there are circumstances where the Commissioner is required to act personally. For example, assessments to additional tax under Sec. 82A consequent upon incorrect returns made without reasonable excuse can only be made by the Commissioner or the Deputy Commissioner personally. Consequently, all "enquiry" cases are seen and judged personally by the Commissioner or Deputy Commissioner. Similarly, before a statement of assets and liabilities can be requested from a person under Sec. 51A, the Commissioner or Deputy Commissioner must be personally of the opinion that the person has made an incorrect return or supplied false information without reasonable excuse.

Although the Commissioner is charged with the responsibility of administering the IRO as enacted he nevertheless in practice adopts a number of extra-statutory practices and concessions where he considers that equity or expedience dictates such a course. Some of these practices and concessions are published and some are not. It is also inevitable that many parts of the IRO are capable of alternative interpretations and the Commissioner has accordingly issued a number of Departmental Interpretation and Practice Notes giving the Department's views and related practices. These are as follows and are reproduced as an appendix to this book:—

(1)   Valuation of Stock-in-Trade and Work-in-Progress and Ascertainment of Profit and the Valuation of Work-in-Progress in Building and Engineering Contracts, Property Development, and Property Investment Cases.
(2)   Industrial and Commercial Buildings Allowances.
(3)   Apportionment of Expenses.
(4)   (Now withdrawn)
(4A) Business Receipts – Lease Premiums, Unreturnable Deposits, Key Money, Construction Fees, etc.
(5)   Scientific Research & Technical Education.
(6)   Objection and Appeal Procedure.
(7)   Machinery & Plant (Depreciation Allowances).
(8)   Out of print as redundant.
(9)   Expenses Deductible for Salaries Tax.
(10) The Charge to Salaries Tax.
(11) Elements of a Tax Investigation.
(12) Commissions, Rebates and Discounts, Payment of Illegal Commissions.
(13) Interest Tax and Profits Tax on Interest.

The notes have no binding force in law and are issued only for the information and guidance of taxpayers. A taxpayer always has the right to object or appeal against the interpretation and practice stated therein. From the Inland Revenue Department's point of view however a taxpayer can expect that the Department will act in accordance with the notes which, where subsequently found by a legal decision to be incorrect, will be amended although not retrospectively. This is because an assessment made under a prevailing practice cannot be re-opened by virtue of the fact that it is subsequently found that the practice is incorrect. (Sec. 70A(1) proviso)

The Department also publishes a number of other explanatory pamphlets for the guidance of taxpayers. The Commissioner issues an annual Departmental Report containing useful information and a summary of the Department's work in the past year including its work in respect of taxes other than the income taxes under the IRO.

All employees of the Department have an obligation of secrecy under Sec. 4 of the IRO with limited official exceptions. The penalty for breach of secrecy is a fine of $50,000.

17. Administration Chart of Inland Revenue Department

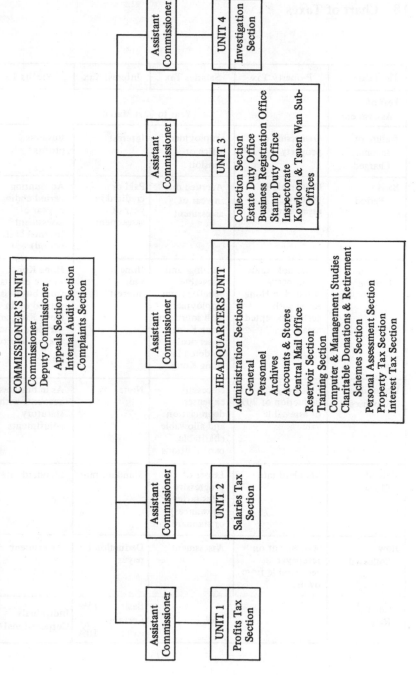

COMMISSIONER'S UNIT
Commissioner
Deputy Commissioner
Appeals Section
Internal Audit Section
Complaints Section

Assistant Commissioner — **UNIT 1**
Profits Tax Section

Assistant Commissioner — **UNIT 2**
Salaries Tax Section

Assistant Commissioner — **HEADQUARTERS UNIT**
Administration Sections
General
Personnel
Archives
Accounts & Stores
Central Mail Office
Reservoir Section
Training Section
Computer & Management Studies
Charitable Donations & Retirement Schemes Section
Personal Assessment Section
Property Tax Section
Interest Tax Section

Assistant Commissioner — **UNIT 3**
Collection Section
Estate Duty Office
Business Registration Office
Stamp Duty Office
Inspectorate
Kowloon & Tsuen Wan Sub-Offices

Assistant Commissioner — **UNIT 4**
Investigation Section

18.   Chart of Taxes

The Taxes	Property Tax	Salaries Tax	Interest Tax	Profits Tax
Year of Assessment	Year to 31st March			
Nature of Income Charged	Ownership of property	Employment, office or pension	Interest	Business profits
Basis Period	Ownership in year of assessment	Accrued due in year of assessment	Paid or credited in year of assessment	Accounting period ending in year of assessment (normal basis period)
Assessable Income	Assessable value of property situated in Hong Kong with certain excepted areas	Earnings and assessable benefits from employment with source in Hong Kong or services rendered in Hong Kong	Hong Kong source interest	Hong Kong source profits from business carried on in Hong Kong and certain deemed taxable sources.
Deductible Expenses	Statutory deduction of 20% of assessable value	Necessary expenses, depreciation and allowable charitable contributions	None	As in business accounts with statutory adjustments
Rate of Charge	Standard rate	Lesser of progressive rates (after allowances) or standard rate	Standard rate	Standard rate
How Collected	Assessment on ratepayer recoverable from owner	Assessment	Deduction by payer	Assessment
Standard Rate		15%	Basic 15% Certain cases 10%	Individuals 15% Corporations16½%

Progressive Rates	Upon the first $10,000	5%
	Upon the next $10,000	10%
	– do –	15%
	– do –	20%
	Upon the remainder	25%
Personal Allowances	See paragraph 10 and Chapter 7	

Note that a permanent or temporary resident of Hong Kong may elect Personal Assessment if advantageous so that total income less personal allowances is assessed and charged at the progressive rates.

Progressive Rates	Upon the first $10,000	5%
	Upon the next $10,000	10%
	—do—	15%
	—do—	20%
	Upon the remainder	25%
Personal Allowance	See paragraph 10 and Chapter 7	

Note that a permanent or temporary resident of Hong Kong may elect Personal Assessment if advantageous so that total income less personal allowance is assessed and charged at the progressive rates.

Chapter 2
PROPERTY TAX

1. Legislation

The relevant law concerning the charging of Property Tax is in Part II of the IRO, Secs. 5 to 7B. The provisions governing assessment and collection of tax contained in Parts X and XII are applicable to Property Tax although Part II contains provisions relating to collection which are peculiar to Property Tax. The provisions of Part XI relating to objections and appeals are applicable as are various other administrative provisions contained elsewhere in the IRO.

2. Scope of the Tax

Property Tax is charged for each year of assessment on the owner of land or buildings situated in Hong Kong at the standard rate on the net assessable value of such land or buildings (Sec. 5(1)). Land and buildings thereon is assessed as a single unit where both the land and the buildings have the same owner otherwise they are assessed separately (Sec. 5(1) proviso (b)). Note that the concept of the owner of land being also the owner of buildings thereon is not applicable, this is discussed further in paragraph 4 on page 26.

Not all land and buildings in Hong Kong is within the scope of Property Tax as certain areas in the New Territories are outside of the charge until such time as the Governor by proclamation in the Gazette declares them to be chargeable (Sec. 5(1) proviso (e)). This is a matter of Government policy and these areas are progressively being brought into Property Tax by proclamation.

The term "land or buildings" includes piers, wharves and any other structure which might not otherwise come within the normal understanding of what constitutes a building and, furthermore, building includes a part of a building except when considering certain exemptions (Sec. 7A). In practice, all parts of buildings which are separately rated under the Rating Ordinance are separately assessed to Property Tax and accordingly the single owner of a block of flats may receive a number of assessments on individual units which makes the tax administratively cumbersome.

A husband and wife are separate persons for the purposes of Property

Tax (unlike Salaries Tax and Profits Tax) and accordingly will receive separate assessments where they each own separately rated properties. Where however property is owned jointly or in common by two or more persons, although only a single assessment will be raised on each rateable unit, the allocation of the tax between them may be relevant when considering exemptions (see pages 30 to 33).

3. The Charge

The charge to Property Tax is at standard rate on the net assessable value.

NET ASSESSABLE VALUE is the assessable value less a statutory deduction of 20% as a fixed allowance for repairs and outgoings. (Sec. 5(1A)). This percentage may be amended at any time by a resolution of the Legislative Council (Sec. 5(1B)). Accordingly, neither actual rent received nor actual outgoings figure in the assessment of Property Tax which is therefore entirely notional.

Example 1

Gross rents received by flat owner	$60,000
Outgoings (Rates, repairs etc.)	$10,000
Assessable value fixed by IRD	$55,000

Assessable value	$55,000
Less: Statutory deduction 20%	11,000
Net assessable value	$44,000
Property Tax @ 15% =	$ 6,600

ASSESSABLE VALUE. Sec. 5A provides the rules for ascertaining the assessable value of land or buildings or land and buildings. As a general principle the intention is that the assessable value should be equal to the current rent which the property can command given that the landlord and the tenant both assume certain liabilities. It is therefore provided that the assessable value for a year of assessment is the amount for which the property could be expected to be let on the first day of the year of assessment on the assumption that:–
(1) the tenant pays all the usual tenant's rates and taxes; and
(2) the landlord pays the Crown rent, repairs, insurance and all other expenses which are necessary to command the market rent. (Sec. 5A(2)).

In the case of CIR v Wan Yam-yin (HKTC 1104) it was held that the valuation must have regard to the impact of rent control legislation if the property is within its scope, whether or not it is actually let.

Where a property becomes chargeable to Property Tax during a year of assessment, its assessable value is fixed by reference to the date upon which it becomes chargeable (Sec. 5A(2) proviso (i)) instead of the first day of the year of assessment.

Certain properties have their rents controlled under the Landlord and Tenant (Consolidation) Ordinance and as it would be inequitable to base an assessment upon a rent which could not be obtained, there are therefore provisions to ensure that the assessable value cannot exceed the controlled rent obtainable. Sec. 5A(1) therefore provides that the assessable value in these cases is to be the estimated annual rent which is permitted under Part I or authorised under Part II of the Landlord and Tenant (Consolidation) Ordinance given the same assumption as to the landlord's and tenant's liabilities as in respect of non-controlled properties. The fixing of assessable value in this way under Sec. 5A(1) is however only applicable where:—

(1) the property or unit being assessed is wholly let on the first day of the year of assessment; and

(2) Part I or Part II of the Landlord and Tenant (Consolidation) Ordinance applies to that letting on the first day of the year of assessment; and

(3) the Commissioner is satisfied that no consideration, in any form whatsoever has been given or is obtainable under the lease, other than the rent permitted or authorised by the Landlord and Tenant (Consolidation) Ordinance (Sec. 5A(4)).

Because the situation may arise that, once an assessable value has been fixed, the property may for good economic reasons be let at an annual rent which is less than the assessable value which forms the basis of the assessment, provisions have been introduced with effect from 1981/82 to correct such an anomaly. Sec. 5A(3A) therefore provides that, if land or buildings or land and buildings are wholly let on the first day of a year of assessment after 1980/81 and the assessable value for that year of assessment exceeds the annual rent in force, the assessable value is reduced to that annual rent. This only applies to leases where the tenant and landlord each bear their liabilities as in (1) and (2) on page 24. In fixing the amount of the annual rent it is of course necessary to annualise any rent fixed for a shorter period and it is also necessary to to include any consideration in cash or kind which has been given or required in connection with the granting or continuation of the lease. If any consideration requires apportionment, the CIR has the power to do this in a reasonable and appropriate manner (Sec. 5A(3B)).

In ascertaining the assessable value under these rules it is correct to include in the valuation, use of machinery which is part of the structure of or otherwise associated with the building but it is not appropriate to include any machinery which is for the purpose of manufacturing operations or any trade process. Normally therefore this will include such machinery as lifts and air-conditioning. Furthermore, in fixing the valuation it is correct to take account of the reasonable cost of operating the machinery included in the valuation (Sec. 5A(3)). This provision could not be interpreted to require the inclusion of furniture which, although it falls within the definition of "plant and machinery" for depreciation allowance purposes (see Chapter 6) could not be regarded as machinery for this purpose.

The intention of the legislation is that the assessable value can be fixed annually in order to keep up with increasing market rents. However, in practice it is not possible for annual revaluations to be made and these are therefore only made at intervals; the last general revaluation had effect for the year 1981/82 and is not expected to be made again in less than four years. As Sec. 5A(1) and (2) requires the assessable value to be fixed at the beginning of each year of assessment, it is further provided that, if no new valuation is made, the one that was last ascertained may be applied (Sec. 5A(2) proviso (ii)).

4. Ownership

As the ownership of land or buildings or land and buildings is fundamental to the charge to Property Tax it is essential to be able to determine who is the owner and the date on which ownership commences and ceases. The IRO does not attempt to fully define ownership but it is first of all necessary to turn to the definition of owner in Sec. 2 which is fully reproduced as follows:—

> "Owner in respect of land or buildings or land and buildings, includes a beneficial owner, a tenant for life, a mortgagor, a person who is making payments to a co-operative society registered under the Co-operative Societies Ordinance for the purpose of the purchase thereof, and a person who holds land or buildings or land and buildings subject to a ground rent or other annual charge".

It is necessary to understand two points of law before proceeding to consider the question of ownership further. Firstly, land is subject to a ground rent where it is leased on condition that certain buildings be erected on it or that other improvements be made. All land in Hong Kong with only minor exceptions is owned by the Crown and is let under Crown leases for varying periods although current Crown leases are normally for periods no longer than the period to 1997 in respect of the New Territories and for periods of 75 years renewable for a further 75 years in respect of other land in Hong Kong. Fundamentally therefore the Crown is the true owner of virtually all the land in Hong Kong but the holder of the Crown lease falls within the definition of owner in Sec. 2 because he holds subject to a ground rent. There are also persons who are permitted to occupy Crown land and erect buildings thereon without the formality of a Crown lease. These persons too fall within the definition of owner. Secondly, it is a basic concept of the law of property relating to land and buildings that the owner of land also has title to all buildings, erected thereon and any other person can only have an interest in the buildings as a lessee. However this concept is not applicable in determining ownership for Property Tax purposes in view of the provision in Sec. 5(1) proviso (b) that the owner of land and the owner of buildings thereon, if different persons, are to be assessed separately.

It is of course the case that the Crown lessee who, as we have seen, is the owner for Property Tax purposes, may assign all or part of his interest in the Crown lease and accordingly subsequent assignees acquire ownership of the land or buildings or part thereof as appropriate. Any other person who merely takes an interest in land or buildings without taking an assignment of an interest in the Crown lease is not an owner but a lessee.

Where property is purported to be held on trust for other persons it is important to establish who has interests therein and the nature of their interests in view of the inclusion of "life tenant" and "beneficial owner" in the definition of owner in Sec. 2 of IRO. It is therefore always desirable to have proper documentation of the terms of a trust.

In view of the fact that a property can have more than one owner during a year of assessment and that not only is the tax divisible between those owners, certain classes of owner can claim exemption from Property Tax (see pages 28 to 33) and it is therefore essential to be able to identify the date of change of ownership. This is largely a question of fact to be determined in the circumstances from available documents. The ownership of a property can pass for this purpose even where the purchase price is paid by extended instalments and assignment is deferred until the final instalment is paid. Sec. 2 of IRO identifies these circumstances particularly in the case of instalments payable to a co-operative society. For a discussion on payments by instalments see a Profits Tax case, CIR v Montana Lands Ltd. (HKTC 334). The date of acquisition of ownership is normally the date on which the purchase and sale agreement is concluded or when it becomes unconditional, if later.

Taxpayers may be required to produce evidence of title and change of ownership and documentation is therefore important as it is not necessary for the title to be registered in the Land Office. This is particularly important in cases of "beneficial ownership" where there has been no formal conveyance of title. It would be usual therefore, lacking any other evidence, to produce documents amounting to a purchase and sale agreement although these must be duly stamped under the Stamp Ordinance before they can be valid as an instrument of sale. (Sec. 7(2) Stamp Ordinance)

5. Exemptions and Reliefs

Various forms of exemption and relief from the charge are provided in the IRO and elsewhere and these are as follows:—

GOVERNMENTS. The charge is not levied where the owner of property is the Hong Kong Government or a Commonwealth Government. Furthermore, under the Consular Privileges Ordinance and the Trade Commissioners Privileges Ordinance, the prescribed foreign powers owning property are also exempt from the charge, but this is only applicable to property actually used for consular purposes.

CORPORATIONS CARRYING ON BUSINESS. A corporation which is carrying on a trade, profession or business in Hong Kong is normally liable to Profits Tax on its profits (see Chapter 5) and if it owns land or buildings which satisfy certain conditions, it will be exempted from Property Tax. (Sec. 5(2)(a))

A corporation is defined by Sec. 2 of IRO as:—

"Any company which is either incorporated or registered under any enactment or charter in force in the Colony or elsewhere but does not include a co-operative society or a trade union".

The conditions are that it either:—
(1) Brings the profits from the property into its Profits Tax computation, or
(2) Occupies the property for the purposes of producing profits subject to Profits Tax. (Sec. 25 proviso (a))

The application for exemption must be made in writing and if substantiated, the exemption will remain in force for all subsequent years of assessment throughout which the relevant circumstances apply. Where the relevant circumstances only apply for part of a year of assessment then the Property Tax chargeable for that year of assessment is reduced on a time basis in accordance with the precise number of days for which the circumstances do apply (Sec. 5(2)(b)). In order to administer this, it is provided that a corporation which has been granted exemption must notify the Commissioner in writing within 30 days after change of ownership or of any other event affecting the exemption. (Sec. 5(2)(c)). It will be seen that the exemption relates to the circumstances of each property and therefore a corporation cannot claim a blanket exemption from Property Tax but must make separate application in respect of each of its properties.

Where a corporation has not claimed exemption or is not in a position to claim exemption because it is only a co-owner or joint owner of a property and has paid Property Tax for a year of assessment, if the conditions stated above for exemptions are satisfied or at least satisfied in respect of its part of the property, it can set off the Property Tax which it has paid against its

Profits Tax payable and so far as it exceeds the Profits Tax payable, claim repayment of the excess (Sec. 25).

Because of the wide interpretation of the term "business" (see Chapter 5), virtually every corporation is in a position to claim exemption from Property Tax.

Example 2

Ona Property Ltd. carries on a trade but also owns a flat which is rented out to give a net profit of $58,000 in its accounting period ended 31st December, 1978. The net assessable value of the property is $50,000 on which it has paid Property Tax for 1978/79 of $7,500.

So long as it brings the rental profit of $58,000 into its Profits Tax computation it can claim exemption and this will be effective for all years for which it owns the flat and brings the rental income into its Profits Tax computation.

For 1978/79 it can either claim a refund of $7,500 under Sec. 79(1) or a set-off against its Profits Tax liability under Sec. 25.

Notes:—
(a) It would in fact have no option but to bring the rental income into its Profits Tax computation because this income is within the definition of business profits (see Chapter 5).
(b) If the flat was not let but was occupied by an employee rent free, the exemption would still be available because the company would be occupying the property through its representative for the purposes of its business. This position can however be contrasted with the decision in BR 13/73 where a non Hong Kong company owned a property in Hong Kong which was occupied by an employee rent free. The company was not carrying on business in Hong Kong and therefore could only rely upon the owner occupier exemption. It was held that, although the employee occupied it for residential purposes, the owner did not and could not and the claim therefore failed.

Example 3

Onapart Property Ltd. is joint owner of a building in which it has a 50% interest and uses the building in its trade, the profits of which are subject to Profits Tax. The other joint owner is a non Hong Kong company which does not carry on business in Hong Kong and does not charge Onapart any rent for its use of the whole building. A Property Tax demand is received on which tax of $75,000 is payable.

Onapart cannot claim exemption because the whole of the property does not meet the necessary criteria for exemption under Sec. 5(2)(a).

However, the provisions of Sec. 25 are satisfied and Onapart can therefore set $37,500 against its Profits Tax liability.

Notes:—

(a) If the other joint owner charged and received a rent (either to Onapart or some other tenant, it would be liable to Profits Tax thereon. Accordingly the whole property would meet the exemption criteria in Sec. 5(2)(a).

(b) In practice, it is quite possible that if Onapart has an interest in a severable part of the building and that part is separately rated under the Rating Ordinance, that part will therefore be separately assessed to Property Tax and exemption in the above circumstances would be available.

OWNER/OCCUPIER. An owner who occupies a building or part of a building throughout the whole of a year of assessment is granted exemption from Property Tax in the following circumstances:—

(1) If he is the sole owner, and

(2) Occupies it solely and exclusively for residential purposes (Sec. 5(3)(a)).

For this purpose, ownership and occupation of a part of a building only qualifies for the exemption where the part is separately rated under the Rating Ordinance in which case it is quite likely that it is also separately assessed to Property Tax (Sec. 5(5)(c)). The position of joint owners or co-owners is not however ignored and is dealt with below. If an owner occupier does not satisfy the rules for exemption throughout the whole of a year of assessment, relief is granted by reducing the Property Tax on a time proportion basis in accordance with the precise number of days for which he does qualify (Sec. 5(3)(b)).

Very often, the tests of occupation "solely by the owner" and for "residential purposes" are not as straightforward as they might appear at first. Occupation by an owner's immediate family is obviously ignored so long as the owner himself occupies with them, even allowing for temporary absences. However, if a person or persons who are not part of the owner's immediate family are occupying a part not separately rated, the exemption will not apply, even if they occupy rent free. Where a part, which is not separately rated, is let, even perhaps to close relatives, the exemption also cannot apply.

Example 4

Mr. X owns a flat, rated as a single unit and occupies it with his wife and children. He allows his brother and his wife to occupy one room rent free as their home and has made that room self contained and it has its own entrance.

Notes:—

(a) Dividing the property up into separately identifiable portions is not sufficient to create separate parts for purposes of the exemption unless those parts are separately rated.

(b) In this case however, Mr. X can claim exemption because his brother and wife would be accepted as immediate family.

(c)   If his brother paid him rent for the occupation, however, the claim would fail.

(d)   If the separate room had been occupied rent free by, say, a friend, in strictness the claim would fail, but in practice the Inland Revenue Department would allow the claim.

If an individual occupies his property for business purposes, even though he may also occupy it as his residence, he cannot be said to have occupied it solely for residential purposes and therefore cannot claim exemption. He can however set the relevant business proportion of the Property Tax against his Profits Tax payable (Sec. 25).

It is of particular note that a husband and wife are separately assessed for Property Tax purposes and, subject to the rules already discussed, can therefore each own and claim exemption for residential property. Up to and including 1980/81 an owner who occupied more than one building or separately rated part of a building for residential purposes could only claim exemption for one such building or part and he had to nominate in writing the one of his choice (Sec. 5(3A)). The Commissioner however had power to extend the exemption to additional parts of a building where they satisfied the rules for residential occupation in total and were reasonably necessary for this purpose (Sec. 5(3A) proviso). From 1981/82 this limitation has been removed and an owner can claim exemption for all properties which satisfy the tests. The main beneficiaries of this change are those who own adjacent flats and occupy the whole as one.

Where a building or part of a building is owned by joint or co-owners, for the purposes of the owner occupier exemption they are treated as if they are separately charged to Property Tax, in the case of joint owners, in equal shares, and in the case of co-owners, in the proportions in which they are interested in the property. The rules and qualifications already described for claiming full year or part year exemption are then applied to their shares of the property, to the extent that they qualify (Sec. 5(3)(c)). For this purpose it is specifically provided that the sole occupation rule is not offended merely by the fact that more than one owner may occupy the same building or part of building at the same time (Sec. 5(5) (b)).

Example 5

X, Y and Z are equal co-owners of a building on which the Property Tax payable is $15,000. During the year of assessment they each occupy a part of the building for 25, 75 and 155 days respectively for residential purposes. They have no other residence for which they claim exemption and the building is let when not occupied by them.

The Property Tax is first of all divided between them as to:—

X $5,000
Y $5,000
Z $5,000

and then their individual exemptions are considered in relation to each share as:—

$$
\begin{aligned}
&\text{X Exempt } 25/365 \times \$5{,}000 = \quad \$\ 342 \\
&\text{Y Exempt } 75/365 \times \$5{,}000 = \quad 1{,}026 \\
&\text{Z Exempt } 155/365 \times \$5{,}000 = \quad \underline{2{,}123} \\
&\hspace{7cm} \underline{\underline{\$3{,}491}}
\end{aligned}
$$

Notes:—
(a) Net Property Tax of $11,509 is therefore payable on the building.
(b) Their individual claims are unaffected if it happens that more than one of them occupies parts of the building at the same time (Sec. 5(5)(b)).

To administer these provisions, the Commissioner must be notified within 3 months of cessation of occupation by a sole owner or co-owner where an exemption is in force (Sec. 5(4)). See page 35 regarding time limits.

The position of certain clans, families and t'ongs has been separately legislated for with effect from 1979/80 and is dealt with as follows.

CLANS/FAMILIES/T'ONGS. The owner-occupier provisions are not such as to confer the opportunity for claiming exemption in respect of ancestral homes owned by clans, families or t'ongs; therefore with effect from 1979/80, a provision included as Sec. 5(3)(d)(iii) allows such exemption where the property is occupied throughout the year of assessment for the purposes of the clan, family or t'ong. The property must be certified to be the ancestral property by the Secretary for the New Territories or the Secretary for Home Affairs (in respect of property in the urban areas) as appropriate.

Where however any rent is received, other than from a member of the clan, family or t'ong, the exemption is reduced accordingly. In fact, Property Tax is charged by first ascertaining the proportion of the new assessable value which is subject to the letting, on an area basis, and then sub-apportioning to the portion of the year for which the letting is effective, on a days basis. See page 35 regarding time limits.

CLUBS AND TRADE ASSOCIATIONS. Clubs and trade associations are mutual trading bodies and are only considered to be carrying on business and thereby subject to Profits Tax in certain specified circumstances (see Chapter

5). When subject to Profits Tax they can claim exemption from Property Tax (see "Corporations Carrying on Business" on page 28). If not subject to Profits Tax they were nevertheless subject to Property Tax up to 1978/79 on property owned by them, whether let or not.

With effect from 1979/80, a provision included as Sec. 5(3)(d)(i) and (ii) allows such exemption where the property is occupied for the purposes of the activities of the club or trade association throughout the year of assessment.

Where rent is received other than from a member of the club or trade association, Property Tax is charged by first ascertaining the proportion of the net assessable value which is subject to the letting, on an area basis, and then sub-apportioning to the portion of the year for which the letting is effective, on a days basis. See page 35 regarding time limits.

VOID OCCUPATION. If it can be proved that any land or buildings or land and buildings have not been occupied during some part of the year of assessment, the Property Tax payable will be proportionately reduced (Sec. 7). For this purpose, "occupied" is specifically defined as "being put to beneficial use" (Sec. 7A). In particular, the fact that a building has no person living in it will not of itself satisfy the claim and if it is furnished it will be regarded as put to beneficial use and the claim disallowed if the occupier is merely temporarily absent. See page 35 regarding time limits.

Example 6

Mr. Y owns a flat which he lets unfurnished. For a year of assessment he has paid the usual Property Tax of $9,000. During the year however there was a vacant period of 2 months when he could not find a tenant and the flat was empty.

Notes:—
(a) On the assumption that he did not put it to any other use during the vacant period, the Property Tax will be reduced by 1/6 x $9,000 and $1,500 refunded.
(b) If the flat was let furnished and the furniture remained there during the vacant period, the Inland Revenue Department would refuse the claim on the basis that the property is being put to beneficial use in storing furniture but the point is open to dispute.
(c) The claim is normally evidenced by production of a vacancy notice issued by the Rating Department because a similar claim is also applicable for relief from rates.

It is a question of fact when beneficial occupation commences and it is debatable whether or not the receipt of rent disqualifies a claim for void occupation where the circumstances are otherwise satisfied.

Example 7

Mr. Z owns a flat which he lets furnished. He entered into a new lease with a tenant on 1st April, 1978 and although the tenant paid his rent from that date he did not move in his furniture until 1st May, 1978; he moved in himself a week later. The tenant found a better flat and moved out on 28th February, 1979 although he had to pay the rent for March, 1979. The flat was empty when not occupied by the tenant. Mr. Z has paid the usual Property Tax of $9,000 for 1978/79.

Notes:—
(a) Although rent was received for April, 1978 and March, 1979, it might be claimed that the flat was not put to beneficial use in those months and therefore Mr. Z might claim to reduce the Property Tax for 1978/79 by 1/6 x $9,000 and receive a refund of $1,500. The Inland Revenue Department are however likely to oppose the claim.
(b) The date of commencement of occupation would normally be when the tenant moved in his furniture rather than when he personally began to live in it.

BUSINESS USE. Although the exemptions available for business use have been dealt with under various headings above it is useful to recap the general position, mainly because of the difference in treatment between corporations and individuals. Where a corporation uses a property in connection with its business, it can normally claim exemption (see "Corporations Carrying on Business" on page 28) under Sec. 5(2). Individuals or partnerships cannot however make such a claim, even if the property is used wholly for business purposes, they must rely on setting off the Property Tax against their Profits Tax liability under Sec. 25.

If an individual uses his residence partly for business purposes, this will disqualify his owner occupier exemption (see "Owner/Occupier" on page 30) and he can only claim the relevant business proportion of the Property Tax against his Profits Tax liability under Sec. 25. Note that the letting of property by an individual does not automatically constitute a business unless he is sub-letting (other than from a Crown lease) when Sec. 2 includes his sub-letting within the definition of business.

6. Payment of Tax

Although Property Tax is assessable on the owner of property, the tax must be paid, in the first instance, by the person who pays the rates whether he is the owner or occupier or the agent for the property. (Sec. 6(1))

If the tax is paid by a person other than the owner, he then has a statutory right of recovery from the owner (Sec. 6(2)) unless he has agreed with the owner to bear it when it merely becomes additional rent in the case of payment by a tenant. Normally, recovery would be effected against the next rental payment if there is no agreement to the contrary. Where no rates are payable in respect of the property, collection of Property Tax is directly from the owner. (Sec. 6(3))

Otherwise, all of the rules concerning assessment and payment of tax and their enforcement contained in Parts X, XA, XB and XII of the IRO are applicable (see Chapter 9).

7. Time Limits and Objections

When an assessment is made, unless a valid objection is submitted within the appropriate time limit, it becomes final and conclusive in accordance with the rules applicable to all assessments under the IRO and such assessments can only be re-opened in prescribed circumstances (see Chapters 9 and 10).

In the case of owner occupier exemption claims, void occupation claims and relief claimable by clubs, trade associations, clans, families and t'ongs (see pages 30 to 33), circumstances are specifically provided where, in the event of a claim made for a year of assessment after the assessment for that year has become final and conclusive, the assessment may be re-opened to put the claim into effect (Sec. 7B). The specified time limit is the later of:—

(1) Within 90 days after the end of the year of assessment, (Sec. 7B(1)) or
(2) Within 90 days after the notice of assessment to Property Tax is given. (Sec. 7B(2))

These claims have of course to be made by the owner, not by any other person who may be interested in the property and, in effect, the normal time limit for objection of one month is extended to 90 days in the case of these claims. The period of 90 days can be extended at the Commissioner's discretion if the delay in submitting the claim has been occasioned by absence from Hong Kong, sickness or other reasonable cause. In practice, this discretion is exercised sparingly and will not be entertained for example where the claim has been overlooked by the taxpayer. This extended objection period does not apply for exemption claims by corporations carrying on business but of course they have the equivalent remedy of set-off against Profit Tax under Sec. 25 in respect of any Property Tax assessment which has become final and conclusive.

If a claim made within the time limits is rejected by the Assessor, it is to be treated as a valid objection under Sec. 64 of the IRO (Sec. 7B(2)) and therefore follows the procedure for processing objections in Part XI of the IRO. (See Chapter 10.)

Chapter 3
SALARIES TAX

1. Legislation

The law governing Salaries Tax is primarily contained in Part III of the IRO, Sections 8 to 13. Also relevant is the Second Schedule to the IRO which covers the progressive rates of tax, and Part XA which covers Provisional Salaries Tax. Apart from Part III, the general provisions covering returns in Part IX, assessments in Part X, objections and appeals in Part XI and payment of tax in Part XII are applicable to Salaries Tax.

2. Scope of the Tax

Salaries Tax is imposed upon income which arises in or is derived from Hong Kong from any office or employment of profit and from pensions (Sec. 8(1)).

Ascertainment of the source of employment income depends upon a number of factors and the IRO gives no guidance apart from indicating that earnings from services rendered in Hong Kong are included (Sec. 8(1A)(a)) and certain other circumstances are to be excluded.

An examination of what is included in the definition of assessable remuneration involves an extensive study of relative case law but the IRO itself is also specific in a number of types of income which are included in assessable remuneration (Sec. 9(1)) or excluded (Secs. 8(2) and 9(1)(a)(i)(ii) & (iii)). Only two types of benefit-in-kind are statutorily taxable: rent free or subsidised accommodation and share options. All other benefits in kind are only taxable under the general rule, established by case law, of whether or not the benefit can be converted into cash or whether it represents an assumption of a personal liability of the employee.

Tax is levied for a year of assessment on the actual income for the year of assessment although it cannot be assessed until it is actually received (Secs. 11B and 11D). For the purposes of an assessment to Salaries Tax, the income of a wife who does not live apart from her husband is deemed to be the income of her husband and he is accordingly assessed (Sec. 10). In the event of default however there are provisions for collection of tax from the wife (Sec. 75A).

The charge to tax is the lesser of:—

(1) Assessable remuneration less expenses wholly, exclusively and necessarily incurred (Sec. 12(1)(a)), depreciation allowances (Sec. 12(1)(b)) allowable charitable donations (Sec. 12(1)(c)), losses computed under Salaries Tax rules (Sec. 12A), and personal allowances (see Chapter 7), charged at progressive rates of tax, and

(2) the same net income before personal allowances, charged at the standard rate (Secs. 12B and 13).

Salaries Tax is collected by direct assessment based on a return made at the end of the year of assessment and there is a system of Provisional Salaries Tax for the current year of assessment which is based on the previous year's agreed assessment and is combined with the final assessment for the immediately preceeding year of assessment. Provisional Salaries Tax is normally payable in two instalments.

3. Source of the Income

GENERAL. Salaries Tax is charged on employment, office or pension income which arises in or is derived from Hong Kong (Sec. 8(1)) and it is therefore initially important to determine the source of any such income to see whether it is within the scope of Salaries Tax. The IRO isolates certain circumstances where income is to be treated as arising in Hong Kong and also circumstances where it is not to be so treated. It is however usually necessary to determine whether the fundamental source of an employment is or is not in Hong Kong and here the IRO gives no guidance. Furthermore there are no legal decisions in Hong Kong or elsewhere of any direct relevance which assist; however there are numerous decisions of the Board of Review in Hong Kong which form the basis of the present attitude of the Inland Revenue Department on fundamental source of employment. Company directors are subject to special considerations and are dealt with separately on page 42 under the heading of "Holder of an Office". Pensions are also considered separately in this chapter.

The following general principles can be stated for employments:—

(1) Where the source of employment is fundamentally outside Hong Kong, remuneration for duties performed in Hong Kong is within the scope of Salaries Tax including leave pay which is attributable to services performed in Hong Kong (Sec. 8(1A)(a)). However, if an individual only performs services in Hong Kong during visits, so long as those visits do not amount to more than 60 days in the year of assessment he will not be charged to Salaries Tax on any of his remuneration (Sec. 8(1B)). For

this purpose, the individual must be a visitor to Hong Kong, not a person who has some form of permanent base there and merely spends most of his time travelling abroad on business. Also, as a matter of practice, normally one of the two days of arrival and departure is ignored but not both. In borderline cases it may be necessary to consider hours and the actual time of arrival and departure will be critical along the lines of Wilkie v CIR (32 TC 495).

(2) Where the source of employment is fundamentally in Hong Kong, all remuneration for services, wherever rendered, is within the scope of Salaries Tax. However if all the services under the employment are rendered outside of Hong Kong, notwithstanding the fundamental existence of the source of income in Hong Kong, the earnings are specifically excluded from the scope of Salaries Tax except for Government employees and seafarers or aircrew (see separate heading on page 43) who are subject to separate rules (Sec. 9(1A)(b)). Furthermore, in determining whether all services are rendered outside Hong Kong the 60 day rule mentioned in (1) above is applicable but this is less likely to be applicable to these cases because an individual with a fundamental source of employment in Hong Kong is more likely to be a resident of Hong Kong, even if he spends most of his working days outside Hong Kong.

Example 1

Herr Kutt is a German national living in Germany and employed by a German company with no permanent establishment in Hong Kong and all factors are consistent with his source of employment being outside Hong Kong. He however has to make regular business trips to Hong Kong to confer with his Company's suppliers. During year of assessment 1, he visited Hong Kong for a total of 53 days and during year 2 his visits totalled 121 days. His annual earnings from the employment are DM48,000. His Salaries Tax position is:—

Year 1

He is exempt under the rule treating visits of not more than 60 days as if they represented services performed outside Hong Kong (Sec. 8(1B)). See note below.

Year 2

He is liable on remuneration for services performed in Hong Kong (Sec. 8(1A)(a)) and this is normally ascertained on a time basis.

Income for Salaries Tax purposes $\frac{121}{365}$ x DM48,000 = <u>DM16,000</u>

Converted to HK$ at average rate of exchange for the year.

Note:—

If he established Hong Kong as his base and made his home there, he may not be classed as a visitor in which case his liability for year 1 would be on:—

$$\frac{53}{365} \times DM48,000 = \underline{DM6,970}$$

Example 2

Mr. Wong is employed by a Hong Kong company and all factors are consistent with his source of employment being in Hong Kong. He is however their representative in London where he has now made his home. He visits Head Office in Hong Kong at regular intervals to report and participate in management meetings. During year of assessment 1 he visited Hong Kong for a total of 53 days and during year 2 his visits totalled 121 days. His annual earnings from the employment are £12,000. His Salaries Tax position is:—

Year 1

As a bona fide visitor he is exempt under the rule treating visits of not more than 60 days as if they represented services performed outside Hong Kong (Sec. 8(1B)). See note below.

Year 2

Because the fundamental source of his employment is in Hong Kong, there is no question of limiting his liability to services performed in Hong Kong as in Example 1 above. He has a full Salaries Tax liability of £12,000 converted at the average rate of exchange for the year.

Note:—

If, despite his absence abroad, he maintained his base and home in Hong Kong, he may not be classed as a visitor in year 1 in which case he would be fully liable on £12,000.

The general principles stated above are as far as the IRO goes in respect of an employment (see separate headings re Holder of an Office, Pensions, Seafarers and Aircrew on pages 42 to 45). Beyond that, it is necessary to resort to case law, in particular to determine the fundamental source of an employment. Unfortunately there is as yet no decision of the Courts on the Hong Kong law and although guidance is sought from decisions in other countries, primarily the U.K. and Australia, the present IRD attitude is governed by a large number of decisions of the Board of Review, many of which are conflicting in detail but from which a general pattern has emerged.

The source of earnings has not been considered in other jurisdictions in the same context as we have to consider it for Salaries Tax purposes. This is why we can do no more than be guided rather than draw conclusions. The following give an indication of factors that have been taken into account elsewhere:—

(1) The source is not outside the U.K. where the only thing that is foreign is the place where the duties are performed and the contract was made in the U.K. and he was paid in the U.K. (Pickles v Foulsham 9 TC 261).

(2) Where the employer is resident outside of the U.K. and the salary was payable outside of the U.K., the source of the employment was accordingly outside of the U.K. (Bray v Colenbrander 34 TC 138 following the decisions in Bennett v Marshall 22 TC 73).

(3) In Australia, the source of remuneration under a contract of employment is normally the place where the work is performed (FC of T v French 11 ATD 288).

The legislations under which the above cases were decided are not the same as that in Hong Kong so they cannot be quoted as direct authorities. Although the Australian law under which the case in (3) above was decided seems closest to the Hong Kong position, the IRD favours the U.K. decisions. If any general pattern can be drawn from the numerous Board of Review decisions it is that the place of performance of the work is ignored and that a totality of sundry facts must be considered. The facts which are considered are as follows:—

(1) The place where the contract is enforceable;

(2) The nature of the taxpayer's duties and exactly what he is remunerated for;

(3) Whether he holds an office in or has an employment with a Hong Kong company, organisation, or Hong Kong branch of a foreign business;

(4) Who remunerates him and where the cost is ultimately borne;

(5) Whether the cost of his remuneration is part, directly or indirectly, of the expenses of a Hong Kong company or branch; and

(6) Whether the duties performed outside Hong Kong were merely incidental to those performed in Hong Kong.

Apart from (6), these factors seem to bear no relationship to the fundamental principle of determination of source of all types of income which was established in CIR v Lever Bros. & Unilever Ltd. (14 SATC 1) that the originating cause is the source, namely the thing which one party must do in order to receive the income. In the case of personal service contracts what the party must do of course is to perform the contract, namely carry out the work. This principle is backed up in Australia by C of T (NWS) v Cam & Sons Ltd. (4 ATD 32). Where the contract is concluded and what the employee is called are only factors precedent to him earning income and, of themselves, bring him nothing at all. Where he is paid and who suffers the cost are merely the mechanics of paying the consideration. He earns nothing unless he does the work which is therefore the originating cause. Clearly, a legal decision of the highest authority is required if this matter is not to remain confused.

See also Appendix 9.

HOLDER OF AN OFFICE. It may not be readily apparent that there is a distinction, in fact a substantial distinction, in the treatment for Salaries Tax purposes between income from an office and from an employment. The distinction lies in the ascertainment of source and the statutory distinction in Sec. 8. An "office" is a position which is independent from the individual holding it and which continues to exist even though unfilled. The source of income from an office is the place where the office legally exists and in the obvious example of a directorship it has been held that the office of director is located at the place where the central management and control of the company is located and that the director's services are deemed to be rendered at that place (McMillan v Guest 24 TC 190).

Sec. 8(1A)(b)(ii) which grants freedom from Salaries Tax where all the services are performed outside Hong Kong or which with Sec. 8(1B) grants the same thing where services are performed in Hong Kong only during visits not amounting to more than 60 days in fact only apply to an employment. A director of a company centrally managed and controlled in Hong Kong is therefore liable to Salaries Tax on his director's remuneration, even if he never visits there. It is however important to recognise that although an individual may be a director of a company he may in fact draw remuneration from the company in a dual capacity; as an employee in addition to his directorship. This is particularly likely to be the position in the case of private companies which are in fact nothing more than an incorporated sole pro-prietorship. The duties of a director are statutory as laid down by the Companies Ordinance or by the company's articles whereas the duties of an employee are as laid down from day to day by his employer. The division of his remuneration between the office of director and the employment is important because the source of each may be separately determined and, in any event, the remuneration from the employment may be exempt under Sec. 8(1A)(b)(ii). This important principle of duality, even where there is no formal division, was established in BR 19/74 following the authority of Lee v Lee's Air Farming Ltd. (3 All E.R. 420).

The IRD will regard any individual who has obligations under the Companies Ordinance or similar obligations under the laws of another country, as the holder of an office. Note that although some Government employees may in fact be office holders there is not usually any necessity to consider this position because Sec. 8(1A)(b)(i) in any event denies Government employees the benefit of exemption in respect of services performed wholly outside Hong Kong.

See also Appendix 9.

Example 3

Ivan Orfiz is a director of a company which has its registered office in and holds its directors' meetings in Hong Kong. He draws fees of $50,000 per annum but during the year under review only visited Hong Kong for a total of 20 days during which he attended Board meetings, signed accounts and attended to various statutory duties.

Notes:—
(a) He will be liable to Salaries Tax on $50,000 because the source of his earnings is the place where the company is managed and controlled, i.e. Hong Kong.
(b) As the holder of an office and drawing remuneration therefrom, he is denied the exemption granted by Sec. 8(1A)(b)(ii) and Sec. 8(1B) to employees.

Example 4

Herr Lein is the owner and chief Executive of a trading company in Europe. That company has a Hong Kong subsidiary the business of which is to make local purchases of goods for the European company. The Hong Kong company has local directors and Herr Lein is also a director. Herr Lein visits Hong Kong for about 30 days each year during which he seeks out and interviews new suppliers and negotiates terms for the ensuing year and also checks on existing suppliers and re-negotiates their terms. He leaves the legal and administrative duties to his local directors. He draws remuneration of $150,000 per annum from the Hong Kong company.

Notes:—
(a) He is in fact the brains behind the Hong Kong business and his position as director is purely nominal. On the authority of BR 19/74 he should be able to claim exemption from Salaries Tax In accordance with Sec. 8(1A)(b)(ii) and Sec. 8(1B) as his income is from a separate employment.
(b) Even if he is allocated a nominal director's fee of say $10,000, this should be covered by personal deductions so that he still pays no Salaries Tax.

SEAFARERS AND AIRCREW.   The IRO lays down special rules for seafarers and aircrew because of their special position as regards performance of duties outside Hong Kong. Sec. 8(1A)(b)(i) denies them the exemption granted by Sec. 8(1A)(b)(ii) for services performed wholly outside Hong Kong, as extended by Sec. 8(1B), where duties are performed in Hong Kong during visits of not more than 60 days. Instead, they are granted exemption under Sec. 8(2)(j) where the rules in fact extend to a test of physical presence in Hong Kong over two years of assessment.

The tests for exemption for a crew member of a ship or aircraft are that he must not have been present in Hong Kong for more than:—
(1) a total of 60 days in the year of assessment (Sec. 8(2)(j)(i)); *and*
(2) a total of 120 days over 2 consecutive years of assessment, one of which is the year under review (Sec. 8(2)(j)(ii)).

It is important to note that the test here is purely of physical presence in Hong Kong whereas the test in the 60 day rule applicable to other employees under Sec. 8(1B) is of visits during which duties are performed. Also, in reviewing the position of a year of assessment under test (2) above there are in fact two tests by aggregating physical presence during the year of assessment and the immediately preceeding year and then the year of assessment and the immediately succeeding year. Although it could be interpreted that it is necessary to satisfy the 120 day test in respect of both possible pairs of years, the IRD interpretation is that satisfying one pair of years is sufficient for exemption to be granted. These rules apply whether the fundamental source of the employment is in Hong Kong or not but if the source is outside Hong Kong and the individual fails the exemption tests his liability cannot exceed tax on the remuneration which relates to services performed in Hong Kong. If the source is in Hong Kong, failure to satisfy the exemption tests will mean liability on the whole of the earnings.

See also Appendix 9.

Example 5

Eva Stone is an air hostess employed by a Hong Kong company which operates an airline. All factors are consistent with her earnings having a fundamental source in Hong Kong. During the consecutive years of assessment 1, 2 and 3 her physical presence in Hong Kong was 75, 50 and 55 days respectively. Her earnings for each year were $75,000.

Her Salaries Tax position for the three years is:—

Year 1

She fails the 60 day test in Sec. 8(2)(j)(i) and therefore whatever her presence in adjacent years, she will be fully liable on $75,000.

Year 2

She satisfies the 60 day test in Sec. 8(2)(j)(i) but fails the 120 day test in Sec. 8(2)(j)(ii) in respect of the aggregate of years 1 and 2.

However, she satisfies the 120 day test in respect of years 2 and 3 and the IRD will allow her exemption for year 2, cancelling any existing final assessment if necessary.

Year 3

She satisfies the 60 day test in Sec. 8(2)(j)(i) and also the 120 day test in Sec. 8(2)(j)(ii) in respect of the aggregate of years 2 and 3.

The IRD will therefore grant exemption for year 3 whatever the amount of her presence in year 4.

Notes:—

If she was employed by a non Hong Kong airline and the factors consistent with the fundamental source of the employment being outside Hong Kong, the position for Year 1 would depend upon services performed in Hong Kong. Unless she could prove having taken a holiday in Hong Kong or come to Hong Kong not in connection with her employment, the 75 days would be assumed to be in the course of her employment and her liability for year 1 would be on:—

$$\frac{75}{365} \times \$75,000 = \$15,410$$

PENSIONS. The assessment of pensions to Salaries Tax is also limited to those pensions which arise in or derive from Hong Kong. Again the IRO gives no guidance as to the source of a pension although it may be implied from the fact that there is a provision whereby, except for Government pensions, the part of a pension which is attributable to services outside Hong Kong is to be exempt (Sec. 8(2)(ca)), that the place where services were rendered is not a criterion in determining source because, if it were, the exemption clause would not be necessary.

The IRD adopts the view that the dominant factor in determining the source is the location of the fund from which payments are made. This can of course be the location of the employer's business if he funds the pension himself or, somewhat artificially, the location of an independent fund. Nevertheless, even if the fund is situated outside Hong Kong the IRD will seek to assess that part of a pension which relates to service in Hong Kong although if the pensioner is not resident in Hong Kong, collection proves impractical and is not therefore normally pursued. There must be doubt whether the assessment, based solely on place of previous service is valid and in the absence of authority must therefore be disputable. When it is necessary to divide a pension between service in Hong Kong and service elsewhere this is normally done by simple time apportionment but it is appropriate, where possible, to make the division on some other factual basis.

4. What Constitutes Assessable Remuneration

Having determined the source of income from employment, office or pension, the next most important thing to ascertain is what remuneration is assessable and what is not. For example, not all payments coming from an employer to an employee represent assessable remuneration and some receipts by an employee from sources other than his employer must be included as assessable. Furthermore there are numerous statutory and case law rules governing the assessability of cash benefits and benefits-in-kind.

The best way to consider the whole question therefore is to consider it in compartments, what the IRO specifically includes and excludes, how this is modified by case law and, separately, the position of certain benefits-in-kind and cash benefits and pensions.

WHAT THE ORDINANCE INCLUDES. Section 9 of the IRO deals with the definition of income from employment for the purposes of Salaries Tax but significantly it begins with the words "Income from any office or employment *includes*" –. It is not therefore exhaustive and accordingly it is necessary to revert to case law for a full understanding of what remuneration can be assessed. Reference is made mostly to U.K. case law because the legislation is substantially based on the U.K. Schedule E provisions although with the added territorial concept and material simplification.

The general charging provision in Sec. 9(1)(a) includes "any wages, salary, leave pay, fee, commission, bonus, gratuity, perquisite or allowance". Furthermore, it is specifically provided that such income is to be included whether it comes from the employer or from some other person. This obviates reference to case law on the particular point but it must not be assumed that all such payments received by an employee are therefore subject to Salaries Tax; there are other important tests which are considered under "Case Law Discussion" on page 54.

Most of the headings included under Sec. 9(1)(a) are easily understood and ascertainable but the one which gives rise to the most difficulty is "perquisite". There has been a considerable amount of U.K. case law on the definition and taxable extent of perquisites and this is therefore considered in detail under "Case Law Discussion" on page 54. Apart from the general charging provisions, only three types of other benefit are specifically included as taxable. These are:–

(1) Lump sums received from a pension scheme or provident fund, so far as they represent employer's contributions to the fund and not wholly a return of the employee's own contributions, unless the scheme or fund has been approved by the Commissioner under Sec. 87A (see Chapter 11). The lump sum is taxable whether it is received during or after the period of employment and whether by way of a commutation of an annuity entitlement or otherwise. Sums received after the employment ceases are treated as having been received on the last day of employment and taxed accordingly, although there is a right to spread back certain lump sum payments where this proves beneficial (see page 62). Of course, if an annuity is drawn, whether from an approved or unapproved fund, it is taxable in full as a pension (Sec. 9(1)(aa)).

(2) The personal benefit derived from occupying a subsidised or rent-free place of residence provided by the employer or an associated corporation is taxed according to a simple formula. This is discussed in detail under the heading "Housing Accommodation Benefit" on page 48.

(3) Any gain realised upon the exercise or disposal of an option to acquire shares, granted to an employee by virtue of his employment, is taxable. This is also discussed in detail under the heading "Share Option Benefit"

on page 52.

The only specific inclusion as regards pensions is the provision in Sec. 9(3) that a pension is to include an ex-gratia pension or one that is capable of being unilaterally discontinued because, without this provision, a series of voluntary payments does not constitute a pension.

WHAT THE ORDINANCE EXCLUDES. The IRO provides a number of specific instances where receipts, which would otherwise fall within the scope of Salaries Tax, are not to be taxed. These are:—

(1) The Governor's official emoluments (Sec. 8(2)(a)).

(2) The official emoluments of consuls, vice-consuls and all persons on the staff of those foreign agencies provided that they are subjects or citizens of the country which they represent (Sec. 8(2)(b)). In practice the exemption is extended to staff of all official foreign government agencies provided that they satisfy the nationality rule. See also (6) and (10) below.

(3) Lump sums received by way of commutation of pensions under a retirement scheme approved by the Commissioner under Sec. 87A of the IRO or under the Pensions Ordinance (Sec. 8(2)(c)). See also (5) below.

(4) Pensions attributable to services outside Hong Kong, other than Hong Kong Government servants (Sec. 8(2)(ca)). See page 45 for further discussion on this.

(5) Any amount, other than as a pension, withdrawn from a retirement scheme approved by the Commissioner under Sec. 87A of the IRO. However, in the case of an employer who is not chargeable to Profits Tax, there is a limitation in respect of schemes set up by him even if approved. In those cases the exemption applicable to that part of the sum withdrawn which represents the employer's contributions must not exceed a sum equal to 15% of the employee's income from the office or employment for the 12 months up to the date of the withdrawal, multiplied by the number of his complete years of service with that employer (Sec. 8(2)(cb)). In effect therefore, the excess of the portion of the sum withdrawn which represents employer's contributions over the above limit is taxable if the employer is not subject to Profits Tax.

(6) Emoluments paid by Commonwealth Governments to members of Her Majesty's forces and permanent civil servants in the employ of those Governments. This does not apply to Hong Kong Government servants (Sec. 8(2)(d)). See also (10) below.

(7) Wound and disability pensions received by members of Her Majesty's forces (Sec. 8(2)(e)).

(8) War service gratuities to members of Her Majesty's forces (Sec. 8(2)(f)).

(9) Any amount arising from a scholarship, exhibition, bursary or similar educational endowment held by a person receiving full time education

　　　　at a recognised educational establishment (Sec. 8(2)(g)).

(10)　Emoluments payable by the U.K. Government to temporary servants who in the Commissioner's opinion satisfy one of the following criteria:—

　　　(i)　Serving in Hong Kong on U.K. based terms because they normally serve in the U.K. but are liable for overseas tours of duty; or

　　　(ii)　Recruited in the U.K. specially for service in Hong Kong (Sec. 8(2)(h)).

　　　　See also (6) above.

(11)　Alimony or maintenance payments received by a woman from her husband or ex-husband (Sec. 8(2)(i)).

(12)　Seafarers and aircrew who satisfy minimum presence rules (Sec. 8(2)(j)). See page 43 for a full discussion.

(13)　Any pension granted under Regulation 31 of the Pensions Regulations. This is an exemption order granted by the Governor under the power contained in Sec. 87 of the IRO.

(14)　The value of any holiday warrant or passage granted to an employee or any allowance for the purchase of such provided that it is expended for that purpose (Sec. 9(1)(a)(i) & (ii)). There is no limit to the amount or frequency of such tax free benefits, the only qualification is that it is actually expended for the given purpose. There is also included as exempt, any allowance for the transportation of personal effects in connection with such journeys (Sec. 9(1)(a)(iii)).

(15)　Refunds of rent to an employee in respect of his residence (Sec. 9(1A)(a)). A taxable benefit may arise in these cases under a separate formula, see below under "Housing Accommodation Benefit".

　　　　HOUSING ACCOMMODATION BENEFIT.　One of the benefits specifically provided as taxable by the IRO is that derived by an employee from the occupation of rent free or subsidised accommodation at the expense of his employer. The taxable benefit is defined as:—

　　　(1)　the *rental value* of any place of residence provided rent free by the employer or an associated corporation (Sec. 9(1)(b)).

or　(2)　where some rent is paid by the employee, the excess of the *rental value* over the rent paid (Sec. 9(1)(c)).

　　　　In order to cover the equivalent circumstances where the employee rents the property himself and looks to his employer for full or partial reimbursement, the reimbursement is exempted from tax (Sec. 9(1A)(a)) and a full reimbursement is treated as giving rise to a rental value as in (1) above (Sec. 9(1A)(b)) and a partial reimbursement as giving rise to a reduced rental value as in (2) above (Sec. 9(1A)(c)). There is however a substantial difference in the tax treatment of a rent allowance, which may be disbursed at the discretion of the employee, and a rent reimbursement which is nothing more than a replacement of a specific expense already incurred. The latter is specifically not taxable, and is replaced by the *rental value,* but the former falls within the definition of allowance in Sec. 9(1)(a) and is fully taxable as income. Provided therefore that any payment by an employer to an employee in this respect is strictly a reimbursement, there is no difference in the tax treatment between a residence owned or rented directly by the employer and one rented in the first instance by the employee himself.

In the case of CIR v Chow Hung-Kong (HKTC not yet published) the employee successfully claimed that accommodation occupied as part of the duties of the employment, i.e. "representative occupation" is not a residence for purposes of the salaries tax charge. This has now been negated by the inclusion of a definition of "a residence" in Sec. 9(6) to include such accommodation.

The *rental value* upon which tax is charged is a fixed percentage of assessable income after excluding any lump sum or gratuity paid upon the retirement or termination of the employee's employment,and deducting any expense allowance or depreciation allowance (see page 64). The relevant percentages are:—

4% where the accommodation consists of not more than one room in a hotel, hostel or boarding house.

8% where the accommodation consists of not more than two rooms in a hotel, hostel or boarding house.

10% in all other cases except that the assessable value for Property Tax purposes (see paragraph 3 in Chapter 2) may be substituted if smaller. (Sec. 9(2))

If the employee's fundamental source of employment is outside Hong Kong and he performs part of his duties outside Hong Kong with the result that only a part of his income is liable to Salaries Tax (see paragraph 3), the rental value is computed, not on the total earnings but only on the proportion liable to Salaries Tax (BR 20/76). Any rent contribution by the employee or portion of rent suffered is not to be similarly pro-rated but is deducted in full per CIR v R.P. Williamson (HKTC 1215).

See illustration in example 10.

Example 6

Benny Fitt received a salary of $120,000 during the year of assessment and also received re-imbursement from his employer of $6,000 per month of the $6,500 which he pays to his landlord for his flat. He also pays rates and maintenance charges of $200 per month. The assessable value of the flat for Property Tax purposes is $60,000. He retired in the following year and elected to relate back $20,000 of the terminal gratuity to this year of assessment. (See page 62.)

His income assessable to Salaries Tax is as follows:—

1)	Salary		$120,000
2)	Rental Value 10% x $120,000 =.	$12,000	
	Less Rent Paid	8,400	
	Net Rental Value	$ 3,600	3,600
3)	Terminal gratuity related back		20,000
	Total Income Assessable to Salaries Tax		$143,600

Notes:—

(a) Although the benefit costs the employer and benefits Benny by $72,000, the assessable benefit is only $3,600.

(b) Although not strictly rent, the rates and maintenance charges are treated as such. However, the Inland Revenue Department examines maintenance charges carefully in case they should be artificially inflated for avoidance purposes.

(c) The Property Tax assessable value is larger than the rental value of $12,000 and therefore the election does not apply. In practice the election is rarely appropriate since the 1981/82 revaluation of Property Tax assessable values.

(d) The terminal gratuity of $20,000 related to this year is ignored in computing rental value (Sec. 9(2)).

(e) Note that it would have been marginally advantageous for Benny to have had a full re-imbursement of $6,700 per month and his salary fixed at $700 per month lower. The cost to the employer would have been the same but Benny's total income assessable to Salaries Tax would be:—

Salary	$111,600
Rental Value (10%)	11,160
Gratuity	20,000
	$142,760

It is always more advantageous from a tax point of view to have a smaller salary than to contribute to rental cost.

The rental value is ascertained according to the period during which the benefit is enjoyed based on the actual assessable income and allowable outgoings for that period. There may be different residences attracting different rates of rental value during one year of assessment and although it is correct to apply the percentages to actual income and outgoings for the relevant periods, in practice this is often done by simple time apportionment.

Example 7

Ernie Nuff came to Hong Kong for employment on 1st April 1978 at a salary of $8,000 per month for the first six months and $10,000 per month thereafter. He also received a bonus of $24,000 in March for the year ended 31st March 1979. During the first three months his employer paid $18,000 for him to live in a single hotel room and also gave him a meals allowance of

$600 per month. He then moved into a flat for which he paid rent, rates and maintenance of $6,200 per month and the employer agreed to re-imburse a maximum of $6,000 per month. His allowable expenses and outgoings for the year were $6,000. The assessable value of the flat for Property Tax purposes is $60,000.

His income assessable to Salaries Tax for 1978/79 is as follows:—

			First 3 months	Last 9 months
1)	Salary	$ 8,000 x 3	$24,000	
		$ 8,000 x 3		$ 24,000
		$10,000 x 6		60,000
2)	Bonus (Time apportioned)		6,000	18,000
3)	Meal Allowance		1,800	–
	Total Employment Income		$31,800	$102,000
4)	Allowable Expenses (Time apportioned)		1,500	4,500
			$30,300	$ 97,500
5)	Rental Value:			
	4% x $30,300		1,212	
	10% x $97,500 =	$9,750		
	Less Rent Paid	1,800		
		$7,950		7,950
			$31,512	$105,450
	Total Income Assessable to Salaries Tax		$136,962	

Notes:—
(a) Although the benefit costs the employer and benefits Ernie by $72,000, the assessable benefit is only $9,162.
(b) The meal allowance is taxable as an allowance under Sec. 9(1)(a).
(c) Although not strictly rent, the rates and maintenance charges are treated as such. However, the Inland Revenue Department examines maintenance charges carefully in case they should be artificially inflated for avoidance purposes.
(d) The Property Tax assessable value of $45,000 (9 months) is larger than the rental value of $9,750, therefore the election does not apply.

It would be easy to avoid or minimise the benefit assessable by arranging for an employee to have a separate employment with an associated company which provided the residence and also a minimal or nil salary. This opportunity has been prevented by the inclusion in the charging sections of the wording "by an employer or an associated corporation". This has the effect of aggregating his earnings from all associated corporations for the purposes of applying the percentage to arrive at rental value. For this purpose an associated corporation is:—
(1) A corporation over which the employer has control or,

(2) if the employer is itself a corporation, a corporation which has control over the employer or which is under the control of the same person as controls the employer corporation.

In this context, control is widely defined as the ability to conduct the affairs of a corporation in accordance with ones wishes whether by the holding of shares, by direct or indirect voting power or by virtue of any power conferred by the articles of association or any other document which confers similar powers directly or indirectly (Sec. 9(6)). It is important to note here that the employer could be an individual and the residence could be provided by a company associated with that individual for the anti avoidance provision to apply, it is certainly not a precondition for its application that both parties be companies. However the provision does not apply in reverse, in other words, the associate must be a corporation.

Example 8

Mr. U.B. Court is employed by a Hong Kong company (1) which pays him a salary of $120,000 per annum. He is also employed as a consultant to a subsidiary company (2) which pays him an annual fee of $5,000 and provides rent free accommodation.

His Salaries Tax position is:—

Salary (1)	$120,000	
Rental Value 10%	12,000	(Note (a))
Salary (2)	5,000	
Rental Value 10%	500	(Note (b))
Total Assessable to Salaries Tax	$137,500	

Notes:—
(a) As the residence is provided by an associated company of company (1), the rental value is computed on the salary from company (1).
(b) The residence is provided by the employer in this case and therefore the rental value is also calculated on the income from that employer.
(c) If Mr. Court's consultancy had instead been with the controlling shareholder of company (1), on the assumption that such shareholder is an individual, the residence is not provided by an associated *company* but an associated individual. His rental value would therefore be limited to $500.

SHARE OPTION BENEFIT. The IRO contains a provision to overcome the decision in Abbott v Philbin (39 TC 82) wherein an employee was granted an option by virtue of his employment, to acquire shares at a given price and when the market value of the shares exceeded the option price, he exercised the option and was able to make a profit which was held not to be a perquisite of his employment. It is therefore provided in Sec. 9(1)(d) that any gain realised by the exercise of, or by the assignment of or release of, an option to acquire stock or shares, is to be a taxable emolument if the option was granted to an individual because of his employment or office. It is of course always open to him to show that the option was obtained at arm's length as a normal investment opportunity not granted as a special opportunity to him because of his position. It should also be particularly noted that it only applies to employees or office-holders of corporations although the subject stock or shares can be with any corporation.

The taxable moment is triggered by the exercise, assignment, or release of the option and a computation of the gain must be made at that time. In the case of an assignment or release, consideration will be received and the gain is simply the consideration received less the amount, if any, paid for the right (Sec. 9(4)(b)). In the case of the exercise of an option there will of course be no consideration received and no actual gain made until such time as the shares are sold, when of course the gain may have disappeared. Nevertheless, the gain to be assessed is the open market value of the shares at the date of exercise of the option less the consideration paid, if any, for the option and the amount paid for the shares (Sec. 9(4)(a)). No value can be put upon services rendered in fixing the amount "paid" for the grant of the option. Only actual payment for the grant can be deducted (Sec. 9(4) proviso).

Were it not for this provision, a benefit might arise on the date of granting the option if the value of the option at that date exceeded the amount paid for it (see Abbott v Philbin and also "Case Law Discussion" on page 54). Because of this it is provided that where Sec. 9(1)(d) may be applicable to the grant of an option upon its exercise etc., Salaries Tax is not to be chargeable by virtue of the earlier event (Sec. 9(5)).

Example 9

Percy Vere is a Director of Stocks Ltd. and in consideration of his services he is given a special opportunity to invest in the parent company Shares Ltd. He pays $50 for an option to acquire 2,000 shares in Shares Ltd. at $10 each. At the time of taking up the option the shares have an open market value of $20 each. Unfortunately the value drops and a month later Percy exercises his option when the value is $15.

The "profit" assessable to Salaries Tax is:—

Open Market Value at date of exercise 2000 @ $15 =		$30,000
Consideration given for Shares 2000 @ $10 =	$20,000	
Consideration given for Option	50	$20,050
Subject To Salaries Tax		$ 9,950

Notes:—
(a) On the principle of Abbott v Philbin there is a taxable profit at the time of granting
     the option because the market value of the shares at that time exceeds what he has
     to pay for them. The "income" is not however assessed because Sec. 9(5) exempts
     it.
(b) If it had not been clear that the option had been granted to him because of his
     directorship, this question would have to be considered on the facts.

This benefit charge should not be confused with the position where a
person is allowed to subscribe for shares at a price where the market value at
the time is in excess of the price paid. There is an immediate taxable benefit
in that case on the principle of Weight v Salmon (19 TC 174). See also BR
27/69.

CASE LAW DISCUSSION.   Whilst the IRO describes the general charging heads for Salaries Tax and also provides specific exemptions and includes
specific benefits as chargeable it is nevertheless essential to look to case law
for a full understanding of the scope and limitations of what constitutes
assessable remuneration. In particular it is necessary to look to case law to
determine upon what basis benefits in kind are subject to Salaries Tax.

First of all however there are a number of general principles which legal
decisions have brought to light.

The income must come to the employee as income from an office or
employment which involves a contractual relationship, not necessarily reduced to writing, between the individual and an employer. In most cases of
course this can be established beyond doubt but there will be a number of
cases where the dividing line between employment and self employment is
difficult to determine. For a discussion of the principles involved see Mitchell
and Edon v Ross (40 TC 11) and Fall v Hitchen (1973 Simon Tax Cases
66) from which the general rule arises that an employee has a master/servant
relationship under which *duties* arise whereas a self-employed person performs services in the course of his trade or profession. These rules also help to
determine the nature of spare-time work carried out by an otherwise full time
employee. It may be that they are so related to the individual's regular
employment that they are to be regarded as casual employment falling within
the scope of Salaries Tax or they may properly represent a separate business
activity falling within Profits Tax. See the discussion in Fuge v McClelland
(36 TC 571). For a discussion of what constitutes a trading activity see
Chapter 5.

It is also a fundamental principle of income from employment being
taxable that the payments, to be brought into account, must arise as a reward
for the services rendered and not for some other consideration (Reid v
Seymour 11 TC 625) (see also Hochstrasser v Mayes 38 TC 702 and BR
20/71).

An example of a non-taxable receipt would be a wedding gift by an employer to an employee so long as the motive is solely a personal gift and not a reward for services. The employer's motive will generally be to foster and maintain goodwill among the employees in general but that should not prejudice the non-taxable nature in the employee's hands. This should not be confused with an ex-gratia payment made to an employee for services rendered which, although non contractual and of a windfall nature, is still taxable because it comes as a reward for services (Cooper v Blakiston 5 TC 347).

An extension of this principle is the receipt by an employee of a terminal payment. It is primarily essential to determine the reason why the payment was made and, if not for services rendered, cannot be taxable. Payments which are typically not taxable are:—

(1) Ex-gratia gift as a token of personal esteem on the occasion of retirement (principles discussed above)

(2) Compensation for loss of office, cancellation of service agreement, salary in lieu of notice etc. There are numerous legal decisions in the UK on these points of principle but typically see Hose v Warwick (27 TC 459) and Duff v Barlow (23 TC 633). In Hong Kong see BR 116/77. Great care needs to be exercised in reaching a decision on payments representing some form of compensation because the following types have been held to be taxable:—

   (i) A terminal payment which has been pre-arranged as part of the terms of employment is in reality deferred remuneration (Henry v Foster 16 TC 605) even if it is referred to in the service agreement as compensation for termination (Dale v De Soissons 32 TC 118).

   (ii) A payment for agreeing not to resign which is in reality a payment for future services (Cameron v Prendergast 23 TC 122) or for agreeing to serve for a smaller salary which is in reality an advance payment of salary (Tilley v Wales 25 TC 136).

(3) Payment for agreeing to enter into a covenant restricting an ex-employee's activities, for example not to compete in the same field.

Furthermore, certain payments received at the commencement of employment may not be taxable, for example in Pritchard v Arundale (47 TC 680) a payment was made to an individual, not as a reward for future services, but as an incentive to encourage him to leave an existing gainful occupation and commence service with the employer. This was held not to be taxable. In all of these cases where special payments are received it is necessary to consider one main point of principle, that is whether the sum is paid for services past, present or future in which case it is taxable, or whether it is paid for some other consideration in which case it is not taxable. The cases already cited illustrate this principle clearly but sometimes the dividing line is narrow. In Ball v Johnson (47 TC 155) a bank employee took and passed the Institute of Bankers professional examination for which his employer rewarded him with a sum of money. This was held not to be taxable.

It is not only payments which come to an employee from his employer which are within the scope of Salaries Tax, the principle of "reward for services" extends to a reward coming from any person so long as it is in return for the services which the employee is required by his employer to perform. The obvious example is "tips" which a customer may give to a taxi driver or waitress in return for good service. This is in any event covered by the inclusion in Sec. 9(1)(a) of the words "...., whether derived from the employer or others ...." but apart from that, the principle was established in Calvert v Wainwright (27 TC 475).

Finally, there is one further point of principle that, even if an employee performs some special service outside of the normal line of his duties, if his employer pays him for it he is taxable (Mudd v Collins 9 TC 297).

Having established whether value received is in return for services rendered it is necessary to go one stage further and consider the form in which it is received. If it comes to the employee in a cash form it is clearly taxable except where specifically exempted by the IRO (e.g. holiday warrants, rent refunds) but if it comes in a non cash form, the so-called "benefits-in-kind", there are other considerations. The extent to which a benefit-in-kind may be taxed, in the absence of specific charging legislation, was considered in the now classic case on this point of principle, that of Wilkins v Rogerson (39 TC 344) adopting a point of principle established much earlier in Tennant v Smith (3 TC 158). In the Wilkins case the employer purchased a suit of clothes for £15 and gave it to the employee and the tax authorities attempted to assess £15 as an emolument. The principle emerged that "it is not what saves the employee's pocket but what goes into his pocket that forms the taxable emolument", in other words because he saves £15, by not having to buy the suit himself, is irrelevant; what is important is, how can he turn the suit into money's worth? He could only do this by selling it and therefore it was established that it was the second-hand value which was taxable and this was found to be £5 in the particular case. This principle holds good for Salaries Tax in all cases of benefits-in-kind except where otherwise provided as taxable by the IRO. In fact the IRO seeks to specifically tax no benefits-in-kind other than the housing accommodation benefit and share option benefit dealt with under separate headings above.

It has however been further held that "cash equivalents" may be taxable at their face value if they in fact enable an employee to make independent purchases, even if they can only for example be spent at one store, because they nevertheless represent money's worth. The classic example is gift vouchers or luncheon vouchers (Laidler v Perry 42 TC 351). If however an employer provided free meals at his own canteen or contracted for an independent restaurant to supply free meals to employees this would not be taxable because it could not be converted into cash. Similarly, if an employee has the use of a company car and is not entitled to sub-let it to any other person, he is not taxed because he cannot convert the benefit into cash. Other examples of non-taxable benefits are:—

Provision of free medical benefits.

Use of furniture and domestic equipment owned by employer.

Provision of domestic servants employed by the employer.

Provision of gas, electricity and telephone services.

It should be noted however that in all of these cases it is an essential element of the freedom from tax that the liability for the provision of the services is contracted for and paid for by the employer. If, for example, the employee employed his own domestic servants and contracted himself for the supply of gas, electricity and telephone but received a re-imbursement of the cost from his employer, this receipt of cash would be taxable. Similarly, although he may have free use of a car, if he pays his own repair and fuel bills and receives re-imbursement thereof or the employer pays the bill direct, the cash benefit would be taxable whereas if the employer contracted directly with a garage to supply these services free of charge to the employee, the benefit would not be taxable. If a benefit is received in kind but could be converted into cash, it is a question of fact as to the amount for which it could be so converted. If for example an employee was sold some shares at below their market value, the immediate taxable benefit would be the market value less the amount paid (Weight v Salmon 19 TC 174). If however some restriction was placed upon the marketability of these particular shares, it would be proper to suitably discount the market value (Ede v Wilson and Cornwall 26 TC 382).

The following is a comprehensive example of the principles discussed in paragraph 4 above.

Example 10

Ian Mcc has the following remuneration package for a year of assessment. He is employed by a non Hong Kong company and is able to show that all factors are consistent with him having a non Hong Kong source of employment. He is able to show that, during the year of assessment 30% of his services were performed outside Hong Kong.

(1) Salary $120,000
(2) Bonus $30,000
(3) Allowance for high cost of living $15,000
(4) The company rents a car at a cost of $18,000 for the year and allows him to use it wholly for private purposes. They also pay the licence and insurance costing $2,500 and have re-imbursed his garage bills of $2,000 during the year. He pays for his own fuel.
(5) Two years ago he was granted, at a cost of $100, an option to subscribe for 1,000 shares in his employer company at $20 each. This year their market value rose to $25 each and he exercised his option. He still has the shares which also paid a dividend to him of $1,500.
(6) He rents his own flat at a cost of $8,000 per month including rates and service charge and his employer reimburses this in full but deducts 3% from his salary as a rent contribution.
(7) His domestic servant is employed by the Company at a cost of $12,000 for the year and the employer also refunds his electricity bill of $7,500 for the year.
(8) $25,000 holiday travel allowance for himself and family which he wholly spent for that purpose in the year.

His assessable income for Salaries Tax, using the same reference numbers, is:—

1)	Salary			$120,000	
2)	Bonus			30,000	
3)	Cost of living allowance			15,000	
4)	Use of Car			2,000	(Note a)
5)	Share option – Market Value	$25,000			
	Cost, including option	20,100		4,900	(Note b)
6)	Household benefits			7,500	(Note c)
				$179,400	
	Exclusion of services outside Hong Kong (30%)			53,820	(Note d)
	Net Assessable Income before Housing Accommodation benefit			$125,580	
7)	Housing Accommodation benefit (10%)	$12,558			
	Less rent contribution 3% x $120,000	3,600		8,958	(Note e)
	Assessable to Salaries Tax			$134,538	

Notes:—
(a) There is no chargeable benefit in respect of the use of the car or the licence and insurance because these items cannot be converted into cash. However, he incurs his own bills at the garage and reimbursements thereof are therefore taxable. Even if he presented the bills to the employer for direct payment after receiving them

personally, this would be a taxable perquisite. It would be tax free if the employer contracted with the garage and was therefore billed direct.

(b)   The taxable benefit is triggered by the exercise of the option (Sec. 9(1)(d)) irrespective of the fact that he has not yet realised the gain. The dividend is not taxable.

(c)   The same principles as discussed in note (a) apply. As the liability for the electricity bill was incurred by Ian, the reimbursement is taxable.

(d)   See page 38.

(e)   The rental value is calculated on assessable income after excluding the proportion which is exempt because it relates to offshore duties (BR 20/76). The rent contribution is not however pro-rated per the decision in CIR v R.P. Williamson (HKTC 1215).

(f)   The holiday travel allowance is exempt as long as it is fully expended for that purpose (Sec. 9(1)(a)(ii)).

TAX ON TAX.   Where an employer pays an employee's tax for him this constitutes additional remuneration of the year in which the tax is paid which accordingly gives rise to a bigger tax liability in that year which if paid by the employer constitutes further remuneration and an even bigger tax liability in the year in which that is paid and so on with increasing cumulative effect.

Example 11

An employee has a fixed salary of $100,000 and the employer pays his tax.

	Taxable Income	Tax Thereon	
Year 1	$100,000	$15,000	(paid in year 2)
Year 2	115,000	17,250	(paid in year 3)
Year 3	117,250	17,587	(paid in year 4)
Year 4	117,587	17,638	(paid in year 5)
	etc.	etc.	

There is therefore an increasing cost to the employer which is accentuated if the salary is increasing as well. This problem can be obviated in the case of medium or long term employment by fixing the salary at a given net-of-tax figure and reporting the notional gross equivalent for tax purposes. However the fact that the earnings have been computed in this manner should be disclosed to the Inland Revenue Department otherwise the Department could charge that the full facts have not been reported although the Department does not lose because, over the life of an employment, the total tax is the same by either method.

Example 12

The employee in Example 11 is to receive annually $100,000 net of tax.
The amount reported for tax is $\frac{100}{85}$ x $100,000 = $117,647.

Taxable Income Reported	$117,647	
Tax thereon @ 15%	17,647	Paid by Employer
	$100,000	Received by Employee

Obviously the calculation of the notional gross equivalent is more complicated in a case where personal allowances are deductible, tax is payable at progressive rates and rental values are involved, in which case an algebraic calculation is necessary. However, the principle holds good and it will be seen from the above examples that the latter method has the merit of consistency.

5. Quantum of Assessment

Having ascertained what income is chargeable to Salaries Tax, the method of assessment is relatively straightforward. It is first necessary to isolate the assessable income for the basis period and then consider what deductions may be made from assessable income. Sec. 12B provides that the net chargeable income is to be arrived at after deducting certain expenses, depreciation allowances, charitable donations and losses to arrive at net assessable income and then deducting personal allowances to arrive at net chargeable income. It then depends upon the size of the net chargeable income whether it is charged at progressive rates or whether the alternative basis of charging net assessable income at standard rate is applicable. The method of assessment and payment involves a system of Provisional Salaries Tax.

BASIS PERIOD.   The IRO simply states that liability to Salaries Tax for a year of assessment is on the aggregate remuneration from all sources within the scope of Salaries Tax which accrue in that year of assessment (Sec. 11B). As this is an "actual" basis, co-incidental with the year of assessment, there are no commencement or cessation provisions. Because Sec. 10 provides that the income of a wife is deemed to be that of her husband, her income liable to Salaries Tax will therefore be aggregated with his and assessed upon him. This is not the case in respect of a wife living apart from her husband, who would be assessed individually in her own name. The definitions of "wife" and "wife living apart from her husband" are important (see Chapter 7). In the year of marriage the wife's earnings are divided between what has accrued to her as a single person, and is assessed upon her with full personal allowances granted, and what has accrued to her since marriage which is assessed upon her husband.

As the basis is income which "accrues" within a year of assessment it is important to know precisely what accrual means. Income accrues to a person when he is entitled to receive it, whether he actually receives it or not (Sec. 11D(b)). Accordingly the day or date on which salary or wages is payable is the governing factor and in regard to other sources, such as a bonus, it is a question of fact when a person becomes entitled to claim payment. It would be usual to look to a service agreement for evidence of entitlement but in the absence of a written agreement, oral evidence or evidence of an existing code of practice might be relevant. If a bonus contractually relates to the employer's profits that bonus will have been earned day by day during the employer's accounting period and, in the absence of any other specific date laid down will be due at the end of that accounting period. Where a bonus is wholly at the employer's discretion, it will not accrue due until it is made known to the employee that it will be paid and in the absence of a stated date of payment will accrue when actually paid. Apart from this, it is specifically provided by Sec. 11D(a) that income is deemed to have been received by a person when it has either been made available to him or has been dealt with in accordance with his instructions. In other words if it is credited to a current account upon which he can draw or he has been told that it is available when he comes to call at the office, notwithstanding that he may not draw upon it or collect it, it is deemed to be paid. Similarly it is deemed to be paid if he asks the employer to invest it for him or pay it to a creditor.

Leave pay occasionally gives rise to difficulties as to the period or periods in which it accrues. The rule is that if there is some specific reference in a person's service agreement to entitlement of leave pay in one lump at a particular time, then the period into which it falls is governed by that due date. However, as is often the case, the arrangements may be informal in which case the following general rules are applicable:—

(1) A payment in lieu of leave not taken accrues when paid.

(2) A single payment for terminal leave accrues when paid or in the final year of assessment if paid after cessation.

(3) A lump sum payment made at the beginning of a period of leave that is in fact made as an advance for the employee's convenience, is treated as accruing when the usual salary payments would have been made but for the advance.

Nevertheless, although Sec. 11B fixes the year of assessment for which a payment accrues, a person cannot be assessed upon it until he actually receives it, although when he ultimately receives it, the assessment is for the year in which he was due to receive it (Sec. 11D(a)). The Board of Review have on a number of occasions considered the date on which income accrues for Salaries Tax purposes. See for example BR 3/73, 13/74 and 17/76.

Example 13

An individual commences employment in Hong Kong on 1st November, 1978 and his service agreement includes the following:

1) Salary of $7,000 per month payable in arrear on the 5th of the following month.

2) Annual bonus in respect of the company's year to 31st December, payable on 31st March each year. In 1979 he is entitled to $10,000 for the part year and due to the fact that the accounts were not prepared in time, it was not ascertained nor paid until 5th July, 1979 after both he and the employer had submitted their Salaries Tax returns for 1978/79.

3) A high cost of living allowance of $5,000 for a full year payable in advance on the commencement of employment and each anniversary thereafter.

His income for Salaries Tax purposes for 1978/79 is:—

1)	Salary 4 x $7,000	$28,000	(Note (a))
2)	Bonus	10,000	(Note (b))
3)	Allowance	5,000	(Note (c))
		$43,000	

Notes:—

(a)   Although he has earned 5 months salary he is only due to be paid 4 payments.

(b)   Strictly the bonus relates to 1978/79 because that was when it was due. If an assessment had already been raised for 1978/79 on the basis of returns which excluded it, an additional assessment would be raised after 5th July, 1979 (Sec. 11D(a)). In practice it would probably be assessed in 1979/80 on a receipts basis. However, if because of personal circumstances, his marginal tax rate for 1978/79 was lower than for 1979/80 it would pay him to seek statutory treatment.

(c)   Although a substantial part of the allowance relates to 1979/80, it was due in 1978/79 and therefore assessable in that year.

There are two other rules which concern post-cessation receipts and lump sum receipts. If a sum which would otherwise be within the scope of Salaries Tax is paid by an employer to an employee after he has ceased that employment, it is deemed to have accrued to the employee on the last day of that employment (Sec. 11D(b) proviso (ii)). As regards lump sums there is a provision by which these can be related back (Sec. 11D(b) proviso (i)):—

(1) Over the period of service for which the payment is made, or, if less:—

(2) Over the period of 3 years up to the date of accrual of the payment or the date of cessation of employment, whichever is earlier.

This rule is applicable only to two types of payment:—

(1) A lump sum payment or gratuity paid upon the termination of an office or employment, or

(2) A lump sum payment of deferred pay or arrears of pay.

The payment is treated as having accrued evenly over the period in (1) or (2) above and of course there is only a benefit in claiming the application of this rule if the marginal rate of tax in the earlier years is lower than that for the year in which the lump sum would otherwise fall. This may arise because either the income was smaller in the earlier years or there were other reliefs available by personal assessment (see Chapter 7) or otherwise. Even where an assessment is otherwise final and conclusive, it can be disturbed to admit a claim made in writing within 2 years of the end of the year of assessment in which the payment is made. In technical terms, an application within this time limit is treated as a valid objection against the assessment affected and therefore, if the IRD fails to admit the claim, the dispute can be processed under the objection and appeal procedures (see Chapter 10). Note that a lump sum or gratuity paid on retirement or cessation of employment is excluded from the calculation of rental value (see page 49) whether the sum is spread back or not.

Example 14

Ivan A. Ward has worked for his employer for 5 years and on 1st October 1978 receives a lump sum of $36,000 in respect of arrears of pay relating to his whole period of service.

If he elects by 31st March, 1981 for the benefit of Sec. 11D (b) proviso (i), the lump sum will be treated as arising evenly back to 1st October, 1975 as follows:—

1978/79	$ 6,000
1977/78	$12,000
1976/77	$12,000
1975/76	$ 6,000
	$36,000

If his employment had commenced on 1st April 1976, the spread would have been:—

1978/79	$ 7,200
1977/78	$14,400
1976/77	$14,400
	$36,000

DEDUCTIONS FROM ASSESSABLE INCOME. In order to arrive at net income chargeable to tax, deductions may be claimed for certain expenses, depreciation allowances and charitable contributions. These are dealt with under separate headings below.

EXPENSES. A deduction may be claimed for all outgoings and expenses, other than expenses of a domestic, private or capital nature which have been wholly, exclusively and necessarily incurred in the production of assessable income. (Sec. 12(1)(a)).

Admissable expenses under this heading are relatively few because of the stringent conditions attached to their allowance. The provision is very similar to an equivalent provision in U.K. tax law and therefore the numerous U.K. Court decisions which relate to the U.K. equivalent are looked to for guidance. Although the law is sufficiently similar for the U.K. decisions to be authoritative, reliance cannot necessarily be placed upon them where the decision turned upon whether or not, for U.K. purposes, the expenditure had been incurred "in the performance of the duties" because in the Hong Kong equivalent the relevant wording is "in the production of the assessable income" which is materially different although the Hong Kong case of CIR v Humphrey does not identify the distinction. The importance of the phrase "In the production of the assessable income" is illustrated by CIR v Robert P. Burns (HKTC 1181) which involved the payment of legal expenses by a racehorse trainer employed by The Jockey Club for the purpose of regaining his training license. It was held that the expenses were incurred for the purpose of seeing that he was not precluded from earning his assessable income, they were not incurred in the production of it. This is however now somewhat confused by a Board of Review decision (so far unpublished) which has apparently held a Jockey Club trainer to be not an employee but to be self-employed and subject to Profits Tax!

The three tests of wholly, exclusively and necessarily, when taken together, are extremely narrow. In practice the wholly and exclusively tests are not strictly applied e.g. if it is demonstrated that an employee must use his car for business purposes, his claim in respect of repairs, fuel, insurance etc. would fail if he also used the car privately, even if only on rare occasions. Therefore, in practice, these expenses would be apportioned between business and private and the business proportion would be allowed. It is a fundamental principle however that expenditure incurred on travelling between home and office is not deductible because it is not incurred in producing the income but merely enabling the employee to get to work so that he can produce income. The U.K. decisions on this are considered relevant authority but there is also the direct authority of CIR v Humphrey (HKTC 451). However, where the employee has more than one place of business, the cost of travelling between those places is deductible (C v C of T 28 SATC 127). Where an employee must travel in the execution of his duties and he necessarily incurs expenditure on subsistence while away from home on duty, such expenditure is deductible (Nolder v Walters 15 TC 380). The relaxation of the wholly and exclusively test is however not extended to every case where there is a duality of purpose, for example an executive or hotel manager claiming the cost of a suit because of the necessity to appear in business suitably dressed will not be successful because the suit will inevitably be worn on non-business occasions.

The test of necessity is probably the most stringent as the IRD will always want to be satisfied as to why, under a master/servant relationship, if the employer requires the expense to be met, he does not pay it himself or reimburse it. The fact that the employee incurs it because it assists him in his employment or is convenient for him is insufficient to qualify it for deduction, it must be required by the employer to be incurred by the employee. This is more likely to be satisfied where an employee earns gross commission by special effort, e.g. a salesman, and is clearly required to bear all costs of earning that commission such as entertainment. In BR 19/78, a stockbroker's runner on a commission basis was allowed to deduct the cost of paying assistants.

An area which illustrates the stringency of the "production of assessable income" test is professional subscriptions incurred by an individual exercising his profession as an employee. These are not strictly deductible because although they may be very much in connection with and relevant to his employment and also assist him in his work in that he receives regular updating of technical information, the expenditure is not incurred in producing his earnings. The fact that the employer may have chosen him because of his professional qualification is not sufficient. The U.K. case of Simpson v Tate (9 TC 314) is considered as authority for this. However, in practice the IRD will allow such subscriptions where:—

(1) They are a prerequisite of employment; or
(2) Retention of membership is of regular use and benefit to him in his employment.

It is quite common for an employer to pay an employee a regular "allowance" to cover business expenditure, e.g. an entertaining allowance. An allowance is strictly taxable under Sec. 9(1)(a) and it is up to the employee to then make a claim under Sec. 12(1)(a). In practice however, if it is shown that the allowance in fact is normally fully expended by the employee in a manner which qualifies for deduction, the allowance is not assessed and no annual claim is called for. See Departmental Interpretation and Practice Note No. 9 reproduced in Appendix 8.

DEPRECIATION ALLOWANCES.   Also deductible are depreciation allowances in respect of plant and machinery which is necessary for the production of assessable profits (Sec. 12(1)(b)). Rules governing the computation of such allowances are contained in Part VI of the IRO (see Chapter 6). Whilst this is in fact an extension of the expense allowance provision it does not contain the "wholly and exclusively" tests, in fact the IRO specifically recognises the dual purpose asset by providing that the allowances are to be apportioned in a manner which the assessor considers to be fair and reasonable (Sec. 12(2)). Where a disposal of such plant or machinery gives rise to a balancing charge, the charge is treated as income chargeable to Salaries Tax. (Sec. 12(5)).

CHARITABLE CONTRIBUTIONS. A third class of deduction in arriving at net assessable income in fact is entirely unrelated to employment income. If the taxpayer or his wife, who is living with him, have made contributions to approved charities and such total contributions amount to at least $100 in the year of assessment, these may be deducted subject to the following limitations (Sec. 12(1)(c)):–

(1) The maximum deduction is 10% of assessable income after deducting allowable expenses and depreciation allowances (Sec. 12(4)(b)); and

(2) Because there is a similar deduction for Profits Tax purposes and the taxpayer or his wife may have a source of income liable to Profits Tax, it is provided that any contributions allowable for Profits Tax purposes may not also be deducted for Salaries Tax. There is a similar disallowance provision in the Profits Tax rules therefore it is not clear which takes priority. Similarly, any contribution which is deductible under other Profits Tax rules, is disallowable for Salaries Tax (Sec. 12(4)(a)).

For some reason which is not immediately apparent, Sec. 12(3) lays down the rule that a claim for deduction of charitable contributions must be in a specified form and contain certain particulars and be subject to such proof as the Commissioner may require (Sec. 12(3)). The expense allowance claim for example does not have such stipulations.

For the purpose of the above deduction an approved charitable donation is defined in Sec. 2 as a donation of money to the Government for charitable purposes or to any charitable institution or trust of a public character which has been granted exemption from tax under Sec. 88 of the IRO. Such approved charitable institutions are listed in Special Supplements to Hong Kong Government Gazette. It has been held in CIR v Sanford Yung-Tao Yung (HKTC 959) that an inflated price paid to a charity for tickets to a social event does not constitute a donation.

Example 15

A salesman has a salary of $45,000 for a year of assessment and also earns commission of $30,000. In earning this income his employer requires him to bear whatever expenses are necessary and he has incurred entertainment expenditure of $3,500. He also uses his own car 60% for business and submits details of total motoring expenditure of $6,500. Total depreciation allowances on the car for the year amount to $6,000. He makes contributions to approved charitable institutions of $4,500 and his wife makes contributions of $2,000.

1) His Salaries Tax position is:—

Salary		$45,000
Commission		30,000
		$75,000

2) Expenses (Sec. 12(1)(a))

— Entertaining	$3,500		
— Car (60% x 6,500)	3,900		(Note (a))

3) Depreciation Allowances (Sec. 12(1)(b))

— 60% x $6,000	3,600	11,000	(Note (b))
		$64,000	

4) Charitable Contribution (Sec. 12(1)(b))   6,400   (Note (c))

Net Income assessable $57,600

Notes:—

(a) Although there is no statutory right to apportion expenses of dual purpose, in practice this is done with car expenses.

(b) Depreciation allowances can however be statutorily apportioned (Sec. 12(2)).

(c) The total contributions are $6,500 but the allowance is limited to 10% of the assessable income less expenses and depreciation allowances (Sec. 12(4)(b)).

LOSSES.   Although in practice a very rare event, it is quite possible for losses to arise under Salaries Tax rules. This happens where allowable expenses and depreciation allowances exceed the assessable income. Charitable contributions cannot augment the loss because relief is restricted to 10% of the income after expenses and depreciation allowances which in these circumstances is of course 10% of nil.

Losses for a year of assessment are carried forward without time limit and allowed against future assessable income under Salaries Tax (Sec. 12A(1)). They must be set against income for subsequent years in strict chronological order (Sec. 12A(3)).

CALCULATION OF TAX.   Having ascertained the net assessable income, the tax is calculated in one of two ways, whichever turns out to give the smallest liability. The two methods are:—

(1) Net assessable income charged at standard rate (Sec. 13 proviso (b)).

(2) Net assessable income less applicable personal allowances to arrive at net chargeable income per Sec. 12B, then charged at the progressive rates provided in the Second Schedule to the IRO (Sec. 13).

The personal allowances and progressive rates are listed in Chapter 1, on page 12 and the necessary rules for claiming personal allowances are detailed in Chapter 7. Note that if (2) above applies, the entitlement to deduct personal allowances is automatic for Salaries Tax purposes, regardless of the individual's residence status. Salaries Tax is the only one of the four Hong Kong income taxes where there is an automatic entitlement to the personal allowances. If they are required to be claimed against income which is subject to one of the other three·taxes, a Personal Assessment election is necessary for which there is a residential qualification (see Chapter 7).

Example 16

I.Q. Upp has the following personal circumstances: –
1) Salary and bonus for the year of assessment 1981/82 $90,000
2) Rent free accommodation for full year
    (contribution to rent $4,000)
3) Agreed allowable expenses $ 1,500
4) Agreed allowable depreciation allowances for car $ 700
5) Approved Charitable Donations by wife $ 1,000
6) Personal allowances due for wife and 1 child.

His Salaries Tax is computed as follows: –

1)	Salary & Bonus			$90,000
2)	Rental Value (10% of 90,000) less $4,000			5,000
				$95,000
3)	Expenses allowable		$ 1,500	
4)	Depreciation Allowances		700	
5)	Charitable Donations		1,000	3,200
	Net Assessable Income			$91,800
1)	Personal Allowances – Self	$20,500		
	Wife	20,500		
	Additional	15,000		
	Child	8,000		
		$64,000		64,000
	Net Chargeable Income			$27,800
(i)	Salaries Tax per Sec. 13	$10,000 @ 5% =		500
		10,000 @ 10% =		1,000
		7,800 @ 15% =		1,170
		$27,800		$ 2,670
(ii)	Salaries Tax per Sec. 13 proviso (b)	$91,800 @ 15% =		$13,770

Notes:–
(a) The Salaries Tax liability is the smaller of the two alternatives and therefore $2,670.
(b) It will be noted that the marginal rate under alternative (a) is already 15% as compared to the flat marginal rate of 15% under alternative (b). As his income increases, the gap between the alternatives narrows until a break even point is reached beyond which alternative (b) is always advantageous. (See Break-Even Point below).

BREAK-EVEN POINT. As illustrated in Example 16 above, there is a point at which tax charged at progressive rates on net chargeable income is exactly equal to tax at standard rate on net assessable income and beyond which the tax at standard rate will always be less. This is illustrated as follows:—

Net Assessable Income		$190,000		
Personal Allowance				
— Self	$20,500			
— Wife	20,500			
— Additional	15,000	56,000		
Net Chargeable Income		134,000		
		10,000	@ 5% =	500
		10,000	@ 10% =	1,000
		10,000	@ 15% =	1,500
		10,000	@ 20% =	2,000
		94,000	@ 25% =	23,500
		$134,000		$28,500
Alternative $190,000 @ 15%			=	$28,500

Obviously, any increase in net assessable income above $190,000 would be charged at 25% on the progressive rate or 15% on the standard rate basis and therefore the standard rate basis will always be applicable and no deduction will be given for personal allowances. Break-even points will of course depend upon personal circumstances but the following are correct for the stated circumstances:—

Personal Allowances for:	Net Assessable Income Break-Even Point
Single	$120,000
Married	$190,000
Married + 1 Child	$210,000
Married + 2 Children	$223,750
Married + 3 Children	$231,250
Married + 4 Children	$236,250

ASSESSMENT AND PAYMENT OF TAX. The assessing system for Salaries Tax consists of a Provisional Salaries Tax assessment in an estimated amount followed, after a return has been made, by a final Salaries Tax assessment on the true figure in which the Provisional Salaries Tax already paid for the year of assessment is credited. In practice the assessment form is a two part set containing the final Salaries Tax assessment for a year of assessment and also the Provisional Salaries Tax assessment for the immediately succeeding year of assessment (Sec. 63D(1)(b)). A single Provisional Salaries Tax assessment is however quite valid on its own (Sec. 63D(1)(a)).

The charge to Provisional tax is authorised by Sec. 63B and, at the commencement of employment in Hong Kong, the Provisional assessment for the first year of assessment is estimated (Sec. 63C(3)), prepared from figures supplied by the taxpayer in a provisional Salaries Tax Return. However, as is most usual, the administrative machinery does not catch up with new employees soon enough and the first assessment is usually a Final assessment in true figures for the first part year and an estimated Provisional assessment for the following year (Sec. 63C(2)). The estimate for the second year is usually based on a precisely grossed-up equivalent of the actual part year figure for the first year. In subsequent years the Provisional assessment is always in the same figure as the immediately preceeding Final assessment (Sec. 63C(1)).

The Assessor has further powers to estimate, in the case of cessation of employment (Sec. 63C(3)) or where the employee is about to leave Hong Kong or it is otherwise expedient to quickly raise a Provisional assessment (Sec. 63C(5)) or in the absence of a return (Sec. 63C(4)). In practice, by the time the Assessor is aware that an employee is ceasing employment or about to leave Hong Kong, a current Provisional assessment is already in existence and this is usually quickly adjusted to a Final assessment on actual figures.

Once assessed, the Commissioner is empowered to issue a notice of assessment and fix the due dates for payment (Sec. 63C(6)). It is usual for the Provisional tax to be payable in two instalments with 75% being fixed for payment in January or February in the year of assessment and the remaining 25% three months later. However, it is now a matter of policy, if the first instalment is in default, the second instalment becomes immediately due. This enables the Commissioner to impose a surcharge on both instalments and enforce collection of both. There is therefore, apart from the policy in the case of defaulters, no question of payment in advance, in fact in the usual case of an increasing income, tax is usually in arrear. When the Final assessment for a year is raised, the Provisional tax already paid for that year is credited against the Final liability (Sec. 63F(1)(a)). Any balance of liability is added to and payable on the same date as the first instalment of Provisional tax for the following year. Where exceptionally there is an overpayment of Provisional tax the excess is not refunded but is deducted first from the first instalment of Provisional tax for the following year and then from the second instalment. (Sec. 63F(1)(b)). If there still remains a balance of overpayment, this is refunded. In the year of marriage, because the wife's income is deemed to be the husband's, any Provisional tax payable by her may be set against the husband's Salaries Tax liability for the year (Sec. 63F(2)). Where an excess of Provisional tax over the final liability is applied against the Provisional tax for the next year and an opportunity arises to hold over all or part of the Provisional tax (see following paragraphs) which is frustrated by the fact that it is already paid by the over payment set-off, it is departmental practice to refund the amount that would otherwise have been held over.

Because of the estimated nature of Provisional tax, there are provisions to enable collection of the tax to be wholly or partly held over in appropriate circumstances. Given the appropriate grounds, the taxpayer must apply in writing within at least 14 days before the due date of payment for the holdover to be made (Sec. 63E(1)). If the opportunity is missed in respect of the first instalment, all or part of the second instalment may still be held over. The appropriate grounds in Sec. 63E(2) are:—

(1) Where the Provisional assessment is based on the previous year's net chargeable income, i.e. personal allowances were deducted, and during the current year the taxpayer has become entitled to an allowance for a wife or an allowance or additional allowance for a child.

(2) Where the net assessable income of the current year is, or is likely to be, less than 90% of the sum which has been assessed to Provisional tax.

(3) Where during the year of assessment the taxpayer has ceased or will cease before 31st March next to derive a source of income chargeable to Salaries Tax.

(4) Where the Final assessment for the preceeding year (upon which the Provisional assessment is of course based) is under objection (see Chapter 10). As will be seen, this is also an occasion for a holdover claim in respect of the Final assessment as well.

Any holdover is entirely at the discretion of the IRD (Sec. 63E(3)) but in practice, where the rules for application have been complied with and the grounds satisfied, the holdover will be given in all but exceptional cases. The holdover does not automatically apply to the whole of the Provisional tax, only to the part which is shown to be affected by the grounds cited. The IRD must in all cases notify their decision in writing (Sec. 63E(4)).

Where the holdover is granted, it will be effective until the Final liability for the year of assessment is ascertained and due for payment but in the case of ground (4) above, if the objection against the previous year's assessment is determined or settled earlier, the earlier date will apply (Sec. 63E(1)).

Example 17

N.E. Oldiron has received the following composite assessment based on his Return of Income of the year ended 31st March, 1982:—

1981/82 Final Salaries Tax

– Net Assessable Income	$111,000
Personal Allowances (Self & Wife)	56,000
Net Chargeable Income	$ 55,000
Tax Thereon	$ 8,750
Provisional Salaries Tax Paid	8,200
Balance Due	$ 550

1982/83 Provisional Salaries Tax

– Net Chargeable Income	$55,000	
Tax Thereon		8,750
Total Tax Payable		$ 9,300
Due on:– 8th February 1983		$ 7,112*
8th May 1983		2,188

*(75% x $8,750 plus $550)

He has a child born in August 1982 and can therefore apply for a holdover as follows:–

Additional allowance for child $8,000
Reduces Provisional Tax by $8,000 @ 25% = $ 2,000
Holdover notice issued by IRD:–

Tax Due:	8.2.83	8.5.83
1980/81 Final	$ 550	
1981/82 Provisional	6,562	2,188
	$ 7,112	$ 2,188
Less Holdover (75%/25%)	1,500	500
Due and Payable	$ 5,612	$ 1,688

Notes:–

(a) If the baby had been born after 25th January, 1983 or he had otherwise missed the 14 day deadline, the $2,000 could be wholly held over against the second instalment.

(b) No further tax is payable until the Final liability for 1982/83 is established when Provisional tax paid of $6,750 will be credited and any balance due will be payable in early 1984.

Apart from the foregoing, the general provisions governing assessments, objections and appeals and payment of tax, as contained in Parts X, XI and XII of the IRO respectively, are applicable. (See Chapters 9 and 10.) See also Departmental Interpretation and Practice Notes No. 10 reproduced in Appendix 9.

Chapter 4
INTEREST TAX

1. Legislation

The law governing Interest Tax is contained in only a few sections in Part V of the IRO. Also relevant is Rule 6 of the IRR concerning the interest element of annuities and the general provisions covering Returns in Part IX, assessments in Part X, objections and appeals in Part XI and payment of tax in Part XII.

2. Scope of the Tax

Basically, Interest Tax is a withholding tax by deduction at source although there are provisions in appropriate circumstances for a direct assessment to be made upon either the payer or the recipient of interest.

Interest is broadly defined by the IRO and specifically includes the portion of an annuity which is deemed to be interest and also certain profits on the presentment on maturity of a Certificate of Deposit or Bill of Exchange are deemed to be interest.

Although Interest Tax is applicable to payments of interest which have a source in Hong Kong, its application is in fact limited because of the number of specific exemptions which are available and also because, in the nature of Hong Kong's international business, it is not difficult under present law and practice to ensure that the source of interest is outside Hong Kong where circumstances so warrant it.

Where Interest Tax is applicable, there are provisions governing its deduction at source and payment to the Government, supply of certificates of deduction and recovery by persons who have incorrectly suffered deduction at source. As already mentioned, there are also provisions for recovery by direct assessment where the deduction system has failed.

The present rate of Interest Tax is 10% in respect of Hong Kong dollar deposits with financial institutions but 15% in respect of all other chargeable interest (Sec. 28A(a) & (b)). However, an individual who satisfies the rules for personal assessment (see Chapter 7) can include the interest in such assessment if it is advantageous to him. There are no allowable deductions in arriving at an Interest Tax liability, it is a flat rate tax on gross interest income.

3. Source of the Income

As with each of the other Hong Kong income taxes it is of fundamental importance to determine the source of a payment of interest when the question of Interest Tax is being considered. The IRO gives no guidance other than the usual phrase "arising in or derived from Hong Kong" (Sec. 28(1)(a)) and therefore it is necessary to turn to case law for support. There is no case law in Hong Kong on the source of interest nor is there any published Board of Review decision except perhaps for one which is really a Profits Tax decision but does give some guidance as to the source of a particular item of interest. This is mentioned on page 76. This is undoubtedly because the IRD has stated their views, based on case law, as long ago as 1973 and currently published in the Departmental Interpretation and Practice Notes No. 13 (see Appendix 12) and as their view is a reasonable and practical interpretation, no person has seen fit to challenge it.

Before coming to the IRD practice it is however desirable to summarise the various factors which courts have from time to time considered as affecting the source of interest. Case law in South Africa, Australia and New Zealand is particularly fruitful in this respect and all of the following factors have been regarded as contributory to the source of interest, namely:—

(1) The place at which the credit is provided
(2) The place where the loan agreement is concluded
(3) The Country under the laws of which the agreement is enforceable
(4) The place where the interest is paid
(5) The currency of the transaction
(6) The place where the borrower is resident or has his operations
(7) The place where the loan funds are used

In Australia, for example, no single factor is regarded as necessarily persuasive but a totality of the foregoing factors is considered. However, in Hong Kong a principle of importance in determining source throughout all of the Hong Kong income taxes has been drawn from the judgements in CIR v Lever Brothers & Unilever Ltd. (14 SATC 1). The general principle emerges that in determining the source of a given receipt of income, one must look to what the party receiving the income had to do in order to qualify for that receipt, in other words, what consideration did he have to give under the contract? This principle is known as the "originating cause" of income and is in fact best illustrated by looking at the Profits Tax principles (see page 91). However, given the authority of the case just mentioned and also Commissioner of Inland Revenue (NZ) v N.V. Philips Gloelampenfabricken (10 ATD 435) and Commissioner-General of Income Tax v Esso Standard Eastern Inc. (Court of Appeal for East Africa), the IRD adopts the view that in the majority of cases, the originating cause in respect of interest is the provision of the credit to the borrower, it is this availability of money for his own use that causes him to have to pay interest on the use of the money. The question to be asked therefore is, where is the credit made available to the borrower? In practice, this means the time and place at which the borrower may first turn the funds to his own account or otherwise exercise dominion over them. This will of course depend upon the manner in which the loans or deposits are carried through. The following illustrations cover the principles involved although it must be remembered that these illustrations are solely for the purpose of illustrating how the source is identified because in the case of foreign currency deposits with financial institutions, there is, since 24th February 1982 an exemption from Interest Tax, whether the source is in Hong Kong or not:—

Example 1

A deposit is made in cash over the counter in Hong Kong.

The credit is clearly provided in Hong Kong and therefore the interest on the deposit has a Hong Kong Source.

Example 2

A depositor resident in Hong Kong has funds available in US dollars in a bank account outside Hong Kong and makes his deposit by transferring these funds to the bank account in New York of a Hong Kong finance company. The credit is therefore received by the finance company outside Hong Kong and the source of the interest payable on the deposit is outside Hong Kong notwithstanding that the finance company may immediately or subsequently remit the funds into Hong Kong.

Example 3

A depositor resident in New York wishes to make a deposit in US dollars with a Hong Kong finance company and he remits a bank draft or other negotiable instrument to that company through the post.

The receipt of a negotiable instrument physically in Hong Kong by a borrower of funds which that instrument represents amounts to the provision of credit in Hong Kong because the borrower has the ability to exercise dominion over the instrument by indorsement. The source of the interest on those funds is therefore in Hong Kong.

Example 4

A Hong Kong resident borrows US dollars from a finance company in

New York and that company credits a current account opened in his name with a bank in New York.

The borrower has received credit in New York because he has funds there under his control which he can draw upon by signing a cheque. Even if he draws a cheque and brings the funds to Hong Kong, the source of the interest which he pays has its origin in the funds made available to him in New York and is therefore outside Hong Kong.

The reader will observe that in each of the illustrations, the same principle in ascertaining the source of the interest applies to each, namely the place where the borrower can first make-use of or otherwise exercise any control over the funds as beneficial owner of the funds. This principle can be applied in the case of all interest arising from loans or deposits except that the IRD has stated that where there is a mortgage, the originating cause might be the mortgage itself.

In other cases where there is no advancement of money at the time of giving the credit, the question may be more difficult. If for example X is due to pay a sum of money to Y on 30th June but does not pay it until 30th September, Y may charge him interest for the overdue debt. In this case it may be necessary to look to the nature of the debt that was payable in the first instance particularly when this arose in the course of trading between the parties. In BR 20/75 similar circumstances occurred where the original debt arose as the result of sales by Y to X and interest was chargeable as a result of extended credit granted to X. Although the interest was charged separately by means of a bill of exchange accepted outside Hong Kong, the Board of Review held that the "interest" was inextricably bound up with, and therefore became part of, the trading transaction. Accordingly it was held that the "interest" became part of the trading profit and followed the source of those profits. This was not an Interest Tax question but the principle is nevertheless of importance in looking at the source of interest.

In the case of the profit on redemption on maturity or presentment of a certificate of deposit or bill of exchange which is deemed to be interest, these source rules do not apply because Sec. 28(1)(c) refers to any "proceeds" arising in or derived from Hong Kong. It is uncertain precisely what this means and there has been no practice statement in this connection. It is widely believed to apply only to Hong Kong dollar instruments and that was surely the intention in the change of law because Interest Tax could be avoided on foreign currency deposits without resort to the use of these instruments merely by ensuring that the original credit was provided outside Hong Kong. However, on a strict reading of the law it seems likely that it could be said that the proceeds arise in Hong Kong if the presentment or redemption is to take place in Hong Kong, i.e. by the holder calling at or sending the instrument to a financial institution in Hong Kong who will pay out the proceeds, whether or not that financial institution may have been the issuer. However, this question is largely academic since 24th February 1982 since when interest on foreign currency deposits with financial institutions has been exempt from Interest Tax. Accordingly, only Hong Kong dollar certificates of deposit and bills of exchange are subject to Interest Tax, as was probably intended in the first place.

Also, in the case of the interest element of an annuity, the same rules do not apply because the IRO refers to "an annuity payable in Hong Kong" (Sec. 28(1)(b)). This is a straightforward factual matter and it is usually necessary to look at the document which regulates the annuity, or other evidence to see where it is required to be paid. The place where it is received or the places of residence of the payer or recipient are irrelevant. See also Departmental Interpretation and Practice Notes No. 13 reproduced in Appendix 12.

4.   What Is Interest

Disregarding for the moment the interest element of an annuity, which is dealt with separately on page 81, it is necessary first of all to look at what the IRO defines as interest within the charge to Interest Tax and then to look into case law to enquire further into the question of what constitutes interest.

Section 28(1)(a) brings into charge:—

> "interest arising in or derived from the Colony on any debenture, mort-gage, bill of sale, deposit, loan, advance or other indebtedness whether evidenced in writing or not;"

The question of "arising in or derived from" has been considered in paragraph 3 and it therefore remains to be determined whether any given payment is within the definition of interest or not. This becomes a difficulty in the case of payments of "near interest" such as the advance of money at a discount with repayment at full value, advance of money followed by repayment at a premium, acquisition of bills of exchange at a discount, sale of securities "cum interest" etc.

There has been a considerable amount of U.K. case law on the subject of what constitutes interest and on the difference between pure discount and interest. Attempts have been made from time to time to define "interest". In the case of Bennett v Ogston (15 TC at page 379) interest was defined as a payment by time for the use of money and in Re Euro Hotel Belgravia Ltd. (1975 Simons Tax Cases 682) it was stated that certain factors must be present namely:—

(1) that there must be a sum of money by reference to which the "interest" is to be ascertained, and

(2) that sum of money must be due to the person entitled to the "interest".

Example 5

A bank agrees to loan a customer $100,000 and advances him $95,000 on the understanding that he will repay $100,000 in 6 months time. There is no separate interest charge.

The cost to the customer of this exercise is $5,000 and in effect he pays this as consideration for the use of $95,000 for six months. It is therefore interest. This would similarly be the case where the bank advanced $100,000 and received repayment of, say, $106,000.

The position might however be different where a full market rate of interest was charged in addition to the discount or premium. Whilst the presumption would be that the premium or discount was not therefore "interest", it would be necessary to consider why a discount or premium was charged if not solely for the use of the money.

Example 6

A bank agrees to loan a customer $100,000 but the customer has no security to offer against the loan. The bank advances him $98,000 on condition that he repays $100,000 one year later together with interest of $12,000.

Clearly the sum of $12,000 is interest but the discount of $2,000 should not be so regarded on the assumption that the $12,000 is a full commercial rate of interest because it can probably be shown that the $2,000 is for the bank's credit risk. Of course, if the commercial rate of interest normally charged is 12% but only $10,000 interest had been charged to the customer, the position would have been much more doubtful.

For further details and a discussion of these principles see Lomax v Peter Dixon & Co. Ltd. (25 TC 373). The problem of difference between discount and interest assumes greater proportions when transactions involving discounted bills of exchange are concerned. It is true to say that the opinions as to what constitutes interest in these cases are finely balanced. In the case of National Provident Institution v Brown (8 TC 57), wherein it was held that so called discount was in fact interest, the judge said at page 66:—

> "it is clear that it is not every difference in amount between a sum payable in future and the same sum represented by cash down which is an annual profit or gain by way of discount even though popularly the word 'discount' may be used to describe it ....
> It seems to me that in each case one must look at the real nature of the transaction and see whether the purchase of the future obligation at a discount is really an investment of money at interest or not."

In the same case at page 67 he considers the factors that govern the amount of discount in a given case and takes the view that where a security is independently purchased in the market at a discount the purchaser is taking a risk governed by market forces and what he ultimately receives is his profit from the risk that he took and in those circumstances although prevailing rates of interest might be a factor in fixing the amount of the discount, the profit nevertheless is probably not of an interest nature. However, on page 96 he further states that where the party liable under the bill is of such standing that there is in reality no credit risk, it is likely that the discount is wholly interest orientated and, therefore, depending upon the other circumstances relating to the transaction, the discount may well be in the nature of interest.

As a further illustration, Torrens v CIR (18 TC 262) also involved a decision as to whether a "discount" was interest or not. In this case there were two judges and, on the facts one decided that the transaction consisted wholly of the purchase of a security at a discount and the other decided that it was really an advance of money at interest. The moral is that each case will turn on its precise facts and the dividing line is precarious.

CERTIFICATES OF DEPOSIT AND BILLS OF EXCHANGE. With effect from the year of assessment 1981/82, certain profits on the redemption on maturity or presentment of certificates of deposit or bills of exchange are deemed to be interest and therefore subject to Interest Tax (Sec. 28(1)(c)).

For this purpose, a certificate of deposit is defined in Sec. 2 as a document relating to money, in any currency, with the following features:—
(1) It is deposited with the issuer or some other person. This seems to suggest that if the holder keeps it at home, the definition does not apply!
(2) It recognises an obligation to pay a stated amount whether to bearer or to order and whether with or without interest.
(3) It is transferable by delivery, i.e. it is a bearer instrument, with or without endorsement. Accordingly an instrument that must be transferred by written contract is not within the definition.

A bill of exchange is not defined and therefore takes its usual commercial meaning. It is of course usually the case that a certificate of deposit carries interest at maturity and sometimes at earlier intervals as well whereas a bill of exchange carries no interest at all. As the amount chargeable to Interest Tax is the excess of the proceeds on redemption on maturity or presentment over the amount received by the issuer upon first sale, it can be seen that the deemed interest charge would only apply to a certificate of deposit where, exceptionally, it is either issued at a discount or redeemed at a premium. The provisions are therefore really aimed at bills of exchange which carry no interest but are issued at a discount, i.e. the "Bankers Acceptance" devices which were previously not chargeable to Interest Tax.

There is an anti-avoidance provision to counteract a first sale to an associated company at an amount higher than the ultimate sale by that associated company. This provides that the amount to be taken as received on the first sale is that received from the first purchaser who is not associated with the issuer (Sec. 28(1)(c) proviso (i)). For this purpose an associated corporation is one which controls or is controlled by or is under common control with, the issuing corporation. Control means the power to conduct the affairs of a corporation by means of shareholdings, voting power or any other power conferred by the articles or other document which regulates the corporation (Sec. 28(3)).

Because there were affected instruments already in issue when the law was introduced, there is a transitional provision which allows the amount received on first sale to be increased to the open market value of the instrument at close of business on 31st March 1981 (Sec. 28(1)(c) proviso (ii)).

It is important to realise that the Interest Tax charge can only apply on the maturity of a certificate of deposit or bill of exchange, it does not apply to any profit that the holder may make on a disposal before maturity. This profit may however be liable to Profits Tax (see page 107).

Example 7

Icehouse Finance has drawn a bill of exchange for $100,000 payable on 30th June 1981 on its parent company, Townbank Inc, which has accepted it. Townbank Inc. sold it for $98,000 to another subsidiary company, Chater Finance, which in turn sold it to a customer for $90,000 on 1st March 1981.

Although the first sale was for $98,000, this is ignored because Chater Finance is an associated corporation of the issuer, Townbank Inc. The amount received on first sale would therefore be $90,000 and accordingly Interest Tax is chargeable upon presentment on 30th June 1981 of ($100,000 less $90,000) i.e. $10,000 @ 15% but for the transitional provisions.

If the open market value at close of business on 31st March 1981 had been $93,000 and the CIR agreed with this figure, the Interest Tax charge would be ($100,000 less $93,000) i.e. $7,000 @ 15% which Townbank Inc. must deduct from the proceeds of $100,000 payable to the holder on 30th June 1981.

If the foregoing dates had been in 1982, Interest Tax would be:–

$10,000 @ 10% assuming that the currency is Hong Kong dollar (Sec. 28A (a)).

Nil if the currency was other than Hong Kong dollar (Sec. 28(1) proviso (g)).

ANNUITIES.   In certain instances, a proportion of an annuity is deemed to be interest for the purposes of Interest Tax and Rule 6 of the IRR determines how this is established. This applies only to an annuity which has been purchased for valuable consideration because only such an annuity could contain an interest and a capital element. For example, an annuity granted under a will or under a covenant "for natural love and affection" cannot have a capital element. Having identified applicable annuities, it is necessary to make an apportionment between capital and interest and then the apportionment is constant for all subsequent payments (Rule 6(1)).

The Rule provides the manner of ascertaining the capital element in three different cases and, in each case, the interest element is of course the balancing figure. The three cases are:—

(1) Where the term and amount of an annuity are dependent only upon the duration of a life or lives, the capital element is that proportion of the annuity which the consideration for its purchase bears to the actuarial value of the payments at the commencement of the term (Rule 6(2)). Rule 6(3) lays down the rules for fixing the actuarial value.

(2) Where the annuity is payable for a fixed term of years, the capital element for a year is the amount of the purchase consideration divided by the number of years in the term (Rule 6(4)).

(3) In any other case, the Commissioner is empowered to fix the capital element on a basis which having regard to all contingencies affecting the annuity, is just and reasonable (Rule 6(5)).

The above three rules only apply if the purchase consideration is provided by the annuitant or the annuitant's spouse. If the annuity is purchased by any other person, there will be no capital element and the whole will therefore be taxed (Rule 6(6)).

INTEREST OUTSIDE THE SCOPE OF INTEREST TAX. Certain types of interest are for one reason or another not regarded as within the scope of interest as defined in Sec. 28(1)(a), in particular the following:—

(1) In partnerships, interest paid to partners on their capital is treated not as interest but as drawings of profits.

(2) Hire purchase interest is not regarded as true interest but merely as a constituent of a hire charge.

(3) Interest paid by the administrator of an estate in respect of the delayed payment of a legacy is disregarded for Interest Tax purposes because it is payable on a gift and therefore outside of the definition in Sec. 28(1)(a).

(4) Interest paid on advances from one branch of a company to another branch of the same company. This is because it is not in fact interest on the basis that a company cannot lend itself money.

The foregoing should not be confused with the statutory exemptions which are dealt with below.

5. Liability to Interest Tax

Interest Tax is charged for a year of assessment at 10% in respect of Hong Kong dollar deposits with financial institutions (Sec. 28A(a)) where the interest is paid or payable after 24th February 1982 and 15% in respect of all other chargeable interest (Sec. 28A(b)). It is chargeable on the recipient of interest which has its source in Hong Kong and is paid or credited to the recipient in the year of assessment. The interest chargeable is that defined by Sec. 28(1)(a), the interest element of a purchased annuity and the deemed interest on the redemption on maturity or presentment of a certificate of deposit or bill of exchange.

These are however a number of exemptions which further reduce the scope of the tax and these are dealt with below.

Because the IRO charges a "recipient", there is no limitation to any type or class of taxpayer, all are chargeable to Interest Tax. As the tax is normally imposed by deduction by the payer this question is however largely academic. There are however circumstances where a direct assessment is necessary and this is dealt with on page 86.

EXEMPTIONS. Even if a payment of interest is otherwise within the scope of Interest Tax it may nevertheless be exempted and thereby paid gross in a number of circumstances primarily concerning the circumstances of the recipient. The circumstances are:–

(1) Interest paid BY:–
    (i)   the Government;
    (ii) a bank licensed under the Banking Ordinance;
    (iii) The Hong Kong Electric Co. Ltd.;
    (iv) China Light and Power Co. Ltd.; and
    (v)   The Hong Kong and China Gas Co. Ltd.

    provided that the interest is paid at a rate which does not exceed the rate specified from time to time by the Financial Secretary by notice in the Gazette. The specified rate follows the current Savings Deposit rate in practise and is presently 10%. The exemption is granted in practice if the rate at the due date of the interest is not greater than the specified rate notwithstanding that it may have accrued at a greater rate for part of its period of accrual (Sec. 28(1) proviso (a)).

(2) Interest paid TO:–
    (i)   a bank licensed under the Banking Ordinance;
    (ii) a corporation carrying on a trade or business in Hong Kong; and
    (iii) the Government

    In the case of (i) and (ii), the logic is that the interest is liable to Profits Tax in the hands of the recipient. Note that in the case of (ii) the exemption applies whether or not the payment of interest is connected with the recipient corporation's business in Hong Kong. As will be seen in Chapter 5, it is still liable to Profits Tax (Sec. 28(1) proviso (b)).

(3) Interest on Tax Reserve Certificates (Sec. 28(1) proviso (c)).

(4) Interest paid TO:—

    (i)   a licensed pawnbroker; and

    (ii) a registered moneylender;

so long as the interest is payable in the ordinary course of the recipient's business (Sec. 28(1) proviso (d)).

(5) Interest on a Government Bond issued under the Loans (Government Bonds) Ordinance (Sec. 28(1) proviso (e)).

(6) Largely as a matter of administrative convenience, an exemption order under Sec. 87 has been made in respect of interest derived from any account or fund in the names of:—

    (i)   Registrar, Supreme Court;

    (ii) Official Administrator; and

    (iii) Master in Lunacy,

provided the interest does not exceed $1,000.

(7) Interest received by a charitable institution exempt under Sec. 88 or any other person exempt under Sec. 87.

(8) Interest received by a credit union in respect of a loan to a member (Sec. 28(1) proviso (f)).

(9) Interest which is paid or payable after 24th February 1982 on a deposit in a currency other than Hong Kong dollars with a financial institution carrying on business in Hong Kong (Sec. 28(1) proviso (g)). For this purpose, a deposit is as defined in Sec. 2(1) of the deposit-taking companies ordinance. It is by no means clear that a deposit includes the bill of exchange devices that are now subject to Interest Tax (see page 79) but in practice the CIR has confirmed that they will be so treated.

DEDUCTION AND PAYMENT OF TAX. Taking into account the criteria necessary to establish liability to Interest Tax and the numerous exemptions applicable, in those cases where a person in Hong Kong pays or credits to any other person any interest which is subject to Interest Tax, he is required to deduct the tax when making the payment or credit (Sec. 29(1)).

The liability to deduct applies where a "person" pays to a "person" as opposed to a "recipient". A "person" is defined by Sec. 2 as including a corporation, partnership or body of persons.

Note that the liability to deduct is triggered not only by actual payment but by the payer crediting the interest to the recipient which broadly means placed at his disposal, for example where a bank adds interest to a customer's account. Problems may arise as to whether any given payment by a debtor to a creditor represents outstanding interest or repayment of principal or a mixture of both. Where it is not otherwise clear, it is necessary to look at how either the debtor or creditor has appropriated the payment in which case treatment for tax would normally follow that. Failing appropriation by either party, it is normal to treat outstanding interest as paid before outstanding principal.

There is a specific exception from liability to deduct Interest Tax granted by Sec. 29(5) with effect from 1st April 1980 to a trustee in respect of the distribution to a beneficiary of a trust of sums which have suffered Interest Tax on receipt by the trust. Whilst this is intended to avoid a double charge, it is considered that there is in any event no basis in law for charging the distribution to Interest Tax because there is no loan of money from the beneficiaries to the trust.

Where a person has deducted tax as required, he must pay it to the Government within 30 days and, unless he is a licensed bank or other corporation specifically identified by the Commissioner by notice in the Gazette, he must supply the recipient with a deduction certificate within 42 days of making the deduction. The deduction certificate must contain the following information:—

(1) Gross amount of interest;
(2) Net amount paid or credited;
(3) Period of accrual;
(4) Date of payment or credit; and
(5) An acknowledgement by the Commissioner of the receipt by the Government of the tax deducted. (Sec. 29(2)(a))

Because the issue of a certificate in every case would be onerous, licensed banks and certain other specified corporations are only required to do so where specifically requested by the recipient. The information required in this certificate is (1) to (4) as above (Sec. 29(2)(b)). The following major corporations have been specified by the CIR, but there are numerous others:—

Chartered Finance (Hong Kong) Ltd.
Harper Finance Ltd.
Hang Seng Finance Ltd.
Wayfoong Credit Ltd.
Mass Transit Railway Corporation.

A recipient would only normally require a certificate where he was entitled to a refund either because he was not liable to Interest Tax or is claiming Personal Assessment (see Chapter 7). If a person is not liable to Interest Tax he may, within 90 days of receiving a certificate of deduction, notify the Commissioner that he disputes the deduction. The Commissioner will then institute the somewhat cumbersome procedure of raising an Interest Tax assessment on the interest in question and crediting the tax already deducted. This enables the person to object against the assessment and recover the Interest Tax by refund (Sec. 29(3)). The most common situation where this applies is where the recipient is a corporation carrying on business in Hong Kong and therefore liable to Profits Tax on the interest and exempt from Interest Tax under Sec. 28(1) proviso (b). In practise the IRD does not strictly enforce the 90 day time limit but are unwilling to depart from the cumbersome repayment procedure; the Interest Tax is not credited in the Profits Tax assessment although this would be the most practical route.

If a person who is entitled to a deduction certificate does not receive it within the prescribed time, he must notify the Commissioner within 14 days after the expiry of the prescribed period and also supply the following particulars in writing:—
(1) Name and address of the payer;
(2) Gross amount of interest;
(3) Net amount paid or credited; and
(4) Date of payment or credit. (Sec. 29(4))

Most persons are ignorant of this obligation and therefore it is unlikely that most such situations are in fact reported. However, failure to notify the CIR as required may lead to a direct assessment on the recipient (see "Direct Assessment" on page 86).

Where a recipient of interest has been exempted from Interest Tax by order under Sec. 87 or 88, there is in fact no authority which enables the payer to pay gross but under Sec. 29A the CIR may direct the payer to pay gross in which case the deduction provisions of Sec. 29 will not be applicable to that particular interest.

FAILURE TO DEDUCT. Where a person is under an obligation to deduct Interest Tax at source and has failed to do so or he has in fact made the deduction but failed to pay it over to the Government, the amount due becomes a debt to the Government with the usual powers of collection without any further action by the IRD. The IRD however may raise a direct assessment upon the payer (Sec. 30). This provision emphasises the need for the payer to satisfy himself without doubt that an exemption is really applicable before paying gross. For instance it cannot be assumed that, if the recipient is a corporation, the exemption applicable to corporations carrying on trade or business in Hong Kong will apply because the company may be dormant or wholly active outside Hong Kong. However, in practice, where a payment has actually been made gross, the IRD will normally look first to the recipient for the tax by direct assessment. If however this fails or is otherwise not a practical proposition, the IRD will fall back on Sec. 30. Where a payer has to pay the tax under Sec. 30 which he failed to deduct, he has a right of recovery against the recipient of the interest (Sec. 32).

There is occasionally some doubt as to whether, where interest has been paid gross to a recipient, this sum should be grossed up in arriving at the amount of tax due. This position is not however taken by the IRD unless there is a specific agreement between the payer and the recipient for the payer to bear the tax.

Example 8

A deposit-taking company accepts a deposit of HK$100,000 from Indamunny Ltd. and agrees to pay interest of 12% thereon.

When the interest of $12,000 is paid it is assumed that Indamunny is carrying on business in Hong Kong and the interest is paid gross. On enquiry the IRD discovers that Indamunny is inactive and the $100,000 represents its share capital.

The interest is not covered by the exemption in Sec. 28(1) proviso (b) and, assuming that it has a Hong Kong source, Interest Tax of $1,200 should have been deducted. Normally the IRD will assess this directly upon Indamunny but they are entitled to look directly to the deposit-taking company under Sec. 30 for payment without assessment. If the deposit-taking company pays, it is entitled to collect $1,200 from Indamunny which it would presumably do out of the next payment of interest plus a further deduction representing Interest Tax on that interest.

Example 9

The facts are the same as Example 8 except that the deposit-taking company has agreed with Indamunny to pay 12% "free of all taxes thereon."

As there is a specific agreement for the payer to bear the Interest Tax, the true gross interest is $\frac{100}{90}$ x $12,000 = $13,333 and therefore the Interest Tax collectible from the payer or assessable on the recipient is $1,333.

DIRECT ASSESSMENT. A direct assessment for Interest Tax is rather the exception than the rule but provisions are laid down to authorise direct assessment where the deduction system is, or is likely to be, ineffective. The following is a summary of the circumstances in which direct assessments might be raised.

(1) Where Interest Tax has been deducted from a recipient who is not liable to Interest Tax and he applies for the refund procedure under Sec. 29(3).

(2) Where a payer has failed to deduct tax or to pay over tax which he has deducted, he may be assessed under Sec. 30.

(3) Where the deduction system has failed to produce payment of tax, or is likely to fail (perhaps because the payer is outside of the IRD's jurisdiction), Sec. 33 empowers the Commissioner to assess the recipient or his "agent". Sec. 2 defines "agent" in relation to a non resident person as including:—

  (i)   the agent, attorney, factor, receiver, or manager in Hong Kong of
        such person, and
  (ii) any person in Hong Kong through whom such person is in receipt of
        income arising in or derived from Hong Kong.

It is therefore possible for a non-resident recipient of interest to be
assessed under Sec. 33 through the payer as agent, where the payer is in
Hong Kong. In these circumstances however, a direct assessment on the
payer under Sec. 30 may be more appropriate.

A recipient can however protect himself from assessment under Sec. 33
by notifying the Commissioner under Sec. 29(4) when he has failed to receive
a deduction certificate within the prescribed time. If he has done this,
whether or not Interest Tax has been deducted, he cannot be assessed under
Sec. 33.

All of the general provisions concerning assessments in Part X, objections
and appeals in Part XI and payment of tax in Part XIII are applicable to
Interest Tax Assessments as are the penalty provisions in Part XIV for failure
to submit returns or deduct and pay over the tax (see relevant chapters).

Chapter 5
PROFITS TAX

1. Legislation

Profits Tax has the greatest amount of legislation of the four income taxes, the main provisions being in Secs. 14 to 27 under Part IV of the IRO. Also, directly relevant are Rules 2A to 2D of the IRR governing apportionment of allowable deductions and Rules 3 and 5 of the IRR governing the ascertainment of branch assessable profits and Part XB governing Provisional Profits Tax. The provisions governing depreciation allowances in Part VI are primarily concerned with Profits Tax but these are dealt with separately in Chapter 6.

The general provisions governing returns in Part IX, assessments in Part X, objections and appeals in Part XI, payment of tax in Part XII and penalties in Part XIV are applicable to Profits Tax.

2. Scope of the Tax

Individuals, corporations, bodies of persons and partnerships are liable to Profits Tax in respect of assessable profits from a trade, profession or business carried on in Hong Kong and giving rise to a source of profits in Hong Kong. The source of profits is ascertained in accordance with case law principles and, in addition, the IRO lays down a number of deemed sources of profit. There is no distinction in the scope of the charge between residents and non-residents but certain rules are laid down concerning dealings between residents and non-residents and the ascertainment of the assessable profits of non-residents. There is a distinction between the taxation of corporations and of other persons whereby corporations are charged at 16½% and others at 15% but this is the only distinction. Furthermore there is no difference in the charge between a resident and a non-resident corporation.

In general, assessable profits are profits arrived at under normally accepted accounting principles, as adjusted to comply with the specific requirements of the IRO, e.g. a difference in depreciation rates for accounting and tax purposes, the exclusion of net profits from a source outside Hong Kong and adjustments where accounting principles and taxation principles conflict as to what constitutes capital and revenue expenditure and profits. Dividends are specifically excluded from assessable profits.

The tax is assessed on the basis of years of assessment ending on 31st March and assessable profits are ascertained on the basis of the accounting period ending in the year of assessment. There are provisions governing the basis of assessment which is applicable in the commencement and cessation years and also where there is a change in a previously established accounting date.

Losses are computed in the same way as profits and can be carried forward indefinitely, in the case of companies, against any source of profits liable to Profits Tax but, in the case of individuals and partnerships, there are restrictions in the classes of income against which they can be offset.

Partnerships are assessed as a single entity with no separate assessments on the individual partners. Normally, the manner in which partners share profits and losses is not of importance except where:
(1) A company is a partner when the companies' rate of Profits Tax will apply to its share or its share of losses may be treated differently;
(2) A partner wishes to claim personal assessment; and/or
(3) There are changes in the partners and losses are carried forward.

There are provisions which allow for the basis of assessment to remain undisturbed notwithstanding withdrawal or addition of a partner.

Depreciation allowances are separately computed for tax purposes and governed by the detailed rules in Part VI of the IRO.

In addition to the general rules for the ascertainment of assessable profits, the IRO recognises that certain types of business need special rules for the ascertainment of source of profits and computation of assessable profits and, in particular, lays down special rules for:
(1) Life Insurance Business;
(2) Other Insurance Business;
(3) Shipping and Aircraft Business; and
(4) Financial Institutions.

Profits Tax is payable by direct assessment and there is a system of Provisional Profits Tax under which a provisional assessment is based on the agreed assessable profits of the immediately preceding year of assessment. Provisional Tax is normally payable in the final quarter of the year of assessment and, where the date of payment normally falls due within the currency of the accounting period which will form the basis for the final assessment; to avoid any element of payment in advance, the tax is payable in two instalments, the first being 75% of the liability and the second, about three months later, is the remaining 25%.

When the actual assessable profits for the year of assessment are agreed, a final assessment is issued and credit is given for the Provisional Tax paid. Any excess of final liability over Provisional Tax paid or vice versa is added to or subtracted from the first instalment of Provisional Tax for the following year. Provisions exist for the Provisional Tax or part of it to be held over in a number of situations and it is at the discretion of the CIR whether the holdover is granted although it is exceptional for a holdover to be refused.

3. Source of the Income

As with each of the other Hong Kong income taxes, the determination of the source of profits is fundamental to ascertaining whether a liability to Profits Tax arises. As will be seen on page 95 there are two major tests to determine liability to Profits Tax, whether a business is being carried on in Hong Kong and whether a Hong Kong source of profits is derived from that business (Sec. 14).

Concentrating upon source, the IRO gives little guidance. In Sec. 14 it refers to profits "arising in or derived from Hong Kong" and in Sec. 2 this phrase is further defined for the purposes of Profits Tax to, "without in any way limiting the meaning of the term, include all profits from business transacted in Hong Kong, whether directly or through an agent". In other words it includes such specific profits but can also include much more, which it in fact does after reference to the substantial amount of case law which is relevant. As to what is meant by "business transacted in Hong Kong" it is necessary to refer to case law in Hong Kong. The point is discussed at length in two of the most prominent Hong Kong cases on source of income, namely CIR v Karsten Larssen & Co. (HK) Ltd. (HKTC 11) and CIR v The Hong Kong & Whampoa Dock Co. Ltd. (HKTC 85), the latter particularly contains a very good summary of the law and other authorities in various countries on the source of profits.

The principle emerged that "business transacted" meant neither the place where contracts were concluded nor the place where the business infrastructure of the taxpayer existed but the place at which the operations take place from which the profits in substance arise. The phrase is in fact taken from the judgement in Smidth & Co. v Greenwood (8 TC 193) which also determined some important principles concerning the law of source of income which remain good to this day.

Having determined therefore that the meaning of "business transacted" in Sec. 2 is in fact an operations test, it is desirable to go back to first principles and see how this test developed from case law. In the case of Rhodesian Metals Ltd. v Commissioner of Taxation (11 SATC 244) it was said that:—

"Source means not a legal concept but something which a practical man would regard as a real source of income .... the ascertaining of the actual source is a practical hard matter of fact."

The argument can then be taken one stage further as illustrated in the following passage from CIR v Lever Brothers & Unilever Ltd. (14 SATC 1):—

"The word source has several possible meanings. In this section it is used figuratively and when so used in relation to the receipt of money one possible meaning is the originating cause of the receipt of the money, another possible meaning is the quarter from which it is received. .... the inference which I think should be drawn .... is that the source of receipts, received as income, is not the quarter whence they come, but the originating cause of their being received as income and that this originating cause is the work which the taxpayer does to earn them, the quid pro quo which he gives in return for which he receives them. The work which he does may be a business which he carries on, or an enterprise which he undertakes, or an activity in which he engages and it may take the form of personal exertion, mental or physical or it may take the form of employment of capital either by using it to earn income or by letting its use to someone else. Often the work is some combination of these."

This is the "originating cause" or "operations" test which is what is meant in Sec. 2 by "business transacted" and which applies in determining source in respect of all types of profit or income. What is then necessary is to analyse the operations which actually cause the income to be received and ask two questions:—

(1) What is the originating cause of the income, and
(2) Is the orginating cause in Hong Kong?

In making this analysis, income can be drawn into two broad classes, active income and passive income although, inevitably, some sources are a mixture of the two. Very broadly, active income is earned by the performance of some active function such as professional advice or construction work and the question therefore to be answered is where is the work carried out? Passive income requires a legal act rather than a physical act such as a sale which involves only the conclusion of a contract in which case the question is where is the legal act completed?

In the case of a pure merchanting business the profit is derived from the conclusion of contracts of sale and in the case of Maclaine & Co. v Eccott (10 TC 572), the following comments were made:—

"In the case of a merchant's business, the primary object of which is to sell goods at a profit the trade is (generally speaking) exercised or carried on at the place when the contracts are made. No doubt reference has sometimes been made to the place where payment has been made for the goods sold or to the place where the goods are delivered and it may be that in certain cases these are material considerations but the most important and indeed the crucial question is where are the contracts of sale made."

Under the law of contract applicable in Hong Kong, a contract is concluded by the acceptance of an offer and therefore in cases where the place of conclusion of the contract is relevant it is necessary to ascertain how and where the acceptance was notified. For a further example of the principles involved here, see Firestone Tyre & Rubber Co. Ltd v Lewellin (37 TC 111).

However, the place where the contract is concluded is valid in determining source only in those cases where no other action is required to earn the profits. This is illustrated from the following comments made in Smidth & Co. v Greenwood (8 TC 193).

> "The contracts in this case were made abroad. But I am not prepared to hold that this test is decisive. I can imagine cases where the contract of resale is made abroad, and yet the manufacture of the goods, some negotiation of the terms, and complete execution of the contract takes place here under such circumstances that the trade was in truth exercised here. I think that the question is where do the operations take place from which the profits in substance arise."

The "operations" test which constantly crops up, when applied to a business that consists of the performance of an active function, means that the source is governed by where those activities are performed, regardless of where any underlying contract may have been concluded. This is clearly illustrated by the Hong Kong & Whampoa Dock Co. case (HKTC 85) wherein, notwithstanding that the company's infrastructure was in Hong Kong and the original instructions were negotiated and concluded there, it was held that the profit arose from the salvage operation which was carried out on the high seas and therefore the source was not in Hong Kong. In other words, nothing could have been earned without actually going to sea and performing the rescue act, no amount of negotiations or contract could have earned the profits in question, these were only conditions precedent to the actual earning operation.

In the case of CIR v Karsten Larssen & Co. (HK) Ltd. (HKTC 11), the company shared commission with ship brokers outside Hong Kong and claimed that this arose solely from the conclusion of charter parties outside Hong Kong by the brokers. It was held that the company earned its share of the commission in fact by the performance of certain subsidiary and administrative functions in Hong Kong and therefore its share of the income arose there. For a further discussion of the source of commission income, CIR v International Wood Products Ltd. (HKTC 551) is essential reading.

Following this decision, the Commissioner issued a circular, dated 25th August 1971, of departmental practice which illustrates a number of typical situations where the profits will be regarded as arising outside Hong Kong. This is reproduced as Appendix 13. This group of Hong Kong tax cases spans a wide area of the law taking in reference to, and comment on, all the important cases of relevance from other countries.

The source of interest income is determined in accordance with the same principles as for Interest Tax (see page 74), but in the case of banks and financial institutions, this is now affected by a deeming provision. The position of banks and financial institutions is considered separately on page 156. There are a number of deeming provisions affecting other classes of income and these are dealt with on page 102.

Apart from the cases already mentioned, there are a number of other decisions, both of the Courts and of the Board of Review in Hong Kong which touch upon the question of source of income for Profits Tax purposes. The more important of these are as follows:—

(1) In CIR v Hang Seng Bank (HKTC 583) it was held that, notwithstanding that a source of interest income arose outside Hong Kong and was there-fore not liable to Profits Tax, an exchange loss on the underlying invest-ment was deductible because the trading stock (money in the case of a bank) of a company carrying on business in Hong Kong did not lose its character by being temporarily invested elsewhere. Contrast this with (2) below.

(2) A company carrying on business in Hong Kong, inter alia, as a share dealer sold, at a loss, shares quoted on the New York Stock Exchange. The loss was disallowed on the grounds that the sale contract was con-cluded outside Hong Kong by the New York brokers. Although the decision to sell was taken in Hong Kong after studying the market and seeking professional advice in Hong Kong, nevertheless it was held that "it is the entering into and the completion of a transaction that produces a profit or loss rather than the studies or exertion antecedent to it" (BR 18/73). Contrast this with (1) above.

(3) A trader with Hong Kong source profits on sales to foreign customers, charged interest to those customers on extended credit. The interest was charged under a separate transaction whereby a bill of exchange was drawn on the foreign customer for the amount of the interest and, not-withstanding that these bills were accepted outside Hong Kong, the in-terest was regarded as having its source in Hong Kong because it was nothing more than an accrual to the trading profit and therefore not separable therefrom (BR 20/75).

(4) The source of commission income must in each case be considered on its

merits and the fact that it may be paid on the occasion of sales made outside Hong Kong between parties outside Hong Kong will not of itself give the commission a non-Hong Kong source if the recipient performs some activities in Hong Kong (BR 2/75). Contrast with the facts in CIR v International Wood Products (HKTC 551). See also BR 68/77.

It can therefore be seen that each case must be carefully considered on its merits and there is a danger in drawing too broad a conclusion from any single decision. However, the "operations" test is a firm guideline and a common sense application of this principle following a careful analysis of the steps involved in earning the income is all that is required in most cases to identify the source.

4. Liability to Profits Tax

Section 14 contains the charging provisions for Profits Tax and, in general, two things must be satisfied before a liability can arise, namely that a person:—

(1) is carrying on a trade, profession or business in Hong Kong, and
(2) is deriving a source of assessable profits in Hong Kong from that trade, profession or business, other than profits arising from the sale of capital assets.

If a liability arises, tax is charged on the profit, as adjusted for tax purposes, at 16½% (since 1980/81) in the case of corporations and the share of partnership profits beneficially owned by a corporation and at 15% in respect of other persons.

Therefore, whether or not a liability arises to Profits Tax depends upon a consideration of a number of basic principles. First there is the question of who can be chargeable. Sec. 14 refers to a "person" which is defined in Sec. 2 as including a corporation, partnership or body of persons. A "corporation" is also defined as any company which is either incorporated or registered under any enactment or charter in force in Hong Kong or elsewhere but does not include a co-operative society or a trade union. Furthermore a "body of persons" means any body public, corporate or collegiate and any company, fraternity, fellowship and society of persons whether corporate or not corporate. There is therefore a wide coverage of chargeable persons.

A wife who does not live apart from her husband is treated as the same person as her husband and her profits are therefore assessed upon him (Sec. 15B). This is a different provision to that for Salaries Tax where a wife's income is merely deemed to be that of the husband and this gives rise to particular problems where, for example, a husband and wife are in partnership.

CARRYING ON TRADE, PROFESSION OR BUSINESS. The next question of importance is whether a trade, profession or business is being carried on by the person in Hong Kong and this is largely a question of fact. It does not of course follow that because a person is deriving a source of income from Hong Kong that he is necessarily carrying on business there, except in the cases where a business is deemed to be carried on (see page 102 under "Deemed Business Receipts"). It is therefore important to distinguish between carrying on business *with* Hong Kong and carrying on business *in* Hong Kong. For example, a manufacturer in America may sell his products in Hong Kong and visiting salesmen may spend a considerable amount of time there tracing and negotiating outlets. Nevertheless, the manufacturer is only doing business with Hong Kong and cannot be taxed there on his profits. If however he opens a warehouse in Hong Kong and has salesmen resident there, the facts would need to be looked at more closely to see whether this was nothing more than an on-the-spot stock to speed up the fulfillment of orders concluded outside Hong Kong or whether in fact it was a means of concluding and executing sales in Hong Kong. Rule 5 of the IRR which deals with the ascertainment and determination of the profits of a branch in Hong Kong of a person whose head office is elsewhere introduces the concept of a "permanent establishment" which is a familiar feature of double taxation agreements, although Hong Kong has no such agreements. Permanent establishment is defined as:—

> "a branch, management or other place of business, but does not include an agency unless the agent has, and habitually exercises, a general authority to negotiate and conclude contracts on behalf of his principal or has a stock of merchandise from which he regularly fills orders on his behalf" (Rule 5(1)).

Accordingly, the existence of an agent in Hong Kong is important and will affect the Profits Tax liability whether the agent is an employee of the principal or whether he is an independent third party. The fundamental question is the extent of his authority to contract on behalf of his principal. An isolated and specific authority to conclude a contract on behalf of the principal is not enough to trigger the permanent establishment rule, it must be a general authority to negotiate *and* conclude and one which is regularly exercised. In these circumstances, not only does the principal come within the scope of Profits Tax, assessments can be made upon the agent (see page 169).

If an office is opened by a non-resident person it is also important to establish its purpose to see whether it is in fact for doing business or whether it has some other function. For example, numerous non-resident banks have a representative office in Hong Kong and these offices are only for the purposes of liaising with customers and introducing them to branches elsewhere with whom they do business. This gives rise to no taxable profits in Hong Kong. Similarly a "buying" office set up in Hong Kong to supervise purchases for shipment elsewhere does not amount to carrying on business (Sully v Attorney-General 2 TC 149).

There is generally no necessity to distinguish between trade, profession and business although each has entirely different meanings and the date of commencement of a trade, profession or business is largely a question of fact. It is however important to establish the date of commencement because it affects the establishment of the basis period (see page 136) and the treatment of expenditure incurred before commencement.

The circumstances constituting a trade are, in general, fairly easy to identify, and also, as a question of fact and by applying the principles already mentioned, whether it is carried on in Hong Kong. The more difficult question of what constitutes a trade in isolated cases is considered under "What Constitutes Trading" on page 100.

In the case of an individual carrying on a profession outside Hong Kong who visits Hong Kong on business, there is more difficulty in deciding what amounts to carrying on a profession *in* Hong Kong. The IRD takes the view in practice that the performance in Hong Kong of any professional service gives rise to a liability to Profits Tax on the fee earned. This is extremely doubtful except in the cases where, for example, an entertainer may perform a whole season in Hong Kong. For a discussion of the principles involved see Davies v Braithwaite (18 TC 198) where an actress was held to be carrying on a single profession in her home country notwithstanding various performances given in other countries. As to the meaning of "profession" this is not statutorily defined but is discussed in IRC v Maxse (12 TC 41). It is yet another question as to what constitutes "business".

MEANING OF BUSINESS.   The scope of Profits Tax extends to the carrying on of "business" which is a term vastly wider than trade or profession. It is defined in Sec. 2 as including:—

> "agricultural undertaking, poultry and pig rearing and the letting or sub-letting by any corporation to any person of any premises or portion thereof, and the sub-letting by any other person of any premises or portion of any premises held by him under a lease or tenancy other than from the Crown".

Note therefore that a corporation which lets any property is immediately regarded as carrying on business whereas any other person is not so regarded unless he sub-lets property, in other words letting of the Crown leaseholder (who is regarded as the "owner" under the IRO — see Chapter 2) who is not a corporation is not necessarily regarded as carrying on business. However, care should be exercised in applying the definition in Sec. 2 because it is only stated to "include" the things which it mentions, therefore its scope can be much wider. Although the decision in Lam Woo Shang v CIR (HKTC 123) is now superceded by a change in the definition of business in Sec. 2 it nevertheless contains a good summary of the principles involved in defining business.

Example 1

Mr. O. Nurr owns a flat on which the net assessable value for Property Tax is $50,000. He lets it to Mr. Smarty at $75,000 per annum who immediately sub-lets it to Mr. A. Sucker for $100,000 per annum. Rates and repairs are paid by Nurr.

O. Nurr is not carrying on business and therefore pays Property Tax on $50,000.

Smarty is carrying on business and pays Profits Tax on $25,000 profit.

Whereas trade and profession are normally associated with some active function, the wider term business includes those circumstances where there is a purely passive receipt of income. For example, a holding company whose function solely is to hold shares in other companies, even subsidiaries, is carrying on business whether or not there is any active management participation in the companies in which it has interests. For an examination of the principles in borderline cases see IRC v Korean Syndicate (12 TC 181). Note that a corporation may commence business before it commences trading.

The ascertainment of whether or not a corporation is carrying on business is most significant in the cases where it is in receipt of interest when, if it is carrying on business, it is liable to Profits Tax on net income after deducting relevant expenses and, if it is not carrying on business, is liable to Interest Tax on the gross interest before any deductions.

Although mutual trading bodies such as clubs, trade associations and mutual insurance corporations are not regarded as carrying on business to the extent that they trade only with members, Sec. 24 treats clubs and trade associations as carrying on business for Profits Tax purposes in certain circumstances and Sec. 23A also treats mutual insurance corporations as subject to Profits Tax.

COMMENCEMENT OF BUSINESS. The commencement of a trade, profession or business triggers the first basis period (see page 136) and is also relevant in ascertaining the treatment of pre-commencement expenditure.

The date of commencement is largely a question of fact, for example a retail shop business does not commence to trade until it opens its doors to the public and a manufacturing business commences to trade when raw materials are first purchased for the manufacturing operations. The mistake should not be made of looking for the first sale or receipt of income because this may be a long time after the commencement of operations which lead up to it. For example, a property development and resale company commences to trade when it first acquires land for development and the sale may be years away. Similarly a commission agent must set up an office and go out to seek business long before he receives his first commission. A property development for investment business does not however commence its property letting business until such time as it has property available for letting, nevertheless if its objects are also "to develop" the property, the commencement of the development probably amounts to the commencement of business, albeit one that gives rise to no income, and then ultimately it commences its property letting business. The earlier commencement of business may be significant if it is in receipt of interest prior to commencement of letting because that interest may then be subject to Profits Tax instead of Interest Tax (see Chapter 4 paragraph 5).

Note that interest incurred during the construction period on loan funds for construction of a building is treated as capital expenditure and not therefore deductible for Profits Tax (CIR v Tai On Machinery Works HKTC 411). Similarly, the strict legal position on all expenditure incurred before the commencement of a business is that such expenditure is not deductible, however in practice the IRD will allow pre-commencement expenditure of a revenue type that would be allowable after commencement to be deducted in the first basis period. Examples of such expenditure are office rent and wages of staff to install and test machinery.

Example 2

Impex Ltd. is incorporated on 1st June 1978 for the purpose of carrying on an import and export business. Due to delay in finding suitable office premises the directors actively engage in investing the Company's funds in interest earning deposits. On 1st January 1979 office premises are found and staff are employed to establish office routines and set up book-keeping procedures. On 1st March 1979 the first import transaction is entered into and commission is received on 15th April.

The trade commences on 1st March 1979 and, in practice the rent and wages for the period 1st January 1979 to 1st March 1979 will be treated as if they were incurred on 1st March 1979.

Also, the Company was carrying on an investment business in the period before it commenced the import/export trade therefore it would be subject to Profits Tax and not Interest Tax on any onshore interest earned in that period.

CESSATION OF BUSINESS.   It is also important to be able to establish the date of cessation of business because upon this depends the final basis period (see page 138) and in addition ·it governs the treatment of post cessation payments and receipts and the treatment of trading stock upon cessation (see pages 117 to 119).

Again, the date of cessation is largely a question of fact and it is particularly important to distinguish between the temporary suspension of a trade and its final cessation. This is particularly difficult in the case of property development when the completion of a development does not of itself signify cessation of trade because there could be a considerable period of inactivity while further suitable property is sought out. Furthermore, the appointment of a liquidator does not of itself signify cessation of trade, this must be judged on the facts because a liquidator may continue the trade for a period of time in order to protect the assets. However if the liquidator is merely realising assets, including trading stock, in order to wind up a company this is unlikely to constitute trading (see Tai Shun Investment Co. v CIR HKTC 370). The circumstances could also exist, for example, in the case of a property developer who sells his last property on an instalment basis and, although he does not seek to acquire or develop any more property, continues to collect the instalments. As it is proper to bring in the profit on sale only in relation to each instalment received (CIR v Montana Lands HKTC 334) it is quite likely that the business can be said to continue until the final instalment is received although this should be contrasted with the facts in the Tai Shun Investment Co. case where only a few instalments remained to be collected and the liquidator was held to be merely tidying up.

Payments made with a view to going out of business are obviously not for the purposes of earning assessable profits and are therefore not deductible (James Snook & Co. v Blasdale 33 TC 244 and see also BR 13/70). However, where a company was about to merge its business with another company and paid out large sums of money to avert a strike which would have damaged its business prior to transfer, those sums were held to be deductible because they were for the purpose of enabling the business to continue, notwithstanding that the paying company could not make a profit (CIR v Swire Pacific Ltd. HKTC 1145).

The circumstances in Example 2 on page 99 could equally apply in reverse so that a company could cease trading yet still be in business.

WHAT CONSTITUTES TRADING. It is often difficult to determine whether an isolated transaction or series of transactions constitutes a trade giving rise to a profit subject to Profits Tax. Section 2 defines trade as including "every trade and manufacture and every adventure and concern in the nature of trade". The tax payer may claim that the purchase and sale of a property or of shares was an investment giving rise to a capital profit whereas the IRD may claim that it was an adventure in the nature of trade giving rise to a revenue profit. The matter has to be judged on the facts and, as the U.K. definition of trade is similar, there is a considerable amount of U.K. case law to which the reader is referred. So far as general rules are applicable the problem boils down to one of circumstances and motive and the latter can only be judged from oral evidence and documents prepared at the time of the transactions in question. The numerous legal decisions were considered by the Royal Commission on the Taxation of Profits and Income which reported in 1955 and the main principles were conveniently summarised under what the Committee referred to as the six "badges of trade". Their verbatim report on this aspect is as follows:—

"(1) The subject matter of the realisation. While almost any form of property can be acquired to be dealt in, those forms of property, such as commodities or manufactured articles, which are normally the subject of trading, are only very exceptionally the subject of investment. Again property which does not yield to its owner an income or personal enjoyment merely by virtue of its ownership is more likely to have been acquired with the object of a deal than property that does.

(2) The length of the period of ownership. Generally speaking, property meant to be dealt in is realised within a short time after acquisition. But there are many exceptions from this as a universal rule.

(3) The frequency or number of similar transactions by the same person. If realisations of the same sort of property occur in succession over a period of years or there are several such realisations at about the same date a presumption arises that there has been dealing in respect of each.

(4) Supplementary work on or in connection with the property realised. If the property is worked up in any way during the ownership so as to bring it into a more marketable condition; or if any special exertions are made to find or attract purchasers, such as the opening of an office or large-scale advertising, there is some evidence of dealing. For when there is an organised effort to obtain profit there is a source of taxable income. But if nothing at all is done, the suggestion tends the other way.

(5) The circumstances that were responsible for the realisation. There may be some explanation, such as a sudden emergency or opportunity calling for ready money, that negatives the idea that any plan of dealing prompted the original purchase.

(6) Motive. There are cases in which the purpose of the transaction of purchase and sale is clearly discernible. Motive is never irrelevant in any of these cases. What is desirable is that it should be realised clearly that it can be inferred from surrounding circumstances in the absence of correct evidence of the seller's intentions and even, if

necessary, in the face of his own evidence."

The question has also come before the Courts in Hong Kong and the reader is therefore referred to CIR v Jebsen & Co. (HKTC 1) and, for a discussion on the special circumstances of an insurance company which owns real property, CIR v Sincere Insurance and Investment Co. (HKTC 602). There are also a number of Board of Review decisions where the principles are discussed. In respect of dealing in land see BR 20/73, 9/74, 12/74, 23/74, 6/75, 6/76 and 20/78 and in respect of share dealing see BR 11/76.

In the case of profits from the purchase and sale of shares and whether this constitutes a share dealing activity it is difficult to lay down general rules because inevitably this introduces an element of gambling. It has been held that gambling winnings do not necessarily constitute the carrying on of a trade (Graham v Green 9 TC 309) but where the gambling is related to a trading activity in which the person has some knowledge or expertise the profits may be taxable (Burdge v Pyne 45 TC 320). However, see CIR v Dr. Chang Liang-Jen (HKTC 975) where an economist was held not to be share dealing. Accordingly there may be some authority for assessing the profits on purchase and sale of shares by a person connected with stockbroking or investment business but much must depend upon the facts. There are also cases establishing that betting winnings are assessable in the case of jockeys and trainers. Where however there is no link with an existing trade or expertise and it is mere speculation it is much more difficult for the taxing authority to show that the profits are taxable. Care should however be exercised in comparing decisions in other countries, particularly the U.K., with facts in Hong Kong because many such decisions are based on the question of whether a "trade" is carried on whereas in Hong Kong the much wider term "business" may catch the transactions in question. Where a business of share dealing is established, see CIR v Ting Kwan-Che (HKTC 901) as to the treatment of bonus shares.

Note that the fact that the activity giving rise to a profit may be illegal does not disqualify it as taxable. See for example Mann v Nash (16 TC 523) where profits were made from the illegal operation of gaming machines.

DEEMED BUSINESS RECEIPTS. Apart from the principles already discussed as to what constitutes the carrying on of a business in Hong Kong and also the factors that determine the source of profits arising, there are a number of types of receipt which, if not otherwise subject to Profits Tax, are treated as if they were Hong Kong source income of a business carried on in Hong Kong. Accordingly, non-residents in receipt of such sources of income even if they have no presence in Hong Kong at all, are assessed on those receipts as if they were carrying on business there. In addition there are deemed business receipts applicable to persons who are actually carrying on business in Hong Kong but who would not otherwise be obliged to bring them into their Profits Tax computation. Needless to say, the deeming provisions are only applicable where the receipts are not already liable to Profits Tax.

The deemed sources are as follows:—

(1) Payments for the use in Hong Kong of any cinema or television film or any tape or sound recording or any advertising material connected with any of these things (Sec. 15(1)(a)). This is a straight-forward factual matter and is most commonly applicable to payments made by cinemas and television companies to non-resident film distributors. The assessable profit is, further, deemed by Sec. 21A to be 10% of the payment and the recipient's liability is therefore effectively 1.65% of the payment if the recipient is a company, otherwise it is 1.5%.

(2) Payments for the use, or right to use, in Hong Kong a patent, design, trademark, copyright material or secret process or formula or any other similar property or for imparting know-how in connection with the use of any of those things (Sec. 15(1)(b)). This speaks for itself and catches a number of payments by trading companies for the use of another's property. Note that it is applicable to the "right to use" even when there is no actual use. However in those cases where there is no actual use but Hong Kong is merely not excluded from the worldwide right to use, it would be unreasonable to assess the whole payment as it could only be said that a small part of the payment related to the right to use in Hong Kong. There is occasionally difficulty in determining when a patent or copyright is used. Broadly, a payment is made for the right to manufacture something in a particular pattern or design and therefore it is the place at which the manufacture takes place that is the place of use. For a copyright this would be where the book was published. The place of sale should not be relevant.

Again Sec. 21A fixes the assessable profit at 10% of the payment.

Example 3

Electronigames Ltd. is a Hong Kong company and manufactures toys including one particular design under license from a German company. It pays the German company 3% on sales which in the year 1978/79 amounted to a payment of $60,000. The German company has no other interests in Hong Kong.

The German company is deemed to be carrying on business in Hong Kong and to have profits arising in Hong Kong from that business of 10% of $60,000, namely $6,000 (Sec. 15(1)(b) and Sec. 21A). It therefore has a

Profits Tax liability of $1,020. Normally this will be assessed upon Electronigames Ltd. as agent (see para. 8 on page 165).

Example 4

If in the first year Electronigames Ltd. had paid the German company say $100,000 for advice on initial assembly of equipment for manufacturing the toy, notwithstanding that this is a once and for all payment it is still caught by Sec. 15(1)(b) and the measure of the assessable profit in that year is $10,000 plus 10% of any royalty also paid.

(3) Payments by way of grant, subsidy or similar financial assistance in connection with a trade, profession or business carried on in Hong Kong but excluding any such payment which is connected with capital expenditure (Sec. 15(1)(c)). In other words any sort of grant or aid from a public body or otherwise that is trade related must be brought in as part of the trading income except where the grant is related to capital expenditure when, if that expenditure attracts depreciation allowances (see Chapter 6) the cost will be reduced by the grant etc. This obviously only applies to a person who is already carrying on business in Hong Kong and merely sets aside the general rule that capital receipts are not within the scope of Profits Tax so far as this type of capital receipt is concerned.

(4) Payments for the use or right to use moveable property in Hong Kong (Sec. 15(1)(d)). This is a plain factual matter and is really an extension of (2) above except that Sec. 21A does not apply in fixing the assessable profit. The assessable profit must therefore be ascertained on a commercial basis and normally any direct expenses incurred by the owner of the asset would be deductible from the payment together with depreciation allowances if appropriate. Where there is no actual use of the asset in Hong Kong the payment is caught because nevertheless there is a "right to use", consideration must be given to how much of the payment is applicable to the right to use in Hong Kong having regard to where else the asset may also be used in consideration for the payment. Cases can arise where, for a single payment, an asset is used partly in Hong Kong and partly elsewhere in which case apportionment on some practical basis is necessary.

Example 5

Diganole Ltd. is a Hong Kong building contractor and it hires some heavy machinery from a French company for which it pays an annual rental of $200,000. The French company has no other interests in Hong Kong.

The French company is deemed to be carrying on business in Hong Kong and to have profits arising in Hong Kong from that business. The measure of its assessable profits is determined by the receipt of $200,000 per annum less direct expenses and depreciation allowances. It may also be able to justify an allocation of overhead expenses.

Example 6

A Hong Kong exporting company hires containers from a Swiss company which it loads in Hong Kong and sends to various parts of the World. The Swiss company has no other interests in Hong Kong.

Strictly the Swiss company is deemed to be carrying on business in Hong Kong to the extent that the containers are used there. As the containers are used both in Hong Kong and on shipments outside Hong Kong, if the liability is pursued, there will have to be a practical apportionment of the rental payment and associated expenses and depreciation allowances.

(5) Interest derived from a Hong Kong source which is received by a corporation carrying on a trade profession or business in Hong Kong (Sec. 15(1)(f)). This is the corollary to the Interest Tax exemption (see Chapter 5 paragraph 5). Therefore, even an investment company is subject to Profits Tax on its interest income provided that the interest has a source in Hong Kong. The source of interest for this purpose is determined in accordance with the "provision of credit" rule (see Chapter 4 paragraph 3). In order to parallel the exemption from Interest Tax that is applicable to interest derived from a foreign currency deposit with a financial institution (as defined in Sec. 2 – see page 157) with effect from 25th February 1982, there is a similar exemption from Profits Tax that would otherwise be applicable under Sec. 15(1)(f). This exemption is not however applicable to a company whose business comprises or includes the taking of deposits (Sec. 15(1B)). Note that this exclusion from exemption does not only apply where the investor company is itself a financial institution because a company's business can comprise or include deposit-taking without it being within the definition of financial institution, for example, a company can take deposits from registered or licensed deposit-taking companies or licensed banks without being required to register under the deposit-taking companies ordinance.

Note also that the reduction in rate of Interest Tax that relates to Hong Kong dollar deposits with financial institutions has no effect for Profits Tax, the applicable rate remains at 16½%.

(6) Interest derived from a Hong Kong source which is received by a person other than a corporation where the interest is exempted from Interest Tax and is in respect of the funds of the person's trade, profession or business (Sec. 15(1)(g)). This is so that the interest which is in effect really a part of the business profits, because it derives from investment of the business funds, will not escape tax altogether. Again, as in (5), interest

on a foreign currency deposit with a financial institution which arises after 24th February 1982 is not chargeable to Profits Tax under Sec. 15(1)(g) unless the recipient's business is one of deposit-taking (Sec. 15(1B)). Equally, the reduced rate of Interest Tax that is applicable to Hong Kong dollar deposits does not apply to Profits Tax under Sec. 15(1)(g).

Example 7

Lotsaloot Ltd. carries on a retail trade in Hong Kong on which it has an adjusted profit for 1982/83 of $120,000. It also has surplus funds which it has placed on deposit with a bank in Hong Kong, partly in Hong Kong dollars and partly in US dollars, receiving interest of $15,000 on each deposit.

The Hong Kong dollar interest is exempt from Interest Tax and is included in the total Profits Tax assessment of $135,000. The US dollar interest is not liable to tax in Hong Kong at all.

Example 8

A partnership of architects has some funds temporarily available before being required again in the business and invests these in a Savings Deposit account for one month. The interest is not in excess of the rate at which such interest is exempt from Interest Tax.

Because the interest is exempt from Interest Tax and arises out of the funds of the business it is included in the partnership Profits Tax assessment. If it had not been exempt from Interest Tax, tax would have been deducted at source at 10% and it would not have been included in the Profits Tax assessment. Clearly it would be a bad investment decision that yielded interest at a low rate subject to tax at 15% instead of higher interest subject to tax at 10%!

(7) Refunds of contributions from an approved retirement scheme to the extent that the recipient obtained a deduction for Profits Tax purposes for such contributions (Sec. 15(1)(h)). Were it not for this provision an employer could obtain deductions for contributions and then close the scheme and receive back all the contributions tax free. The provision however applies only to approved retirement schemes, an employer can still obtain deductions for contributions to a non-approved retirement scheme which is subsequently wound up in a manner which does not give rise to a tax liability.

(8) Interest income that would otherwise be regarded as having a non-Hong Kong source which arises through or from the carrying on of business in Hong Kong by a bank or financial institution (Sec. 15(1)(i)). This is a complicated matter and is dealt with separately on pages 156 to 160

under the heading "Banks and Financial Institutions".
(9) Profits arising in or derived from Hong Kong by a corporation carrying
on a trade or business in Hong Kong from the disposal of or on the
redemption on maturity or presentment of a certificate of deposit or bill
of exchange (Sec. 15(1)(j)). For this purpose, certificate of deposit is as
defined for Interest Tax purposes in Sec. 2 (see page 79) but bill of
exchange is not defined therefore it takes its usual commercial meaning.
Where the profit on maturity is in fact interest as it would be on a
certificate of deposit, it is Sec. 15(1)(f) that applies (see (5) on page 105)
and not Sec. 15(1)(j). Where the certificate of deposit is sold before
maturity, the profit is not interest therefore Sec. 15(1)(j) applies. These
points give rise to some interesting anomalies as illustrated in this
example:—

Example 9

Kash-my-chek Ltd. is a real estate investment company in Hong Kong
which has temporary surplus cash. If it has, say, HK$100 to invest it may:—
(a) Place HK$100 on deposit and receive a CD which it holds to maturity
and receives HK$110.
The profit of HK$10 is interest on which it pays Profits Tax of HK$1.65
(Sec. 15(1)(f)).
(b) Buy in the secondary market for HK$100 a CD originally issued for
HK$90 which it holds to maturity and receives HK$110.
Its profit is HK$10 but the HK$110 includes interest of HK$20 which
Kash-my-chek must report for Profits Tax, paying HK$3.30 tax (Sec.
15(1)(f)).
(c) As for (b) but it sells again in the secondary market one day before
maturity for HK$109.9.
Its profit is HK$9.9 and it pays Profits Tax on this of HK$1.65 (Sec. 15
(1)(j)).
(d) If it converts the HK$100 into foreign currency and carries out the same
transactions in that currency, it pays no tax in any of the cases (a), (b) or
(c) because of the exemption offered by Sec. 15(1B) for deposits in
foreign currency with financial institutions with effect from 25th
February 1982.

The provisions refer only to profits which arise in or derive from Hong
Kong, i.e. which have a Hong Kong source. It is likely that it would only have
a non Hong Kong source if the sale is concluded outside Hong Kong by an
agent outside Hong Kong along the lines of the decision in BR 18/73. It
would not have an offshore source merely because it was in a non Hong Kong
currency nor would it necessarily be so if it was sold directly to an offshore
counterparty. However, this is largely academic since 24 February 1982 after
which interest, deemed interest and profits from disposal of certificates of

deposit and bills of exchange in respect of deposits in foreign currency with financial institutions are exempt from Profits Tax (Sec. 15(1B)).

Because affected certificates of deposit and bills of exchange would have been in issue when the change of law occurred with effect from 1st April 1981, there are transitional provisions (Sec. 15(1A)). These provide that any part of the profit which is otherwise liable to Profits Tax but which relates to a period held before 1st April 1981 is not to be chargeable. This is achieved by substituting the open market value of the security as at the close of business on 31st March 1981. This exclusion does not however apply to a corporation which is carrying on a trade of dealing in securities for the obvious reason that it would have been liable to Profits Tax on the profits before the change in law so there is no question of any new imposition with effect from 1st April 1981.

(10) Profits arising in or derived from Hong Kong, identical to those dealt with in (9) above but where the investor is any person other than a corporation but who is carrying on a trade, profession or business in Hong Kong and where:—

(a) The profits from the disposals of the certificates of deposit or bills of exchange are in respect of the funds of the business.

(b) The profits are exempt from Interest Tax.

(Sec. 15(1)(k)).

This provision mirrors the subjection of Hong Kong source interest to Profits Tax in the same circumstances (see (6) above). Accordingly it only applies where the profit in question is not interest, i.e. disposal of a bill of exchange at any time and disposal of a certificate of deposit before maturity. Note however that if the funds used are not funds of the business, the Profits Tax charge does not apply. Therefore where an individual is carrying on a business it is important to determine whether funds used have been permanently extracted from the business for investment or whether they have been temporarily invested prior to further business requirements.

As these provisions are identical to the deemed charge described in (9) above, the only difference being the status of the person chargeable, the following principles which are fully described in (9) above are equally applicable:—

(i) Determination of source.

(ii) Exemption from Profits Tax with effect from 25th February 1982 in respect of funds placed with a financial institution in a foreign currency (Sec. 15(1B)).

(iii) Transitional provisions (Sec. 15(1A)) in view of commencement on 1st April 1981.

Example 10

The partnership in example 8 has, during 1982/83, invested business funds partly in a HK$ certificate of deposit and partly on a simple deposit with a bank in HK$.

The CD is sold before maturity at a profit of $10,000. The interest on the deposit is $11,000.

The profit of $10,000 is subject to Profits Tax at 15% (Sec. 15(1)(k)). The interest of $11,000 is subject to Interest Tax at 10% if the interest is in excess of the exempt rate (see page 82). If below the exempt rate it is exempt from Interest Tax and therefore subject to Profits Tax at 15% (Sec. 15(1)(g)).

If however the funds were identically invested in US dollars or other foreign currency, no tax would be chargeable at all (Sec. 15(1B)).

(11) Where a deduction has been allowed for a debt incurred in the course of a trade, profession or business and that debt is subsequently wholly or partly released, the part released is treated as a receipt of the trade, profession or business in the basis period in which the release is effected (Sec. 15(2)). This provision applies only to the release of a debt which implies some act of forgiveness on the part of the creditor. For example, in a bankruptcy where only a percentage of the debt is paid, the balance is not released but in effect remains uncollectable. The provision is included to nullify the decision in British Mexican Petroleum Co. Ltd. v Jackson (16 TC 570).

Of the above eleven deeming provisions, (3), (5), (6), (7), (8), (9), (10) and (11) in fact apply to persons already carrying on business in Hong Kong and merely supplement the taxable profits in circumstances where the receipt in question would otherwise not be within the scope of Profits Tax. Headings (1), (2) and (4) create a position, mostly applicable to non-residents, where a business is deemed to be carried on. Because of the difficulties of collection, extensive powers are provided for assessing upon and collecting from agents in Hong Kong and, for this purpose, "agent" is widely defined. These provisions are dealt with on page 169.

Under headings (1) and (2) the ascertainment of the amount of the taxable profit is clearly identified by Sec. 21A but it would be open to a non-resident to show that he was in fact carrying on a business in Hong Kong and that his actual assessable profits were less than as provided by Sec. 21A because if he is carrying on business, Sec. 14 is applicable and, automatically, Sec. 15(1) is not applicable. Under heading (4) there is no specifically identifiable assessable profit and this must therefore be ascertained as a question of fact. Failing an ascertainment of the true profit arising in Hong Kong, Sec. 21 provides that it may be computed on a fair percentage of the receipt in question.

The identification by the IRD of sources arising to non-residents under headings (1), (2) and (4) is usually from an examination of the tax returns of the payer who is in fact obliged to report the existence of any such payments in accordance with specific questions on his return form.

5.   Ascertainment of Assessable Profits

The usual starting point for the ascertainment of the assessable profits of a business venture is the profit revealed by the commercial accounts and it is fairly well established law that ordinarily accepted accounting principles are acceptable in determining profits or losses for tax purposes except where the tax statutes require specific adjustments to those profits or losses (see Usher's Wiltshire Brewery v Bruce 6 TC 399). Inevitably there are differences in interpretation in the application of accounting principles and there is therefore a wide body of applicable case law on this subject, particularly in the area of greatest contention, i.e. whether a given transaction is on revenue or on capital account.

The IRO deals very little with the receipts side of the account except to exclude profits from the sale of capital assets and income derived from a non-Hong Kong source (see pages 91 to 95) and to include certain receipts as deemed business receipts (see page 102). Whether or not the sale of an asset is an adventure in the nature of trade giving rise to a revenue profit or loss or whether it is an investment giving rise to a capital profit or loss is a contentious area on which there is a considerable amount of U.K. case law and this is discussed on pages 100 to 102.

On the expenditure side the IRO contains a number of regulating provisions for adjusting the commercial accounts and these are dealt with in detail under various headings later. There are also a number of general principles on which there is a considerable amount of law and practice and these are also covered under suitable headings.

CAPITAL OR REVENUE.   As most capital receipts and capital expenditure must be excluded from the commercial profit in arriving at the profit assessable to Profits Tax, it is a matter of fundamental importance to be able to identify them. This is a very wide area of the law with probably more legal decisions related to this question than to any other single tax question. Certain general principles can be drawn but, in border line cases, there is no substitute for analysing the facts and researching the numerous decisions for parallel or similar circumstances.

On the income side the IRO excludes only profits from the sale of capital assets so in the circumstances where a receipt is of a capital nature but is not from the sale of an asset it seems there is no authority to exclude it if it arises from the trade, profession or business. This point has been considered by the Privy Council in the case of CIR v Far East Exchange (HKTC 1036).

On the expenses side, Sec. 17(1)(c) disallows expenditure of a capital nature and it is only appropriate to consider here the general principles which govern the identification of capital expenditure; the reader is referred to the substantial body of case law in the U.K. and elsewhere.

One of the earliest tests was put forward by Lord Dunedin in Vallambrosa Rubber Co. v Farmer (5 TC 529) when he suggested that capital expenditure is that which is made "once and for all" whereas revenue expenditure will "recur year by year". Unfortunately this test is really much too simple and has so many exceptions that it cannot be regarded as a general rule standing on its own. A little later the test was expanded and qualified into what is now regarded as the classic and most often quoted rule, that of Lord Cave in British Insulated and Helsby Cables v Atherton (10 TC 155) when he stated:—

> "But when an expenditure is made, not only once and for all but with a view to bringing into existence an asset or an advantage for the enduring benefit of a trade, I think that there is very good reason (in the absence of special circumstances leading to an opposite conclusion) for treating such an expenditure as properly attributable, not to revenue, but to capital."

From this rule most decisions flow and can be reconciled with but nevertheless it must be treated with caution lest its wording be given too wide a meaning. It is perhaps relatively simple to identify the cases in which an asset is brought into existence whether it be a tangible or intangible asset. As regards the creation of an enduring advantage, it is a failing of tax officials to refer to the Atherton case and state that an expenditure in question gives rise to an advantage and is therefore of a capital nature. What must be remembered is that all expenditure gives rise to an advantage or it would not have been incurred. What is important is whether the advantage is enduring in nature and this implies something which is not necessarily permanent but of which the span is appreciably longer than that created by the normal revenue charge. In other words an annual bonus to employees certainly creates the advantage of willing service for a full year but if it is not paid next time, the advantage quickly fades whereas a payment to a departing employee in order to secure his covenant not to compete after he has left is a long lasting advantage and therefore of a capital nature (Associated Portland Cement Manufacturers v IRC 27 TC 103). Similarly, regular contributions to maintain an employee pension scheme are of a revenue nature but the initial contribution to create the nucleus of the fund is of a capital nature (the Atherton case and also Rowntree & Co. v Curtis 8 TC 678).

The fact that the intended advantage does not materialise or that the intended asset is not acquired and therefore expenditure laid out in anticipation is abortive is not however a ground for regarding it as revenue expenditure (Southwell v Savill Bros. 4 TC 430). It has in fact from time to time been urged upon the Government both in the U.K. and Hong Kong to legislate for this fact but nevertheless it remains that abortive capital expenditure attracts neither deduction in arriving at assessable profits nor depreciation allowances. There are also a number of cases on the principle that depreciation of capital assets whether tangible or intangible is of a capital nature. This is in fact replaced by the statutory depreciation allowances (see Chapter 6).

There are then the rules related to the cost of getting rid of some undesirable factor that is a hindrance to business. The cost of removing an undesirable capital asset has been held to be of a capital nature (Mallett v Staveley Coal and Iron Co. 13 TC 772) because this creates an advantage as enduring as the asset itself whereas the cost of commuting a future onerous revenue charge in fact does nothing more than replace that revenue expenditure and therefore is itself of a revenue nature (Hancock v General Revisionary and Investment Co. 7 TC 358). Similarly a payment to terminate an onerous trading agreement is of a revenue nature (Anglo-Persian Oil Co. v Dale 16 TC 253). Although the cost of bringing into existence or improving or adding to an asset, together with all related incidental expenditure such as legal fees, is of a capital nature, once in existence, the cost of protecting that asset is of a revenue nature (Southern v Borax Consolidated 23 TC 597).

Where a payment is in the nature of compensation or damages, it is necessary to consider to what it relates and it in fact normally follows the treatment of the transaction upon which the liability arose. In other words, if it is damages arising out of a trading contract, say for the supply of faulty goods, it is of a revenue nature but if it is in respect of a capital asset, as in the case of a deposit paid for the acquisition of a ship and that contract is not pursued, in fact a further sum is paid to secure the release of the obligation to buy the ship, it is of a capital nature (Countess Warwick Steamship Co. v Ogg 8 TC 652).

Notwithstanding this wealth of legal decisions they should be treated as no more than guidelines in given cases unless the exact parallel can be found. For example, some decisions may appear to be exactly contrary to the rules quoted above and, whilst this does happen, usually a close examination of the facts and the judgement will indicate why. For a review of many of the more important decisions see the more recent case of Regent Oil Co. v Strick (43 TC 1). These rules of case law are modified in certain circumstances by specific provisions in the IRO (these will be identified in their context) and by concession and practice. For example, the Third Inland Revenue Ordinance Review Committee considered two examples where strictly the expenditure is of a capital nature but the IRD practice is in fact more flexible. In the case of the cost of removal of a business to a new location they reported the IRD practice as follows:—

"In considering any claim for removal expenses it is necessary to look into the circumstances and the nature of the expenditure incurred. The cost of removal of trading stock is normally admitted as a revenue expense. Where the removal has been undertaken wholly or mainly as part of a scheme for improvement and expansion or in the interests of the business, and the removal has been made voluntarily, the removal expenses should normally be regarded as of a capital nature. In such circumstances, the part of the expenditure which relates to the dismantling, transport and re-erection of machinery, etc. would be treated as qualifying for initial and annual allowances. Where, however, the removal is not voluntary but is primarily forced upon the trader by circumstances such as the refusal of a landlord to renew a lease or the redevelopment of the site, the cost of removal is normally allowed as a revenue charge. In such cases, the cost may include not merely the actual transport between the old and new premises, but also the cost of dismantling and re-installing plant, machinery, fittings, etc."

Similarly in the case of pre-commencement expenditure they reported the IRD practice as follows:—

"The owner of a business may thus incur outlay on wages or on rent for some time before the technical date of commencement. We understand, however, that the Inland Revenue Department does not adopt a rigid attitude in this matter. In general, we are informed, expenditure of the type that would normally qualify as revenue outlay may be deducted as an expense of the first accounting period. In particular, the wages of office staff engaged before trading begins and of operatives taken on in readiness for the start of production would qualify for this statement. An exception occurs when maintenance engineers are set to work on the installation of machinery; but in this case their remuneration will be effectively allowed in the long run by adding it to the capital cost of the machinery so that the capital allowances are based on the cost as so increased."

In the particular circumstances of Hong Kong, the treatment of trade "quotas" is important. There are two types of quota, the "permanent quota" which is issued by the Trade, Industry and Customs Department and entitles the recipient to export a given quantity of goods and the "temporary quota" which a holder of a permanent quota grants temporarily to another trader when he is unable or does not wish to fulfill his permanent quota. The cost of acquiring a permanent quota is treated as capital expenditure, being the acquisition of an asset (BR 29/69) whereas the cost of a temporary quota is a revenue expense being the cost of making use of an asset owned by somebody else. The treatment in the hands of the recipient of the payment is the same.

Another area of particular significance in Hong Kong is that of the treatment of foreign exchange gains and losses. It follows that, where a business of dealing in foreign currencies is carried on, the profits therefrom must be of a revenue nature. The more difficult questions arise out of other foreign exchange gains and losses that arise out of keeping accounts in foreign currencies and/or incurring liabilities in and earning income in, foreign currencies in the course of carrying on some trade or business. Two main questions arise:–

(1) Are the gains/losses of a capital or revenue nature?

(2) Are they realised or unrealised?

If they are of a revenue nature they are potentially assessable/deductible but whether or not they are realised determines the timing or assessability/ deduction (see "Date Income arises and Expenditure Incurred" in following pages).

A full discussion of the principles governing whether or not the gains/ losses are of a capital or revenue nature is highly complicated and outside the scope of this book. However there are some general guidelines by which these problems can be solved. The most important rule in dealing with an exchange gain or loss which is not derived from a purchase and sale of foreign currency for speculative purpose is that it always arises out of some other transaction and is therefore tied to it such that the gain or loss has the same character as the transaction to which it is related. For example, a profit on sale of goods is of course a revenue transaction and if the purchaser pays his debt in US dollars and during the period between payment and realisation of the US dollars by the seller, the movement in exchange rates creates a profit on exchange, that profit is merely an addition to the profit on sale of goods. In this context, realisation does not necessarily mean conversion into Hong Kong dollars, it may be realised at the moment the US dollars are used to pay a US dollar liability, appropriated as an investment in US dollars or switched into another foreign currency. As another example, if a US dollar loan is taken out to finance the fixed assets of a business and between the date of taking up the loan and repaying it some years later there is an upward movement of US dollars against Hong Kong dollars. The loss on exchange is in effect a loss on fixed capital. Alternatively, if the loan had been a temporary overdraft to finance working capital, it would have been a loss of working or circulating capital and of a revenue nature.

The following legal decisions illustrate these principles further:–

(1) Golden Horseshoe (New) Ltd. v Thurgood (18 TC 280) – The distinction between and relevance of fixed capital and circulating capital.

(2) Davies v Shell Co. of China (32 TC 133) – Deposits made with a principal by a selling agent to cover future liabilities to account for sales proceeds were regarded as fixed capital and therefore exchange losses on those deposits were capital losses.

(3) Landes Bros. v Simpson (19 TC 62) – Advances made to a principal against sales made on behalf of the principal were regarded as incidental to the sales and therefore of a revenue nature. Contrast this with (2) above.

(4) CIR v Li & Fung Ltd. (HKTC 1193) – Receipts in foreign currency from trade debtors were placed on deposit on 7 day call after which they were either used to meet debts in that currency or remitted to Hong Kong. The funds were regarded as having changed their character from trading debts to capital investments at the time they were placed on deposit. Therefore foreign exchange losses on the deposits were of a capital nature.

(5) Pattison v Marine Midland Ltd. (1981 Simons Tax Cases 540) – An exchange loss on repayment of a long term borrowing by a bank was held to be a loss of fixed capital notwithstanding that the proceeds of the loan had been invested in current assets.

DATE INCOME ARISES AND EXPENDITURE INCURRED. It is important to ascertain the date on which income arises and on which liabilities are incurred for tax purposes because this does not always coincide with the accounting treatment and adjustments may therefore be necessary.

For tax purposes income arises or liabilities "accrue" on the date on which they become due and payable notwithstanding that actual payment may be deferred for a period of time or may even be made in advance. Generally the accounting treatment follows this principle but there are circumstances in which income and expenses are brought into account before or after they in fact "accrue". It is often the case, for example, that an interest receipt which falls due after the balance sheet date is accrued on a time basis up to that date. Strictly the accrued interest should be excluded because it does not accrue for tax purposes until the due date and furthermore, on the authority of CIR v Lambe (18 TC 212) it cannot in fact be assessed until it is received although the assessment is still for the year in which it was due and payable. Similarly anticipated discount on bills of exchange which mature after the balance sheet date must be excluded and brought into the next period per Willingale v International Commercial Bank (1978 Simons Tax Cases 75). In the case of property sales by instalment, the profit on sale is regarded as arising in pro-rata amounts as the instalments are received if in fact it is accounted for in this way (CIR v Montana Lands HKTC 334). However, it is likely that if all of the profit is accounted for in the basis period in which the sale is made, the whole of that profit would also be taxable in the same period. In the case of sales of property in Hong Kong, the date on which the profit arises on an outright sale is in practice the later of:—

(1) the date of conclusion of the sale and purchase agreement, or
(2) the date of the granting of the occupation permit.

These matters are dealt with in the Departmental Interpretation and Practice Notes No. 1 (see Appendix 1).

In the case of the sale of goods it is a question of fact and of law when the sale takes place and it is irrelevant that payment may be made much later. Furthermore where it is subsequently agreed to make an additional payment, that payment relates back to the original date of sale per Frodingham Iron-stone Mines v Stewart (16 TC 728). Supplementary to this is where an exchange profit is made on the realisation of a trade debt; strictly that profit relates back to the original sale on which the debt was created. Where payment for any transaction is made or received in advance of the due date it is not to be taken into account for tax purposes until the period for which it is due (Arthur Murray (N.S.W.) Pty v CIR 9AITR 673).

On the expenditure side it is also a question of fact and of law when an expense becomes due and payable and when a loss arises. The prudency concept of accounting will often necessitate a provision for an anticipated expense or loss and this must be adjusted for tax purposes (Edward Collins and Sons v CIR 12 TC 773). Also, it is the date on which the liability to make payment occurs (either immediately or at some future date) not the date of the circumstances which ultimately give rise to the liability, i.e. if damages to property are suffered, the deduction for repairs expenditure is in the period when the liability is incurred for the repairs not when the damage occurred (Naval Colliery v CIR 12 TC 1017) and not when payment is ultimately made.

Even where a liability has arisen in a year, it is not necessarily the case that it can be quantified accurately, i.e. where a customer has notified a claim for damages which is admitted but not yet agreed in amount. In these circumstances, a provision will usually be made for accounting purposes and that provision will be deductible if:−

(1) it is a specific provision for a liability that has accrued in the basis period; and

(2) it is ascertained with substantial accuracy.

For a discussion on the principles and a summary of earlier authorities see Owen v Southern Railway of Peru (36 TC 602). Where however the liability is contingent upon some future event, it cannot be said to have accrued and is not therefore deductible until the contingency crystallises.

Example 11

Payout Ltd. has an accounting date of 31st December and each year makes a provision in respect of bonuses to employees. The employees fall into two groups.

The office staff have contracts of employment which entitle them to an annual bonus, subject to good conduct, based on the Company's results. If they have not worked for the Company's full year they are paid a pro-rata amount. The bonuses are paid at the Chinese New Year.

The factory staff are paid an additional month's salary at the Chinese New Year provided they are in employment at that date.

The provisions are calculated as accurately as possible at 31st December and the figure is rounded off.

The provision for office staff will be allowed because a liability exists day by day throughout the year and it is ascertained with substantial accuracy.

The provision for factory staff will not be allowed because the liability does not accrue until Chinese New Year being contingent upon being in service at that date. It will be allowed on a cash payment basis in the following period.

Although there is no statutory foundation for the practice, some professional accounts are prepared, and accepted for Profits Tax, on a cash basis.

POST CESSATION RECEIPTS AND PAYMENTS. The receipt of income after cessation, even in a later year of assessment, does not mean that it escapes tax whether the recipient has been on a cash basis or an accruals basis. Equally, expenditure after cessation may still qualify as a deduction.

Sec. 15D(1) provides that sums received after cessation which, had they been received before, would have been within the scope of Profits Tax, are to be included in the Profits Tax computation for the year of assessment in which the cessation occurred. If necessary, an additional assessment is raised. Also, if expenditure is incurred after cessation which would have been deductible if incurred before, it is treated as if it had been incurred in the year of assessment in which the cessation took place (Sec. 15D(2)). If necessary, a final assessment is re-opened to admit the deduction. The treatment of trading stock upon cessation is subject to special provisions (see sub paragraph which follows).

Example 12

Snarlup Ltd. is a road construction company which ceased business on 31st December 1978 and had an assessable profit of $625,000 for 1978/79. On 15th March 1979 it received $15,000 compensation from a concrete supplier for faulty goods supplied in 1978. On 14th June 1979 Smarlup paid out damages of $25,000 to a motorist as compensation for an accident caused by faulty road construction.

When the receipt of $15,000 is reported, if the 1978/79 assessment on $625,000 had already been finalised, an additional assessment for 1978/79 on $15,000 would be raised. Likewise, the payment in 1979/80 can be claimed and, although Sec. 15D(2) does not specifically provide that the 1978/79 final assessment may be re-opened, this is in fact done and repayment made of $25,000 @ 17% (the rate applicable in 1978/79).

TRADING STOCK AND WORK-IN-PROGRESS. Because the inclusion of trading stock and work-in-progress (subsequently referred to as stock) in commercial accounts on a valuation basis can be materially influential upon the results shown by the accounts, the amount at which such stock is brought into the accounts is a very sensitive area from a taxation point of view. As a result there are challenges from time to time as to whether a given basis of valuation is valid for tax purposes. There are therefore a number of relevant legal decisions and, as regards the practice in general in Hong Kong in relation to the stock, the Departmental Interpretation and Practice Notes No. 1 is essential reading (see Appendix 1).

Generally, the treatment for tax purposes follows the accounting treatment but nevertheless there are cases where the method of valuation adopted is not acceptable for tax purposes. For example, the LIFO method of valuation was held to be unacceptable in Minister of National Revenue v Anaconda American Brass (34 TC 330) as was the base stock method in Patrick v Broadstone Mills (35 TC 44) and the replacement value method in Freeman, Hardy & Willis v Ridgeway (47 TC 519). For a discussion on the necessity or otherwise to include overheads in a stock valuation for tax purposes see Duple Motor Bodies v Ostime (39 TC 537) although this has been largely overtaken by the standard accounting requirements now laid down by the accountancy bodies. In general, the IRD accepts the principles laid down in the Statement of Standard Accounting Practice issued by the approved accountancy bodies in the U.K. and the few reservations which the IRD has are dealt with in its Departmental Interpretation and Practice Notes reproduced in Appendix 1.

A number of special points arise out of case law in connection with trading stock. For example, the principle in Sharkey v Wernher (36 TC 275) that where trading stock is appropriated to some other use, perhaps for personal consumption or for use in the business as a fixed asset, it is to be treated as a sale at open market value. See also in this connection BR 21/76. This situation may also arise in reverse, particularly in connection with real property where a property may have originally been acquired as an investment and is then subsequently appropriated as a current asset with a view to resale. For the purposes of arriving at the taxable profit on sale, the acquisition cost is not the historical cost but is the open market value at the time of appropriation. The difficulty is of course in establishing the date when the intentions for the property changed.

A similar principle was established in Petrotim Securities v Ayres (41 TC 389) but for a different reason. Here, valuable investments held as trading stock were sold to an associate at a nominal price to produce a loss. It was held that this could not constitute a trading transaction and therefore the open market value must be substituted. The other side of the coin is that, on the authority of Ridge Securities v CIR (44 TC 373) an equivalent adjustment can be made by the purchaser to raise the purchase cost from the nominal figure to open market value. This is supported in the Hong Kong case of Wing Tai Development Co. Ltd. v CIR (HKTC 1115) where shares were acquired by reference to their nominal value but the taxable profit on subsequent sale had to be measured on the basis of acquisition at their true value.

The IRO also provides for special treatment on the cessation of a business. The treatment applies only to trading stock, not to work-in-progress and is as follows:—

(1) Where the stock is sold to a person who will use the stock in a business carried on in Hong Kong and will be claiming the purchase cost as a deductible expense, the actual sale proceeds are not disturbed, whether they be at open market value or otherwise (Sec. 15C(a)).

(2) In any other situation, the disposal is to be brought in at open market value (Sec. 15C(b)). In other words the Sharkey v Wernher principle is statutorily applied on a cessation whereas otherwise it might not apply.

Example 13

Sharedealers Ltd. holds a number of securities as trading stock with a historical cost of $250,000 and a current market value of $600,000. It is decided to cease the share dealing business and liquidate the company and in doing this the shares are sold to Shareinvest Ltd. for $250,000 and Shareinvest holds these as a fixed asset for income.

If Sharedealers had instead decided to hold the securities as fixed assets for income purposes and had therefore appropriated them to fixed assets, the principle in Sharkey v Wernher would have applied and an immediate taxable profit of $350,000 would have arisen although there would be great practical difficulty in demonstrating that a cessation of sharedealing had actually taken place. It would escape this principle by merely selling them into a separate investment company at cost but for Sec. 15C(b) which ensures that the notional profit of $350,000 is taxable on cessation. If Shareinvest had also been a dealing company, Sec. 15C(a) would have applied and Sharedealers would have had no taxable profit but the new dealing company would have an acquisition price of $250,000.

If Sharedealers had not been ceasing business Sec. 15C would not apply but the sale to Shareinvest at $250,000 might be attacked under Petrotim Securities v Ayres.

ADJUSTMENTS TO COMMERCIAL ACCOUNTS. The IRO provides a number of specific circumstances where a given expense is to be deductible and where a given expense cannot be deductible as well as setting out the general rules for deductibility. Therefore, when starting with a profit or loss shown by commercial accounts it is necessary to add back items deducted in arriving at the profit or loss that are not deductible and to deduct those items which are deductible but have not already been deducted in the commercial accounts. The result is an "adjusted profit" for Profits Tax purposes. Furthermore, in arriving at the adjusted profit it may have been necessary to exclude some of the income as not liable to Profits Tax in which case it is necessary to exclude related expenditure and this may involve arbitrary apportionment which is provided for in the IRR. In the case of non-residents carrying on business in Hong Kong or having a source of assessable income in Hong Kong and the profits therefrom are not readily ascertainable by the usual methods, there are provisions in the IRO and IRR for ascertaining the measure of assessable profits. Also, in the case of certain special types of business there are specific rules for the ascertainment of assessable profits (see paragraph 7).

EXCLUDED INCOME. The following income is excluded in arriving at adjusted profits.

(1) Profits from the sale of capital assets (Sec. 14).

(2) Income not arising in or derived from Hong Kong (Sec. 14).

(3) Dividends from corporations which are chargeable to Profits Tax (Sec. 26(a)). This seems to imply that a dividend from a company which is not subject to Profits Tax because it is not carrying on business, i.e. it might merely be subject to Interest Tax on the investment of its share capital, may be subject to Profits Tax. It is thought however that where a company is carrying on business in Hong Kong but is not liable to pay Profits Tax because all its profits either arise offshore or are not otherwise taxable, it is nevertheless "chargeable" to Profits Tax and its dividends will therefore fall within the exclusion.

(4) Income already charged elsewhere to Profits Tax (Sec. 26(b)). This might arise for example where a company is a member of a partnership. The partnership is independently assessed on its profits (see page 162) and the company will of course bring its share of profits into its accounts. The company cannot be charged on those profits.

(5) Tax Reserve Certificate interest (Sec. 26A(1)(a)).

(6) Interest arising on a Government bond issued under the loans (Government Bonds) Ordinance (Sec. 26A(1)(b)).

(7) Any profit on the sale of a Government bond as in (6) above (Sec. 26A(1)(c)).

(8) Interest arising to a person other than a corporation where Interest Tax has been paid (Sec. 26A(2)). This seems to imply that, if for some reason there was a failure on the part of the payer to deduct Interest Tax, the interest will instead be charged to Profits Tax. In fact this is a sensible practical solution as, at present, the rates of Interest Tax and Profits Tax on persons other than corporations are the same. For corporations, the interest is always included in the Profits Tax computation because it is exempt from Interest Tax (see page 82).

EXPENDITURE DEDUCTIBLE. The general rule for deductibility of expenditure is stated in Sec. 16(1) as all outgoings and expenses to the extent to which they are incurred during the basis period for the year of assessment

in the production of profits chargeable to Profits Tax. The question of when
expenses are incurred has been dealt with in paragraph 4 and the question of
whether or not expenditure is related to the production of assessable profits
is largely a question of fact. The use of the words "to the extent that" is
sufficient to require disallowance of expenditure not related to or only partly
related to assessable profits but the specific apportionment provisions in the
IRR put the matter beyond doubt. See page 128 under the heading
"Apportionments".

Apart from this general rule as to deductibility, Section 16 provides a
number of circumstances where certain expenditure is specifically deductible
as follows. It is important to remember however that it is not only expenditure that meets the following rules which is deductible, these are merely
specific provisions to ensure that the described expenditure is deductible.
Everything else is subject to the general rule quoted above and to case law.

(i)   LOAN INTEREST AND RELATED EXPENDITURE such as legal fees,
      procuration fees and stamp duties are deductible so long as they are for
      the purpose of producing assessable profits (Sec. 16(1)(a)). Whether
      these expenses are for the purpose of producing assessable profits is
      usually judged by how the loan proceeds are applied. In particular, if a
      loan is used to purchase shares in another company, this will not pro-
      duce assessable profits unless the purchaser is a share-dealer therefore
      the interest and related expenses would be disallowed. If a loan is used
      partly to buy shares, a proportionate disallowance is required as laid
      down in IRR2B (see page 128 under "Apportionments").

(ii) RENT paid in respect of land or buildings occupied for the purpose of
      producing assessable profits. This is perhaps obvious and not really
      necessary to have a specific provision for deductibility. It is however
      provided that where the rent is paid by a partnership to one or more of
      the partners, the deduction is limited to rent equal to the assessable
      value of the land or buildings for Property Tax purposes (see pages 24
      to 26). If it was not for this provision, a partner could charge a rent
      greater than the amount on which he is subject to Property Tax because
      the actual amount of the rent is not assessable upon him but would
      otherwise be deductible by the partnership (Sec. 16(1)(b)).

(iii) BAD DEBTS AND DOUBTFUL DEBTS that have become bad during the
      basis period notwithstanding that the debt may have been due and
      payable in an earlier period (Sec. 16(1)(d)). It is necessary to convince
      the assessor of the fact that the debts have become bad because the
      deduction is at his discretion. It is usually necessary to show that posi-
      tive action has been taken to enforce collection and that this has proved
      fruitless, the fact that the debt is doubtful is insufficient, it must have
      become bad and clearly therefore it must be a specific provision.

Furthermore, to qualify for deduction the debt in question must have been originally brought in as a trading receipt, in other words a loan to a customer for example, even if it was defaulted and irrecoverable, would not be deductible because it did not represent a trading receipt. The exception of course is a loan in the ordinary course of a money-lending business because, although there is no equivalent credit to the profit and loss account, it is in the nature of the business to lend money (Sec. 16(1)(d) proviso (i)). For a discussion on what constitutes a moneylending business for the purpose of Sec. 16(1)(d) see Shun Lee Investment Co. v CIR (HKTC 322). If any bad debt that has previously been allowed as a deduction is ultimately recovered, it is treated as a trading receipt of the period in which it is recovered (Sec. 16(1)(d) proviso (ii)).

(iv)   REPAIRS to premises, plant, machinery, implements, utensils or articles which are employed in the production of assessable profits (Sec. 16(1)(e)). The terms implement, utensil or article are defined by IRR1(1) as including the following:—

Belting
Crockery and cutlery
Kitchen utensils
Linen
Loose tools
Soft furnishings (including curtains and carpets)
Surgical and dental instruments
Tubes for X-ray and infra-red machines

As will be seen in Chapter 6, these items do not qualify for depreciation allowances on their initial purchase.

(v)   REPLACEMENT of any implement, utensil or article as defined above (Sec. 16(1)(f)) so long as no depreciation allowance is claimed although this is specifically prohibited by IRR2(1). Without this provision the expenditure would constitute disallowable capital expenditure and the relationship between this provision and the disallowance of depreciation allowances is merely a means of granting relief on the "replacement basis" for a limited class of capital expenditure.

(vi)   REGISTRATION OF TRADE MARKS, PATENTS OR DESIGNS would be disqualified as capital expenditure but for Sec. 16(1)(g) which permits a deduction where the trade mark, patent or design is used for the purposes of earning assessable profits. Note that it is only expenses "for the registration" which are allowable, any expenses in connection with the acquisition of a patent/trade mark etc. are capital expenditure and not deductible.

(vii) CONTRIBUTIONS TO RETIREMENT SCHEMES are deductible, whether approved under Sec. 87A or not, provided that they satisfy the rules as to deductibility and do not offend the rules for exception from deductions (see pages 126 to 128 under the heading "Expenditure Not Deductible"). However, as regards a contribution to an approved fund other than an ordinary annual contribution, Sec. 16A provides a limitation as to its deductibility although in the case of an initial payment, which would otherwise be considered of a capital nature per Atherton v British Insulated and Helsby Cables (10 TC 155), the section provides for a deduction to be given. Where a payment other than an ordinary annual contribution is made to an approved fund it is deductible in five equal instalments over five years of assessment beginning with the basis period in which the payment was made (Sec. 16A(2)). The section applies only to "payments" therefore where there is no independent fund but annual provisions are set aside, the deductibility must follow the rules for deductibility of provisions (see page 116). It is important to note that where there is a binding obligation to pay a pension in due course, the provisions are not contingent upon some future date of retirement but are deductible provided that they are computed with substantial accuracy and this includes a mandatory provision for back years service (IRC v Titaghur Jute Factory, 1978 Simons Tax Cases 166).

(viii) SCIENTIFIC RESEARCH expenditure either of a revenue or a capital nature which is appropriately related to the trade or business (Sec. 16B). In particular, relief is granted for:—

(1) payments to an approved research institute for research which may be specific to the requirements of the trade or business or which may be merely within that class of trade or business. The point is that it must have some relevance, in other words a contribution for cancer research would not be deductible to a textile manufacturer but would be to the operator of a sanatorium (Sec. 16B(1)(a)).

(2) expenditure by the taxpayer on scientific research, including capital expenditure except expenditure on land or buildings because Industrial Building Allowances are separately granted for this (see Chapter 6). Expenditure on plant and machinery for example would attract the full deduction instead of the depreciation allowances normally granted. However upon disposal of the plant and machinery, the sale proceeds or other disposal receipts are brought in as a trading receipt, either in the basis period in which the disposal takes place or as a post cessation receipt (Sec.

16B(3)). Again the expenditure must be related to the trade or business (Sec. 16B(1)(b)). Capital expenditure incurred before the commencement of trading is treated as incurred on the day of commencement and therefore deductible in the first basis period (Sec. 16B(6)(b)).

Scientific research is defined as any activities in the fields of natural or applied science for the extension of knowledge and a research institute is approved if it has been so approved in writing by the Director of Education and the approval may operate from whatever date may be specified by the Director and can equally be withdrawn at any time (Sec. 16B(4)). Whether any given research is appropriately related to a trade or business is largely a question of fact but Sec. 16B(5)(b) specifies some circumstances which are to be specifically regarded as so related and these are:—

(1)   research which may lead to or facilitate an improvement or extension in the technical efficiency of that trade or business, for example research carried out by an approved university into the processing of multifibres would benefit all textile manufacturers;

(2)   medical research which is of special benefit to the welfare of workers in a particular industry, for example research into the harmful effects of and alleviation of excessive noise would be of special benefit to a company employing persons in an enclosed area with noisy machinery. It is not sufficient to say that all medical research is in the interests of the welfare of all employees as in the case of the cancer research mentioned earlier. This may however be achieved by deductible charitable contributions (see pages 125 to 126 under "Charitable Contributions").

Expenditure is not allowed where it is for the purpose of acquiring rights in or arising out of scientific research, only for the original research (Sec. 16B(5)(a)). Also where the taxpayer receives some subsidy or grant from any body or person in connection with the expenditure, only the net expenditure is deductible (Sec. 16B(6)(a)).

Where the expenditure is made or incurred outside Hong Kong and the business is carried on partly in Hong Kong and partly elsewhere, it will be necessary to apportion the expenditure on some reasonable basis (Sec. 16B(2)). However, if the expenditure is made or incurred in Hong Kong, there is no requirement to apportion, even if part of the profits arises outside Hong Kong and is not subject to Profits Tax. This is because the deduction criteria are related to trades and businesses not to profits, presumably to encourage local research. (See Departmental Interpretation and Practice Notes No. 5 reproduced in Appendix 5.)

(ix) TECHNICAL EDUCATION expenditure may be disallowable because it fails to meet the rules for qualifying as a deduction or may specifically fall within the disallowance provisions (see pages 126 to 128 "Expenditure Not Deductible"). However, presumably as an incentive for business to contribute to technical education, it is specifically provided by Sec. 16C that, in the appropriate circumstances, relief is to be given. The circumstances are simply that the payment must be to any university, university college, technical college or other educational institution which has been approved in writing by the Director of Education and must be related to the business against which the payment is to be deducted (Sec. 16C(1)).

There is no requirement that the educational institution be in Hong Kong and the relationship between the nature of the business and the type of education is of course a question of fact although it is specifically stated that it must be education of a kind which is specially requisite for persons employed in the class of business in which the business operates (Sec. 16C(2)).

The approval of the Director of Education can be with retrospective effect if necessary but is also revocable by the Director at any time (Sec. 16C(3)). (See Departmental Interpretation and Practice Notes No. 5 reproduced in Appendix 5.)

(x) CHARITABLE CONTRIBUTIONS would of course not be deductible because they are hardly incurred for the purposes of earning assessable profits as required by Sec. 16 and therefore Sec. 16D introduces specific provisions to enable deductions to be made, subject to limitations.

To qualify for deduction, the payment must be a donation of money to a charitable institution or trust of a public character which has been approved as exempt from tax under Sec. 88 of the IRO or to the Government for charitable purposes (Sec. 2). The payment must be a pure donation and not confer any benefit at all upon the donor. For this purpose, an inflated payment for a ticket for a social function has been held not to be a donation for this purpose (CIR v Sanford Yung-Tao Yung HKTC 959). The limitations are as follows:—

(1) The aggregate of allowable donations must be not less than $100 (Sec. 16D(1)).

(2) Deduction is limited to 10% of assessable profits after depreciation allowances but before charitable donations. Therefore, where there are adjusted losses, there can be no deduction for charitable donations at all (Sec. 16D(2)(b)).

(3)   The sum must not qualify for deduction under other Profits Tax rules or against Salaries Tax under Sec. 12(1)(c) (Sec. 16D(2)(a)).

It must not be assumed that all donations have to be considered for deduction only under Sec. 16D. It is possible that a donation which is not deductible under Sec. 16D may qualify under Sec. 16 if the circumstances and motive fulfil the argument that it is business motivated. Accordingly a payment which would be limited under the 10% rule might qualify in full under Sec. 16.

Example 14

Andouts Ltd. is a textile manufacturer with an adjusted profit for the year of assessment of $65,000 and it has made an approved charitable donation of $8,000 to the Textile Workers Orphans Fund which has not been added back in arriving at the adjusted profit. It also has depreciation allowances of $12,000 and a balancing charge of $4,500 to be taken into account.

The assessable profit is as follows:—

Adjusted Profit		$65,000
Add back donation		8,000
		$73,000
Depreciation Allowances	$12,000	
Balancing Charge	4,500	7,500
		$65,500
Charitable Donation (10%)		6,550
Assessable Profit		$58,950

Note:—

Andouts may have a good case for saying that the donation is for the purpose of fostering and maintaining employee goodwill being directly related to its business and is therefore deductible under Sec. 16(1) instead of Sec. 16D. In this case, the assessable profit would be:—

Adjusted Profit	$65,000
Net Depreciation Allowances	7,500
	$57,500

EXPENDITURE NOT DEDUCTIBLE.   The IRO contains, in Sec. 17, those types of expenses and outgoings which are not to be deductible for Profits Tax purposes and must therefore be added back in arriving at adjusted profits. These are as follows:—

(1) Domestic or private expenses which includes the cost of travelling by the proprietor between residence and place of business (Sec. 17(1)(a)).

(2) Disbursements or expenses which are not for the purpose of producing assessable profits (Sec. 17(1)(b)). This is of course the complement to the exactly opposite deduction contained in Sec. 16(1).

(3) Capital expenditure including capital losses and withdrawals which otherwise do not fall within the meaning of "expenditure" (Sec. 17(1)(c)). As to what constitutes revenue or capital is a question which has had wide coverage in the Courts. The arguments are covered on pages 110 to 115 under the heading "Capital or Revenue". The exclusion of course covers the depreciation charge in the commercial accounts which must be added back and replaced by statutory depreciation allowances (see Chapter 6).

(4) The cost of improvements which is in any event probably capital expenditure already disallowable under (3) above (Sec. 17(1)(d)). Much of this expenditure will qualify for depreciation allowances.

(5) Sums recoverable under an insurance or indemnity policy (Sec. 17(1)(e)). This adjustment should not normally be necessary because the commercial accounts should already contain a credit where an expense or loss incurred is recoverable. In any case, even if it was deductible, it would only be a matter of timing difference because the insurance receipt would be taxable (Green v J. Gliksten & Son Ltd. 14 TC 364).

(6) Rent and expenses for premises which are not used for producing assessable profits (Sec. 17(1)(f)) which is hardly surprising as it would fail the basic test in Sec. 16(1).

(7) Any taxes payable under the IRO except Salaries Tax paid on behalf of an employee which is of course nothing more than additional salary (Sec. 17(1)(g)). It seems that Property Tax paid as occupier could be disallowed under this provision despite the fact that recovery from the owner in accordance with Sec. 6(2) may have been foregone by agreement with the owner in which case the payment is no more than additional rent. Interest Tax paid by a corporation is recoverable (see page 84).

(8) An ordinary annual contribution or an insurance premium in respect of an employees retirement scheme which has been approved under Sec. 87A in so far as it exceeds 15% of the employee's total emoluments for the period in respect of which the payment is made (Sec. 17(1)(h)). The limitation is computed separately in respect of each employee and not in aggregate in respect of total employees' remuneration. The limitation is in respect of total emoluments and it does not specifically mention taxable emoluments, therefore it should be appropriate to include rent reimbursements, leave passages etc. in the calculation.

It is important to appreciate that this limitation does not apply to contributions to unapproved schemes, these are governed entirely by the general deduction test in Sec. 16(1). Furthermore a special contribution other than an ordinary annual contribution is not allowable in the case of an unapproved scheme because it is capital expenditure and, in the case of an approved scheme is governed by the special rules in Sec. 16A.

(9) In the case of a partnership, no deduction is permitted for partners' salaries or interest on capital, these are treated in effect as drawings on account of profit (Sec. 17(2)). As a wife is treated as one and the same person as her husband for Profits Tax purposes (Sec. 15B), a partner's wife's salary is disallowable whether she is a partner or not.

APPORTIONMENTS. Because various sources of income are not taxable in Hong Kong, particularly sources of income which do not arise in or derive from Hong Kong and dividends, wherever they arise, it will be apparent that it would not be correct to exclude items of income from the profit and loss account without making some appropriate adjustment in respect of the expenditure. Whilst authority for disallowing a proportion of expenditure can be inferred from the general deduction test in Sec. 16(1) and its complement in Sec. 17(1) whereby only expenditure incurred in the production of assessable profits is allowable, there are nevertheless some specific apportionment provisions contained in the IRR. These are as follows:—

(i) THE GENERAL RULE in IRR2A provides for the situation where profits are derived partly from a source within Hong Kong and partly from a source outside Hong Kong when outgoings and expenses are to be apportioned "on such basis as is most appropriate to the trade, profession or business".

Where part of the profits is not taxable for some other reason than that it has a source outside Hong Kong or there is some other reason why it is necessary to apportion expenses and outgoings it is provided that this is to be on a "basis as is most reasonable and appropriate in the circumstances".

In neither case therefore is the method of apportionment rigidly laid down, it is left to fact and commonsense although there is a subtle difference in the case of onshore/offshore profits where the circumstances of the business must be considered and in other cases where any reasonable basis is appropriate.

Example 15

Eerzacase Ltd. earns its profits from the sale of textile products both from an office in Hong Kong and an office in Taiwan. The following facts are relevant for the year of assessment:—

1) Total adjusted gross profits $450,000 Turnover $1,400,000
2) Adjusted gross profits (Taiwan) $ 90,000 Turnover $ 200,000
3) Offshore interest income from
   deposit of surplus funds in
   Singapore $ 40,000
4) Overhead expenditure $280,000
5) Taiwan office has 2 sales staff and Hong Kong
   office has 6. Each office is autonomous but
   the directors are in Hong Kong
6) There is an interest charge of $35,000 in the
   profit and loss account which relates wholly to
   bills of exchange.

First of all, no adjustment to overhead expenditure should be necessary in respect of the offshore interest income because a deposit will incur no material management time or other expenditure. Also the interest outgoing is not related to it and should not require adjustment.

There are a number of methods of possible apportionment in respect of onshore/offshore trading profits:—

Method A based on turnover

Total gross profit			$450,000
Less offshore profit			90,000
Onshore gross profit			$360,000
Allowable overheads	12/14 x 280,000	=	240,000
Assessable profit			$120,000

Method B based on profit

Onshore gross profit			$360,000
Allowable overheads	36/45 x 280,000	=	224,000
Assessable profit			$136,000

Method C based on staff

Onshore gross profit			$360,000
Allowable overheads	6/8 x 280,000	=	210,000
Assessable profit			$150,000

Method D more detailed

Onshore gross profit			$360,000
Interest outgoing (by turnover)	12/14 x 35,000	=	(30,000)
Other overheads (by staff)	6/8 x 245,000	=	(183,750)
Assessable profit			$146,250

Equally it can be seen that there are other methods involving a combination of Method D and the other methods, each of which will give a different answer. *None of these methods is necessarily the "right" one.* They all have their merits and demerits and in the end it is a question of judgement and negotiation.

(ii)   INTEREST ON MONEY BORROWED TO BUY SHARES is dealt with in
         IRR2B. Clearly the purchase of shares yields no taxable income, unless
         the business consists of share dealing, because dividends are not taxable.
         Therefore, if shares are purchased with borrowed money, it is obvious
         that the interest incurred thereon is not for the purpose of earning
         assessable profits and should therefore be disallowed under the general
         deduction test in Sec. 16(1). It also seems logical that where money is
         borrowed and is used partly to buy shares and partly for purposes
         which will yield an assessable profit, that the relevant proportion of
         interest be disallowed. Although again this may be inferred from Sec.
         16(1), the point is specifically covered by IRR2B(1) which lays down
         that the proportion used to buy shares is not deductible and is to be
         ascertained on "such basis as is most reasonable and appropriate in the
         circumstances".

             As in the case of apportionments under IRR2A, there is no
         "right" method of doing it although it is easier to be more positive
         under IRR2B because an apportionment is only required where money
         is borrowed and actually used to buy shares. If existing cash resources
         are used to buy shares and a new loan is taken up exclusively to provide
         working capital, IRR2B does not apply but of course it would have to
         be proved that the funds were used in that manner.

             No adjustment is called for in respect of the purchase of shares by
         a share dealing business (IRR2B(2)).

Example 16

   Bishops Investments Ltd. is carrying on a trading business in Hong Kong
as well as a share investment business. During the year it took up a fixed loan
from its bankers, to acquire shares in an associated company (loan 1) and a
further loan of $100,000 (loan 2) of which $60,000 was used to pay off
pressing trade creditors and the balance to purchase a portfolio of share
investments. During the year Bishops Investments paid interest of $9,000 on
loan 1, interest of $12,000 on loan 2 and further interest of $6,500 on its
overdraft which has been used for general trading purposes.

Notes:−
(a)   The interest of $9,000 on loan 1 is disallowable, not under IRR2B but under the
      general deduction test in Sec. 16(1) because the whole of the loan was used to buy
      shares.
(b)   Of the interest of $12,000 paid on loan 2, 40% or $4,800 is disallowable under
      IRR2B being the proportion related to purchase of shares.
(c)   If any shares had been purchased out of the main bank account on which the
      overdraft arises there can be great practical problems in applying IRR2B. If, as is
      often the case, the account is in overdraft from year to year, it would not be proper

to make a disallowance every year based on the current overdraft interest rate and the amount originally withdrawn to buy shares. It must be recognised that an overdraft is constantly changing in character and that withdrawals are ultimately repaid by credits notwithstanding that new withdrawals keep the account in overdraft. A practical solution is to ascertain the amount of the debit balance immediately before buying the shares, e.g.:—

Debit balance at 15.6.79	$165,000
Shares purchased 15.6.79	40,000
	$205,000

and then to ascertain the date by which aggregate credits have amounted to $205,000 which is on the assumption that repayment is on a first-in-first-out basis. The average rate of interest for the period ascertained could be applied to $40,000 for that period to give the disallowance. Even this does not allow for the fact that there will have been a period during which the outstanding principal of $40,000 will have been gradually reduced and more complicated research and computation would be required to allow for this.

(iii)   OVERHEAD COST OF INVESTMENT PORTFOLIOS is covered by IRR2C. The logic of this provision is that where a business which is otherwise earning assessable profits also has a material investment portfolio which does not of course yield assessable income, some of the overhead expenditure charged against business profits must relate to the cost of supervision and management of the portfolio and should therefore be disallowed.

The provision is only applicable if, in the opinion of the assessor, the portfolio is sufficiently substantial (IRR2C(2)) and this must of course be judged in relation to the business as a whole. Where it is decided that an adjustment is required, this is to proceed on the basis of a fixed percentage of the total cost of the investments unless a more practical and suitable basis is available in the circumstances. As a fixed percentage is completely arbitrary, it is often possible to adopt a more practical method, usually related to actual costs. For example a portfolio which undergoes few changes would attract a nominal or nil adjustment because no staff time or other costs are involved in its maintenance.

If the percentage method is adopted the rate is to be such as is most reasonable and appropriate in the circumstances but not exceeding:—

(1)   1/8% where the business is share dealing. This is merely to cover the cost of collection of non taxable dividends.

(2)   1/2% in other cases.

Where the cost of the portfolio is continually changing it is common to apply the percentage to the average cost for the year taking the mean of the opening and closing figures for the basis period.

Because the IRR are in fact no more than an extension to the IRO, any dispute as to their application is subject to the same right of objection and appeal as other provisions (IRR2D). See also Departmental Interpretation and Practice Notes No. 3 reproduced in Appendix 3.

LOSSES are computed in exactly the same way as profits and by reference to the same basis periods (Sec. 19D). In the same way as depreciation allowances and balancing charges decrease and increase assessable profits respectively, so do they increase and decrease allowable losses (Sec. 19E(1)). If a balancing charge exceeds adjusted losses, an assessable profit arises (Sec. 19E(2)). Where depreciation allowances exceed the adjusted profit, an allowable loss results (Sec. 18F(2)).

The treatment of losses depends upon whether the person incurring them is an individual, a partnership or a corporation.

(i)   AN INDIVIDUAL who incurs a loss in a trade, profession or business may either elect for personal assessment and thereby have the loss allowed against his other sources of income assessable under the IRO for the same year of assessment as that in which the loss was incurred (see Chapter 7) or he may have the loss carried forward indefinitely and set off against future profits from the same trade, profession or business in which the loss was incurred (Sec. 19C(1)). If he elects for personal assessment, he is deemed to elect for personal assessment in all subsequent years where an excess of the loss over total income is carried forward (see Chapter 7). This similarly applies where an individual is a member of a partnership consisting of not more than 20 partners in that he can take his share of the loss and claim personal assessment or carry it forward against his share of profits from that partnership for subsequent years of assessment (Sec. 19C(2)). If he withdraws from the partnership while the loss is still unutilised, his share of losses ceases to be available against subsequent profits. The law in relation to partnership losses changed in 1975 prior to which losses were carried forward against partnership profits irrespective of individual partners' shares of the losses and therefore losses incurred in 1974/75 or earlier do not lapse upon the withdrawal of a partner. From 1975/76, although partnerships are still assessed as a single legal entity, profits or losses are identified with the individual partners.

Where a corporation is a member of a partnership consisting of not more than 20 partners, its share of the losses is not treated in the same way as individuals but is subject to the more generous rules applicable to corporations as follows (Sec. 19C(5)).

(ii)   A CORPORATION OR OTHER PERSON other than an individual or partnership is subject to more advantageous rules for relief of losses. For this purpose a partnership is one which does not at any time in the year of assessment have more than 20 partners (Sec. 19C(7)) and therefore a partnership of more than 20 partners which incurs losses is treated in the same way as a corporation or other person who is not an individual (e.g. an association). The loss is automatically set against any other source of income liable to Profits Tax for the year of assessment in which the loss was incurred and, so far as not fully relieved, can be carried forward indefinitely and set off against any profits subject to Profits Tax in subsequent years (Sec. 19C(4)).

Where a corporation or person other than an individual or a partnership of 20 partners or less is a member of a partnership, its share of losses which are not set off against current profits are carried forward indefinitely and set off against profits of any type subject to Profits Tax but must be set off in priority against its share of profits from the partnership. The losses do not however cease to be available if it withdraws from the partnership (Sec. 19C(5)). For further discussion see under "Partnerships" on pages 162 to 165.

(iii) A PARTNERSHIP, although assessed to Profits Tax as a person, has its losses dealt with in accordance with the capacities of its individual partners. Therefore, they are dealt with as described in (i) or (ii) above.

(iv)   A TRUSTEE is now within the definition of person. However, his liability to Profits Tax and therefore treatment of any losses incurred in respect of a trade carried on for the benefit of a trust remain confused. See further comment on page 274.

Example 17

Percy Vere, a married man with no children, carries on a motor repair business and has made an adjusted loss of $25,000 for the year of assessment 1977/78. He is entitled to depreciation allowances of $3,000 for 1977/78. His savings are invested in a Hong Kong dollar bond on which interest of $4,500 arises each year and Interest Tax is deducted. For 1978/79 he has an adjusted profit of $1,500 and depreciation allowances of $2,500. For 1979/80 he has an adjusted profit of $70,000 and depreciation allowances of $2,000. Losses would be utilised as follows:—

(1) If Percy elects for personal assessment for 1977/78 he will obtain repayment of the Interest Tax deducted and the balance of loss will be:—

Adjusted loss	$25,000
Depreciation allowances	3,000
Allowable loss	$28,000

Interest	4,500	(Recovery $675)
Loss carried forward	$23,500	

For 1978/79 he will be deemed to have elected for personal assessment (see Chapter 7) and he will again obtain repayment of the Interest Tax deducted and the balance of loss will be:—

Adjusted profit	$ 1,500
Depreciation allowances	2,500
Allowable loss	$ 1,000
Loss brought forward	23,500
	$24,500
Interest	4,500

(Recovery $675)

Loss carried forward	$20,000

For 1979/80 he will be deemed to have elected for personal assessment (see Chapter 7) and he will pay tax on total income:—

Adjusted profit	$70,000	
Depreciation allowances	2,000	
Assessable profit	$68,000	
Interest	4,500	
Total income	$72,500	
Loss brought forward	20,000	
Taxable income	$52,500	Tax = $1,875

(2) If Percy does not elect for personal assessment for 1977/78, the position is as follows:—

1977/78 Allowable loss carried forward	$28,000	
1978/79 Allowable loss	1,000	
Carried forward	$29,000	
1979/80 Assessable profit	68,000	
Net assessable profit 1979/80	$39,000	Tax = $450

Under method (1) his total tax for the 3 years is $1,875. Under method (2) his total tax for the 3 years is $2,475 ($450 plus 3 years Interest Tax). It would therefore pay him to elect but this would not always be the case.

Example 18

Mr. Hop, Mr. Skip and Jump Ltd. are in partnership as engineers and they share profits and losses equally. Recent results of the partnership are as follows:—

1979/80	Allowable loss	$150,000

```
     1980/81      Assessable profit         12,000
     1981/82      Assessable profit        120,000
```
Mr. Hop withdrew from the partnership at the end of 1980/81 and therefore does not share in 1981/82. Hop and Skip have no other sources of income but Jump Ltd. has other income subject to Profits Tax of $20,000 per annum.

The partnership tax position is as follows:—

		Hop	Skip	Jump Ltd.	Partnership
1979/80	Loss	$50,000	$50,000	$50,000	
	Other income	–	–	20,000	
	Loss C/F	50,000	50,000	30,000	($130,000)
1980/81	Profit	$ 4,000	$ 4,000	$ 4,000	
	Loss B/F	50,000	50,000	30,000	
		46,000	46,000	26,000	
	Other Income	–	–	20,000	
	Loss C/F	46,000	46,000	6,000	($ 98,000)
1981/82	Profit		$60,000	$60,000	
	Loss B/F		46,000	6,000	
	Assessable Profit		$14,000	$54,000	$ 68,000

Notes:—
(a) Hop's share of losses ceases to be available either to him or the partnership upon his withdrawal.
(b) If the individual partners had other income, the position would be the same as above if they did not elect for personal assessment.
(c) Skip would on the above figures elect for personal assessment for 1981/82 because he would then obtain personal allowances against his share of net profits after losses and no liability would arise.
(d) Jump Ltd. must bring in its remaining share of partnership losses against the 1981/82 share of profits in priority to all other income.
(e) Assuming Skip's election for personal assessment for 1981/82, the assessment on the partnership would be $54,000 @ 16½% and Jump Ltd. would be assessed separately on its own profits, i.e. at 16½% on $20,000.
(f) For personal assessment rules see Chapter 7.

6. Basis of Assessment

Because commercial and accounting requirements normally dictate that accounts of business profits and losses are made up for periods of account which do not necessarily coincide with years of assessment, it is necessary to have rules for allocating profits and losses of accounting periods to years of assessment. Also, because accounting periods are open to manipulation, some of the rules are necessarily complicated although the position has been greatly simplified since 1st April 1974 when an "actual" basis has been adopted, superceding the "previous year" basis which applied before that date. The old basis and the transitional provisions to the new basis are not dealt with in this book except in so far as it is necessary to refer to them in clarification of certain of the new provisions.

NORMAL BASIS. From 1975/76, the assessable profits for a year of assessment are to be computed on the basis of the profits arising during the year of assessment (Sec. 18B(1)). This is of course straight forward where the accounting year is co-terminous with the year of assessment, i.e. to 31st March, but where, as is most usual, the accounts are made up to some other date, the basis is the amount of the profits arising in the year which ends with the accounting date which falls within the year of assessment (Sec. 18B(2)). For example:—

A/Cs year to   1. 4.78 = year of assessment 1978/79
A/Cs year to 31.12.78 = year of assessment 1978/79
A/Cs year to 28. 2.79 = year of assessment 1978/79

This basis is in fact not automatically as of right because the section provides that the Commissioner is empowered to direct that this shall be the basis. In fact this basis is adopted from year to year where the accounting date is consistent. Where however the accounting date is changed, there are other considerations as there are in commencement and cessation years.

COMMENCEMENT. If the commercial accounts are made up to 31st March each year there is no problem because the first assessment is in respect of profits arising from the date of commencement to the following 31st March, the next assessment is for the year to the succeeding 31st March and so on. However, where the accounting date is other than 31st March, special rules apply. The following applies to a trade, profession or business which commences on or after 1st April 1974:—

(1) Where the first accounts are for a period of a year or less and:—

    (i)   They are made up to a date within the same year of assessment as the date of commencement of business, the first assessment is based on the profits of that period (Sec. 18C(1)(a)). Subsequent assessments are on the normal basis.

    (ii) They are made up to a date within the year of assessment following the year of assessment in which the date of commencement falls, there is no assessment for the year in which the business commenced (Sec. 18C(2)) but the first assessment is for the year in which the first accounting date falls and is based on the profits of that accounting period.

(2) Where the first accounts are for a period in excess of a year, obviously the accounts embrace at least two years of assessment and, in some cases, more. In these circumstances, the assessment for the year in which the commencement occurred is at the entire discretion of the Commissioner

(Sec. 18C(1)(b)). The section gives the Commissioner no discretion over the following year of assessment which is therefore subject to the rules in Sec. 18B described earlier under the heading "Normal Basis". It is however the normal intention of the IRD to allocate profits to years of assessment in such a way that ensures that total assessments equal total profits earned during the life of a business with no overlap and no falling out of account. Accordingly, they will normally allocate the profits of periods in excess of 12 months by reference to the expected future accounting date (see Example 21).

Example 19

A business commenced on 1st June and future accounts will be prepared to 31st December each year. Adjusted profits are:—

7 months to 31st December 1978	$ 50,000
Year ended 31st December 1979	180,000

The first assessments will be:—

1978/79 Basis Period 1.6.78 to 31.12.78	$ 50,000	(Sec. 18C(1)(a))
1979/80 Basis Period Yr/Ended31.12.79	180,000	(Sec. 18B(2))

Example 20

A business commenced on 1st June 1977 and future accounts will be prepared to 30th April each year. Adjusted profits are:—

11 months to 30th April 1978	$350,000
Year ended 30th April 1979	520,000

The first assessments will be:—

1977/78 No assessment (Sec. 18C(2))		
1978/79 Basis Period 1.6.77 to 30.4.78	$350,000	(Sec. 18B(2))
1979/80 Basis Period Yr/Ended30.4.79	520,000	(Sec. 18B(2))

Example 21

A business commenced on 1st March 1977 and future accounts will be prepared to 30th April each year except that the first accounts are prepared up to 30th April 1978. Adjusted profits are:—

14 months to 30th April 1978	$420,000
Year ended 30th April 1979	500,000

The year of commencement (1976/77) is at the discretion of the Commissioner (Sec. 18C(1)(b)) but he will normally allocate profits by reference to the expected regular accounting date (30th April) and the first assessments would therefore normally be:—

1976/77	Nil	
1977/78	Basis period 1.3.77 to 30.4.77 (2/14)	$ 60,000
	(Sec. 18B(2))	

1978/79	Basis period 12 months to 30.4.78 (12/14)	$360,000
	(Sec. 18B(2))	
1979/80	Yr/Ended 30.4.79	$500,000
	(Sec. 18B(2))	

For a discussion on what constitutes commencement of business see under that heading on pages 98 to 99.

CESSATION. In the case of a cessation, the rules are different depending upon whether the business commenced before 1st April 1974. This is because those businesses which commenced before 1st April 1974 will have been subject to the old system wherein, at the commencement, they may have been assessed more than once on the same profits and therefore, on cessation, are able to redress the balance by allowing some profits to drop out of account.

Business commenced after 1st April 1974. Where a trade, profession or business ceases during 1975/76 or subsequently and which was commenced after 1st April 1974, the assessable profits for the year in which the cessation takes place are based on the period which begins immediately after the end of the basis period for the preceding year of assessment and ends on the date of cessation (Sec. 18D(1)). In other words there is complete continuity with no duplication or drop out.

Example 22

A business which has been carried on since 1975 and for which accounts have annually been made up to 31st December, ceased on 16th June 1979. Adjusted profits are:—

Year ended 31st December 1978	$75,000
Period 1st January 1979 to 16th June 1979	15,500

The final assessments will be:—

1978/79 Basis period Yr/Ended 31.12.78	(Sec. 18B(2))	$75,000
1979/80 Basis period 1.1.79 to 16.6.79	(Sec. 18D(1))	15,500

Where, exceptionally, a business commences in a year of assessment and then ceases in the immediately following year of assessment, special rules apply if there was no assessment for the year of commencement by virtue of Sec. 18C(2). In these circumstances the assessment for the year in which the cessation takes place is based on the whole of the profits from commencement to cessation (Sec. 18D(5)).

Example 23

A business commenced on 15th July 1977 and made up its first accounts to 30th June 1978. The business ceased on 12th December 1978. Adjusted profits are:—

Period to 30.6.78 $84,000
Period 1.7.78 to 31.12.78   25,000

The assessments will be:—

1977/78 Nil per Sec. 18C(2) (See Example 20)
1978/79 $109,000 (Sec. 18D(5))

Business commenced before 1st April 1974. Where a trade, profession or business, which commenced before 1st April 1974, ceases in 1975/76 or before 1st April 1979, the assessable profits from the ceased source for the year of assessment in which the cessation takes place are based on the profits for the period from 1st April in the year of assessment to the date of cessation (Sec. 18D(2)). Accordingly, the profits in the period from the end of the immediately preceding accounting period up to the following 31st March, fall out of account. There is of course no fall out if the basis period for the preceeding accounting period ended on 31st March.

There are some special transitional rules for cessation during 1975/76 where the proviso to Sec. 18D(2) is applicable (Sec. 18D(3)). There are also special transitional rules for cessations in 1975/76 where the commencement was in 1973/74 (Sec. 18D(4)).

Sec. 18D(2) does not apply to all businesses which commenced before 1st April 1974. For example, where a business ceases and is wholly or partly carried on by another person, the basis period for the year in which cessation takes place is the same as for a business which commenced after 1st April 1974, i.e. there is no drop out. This proviso will not however apply if the cessation is the result of the death of an individual, but not a wife living with her husband, who was carrying on the trade, profession or business as the sole proprietor (Sec. 18D(2) proviso).

Because the foregoing rules permit a "drop-out" which is open to manipulation and the fact that this loophole had been widely used to avoid substantial amounts of tax, the law was changed to apply to cessations of business on or after 1st April 1979.

The changes contained in Sec. 18D(2A) are somewhat complicated in detail but the overall effect is that the basis period for the year of assessment in which the cessation takes place is the period from the end of the basis period for the previous year of assessment up to the date of cessation (i.e. the same as for a business which commenced after 1st April 1974) less a "transitional amount". The "transitional amount" is the equivalent of the previous drop-out but is based on a proportion of the assessable profits for the 1974/75 year of assessment and is therefore already fixed in respect of cessations which have not yet taken place although, as will be seen, even this is the maximum amount because there are limitations to the transitional amount depending upon what profits arise in the cessation period. Note that Sec. 18D(2A) only applies where Sec. 18D(2) would have applied, i.e. where the business is transferred upon cessation, Sec. 18D(2) would not have applied, therefore neither does Sec. 18D(2A).

Sec. 18D(2A) contains a number of new phrases which are now briefly explained before their application is explained:—

"Relevant trade, profession or business" means one commenced before 1st April 1974 and to which Sec. 18D(2) applies and where the basis period for the penultimate year of assessment ended on a date other than 31st March. Sec. 18D(2) does not apply to all businesses which commenced before 1st April 1974 as stated earlier.

"Excepted trade, profession or business" means a relevant trade, profession or business for which the basis period for the year of assessment 1974/75 ended on a date other than 31st March and was either the accounting period ended in 1974/75 per Sec. 18(2) or the accounting period ended in the previous year per Sec. 18A(2).

"Relevant period" is the period which otherwise drops out of account under Sec. 18D(2), i.e. from the day following the end of the basis period for the penultimate year of assessment to the following 31st March.

"Relevant profits" are the profits of the relevant period which would be assessable but for Sec. 18D(2) and notwithstanding the deductibility of depreciation allowances.

"Transitional amount" is the equivalent of the drop-out under Sec. 18D(2) but is instead calculated as a proportion of the 1974/75 assessable profits.

Where a person ceases a relevant trade, profession or business before 1st April, 1979, Sec. 18D(2) applies as already described. However where he ceases on or after 1st April 1979, Sec. 18D(2A) applies and the assessable profits for the year of assessment in which the cessation took place are computed as follows:—

(A) Assessable profits to the date of cessation from the immediately preceeding 1st April (i.e. as per Sec. 18D(2))
    plus

(B) Assessable profits of the relevant period (i.e. relevant profits)
    less

(C) The transitional amount
    If (C) is greater than (B) it is limited to (B). In other words, the drop-out cannot be greater than would have been the case if the law had not changed.
    The calculation of the transitional amount proceeds as follows:—

(1) If the basis period for the 1974/75 year of assessment was the profits of the accounting period ended in the preceeding year of assessment (i.e. as per Sec. 18(2)) the amount is the assessable profits from the corres-

ponding date in the year ended 31st March 1975 (not necessarily the accounting date falling in that year, although it usually will be) up to 31st March 1975.

(2) If the basis period for the 1974/75 year of assessment was the profits of the accounting period ended in the year of assessment (i.e. as per Sec. 18A(2)) the amount is the assessable profits from that date up to 31st March 1975.

(3) In the case of any relevant trade, profession or business which is not an "excepted trade, profession or business", in other words where the basis period for 1974/75 was anything other than (1) or (2), the transitional amount is Nil.

Furthermore, where the calculation in (1) or (2) results in a loss, the transitional amount is regarded as Nil. In order to make the necessary apportionments to arrive at the transitional amount, it is necessary to look to the authority of Sec. 18E for the method of apportionment. Sec. 18E(4) now provides that, specifically for the purposes of Sec. 18D(2A), the Commissioner may make divisions, apportionments or aggregations on whatever basis he considers appropriate in the circumstances. Usually this will be done on a time basis but any reasonable option is open to the Commissioner. Before the introduction of Sec. 18D(2A) and thereby Sec. 18E(4) the method of allocation of profits to a specific period was strictly by time apportionment, it was not open to the Commissioner to indicate that the profits arose on a particular date and should therefore be wholly allocated to the period in which that date falls (see BR 5/80). Presumably he can now do so under Sec. 18E(4).

Example 24

The assessable profits of a business since 1972 up to 30th June 1979 when it ceased business have been as follows:—

Year ended 31st December				1972	$186,000
"	"	"	"	1973	$224,000
"	"	"	"	1974	$180,000
"	"	"	"	1975	$196,000
"	"	"	"	1976	$160,000
"	"	"	"	1977	$150,000
"	"	"	"	1978	$120,000
Period to 30th June				1979	$100,000

1) The year of cessation is 1979/80.
2) This is a "relevant trade, profession or business" because it commenced before 1st April 1974 and the basis period for 1978/79 (y/e 31.12.78) ended on a date other than 31st March and Sec. 18D(2) would apply (the business has not been transferred to another person). However, Sec. 18D(2A) applies because the cessation was after 1st April 1979.

3) The 1974/75 assessment was, under Sec. 18A(2), based on the previous year's profits (i.e. $224,000 for the y/e 31.12.73) and therefore this is an "excepted trade, profession or business".

4) The "transitional amount" is as follows:–

End of basis period *for* 1974/75 is 31.12.73

Equivalent date *in* 1974/75 is 31.12.74 (which happens to coincide with the next accounting date as it usually will).

It is necessary therefore to ascertain assessable profits for the period 1.1.75 to 31.3.75, i.e. –

¼ x $196,000 = $49,000

(Note that the Commissioner is not obliged to make the apportionment on a time basis.)

5) The assessment for 1979/80 will be as follows:–

Assessable profits 1.4.79 to 30.6.79 (3/6 x $100,000)   = $ 50,000   (A)
Plus Relevant profits (1.1.79 to 31.3.79)(3/6 x $100,000) = $ 50,000   (B)

$100,000

Less Transitional amount
  (not limited because Relevant profits (B) are greater)   49,000   (C)

Assessable 1979/80 $ 51,000

Notes:–
(a) The assessable profits for 1979/80 would have been $50,000 under Sec. 18D(2).
(b) If in fact the results for the years ended 31st December 1973 and 1974 had been transposed, the basis period for 1974/75 would have been the year ended 31st December 1974 under Sec. 18(2). The transitional amount would therefore have been the same.
(c) If the results for the year ended 31st December 1975 had been a loss, the transitional amount would have been nil.

Example 25

A business which had been in existence for 20 years and which made up its accounts to 31st December each year ceased on 31st August 1978. The assets were disposed of piecemeal. Adjusted profits have been:

Year ended 31st December 1977 $150,000
Period 1st January 1978 to
    31st August 1978   96,000

Final assessments will be:–
    1977/78 year ended 31.12.77 $150,000
    1978/79 period 1.4.78 to 31.8.78 (5/8)   60,000   (Sec. 18D(2))

Note:–
If the business had been transferred to another person, the 1978/79 assessment would have been $96,000 (Sec. 18D(2) proviso).

CHANGE OF ACCOUNTING DATE. Because the normal basis of assessment limits the basis period to one of 12 months up to the accounting date, it would be easy to arrange for large profits to fall out of account by judicially changing the accounting date. This is frustrated by the provisions in Sec. 18E which give the IRD considerable discretionary powers in the situation where the assessable profits of a trade, profession or business have been computed by reference to accounts made up to a particular day in a year of assessment and then either of two possible events occurs, namely:—

(1) accounts are not made up to the corresponding day in the following year of assessment, or

(2) accounts are made up to more than one day in the following year of assessment.

The year of assessment in which (1) or (2) takes place can be referred to as the "year of change" and the Commissioner is empowered to select the basis period for the year of change and the immediately preceding year on whatever basis he considers fit (Sec. 18E(1)). Where the business commenced after 1st April 1974, the Commissioner is entitled to adopt a basis period for the affected years which may be longer than the normal 12 months (Sec. 18E(2)(b)); this is because the intent behind the rules governing basis periods for businesses commencing after 1st April 1974 is that not less than the total profits made over the life of the business are to be assessed. However, because the normal basis period requires a period of at least 12 months to be taken into account, there will be a duplication of profits assessed if a change of accounting date results in an accounting period of less than 12 months (see Example 28).

It is not possible to guarantee how the Commissioner will select a basis period but in fixing the period for the year of change it is usual to take a period of 12 months up to the new accounting date, or longer than 12 months if the business commenced after 1st April 1974 and the accounting date has been put back. The basis period for the preceding year will be adjusted to the equivalent 12 months only if this will result in an additional assessment but in the case of businesses which commenced after 1st April 1974 an adjustment to the preceding year will not normally be required because no profits will have fallen out of account (see Example 27).

Example 26

A business has been carried on for many years, making its accounts up to 30th June. In 1978 the accounting date is changed to 31st December and adjusted profits are as follows:—

12 months to 30.6.77	$220,000
12 months to 30.6.78	350,000
6 months to 31.12.78	250,000

12 months to 31.12.79   300,000

The "year of change" is 1978/79 because it has two accounting dates in that year and therefore the affected years are 1978/79 and 1977/78. It is likely that the assessments would be as follows:—

1978/79 — Year to 31.12.78 — ½ x $350,000		=	$175,000
	plus		250,000
			$425,000
1977/78 — Year to 31.12.77 — ½ x $220,000		=	$110,000
½ x $350,000		=	175,000
			$285,000
Previously assessed (year ended 30.6.77)			220,000
Additional Assessment			$ 65,000

Notes:—
(a) Had the profits for the year ended 31.12.77 been less than those already assessed for the year ended 30.6.77 it is unlikely that the assessment for 1977/78 would be disturbed.
(b) The effect of the change in basis period upon the depreciation allowances is ignored in this illustration for the purposes of simplicity. In fact, the apportionments would be made in respect of adjusted profits before depreciation allowances and then the depreciation allowances would be recomputed in accordance with the new basis periods for the relevant years of assessment (see example 17, Chapter 6).

Example 27

A business which commenced after 1st April 1974 has made up accounts to 30th April until 1978 when it brought forward its accounting date to 31st January. Adjusted profits are as follows:—

12 months to 30.4.75	$250,000
12 months to 30.4.76	275,000
12 months to 30.4.77	300,000
9 months to 31.1.78	210,000
12 months to 31.1.79	400,000

The "year of change" is 1977/78 because it has two accounting dates in that year and therefore the affected years are 1977/78 and 1976/77. It is likely that the assessments would be as follows:—

1977/78 — Existing assessment — Year to 30.4.77	$300,000
Additional assessment — 9 months to 31.1.78	210,000
	$510,000

This is to bring it up to the new accounting date and is for a 21 month period to ensure that no profits fall out of account. This is allowed by Sec. 18E(2)(b).

1976/77 — Year to 30.4.76	$275,000

It would not be adjusted to the year to 31.6.76 because otherwise the profits for the 3 months to 30.4.76 would fall out of account.

Note:—
The effect of the change in basis period upon the depreciation allowances is ignored in this illustration for the purposes of simplicity. In fact, the apportionments would be made in respect of adjusted profits before depreciation allowances and then the depreciation allowances would be recomputed in accordance with the new basis periods for the relevant years of assessment (see example 17, Chapter 6).

Example 28

A business which commenced after 1st April 1974 has made up accounts to 30th September each year until 1978 when the accounting date was brought forward to 30th June. Adjusted profits are as follows:—

12 months to 30.9.76	$250,000
12 months to 30.9.77	280,000
9 months to 30.6.78	175,000
12 months to 30.6.79	300,000

The "year of change" is 1978/79 because an account was not made up to the corresponding date of 30.9.78. The affected years are therefore 1978/79 and 1977/78. It is likely that the assessments would be as follows:—

1978/79 — 9 months to 30.6.78	$175,000
3 months to 30.9.77 (3/12)	70,000
	$245,000

The basis period must be of twelve months, therefore there is a duplication of three months because the 1977/78 assessment will remain undisturbed on the basis of profits for the year ended 30th September 1977:—

1977/78 — Year ended 30.9.77	$280,000

Note:—
The effect of the change in basis period upon the depreciation allowances is ignored in this illustration for the purposes of simplicity. In fact, the apportionments would be made in respect of adjusted profits before depreciation allowances and then the depreciation allowances would be recomputed in accordance with the new basis periods for the relevant years of assessment (see example 17, Chapter 6).

Occasionally accounts are made up to the end of the Lunar Year and therefore will have a different balance date each year. In these circumstances it will not be treated as a change of accounting date (Sec. 18E(2)(a)).

APPORTIONMENT. As will have been seen, there are a number of cases where is is necessary to adopt as a basis period, only a portion of the adjusted profits of a longer accounting period and, furthermore, to aggregate such a portion with a portion of the adjusted profits of another accounting period. Sec. 18E(3) validates these apportionments and provides that such apportionment may be made on the basis of days or months in the respective periods or alternatively the Commissioner may direct that the apportionment is to be made on some other basis if special circumstances should so dictate. The alternative would only be adopted where, for example, a large proportion of profits clearly fell within a specific part of an accounting period and it would be inappropriate to effectively spread it by time apportionment. Note that depreciation allowances are not apportioned, they are, instead, recalculated in accordance with the new basis period (see page 209).

7. Special Classes of Business

Although the general rules for ascertainment of assessable profits, basis periods etc. are applicable to every type of business that falls within the scope of Profits Tax, certain types of business require specific legislation if they are to be adequately taxed and not to escape solely by virtue of the specialised nature of their business. The IRO therefore includes specific legislation in respect of a number of types of business and these are dealt with in following paragraphs. Also included are partnerships, although these are not a special class of business there are nevertheless a number of special points which must be considered when dealing with a partnership.

LIFE INSURANCE CORPORATIONS. Sec. 23 deals with the ascertainment of the assessable profits of life insurance corporations and, for this purpose, life insurance business is specifically defined as including annuity business (Sec. 23(9)) and the provisions apply equally to mutual and to proprietary corporations (Sec. 23(1)). Without the specific inclusion of mutual corporations, the mutual profits would not be taxable on the general principle that a person cannot make a profit out of himself (Faulconbridge v National Employers' Mutual 33 TC 103).

There are two ways of ascertaining the assessable profits of a life insurance corporation, one is a straightforward rule-of-thumb which gives a notional profit but is easy to ascertain and therefore may be acceptable for that reason; the other is a sophisticated computation involving acturial valuations and is only applicable upon specific election; otherwise the simple method automatically applies. The rules only apply to the assessable profits from life insurance (including annuity) business and therefore if a corporation is carrying on other business as well, the ascertainment of the assessable profits of that other business is not affected.

The assessable profits of life insurance business for a given year of assessment are therefore ascertained as follows:—
(1) 5% of the premiums from life insurance business in Hong Kong during the basis period for the year of assessment (Sec. 23(1)(a)), or
(2) if the corporation so elects, that part of the adjusted surplus, ascertained

in accordance with specific rules laid down in Sec. 23, which is deemed to arise in the basis period less any dividends received from corporations which are themselves subject to Profits Tax (Sec. 23(1)(b)). The reason why it is necessary to deem adjusted profits to have arisen in a basis period is explained by the fact that the adjusted surplus will normally cover more than one basis period and has therefore to be allocated as described later.

Under alternative (1) the calculation is limited to premiums from life insurance business in Hong Kong thereby retaining the Hong Kong source concept. For this purpose "premiums from life insurance business in Hong Kong" are specifically defined to include:—

(i)   all premiums received or receivable in Hong Kong whether from residents or non-residents, and

(ii) all premiums, received or receivable elsewhere, from Hong Kong residents where the premiums are in respect of policies the proposals for which were received by the corporation in Hong Kong.

Returned premiums or re-insurance premiums relating to those received may be deducted before applying the 5% (Sec. 23(9)).

THE ELECTION for treatment under Sec. 23(1)(b) is irrevocable and once made is deemed to apply to all subsequent years of assessment (Sec. 23(1) proviso (i)). Furthermore, the election is only effective if certain documents are submitted to the IRD. There is no time limit for the election as such but there is a time limit on the submission of certain documents. In respect of companies which are subject to the requirements of Sec. 12 of the Life Insurance Companies Ordinance, the Ordinance requires an actuaries' report and the election under Sec. 23(1)(b) is only valid if a certified true copy of that report is submitted to the IRD within two years of the date to which the report is made up (Sec. 23(2)(a) and (3)). In the case of companies which are exempt from the requirements of Sec. 12 of the Life Insurance Companies Ordinance, the Assurance Companies Acts 1909 and 1946 require certain other documents to be submitted to the Board of Trade and these also have to be submitted to the IRD within the two year time limit (Sec. 23(2)(b) and (3)).

The procedure is then to ascertain the "adjusted surplus" for the period of the actuarial report and to allocate it between the basis periods for years of assessment. An actuarial report is normally for a period of five years, although it can be less, so a number of years of assessment are affected. In order that collection of tax should not be delayed pending ascertainment of the adjusted surplus, assessments are raised annually on the 5% of premiums basis (Sec. 23(1) proviso (ii)). Although these assessments become final and conclusive it is specifically provided that they may be re-opened and adjusted upon the ascertainment of the adjusted surplus. Such an adjustment may of course involve an additional assessment or a reduction and repayment (Sec. 23(3)).

THE ADJUSTED SURPLUS is obtained by making specified adjustments to the surplus and the surplus is the amount by which the value of the life insurance fund (i.e. the accumulated investments representing invested premia) exceeds the company's estimated liability on its policies which the fund represents (obtained from the actuaries' report) at the end of the period in respect of which the actuarial report is made (Sec. 23(4)(a)).

The adjustments which are required to the surplus are as laid down in Sec. 23(4)(b) and are in effect only to adjust for the surplus or deficit shown by the immediately preceding actuarial report (obviously no such adjustment is required in respect of the first actuarial report covering the opening years of business) and to deduct from or add to the surplus certain other expenses and receipts in accordance with the general rules applicable to Profits Tax. In summary, the adjustments are as follows:—

Deduct from surplus:—

(1) Any surplus of a previous period retained in the life fund;
(2) Any transfer or appropriation to policy holders which has not been charged against the life fund in the actuarial report;
(3) Outgoings or expenses allowable under Sec. 16 which have not already been charged against the life fund;
(4) Capital receipts or transfers from reserve which have been credited to the life fund; and
(5) Depreciation allowances.

Add to surplus:—

(6) Any deficit of a previous period where such deficit is included in the report;
(7) Outgoings or expenses charged against the life fund which are not allowable under Sec. 16 or which are specifically disallowable under Sec. 17;
(8) Other sources of taxable income not already included in the life fund other than non-life-insurance business (because the profits from such a source are computed under the rules in Sec. 23A, they are dealt with from page 152 to page 154 in this chapter);
(9) Any appropriations of profits or transfers to reserve which have been charged against the life fund, other than transfers to policy holders; and
(10)Any balancing charge.

The concept of limiting Profits Tax to those profits which arise in or derive from Hong Kong is effected by apportioning the adjusted surplus between life insurance business within Hong Kong and life insurance business elsewhere, with the latter proportion being exempt from Profits Tax (Sec. 23(5)).

The apportionment is made on the basis of the total premiums arising during the period of the actuarial report from life insurance business in Hong Kong to the total aggregate premiums for the period (Sec. 23(6)). The meaning of premiums from life insurance business in Hong Kong has been dealt with on page 147.

ALLOCATION TO BASIS PERIODS of the proportion of the adjusted surplus which is applicable to life insurance business in Hong Kong is done similarly on the basis of the proportion which the premiums from life insurance business in Hong Kong arising in each basis period bears to the total aggregate of such premiums arising during the period of the actuarial report (Sec. 23(7)).

The ascertainment of adjusted losses their limitation to losses arising from life insurance business in Hong Kong and allocation over basis periods is carried out in precisely the same manner as adjusted profits (Sec. 23(8)).

Example 29

Livelong Life Insurance Ltd. is carrying on life insurance and accident insurance business in Hong Kong which it commenced on 1st January 1975. It makes up accounts to 31st December each year and under Sec. 12 of the Life Insurance Companies Ordinance has submitted an actuarial report for the period 1st January 1975 to 31st December 1978. The following facts are extracted from the actuarial report and accounts:—

Value of life fund at 31st December 1978		$2,875,000
Actuarial liability on policies comprising		
life fund at 31st December 1978		1,850,000

Premiums received and receivable:

	Hong Kong Office	Macau Office
in year ended 31.12.75	$175,000	$ 25,000
31.12.76	230,000	40,000
31.12.77	375,000	65,000
31.12.78	570,000	185,000

Premiums arising to the Macau office derive from proposals made to that office.

The company has incurred management expenses over the four years of $1,200,000 and the proportion which relates to life insurance is $875,000 which has not been charged to the life fund.

The life fund includes credits of $8,700 for profits on disposal of fixed assets, $12,000 for profits on disposal of shares comprising part of the life fund and $15,000 for transfer from reserve for contingencies. There has also been debited to the life fund a transfer to contingency reserve of $75,000 and a general provision for doubtful debts of $35,000. A sum of $50,000 has been appropriated to policy holders from the life fund.

Depreciation allowances on assets of both branches applicable to life business have been computed as:—

1975/76	$80,000
1976/77	45,000
1977/78	40,000
1978/79	35,000

Adjusted profits (losses) of the accident business, after taking into account the relevant proportion of management expenses and relevant depreciation allowances:

1975/76	($ 7,500)
1976/77	($ 1,500)
1977/78	$20,000
1978/79	90,000

Assessments

The basis periods for four years of assessment are covered by the actuarial report as follows:—

year ended 31.12.75	=	1975/76
year ended 31.12.76	=	1976/77
year ended 31.12.77	=	1977/78
year ended 31.12.78	=	1978/79

An election under Sec. 23(1)(b) cannot be made until the actuarial report has been submitted and this must be done within two years of the date to which it is made up. If the election is made it will therefore be made some time between 31st December 1978 and 1980. This would only apply to the life business.

In the meantime assessments on the life business are raised on the basis of Sec. 23(1)(a) as follows:—

		Life	Accident	Assessment
1975/76	5% x $175,000	$ 8,750	($ 7,500)	$ 1,250
1976/77	5% x $230,000	11,500	($ 1,500)	10,000
1977/78	5% x $375,000	18,750	$20,000	38,750
1978/79	5% x $570,000	28,500	90,000	118,500

Note that all other adjustments in respect of life business are ignored, including depreciation allowances because these are deemed to have been made in arriving at the notional profit under Sec. 23(1)(a).

If the election under Sec. 23(1)(b) is made, the first step is to ascertain the:—

Adjusted Surplus

Life Fund at 31.12.78	$2,875,000
Liability at 31.12.78	1,850,000
Excess	$1,025,000

Less:	Management expenses	$875,000	
	Disposal of fixed assets	8,700	
	Transfer from reserve	15,000	
	Depreciation allowances	200,000	1,098,700
			($ 73,700)
Add:	Transfer to reserve	$ 75,000	
	Provision for doubtful debts	35,000	110,000
	Adjusted surplus for period 1.1.75 to 31.12.78		$ 36,300

The next step is to divide the adjusted surplus between onshore and offshore business:—

Total onshore premiums for period	$1,350,000
Total offshore premiums for period	315,000
	$1,665,000

Onshore portion of adjusted surplus =

$$\frac{1,350,000}{1,665,000} \times 36,300 = \underline{\$29,432}$$

The next step is to allocate this portion of the adjusted surplus over the basis periods:—

$$\text{Year ended}\quad 31.12.75 = \frac{175,000}{1,350,000} \times 29,432 = \$3,815 \quad (1975/76)$$

$$31.12.76 = \frac{230,000}{1,350,000} \times 29,432 = \$5,014 \quad (1976/77)$$

$$31.12.77 = \frac{375,000}{1,350,000} \times 29,432 = \$8,176 \quad (1977/78)$$

$$31.12.78 = \frac{570,000}{1,350,000} \times 29,432 = \$12,427 \,(1978/79)$$

The final step is to merge these results with the accident business profits to form the total assessment on the company:—

	Life	Accident	Total
1975/76	$ 3,815	($ 7,500)	Nil
1976/77	5,014	($ 1,500)	Nil
1977/78	8,176	$20,000	$ 28,005
1978/79	12,427	90,000	102,427

Notes:—

(a) A surplus of losses is carried forward from 1975/76 and 1976/77 and used up in 1977/78.

(b) The assessment for each year is automatically reduced from the figure provisionally assessed under Sec. 23(1)(a) and a refund is made.

(c) For subsequent years the election must apply because it is irrevocable but until the next actuarial report is available, assessments are again provisionally made on the 5% basis under Sec. 23(1)(a).

NON-LIFE-INSURANCE CORPORATIONS. The ascertainment of the assessable profits of insurance business other than life insurance is governed by Sec. 23A and is much less complicated than the life insurance provisions.

The computation in most cases probably follows the financial accounts subject to any apportionment between onshore and offshore business and the usual statutory adjustments. It is specifically provided that the assessable profits are to be ascertained as follows:–

Gross premiums from non-life-insurance business in Hong Kong

Less:– Returned premiums

Corresponding re-insurance premiums

Any increase in the provision for unexpired risks as provided in the accounts

Actual losses less recoveries (note: provisions not deductible)

Agency expenses

Head office administration expenses so far as related to that business

Depreciation allowances less balancing charges so far as related to that business.

Plus:– Any interest or other income arising in or derived from Hong Kong.

Where a corporation is carrying on life business and non life business and indeed any other business, apportionments of expenses and depreciation allowances as appropriate are necessary to arrive at the foregoing computation.

In the case of a non Hong Kong resident insurance company, if the Hong Kong business is of a limited extent and it would be unreasonable to attempt to extract the foregoing information relating to Hong Kong business, the assessable profits may be ascertained as the proportion of worldwide profits and income which its premiums from Hong Kong insurance business bears to total premiums. Alternatively, any other equitable basis may be applied. Both of these alternatives are at the Commissioner's discretion (Sec. 23A(1) proviso).

For all these purposes the meaning of "premiums from insurance business in Hong Kong" is defined by Sec. 23A(2) as:–

(1) Premiums in respect of insurance contracts made in Hong Kong, and

(2) Premiums on policies the proposals for which were made to the corporation in Hong Kong.

Note that this definition is narrower than the equivalent definition for life insurance business in Sec. 23 where receivability in Hong Kong is sufficient.

RESIDENT SHIP AND AIRCRAFT OWNERS. Although, in general, the residence concept familiar in other taxation jurisdictions, is not applicable to

Hong Kong taxes, there are separate provisions for the ascertainment of the assessable profits of so called resident ship and aircraft owners and non-resident ship and aircraft owners. Sec. 23B applies to residents although the Section itself does not use the term resident. It is in fact applicable to:—

(1) Shipowning businesses which are normally managed and controlled in Hong Kong, and

(2) Shipowning businesses carried on by companies incorporated in Hong Kong (Sec. 23B(1)).

For the purposes of the section, a ship includes an aircraft and ship-owning business specifically excludes a dealer in ships and a shipping agent but includes a charterer (Sec. 23B(2)). Therefore the section embraces an operator or hirer of ships (or aircraft).

Management and control of the business as in (1) above is not further defined but is assumed to mean the same principles as govern the residence of a company under U.K. tax law, i.e. the place where the directors meet and exercise central management and control over the company. This is however far from clear.

There are two particularly important definitions which have a direct bearing on the liability under Sec. 23B. These are:—

"Charter Hire" which means sums receivable by a shipowner under a charter party which is either a bare boat, voyage or time charter and under which there is a demise of the ship.

"Permanent Establishment" is almost the same as in IRR5 and in double taxation agreements and means a branch, management or other place of business and also includes an agency if the agent has and habitually exercises a general authority to negotiate and conclude contracts on behalf of his principal.

A person whose shipowning business falls within (1) or (2) above is deemed to carry on that business in Hong Kong and his assessable profits from the business for a year of assessment are deemed to be that proportion of the total profits that the income from passengers, mails, livestock and goods taken on board in Hong Kong (other than transhipment unless the outward freight is payable in Hong Kong), income from outward towage undertaken in Hong Kong and charter hire income (except income attributable to a permanent establishment outside Hong Kong) bears to the aggregate of such income from worldwide sources during the basis period. In other words:—

Assessable profits = Worldwide Shipping Profits x A/B

Where A = income from:—

> Passengers, mails, livestock, goods etc. taken on in Hong Kong (except transhipment)
> Outward towage from Hong Kong

Charter hire excluding that applicable to a permanent establishment outside Hong Kong

and B = Total world income from those same sources, including those items of transhipment and charter hire excluded from A.

It has been held that shipping income for this purpose includes certain Government grants (CIR v Zim Israel Navigation Co. HKTC 573). This case was in respect of non-resident shipowners under Sec. 23C but is equally applicable to Sec. 23B.

For the purposes of the foregoing calculation, the total worldwide shipping profits are to be adjusted to conform with the general rules applicable to the ascertainment of assessable profits for Profits Tax. However, because this may be largely impractical, Sec. 23B(3) does provide a measure of flexibility in that it only requires such adjustment where the profit and loss account differs materially from what would otherwise be the adjusted profit and, furthermore, it is only to be adjusted "as nearly as may be". In other words it is not uncommon for example for the depreciation charge in the profit and loss account to be left unadjusted because it represents as nearly as may be the tax depreciation allowances.

Also, where charter hire income does not fall within the earlier definition of charter hire, it is treated as if it was receivable from the carriage of passengers, mails, livestock or goods (Sec. 23B(3)). Therefore if the ship calls at Hong Kong and picks up, the charter hire income will be assessable.

Example 30

Ankazawei Ltd. is a Hong Kong company which owns a number of ships engaged in international shipping activities, many of which never come to Hong Kong. Besides operating its own ships it runs agencies in a number of overseas ports but does not have an agency business in Hong Kong.

The profits shown by the profit and loss account for a basis period are as follows:−

Total profits before tax	$ 1,890,000
Agency profits included therein	270,000

The turnover is analysed as follows:−

(1) Total receipts from carriage of passengers and
goods contracted and invoiced in Hong Kong.   12,500,000

(2) Receipts included in (a) where goods taken
on in Hong Kong.   4,500,000

(3) Charter hire income $500,000 not included
in (1) of which:−
− $400,000 was from charter parties concluded

by the Hong Kong office
- $100,000 was from charter parties concluded
by the Panama office.
(4) Agency receipts $1,500,000 not included in (1).
(5) Interest on investments — Hong Kong   125,000
                                  — elsewhere   250,000
(overhead costs estimated at 5% of income)

The first step is to ascertain the worldwide profit from shipowning business, as follows:—

Total profits before tax		$ 1,890,000
Less: Agency profits	$270,000	
Interest less attributable expenses	356,250	626,250
Shipowning profit		$ 1,263,750

Note:—

This should strictly be adjusted to conform to the rules of Profits Tax, i.e. adjustments of allowable/disallowable expenses and substitution of depreciation allowances for the depreciation charge in the accounts. However this need not be fully done unless there is likely to be a material difference (Sec. 23B(3)).

The measure of the Hong Kong assessable shipowning profit is:—

Goods taken on in Hong Kong	$4,500,000
Charter hire not applicable to permanent establishment outside Hong Kong	400,000
	$4,900,000
Total freight etc. receipts	$12,500,000
Total charter hire receipts	500,000
	$13,000,000

$$\text{Hong Kong assessable shipowning profit} = \frac{4,900,000}{13,000,000} \times \$1,263,750$$
$$= \$476,336$$

Add Hong Kong source interest (less expenses)	118,750
Total profits assessable to Profits Tax	$595,086

Notes:—
(a) The agent in Panama with power to conclude charter parties constitutes a permanent establishment in Panama and therefore charter hire income which he obtains is excluded from Hong Kong turnover.
(b) The agency business is not carried on in Hong Kong and is therefore completely excluded from the calculations.
(c) The Hong Kong source interest in liable to Profits Tax per Sec. 15(1)(f).

NON-RESIDENT SHIP AND AIRCRAFT OWNERS. Sec. 23C covers the position of all ship and aircraft owners who are not covered by Sec. 23B. Once again, the term "resident" is not actually used in the wording of the subsection but, in effect, the provisions cover all ship owners not incorporated in Hong Kong where the business is not normally controlled or managed from within Hong Kong (otherwise it would be within the scope of Sec. 23B) but a ship or ships call at Hong Kong. If the Commissioner can be satisfied that a call of a ship is only a casual call, it will be ignored and no liability will arise (Sec. 23C(3)).

The general impact of the provisions is virtually the same as Sec. 23B in that the assessable profit is based on a proportion of worldwide profit and in fact there is very little difference in the calculation, the only difference being in relation to charter hire income. Under Sec. 23B charter hire income *is only excluded* if it is concluded through a permanent establishment outside Hong Kong and under Sec. 23C it *is only included* if it is concluded through a permanent establishment in Hong Kong. A useful discussion of what constitutes charter hire income is contained in the Report of the Third Inland Revenue Ordinance Review Committee (paras. 170 to 173). Otherwise, all of the definitions, inclusions and exclusions which are applicable to Sec. 23B are also applicable to Sec. 23C and the computation proceeds exactly as in Example 28 when the assessable charter hire income has been established.

The only additional provision is one enabling a simplified method of profit ascertainment which may be desirable where there are practical difficulties in carrying out the apportionment calculation. Sec. 23C(2) therefore provides that where in the assessor's opinion the apportionment formula cannot be satisfactorily applied, the assessable profits may be computed on a fair percentage of the aggregate of the sums which would otherwise form the numerator of the apportionment fraction, i.e. sums from: passengers, mails, livestock and goods taken on in Hong Kong (except transhipment), outward towage from Hong Kong and charter hire attributable to a permanent establishment in Hong Kong. (See CIR v Zim Israel Navigation Co. (HKTC 573) as to the inclusion of certain government grants in income from passengers, mails etc.)

If an assessment has been made on this alternative basis and has become final and conclusive nevertheless it can be re-opened and adjusted to the profit ascertained on the apportionment basis if a claim is made within 2 years of the end of the year of assessment (Sec. 23C(2) proviso). Like Sec. 23B, Sec. 23C also allows for the worldwide profit on shipping as revealed in the financial accounts to remain unadjusted unless there are material differences.

FINANCIAL INSTITUTIONS. Although in all general respects the ascertainment of the assessable profits of financial institutions is the same as for other types of business, there is an important provision, first effective for the year of assessment 1978/79, which deems the source of interest income arising to certain (defined) financial institutions in defined circumstances to be in Hong Kong notwithstanding that under the source rules applicable to interest (provision of credit test — see Chapter 4 paragraph 3) the source is not in Hong Kong. There is a view that, even before 1978/79, the provision of credit test was not applicable to the determination of the source of interest which is a trading receipt but such view has not been advanced by the IRD.

The provisions are contained in Sec. 15(1)(i) and apply to financial institutions as defined in Sec. 2(1). Financial institution means:—

(1) A bank licensed under the Banking Ordinance;
(2) A company registered or licensed under the Deposit-Taking Companies Ordinance;
(3) An associated company of (1) or (2) which would be liable to be registered or licensed under the Deposit-Taking Companies Ordinance but for the fact that it only takes deposits from licensed banks or registered or licensed deposit-taking companies.

The provision in (3) is an anti-avoidance provision but does not apply automatically to all such associated companies unless they are carrying on a deposit-taking business which would normally imply a systematic acceptance of deposits and re-investment at profit. Associated company is further defined by Sec. 2(2) to mean a company controlled by, controlling or under common control with the bank or deposit-taking company. Control is also widely defined.

Sec. 15(1)(i) merely provides that, notwithstanding that credit may have been provided outside Hong Kong, interest income arising to a financial institution through or from the carrying on of its business in Hong Kong is deemed to have a Hong Kong source. Unfortunately there is no further statutory guidance as to what constitutes "through or from the carrying on of business in Hong Kong" but the Inland Revenue Department have issued an Interpretation and Practice Notes No. 13 (see Appendix 12) which gives a certain amount of guidance as to the IRD views. The wording of Sec. 15(1)(i) is fairly widely drawn but the practice note indicates relaxations in that interest which is merely recorded in the books of the Hong Kong business (referred to as "booked" or garaged") will not be taxed. It is in fact not uncommon for all of the work in connection with a loan to be carried out by a head office or initiating branch outside Hong Kong and for that head office or initiating branch to arrange that the funds are made available to the customer through the Hong Kong branch (often for tax reasons or commercial restrictions in another part of the world) without any work being done by the Hong Kong branch other than recording the principal and interest. This will not be taxable, although it could be said that, notwithstanding the work being done elsewhere, the business of the Hong Kong branch is to passively record the interest income. However, there is also an intermediate position where, although the work on a loan is largely carried out by a head office or branch outside Hong Kong, something more is done by the Hong Kong branch than mere booking. The practice note indicates that an apportionment of the interest income between taxable and non-taxable portions would be considered but gives no guidance as to the basis upon which this might be done. At the time of writing the 1982 edition of this book, the practice has still not been fully clarified but it seems likely that the following general pattern will govern compromise settlements of the Profits Tax liabilities of financial institutions and they will certainly all be compromise settlements because a precise decision in legal terms seems impossible.

The factors in the loan making process which are precedent to the receipt of interest are considered and weighted and if more than 50% of those factors relate to intervention in the making of the loan by a bona fide branch or head office outside Hong Kong or by a group company outside Hong Kong, the loan will be regarded as "booked or garaged" in Hong Kong and therefore the interest will not be subject to Profits Tax. If more than 50% of the factors relate to the Hong Kong business, the interest will be regarded, strictly, as wholly taxable, but in cases where there is "substantial intervention" by a bona fide branch or head office or group company outside Hong Kong, only a portion of the interest will be taxed; probably 50%.

The factors which are taken into consideration are:—

(i) who makes first contact with or introduces the customer
(ii) who negotiates the terms
(iii) who assesses country/credit risk
(iv) who decides to take up the loan
(v) who provides the funding
(vi) who does all the paper work up to and including the loan agreement

Although this exercise necessitates a loan by loan study, it is usual to categorise loans into groups of common factors with as few groups as possible.

It can readily be seen that there are too many areas of imprecise definition for these rules to provide anything other than a basis for compromise, e.g.:—

(a) How does one weight the factors and decide where the 50% line falls?
(b) Many other factors might be considered relevant.
(c) Where does substantial intervention end and minor intervention begin because in the latter circumstances the CIR is regarding the interest as fully assessable?

Questions (a) and (c) are being answered solely by compromise.

Even when the question of the assessability of the interest income is settled, there remains to be determined the assessability of other sources of income and the allocation of expenditure, all of which must be determined under the existing rules of Profits Tax. In many ways, Sec. 15(1)(i) is a totally unsatisfactory area of the law because of the high degree of uncertainty as to how it applies in practice.

The position is recognised where a company may only fall within the definition of financial institution for part of a basis period and it is provided that the interest deeming provision applies only for the relevant part of the basis period during which it is caught by the definition (Sec. 15(3)). It may be acceptable to do this on the basis of time apportionment as authorised by Sec. 18E(3) but it would be more correct to identify the due dates of the interest income and allocate it accordingly and then to make consequential allocations of the related outgoings on some suitable basis.

Because of these provisions interest income will often be subject to tax in its country of source as well as to Profits Tax in Hong Kong. Because of this and the fact that the double taxation relief provisions are largely inadequate (see Chapter 11) there is a provision to specifically grant a measure of double taxation relief to financial institutions (Sec. 16(1)(c)). This does not amount to a full credit because the foreign tax is deductible only as a business expense. The tests which must be satisfied to qualify the foreign tax as a deduction are:—

(1) The claimant must be a financial institution;
(2) The tax must be an "income" tax;
(3) The financial institution must be managed and controlled in Hong Kong. In other words a Hong Kong branch of a company which is managed and controlled elsewhere cannot make the claim; and
(4) The financial institution must not qualify for double taxation relief under Sec. 45 in respect of the tax. (See Chapter 11.)

Example 31

Townbank Inc. has a Hong Kong branch which has made a loan to an Australian resident and in the year of assessment 1981/82 has received interest on the loan of $650,000 from which Australian withholding tax of $65,000 has been deducted. Branch officers negotiated and finalised the loan and used branch funds to advance to the customer in US$ through bank accounts in New York.

Notwithstanding that the source of the interest is outside Hong Kong under the provision of credit rule, the interest is subject to Profits Tax under Sec. 15(1)(i) because it arises from the branch business.

Double taxation relief is not available under Sec. 45 (see Chapter 11). Relief for the Australian tax is not available under Sec. 16(1)(i) because it is only a branch of a non-resident company.

Ignoring other expenses, Profits Tax is $650,000 @ 16½%

If the loan had been made by Town Finance (HK) Ltd the autonomous

Hong Kong deposit-taking subsidiary, relief would have been available under Sec. 16(1)(c) and Profits Tax would have been $585,000 @ 16½%. (See page 168 under the heading "Rule 3" regarding the Hong Kong branch of a non-resident bank.)

CLUBS AND TRADE ASSOCIATIONS. If there was no specific provision in the IRO, mutual clubs and trade associations would only be liable to tax (not necessarily Profits Tax) on the income which they derived from non-members. This is because of the principle that a person cannot make a profit from himself (Faulconbridge v National Employers' Mutual 33 TC 103) and therefore that profit which derives solely from sums paid in by members, and belongs to the members on the mutuality principle, would not be taxable. Receipts from non-members are however outside of the mutuality principle and would be taxable (Carlisle & Silloth Golf Club v Smith 6 TC 48).

However Sec. 24 invades this principle, somewhat artificially by deeming the whole of the profits, including receipts that would otherwise not be taxable, of clubs and trade associations to be the profits of a business for Profits Tax purposes when given circumstances apply.

In the case of a club or similar institution the test is based on gross receipts on revenue account which by specific definition includes entrance fees and subscriptions, the former normally constituting capital receipts if they are so treated in the accounts. If less than half of such gross receipts are received from members, the whole of the profits from both members and others and including entrance fees and subscriptions is subject to Profits Tax as if it was derived from a business (Sec. 24(1)). For this purpose, a member is a person who is entitled to vote at a general meeting of the club or institution (Sec. 24(3)). The exclusion of capital receipts from the general scheme of Profits Tax does not override the specific taxing provision in respect of entrance fees in Sec. 24(1) (CIR v Far East Stock Exchange (HKTC 1036) — Privy Council decision which in fact related to a trade association but which nevertheless holds good for clubs as well). It is the test of entitlement to vote which is the artificial element although it was introduced to prevent avoidance of tax by, for example, night clubs which sign in customers as quasi members. A club is not defined and must therefore take its natural meaning but it is interesting that in BR 1/79 a credit union was held to be a club, although in BR 3/80 a stock exchange was held not to be a club but is a trade association.

In the case of a trade, professional or business association, the test is on the basis of its subscription income. Where more than half of the receipts from subscriptions is from persons who either claim, or would be entitled to claim, that their subscriptions are allowable deductions against their own business profits (and this would normally be the case) the association is deemed to be carrying on business and is subject to Profits Tax on the whole of its profits including entrance fees and subscriptions (Sec. 24(2)). Note that entrance fees do not enter into the 50% test, it is only subscriptions (see BR 3/80).

Example 32

The Wanchai Missionaries Club owns a building, one third of which is used by members for club activities and the other two thirds of which is let out to local business. An analysis of the income and expenditure account for a basis period reveals the following:—

Subscriptions from members	$100,000
Catering and bar receipts	85,000
Rental receipts	245,000
	$430,000
General Administration expenses	$250,000
Property outgoings	60,000
	$310,000
Net profit c/d	$120,000

All members are entitled to vote at general meetings and only members can purchase food and drinks.

Entrance fees of $25,000 have been credited direct to the Accumulated Fund.

If it was not for Sec. 24(1) assessable profits would be limited to income from non-members, namely:—

Rental income		$245,000
Outgoings (2/3)	$40,000	
* Administration expenses, say	10,000	50,000
		$195,000

* An arbitrary figure for this illustration. It would be subject to negotiation.

However, the test under Sec. 24(1) is as follows:—

	Members	Non-Members
Subscriptions	$100,000	
Catering etc.	85,000	
Rents		$245,000
Entrance fees	25,000	
	$210,000	$245,000

As less than half derives from members, the whole of the profits are subject to Profits Tax and the assessment would be:—

Profits per income & expenditure account	$120,000
Add entrance fees	25,000
	$145,000

It works out favourably in this case because the rental profits are in fact subsidising club activities and the loss on club activities would not be allowable but for Sec. 24(1).

PARTNERSHIPS. There is nothing different about the ascertainment of the assessable profits of a partnership or about the ascertainment of basis periods for years of assessment. There are however a number of additional rules and special rules which it is convenient to bring together under this paragraph. It is very important to note that, for the purposes of the special rules applicable to losses incurred by an individual as a member of a partnership and allocation of the profits and losses of a partnership among the partners, a partnership is one which comprises not more than 20 partners (Sec. 19C(7)(a) in relation to losses, Sec. 22A(3)(a) in relation to allocation of shares). In counting the number of partners, if a partnership is itself a partner, all those other partners must be included (Secs. 19C(7)(b) and 22A(3)(b)). If a partnership consists of more than 20 partners, the rules for allowance of losses under Sec. 19C follow those applicable to a corporation and Sec. 22A concerning allocation of profits and losses does not apply at all. Therefore, if a corporation is a partner in a partnership consisting of more than 20 partners, the whole of the profits are assessed at the standard rate and that part applicable to the corporate partner is *not* assessed at the higher rate applicable to corporations. Furthermore an individual cannot bring his share into a "personal assessment" computation (see Chapter 7) because in effect he does not have a share.

It is necessary to establish whether a partnership exists between two or more persons, whether they be individuals, companies or a mixture of both because a partnership is assessed to Profits Tax as a single legal entity regardless of the individual identity of the partners (Sec. 22(1)). Furthermore, even where a partnership has ceased or been dissolved, an assessment may be made upon it and the tax recovered from any of the former partners (Sec. 22(5)). Whether a number of persons acting together constitutes a partnership is a question of fact and of law. The law in connection with partnerships in Hong Kong is contained in the Limited Partnerships Ordinance and the Partnership Ordinance. The taxation rules applicable to partnerships apply equally to limited and unlimited partnerships and an individual may be a partner whether he takes a full equity share in profits or whether his share is limited to a fixed amount which may be called a "salary". It is merely a question of law as to whether he has the obligations of a partner. No formal partnership agreement is required in Hong Kong law and, in the absence of a formal agreement, it is necessary to look to the actual course of business between the partners. Very broadly, a partnership is a relationship between persons carrying on business in common with a view to profit and would often include arrangements between two persons, usually companies, termed "joint ventures". It would not however include an arrangement such as an investment club where the purpose is merely to place funds into a common pool and take out profits rateably.

The precedent partner has the responsibility to submit returns of partnership profits and losses but if there is no active partner in Hong Kong, it becomes the responsibility of the resident manager or agent (Sec. 22(2)). However as regards recovery of unpaid tax, The IRD is entitled to collect from any partner (see CIR v Tse Kai-Wan and Sian Wong HKTC 921) or out of the partnership assets (see 22(4)). Precedent partner is defined by Sec. 2 as the first named in the partnership agreement or, failing that, the first named in the usual partnership name or in any statutory statement of the names of the partners.

Although a partnership is assessed as a single legal entity, because of the various ways in which the partners may, or are mandatorily required to, use their individual shares of profits or losses, the final computation of assessable profits or losses of a partnership consisting of not more than 20 partners is of necessity a combination of computations for each individual partner. Of course, if all of the partners are individuals, have been in partnership together throughout the whole of the basis period for the year of assessment and there is an assessable profit and no losses brought forward, there will be no necessity to compute individual shares for tax purposes and a single assessment is made at 15%. It is a matter for the partners themselves as to how they allocate the tax payment between themselves. Even so, however, a partner in a partnership consisting of not more than 20 partners may have reason to elect for personal assessment (see Chapter 7) in which case it will be necessary to ascertain his share of the profit for inclusion in the personal assessment computation. The share is ascertained in accordance with the manner in which they actually shared profits or losses during the basis period for the year of assessment (Sec. 22A(1)), not during the year of assessment itself. Where losses are brought forward from an earlier year, the whole loss is *not* automatically set against the whole profit (Sec. 22A(2)). This would be incorrect because it is necessary to allocate the loss in the same way as profits under Sec. 22A(1) and bring forward each partner's share against his subsequent share of profits. If there has been a change in profit sharing ratio or a partner has retired, the loss may be limited.

Example 33

A, B, C & D have been in partnership many years and recent results, as adjusted for Profits Tax purposes, have been as follows:

Year ended 31.12.77 Adjusted loss ($480,000)
Year ended 31.12.78 Adjusted profit $500,000

They had always shared profits equally until D retired on 31.12.77 and C semi-retired. From 1.1.78 therefore C took 1/5 of the profits and A & B shared the balance equally.

	A	B	C	D	Asst.
1977/78 (Note b)					
Basis period					
– year ended 31.12.77					
– loss ($480,000)	($120,000)	($120,000)	($120,000)	($120,000)	Nil
(Allocation per Sec. 22A(1))	C/F	C/F	C/F	Ceased	
1978/79 (Note b)					
Basis period					
– year ended 31-12.78					
– profit $500,000	$200,000	$200,000	$100,000		
(Allocation per Sec. 22A(1))					
Net	$ 80,000	$ 80,000	–		$160,000
Loss			($ 20,000) C/F		

Notes:—

(a) D's loss can only be set against *his* share of profits (Sec. 19C(2)) and therefore it lapses on his retirement (see "Losses" on page 132). Equally C's loss is limited to his share of profit and the balance is carried forward.

(b) Notwithstanding the retirement of D, the business is treated as continuing, therefore the cessation rules do not apply (Sec. 22(3) – see discussion below).

(c) See also Example 18.

Where a corporation is a partner in a partnership of not more than 20 partners it is always necessary to ascertain that corporation's share of profits and losses because its profits are assessed at the corporate rate of Profits Tax (not separately assessed but embodied in the assessment on the partnership) and its losses are treated differently to those of partners who are individuals. For an illustration of the principles see Example 18 and the more detailed discussion under "Losses" on page 132.

If there is a change in a partnership by virtue of one or more partners withdrawing or the dissolution of the partnership or of the admission of one or more new partners, this would normally constitute a cessation of one business and the commencement of a new business with the consequent adjustments to the basis periods for years of assessment affected by the change. However, Sec. 22(3) provides that, so long as at least one person who was a partner (or sole proprietor) before the change is a partner after the change, the business is to be treated as continuous throughout so that there is no adjustment to basis periods. However, losses applicable to withdrawing partners lapse because of the operation of Sec. 19C(2). See Example 33.

Note that if a husband and wife are in partnership, this is effectively a sole proprietorship by the husband because of the fact that under Sec. 15B a wife living with her husband is deemed to be one and the same person as her husband.

There are some particular provisions in relation to the ascertainment of the assessable profits of a partnership (including a partnership of more than 20 partners) and these are summarised as follows:—

(1) Rent payable to one of the partners in respect of property used for the business of the partnership is only deductible to the extent of an amount equal to the assessable value of the land or buildings for Property Tax purposes (see paragraph 3 of Chapter 2) (Sec. 16(1)(b)).

(2) Nothing can be deducted in respect of salaries or other remuneration of partners or for interest on partners' capital or loan accounts (Sec. 17(2)). This has the effect of disallowing a salary paid to the wife of a partner even though she may be a full time employee carrying out a necessary function, because she is treated by Sec. 15B as being the same person as her husband and therefore the salary is "paid to a partner". Presumably the salary would not be assessed to Salaries Tax on the basis that the partner could not employ himself although this is far from certain.

8. Non-Residents

Other than for isolated reasons such as eligibility to elect for "personal assessment", there is no concept of residence for Hong Kong tax purposes. In whatever way they might be defined, residents and non-residents are subject to tax in Hong Kong if they have a source of income in Hong Kong that is within one of the four income taxes. For the purposes of Profits Tax, if a person is carrying on business in Hong Kong and derives a source of profits in Hong Kong in connection with that business, he is subject to Profits Tax whatever his residence status.

The IRO does however deal with a number of special situations where the potential tax payer is not physically or legally in Hong Kong and sometimes the IRO uses the word "resident" without defining it. Also, a number of provisions are aimed at non-residents by implication, for example the deeming provisions in Sec. 15(1) (see under "Deemed Business Receipts" on pages 102 to 110), many of which are aimed at payments made to persons who are not actually carrying on business in Hong Kong. In practice, where the IRO uses the terms "resident" or "non-resident" it is usually possible to identify the parties affected with no problem but if the question is ever disputed it is possible that the U.K. case law principles would be applicable. A detailed consideration of these is beyond the scope of this book but very broadly, residence in the case of an individual is governed by whether or not he has a place of accommodation available to him as a place of abode or whether he makes visits of a habitual and substantial nature; in the case of a company it is governed by where its central management and control is exercised, i.e. where its directors meet and in the case of a partnership it is governed by where it is managed and controlled.

Rule 5 of the IRR deals, in effect, with the identification of and ascertainment of the assessable profits of, a non-resident carrying on business in Hong Kong but in fact refers to the "profits of a person having a permanent establishment in Hong Kong whose head office is situated elsewhere". For this purpose, the definition of person in Sec. 2 is unnecessarily repeated in Rule 5(1), i.e. that a person includes a company, partnership or body of persons. The definition of permanent establishment in Rule 5(1) is however important and is virtually the same as similar definitions contained in double taxation agreements (of which Hong Kong has none). The definition includes the obviously physical place of business, i.e. a branch, management or other place of business which is purely a factual matter and it also includes an agency. An agent becomes a permanent establishment if:—

(1) He has, and habitually exercises, a general authority to negotiate and conclude contracts on behalf of his principal, or

(2) He has a stock of merchandise from which he regularly fills orders on behalf of his principal.

Note that (1) is not satisfied by a one-off authority to negotiate and conclude a specific contract, it must be a general authority and be regularly exercised for the principal to be regarded as having a place of business in Hong Kong. However, the principle applies equally in the case of an independent agent as to one under the employment or control of the principal, unlike in many double taxation agreements where an independent agent acting in the normal course of his business is excluded from the definition of permanent establishment. Situation (2) covers goods held on consignment by an agent in Hong Kong. Apart from constituting a place of business of the principal, goods sold on consignment give rise to an effective withholding tax liability as discussed under "Goods on Consignment" on pages 168 to 169.

An agent who has power to purchase goods on behalf of a principal for shipment outside Hong Kong does not amount to carrying on business in Hong Kong (Sully v Attorney-General 2 TC 149). Also, offices in Hong Kong which are engaged in liaison or representation for non-resident principals do not constitute a business carried on in Hong Kong.

Once it is established that a non-resident has a place of business in Hong Kong in accordance with Rule 5, the method of ascertainment of assessable profits is laid down by Rule 5(2) as follows:—

(1) If branch accounts are kept which show the true profits arising in Hong Kong, these are adopted and adjusted in accordance with all the rules of Profits Tax. It is quite possible that a large part or even all of the profits may have a non-Hong Kong source in which case no liability would arise on that part.

(2) Failing the provision of accounts for the branch, or where the accounts do not show the true position for the Hong Kong branch, the assessable profits may be ascertained by adjusting the world wide profits to conform to Profits Tax principles and apportioning them on the basis of Hong Kong turnover to world wide turnover.

(3) Failing either (1) or (2), which would be exceptional, the Assessor is empowered to fix the assessable profits as a fair percentage of the Hong Kong turnover. Clearly this is an arbitrary method and a tax payer would normally strive to ensure that his assessable profits could be ascertained under (1) or (2).

Rule 5 is part of the IRO and therefore any assessment made under its authority is subject to the objection and appeal procedure in the same way as assessments made under the authority of Part IV of the IRO.

Example 34

Ahso Ltd. is a Japanese company which sells portable radios around the world. It has no branch or office in Hong Kong but has appointed an independent wholesale agent in Hong Kong to represent it and accept orders from retailers on its behalf. Ahso ships orders direct to the retailers. The results for a year of assessment indicate the following:—

Worldwide profit (as adjusted)	$1,470,000
Turnover — Sales to Hong Kong retailers	840,000
Worldwide sales	5,880,000

If no branch accounts are prepared, the assessable profit is:—

$$\frac{840}{5,880} \times 1,470,000 = \underline{\$210,000}$$

Notes:—

(a) The world wide profit will have been adjusted in accordance with the rules of Profits Tax as required by Rule 5(2)(c).

(b) If, for example, sales were being made into Hong Kong at a lower price than elsewhere, perhaps to break into the market, it would pay Ahso to prepare branch accounts as the profit is likely to be smaller than $210,000.

(c) If the agent only solicited orders which he then submitted to Japan for formal acceptance, Rule 5 would not apply and there would be no Profits Tax liability.

Rule 3 of the IRR is in principle similar to Rule 5 except that it applies specifically to banks whose head office is elsewhere than in Hong Kong. There is no reference to "permanent establishment" in Rule 3, presumably because in the special nature of banking business it is quite clear whether or not a non-resident bank has a branch in Hong Kong. In any event, a license is required from the Banking Commissioner before a banking business can be carried on in Hong Kong.

The methods of ascertaining assessable profits of the Hong Kong branch of a non-resident bank are, apart from straight forward branch accounts, not quite the same as for other types of business under Rule 5. The methods laid down in Rule 3(2) and (3) are:—

(1) If branch accounts are kept which show the true profits arising in Hong Kong, these are adopted and adjusted in accordance with the rules of Profits Tax.

(2) Failing the provision of accounts for the branch, or where the accounts do not show the true position for the Hong Kong branch, the assessable profits may be ascertained by adjusting the world wide profits to conform to Profits Tax principles and apportioning them on the basis of the total Hong Kong assets to world wide assets. Note that in the case of other types of business under Rule 5, the basis of apportionment is turnover.

(3) Failing either (1) or (2), which would be exceptional, the Assessor is empowered to estimate the Hong Kong profits. This is even more arbitrary than the similar provision for the businesses under Rule 5 where at least a fair percentage is applied to Hong Kong turnover, but it would be unusual for a bank to be unable to satisfy (1) or (2).

Rule 3 is part of the IRO and therefore any assessment made under its authority is subject to the objection and appeal procedure in the same way as assessments made under the authority of Part IV of the IRO.

See page 156 for details under the heading "Financial Institutions" for the special provisions which apply in ascertaining the assessable profits of banks.

Goods on consignment which are held in Hong Kong on behalf of a non-resident principal and which are sold on behalf of that principal give rise to an automatic tax liability, often loosely referred to as consignment tax, which is akin to a withholding tax. Sec. 20A(3) requires an agent who makes such consignment sales to submit a quarterly return to the Commissioner showing gross proceeds of such sales and at the same time remitting a sum equal to 1% of the gross proceeds or such lesser sum as the Commissioner may agree. In practice, only ½% of gross proceeds is demanded. The act of selling goods on consignment constitutes a permanent establishment under Rule 5 (see page 166) whereby the non-resident principal is regarded as carrying on business in Hong Kong and his assessable profits are to be ascertained in accordance with Rule 5. Accordingly, his true assessable profits may be ascertained and assessed in which case the consignment tax already paid would be taken into account. In practice, the consignment tax is usually regarded as the final liability but it would always be open to a non-resident principal to produce financial statements to show that his liability was in fact less than ½% of gross sales proceeds. However, he would not be able to continually change methods from year to year.

The Commissioner is given power by Sec.20A(3) to exempt from the consignment tax any person on such conditions as he thinks fit.

Example 35

Billy Kan is Hong Kong agent for Desca Ltd., a Japanese company manufacturing TV sets for worldwide sale. Billy holds a consignment of the sets in Hong Kong and regularly fills local orders from the stock. Sales for the year have been:—

1st	Quarter	$125,000	Billy's Commission	$12,500
2nd	Quarter	60,000	Billy's Commission	6,000
3rd	Quarter	110,000	Billy's Commission	11,000
4th	Quarter	95,000	Billy's Commission	9,500

Billy is required by Sec. 20A(3) to submit a return of these sales to the IRD each quarter and to pay over the following sums which represents Desca's tax liability:—

1st	Quarter	½% x $125,000 =	$ 625
2nd	Quarter	½% x $ 60,000 =	300
3rd	Quarter	½% x $110,000 =	550
4th	Quarter	½% x $ 95,000 =	475
Tax for the year			$1,950

Note that the commission is not taken into account.

Desca is in fact regarded by Rule 5 as carrying on business in Hong Kong and if it could produce a financial statement to show that its true profit from these sales was less than $11,818 ($11,818 @ 16½% = $1,950) that would be to its advantage. Otherwise it is likely that $1,950 will be Desca's final liability for the year and will be paid by Billy deducting it from his remittances.

Assessments upon an agent in respect of the Profits Tax liability of a non-resident principal are competent under the authority of Sec. 20A(1). Sec. 20A(2) authorises the agent to retain out of any assets coming into his possession or control on behalf of the principal, sufficient to reinburse him or to enable him to pay the tax on behalf of the principal.

Sec. 20A(1) gives the IRD wide powers to collect tax in respect of business done by non-resident principals, even when the Department otherwise has little or no jurisdiction, where an agent is or has been involved. The non-resident may be assessed directly or in the name of his agent and the latter applies whether or not the agent has receipt of the profits. Collection may be enforced out of assets in the possession of the agent and, where more than one agent is involved, those agents may be assessed jointly or severally in respect of the non-resident principal's profits and collection may be enforced jointly or severally.

For these purposes, an agent is widely defined by Sec. 2 as including:—
(1) An agent, attorney, factor, receiver, or manager in Hong Kong of a non-resident principal, and
(2) any person in Hong Kong through whom a non-resident principal is in receipt of profits or income arising in Hong Kong, i.e. a payer of a royalty becomes an agent of the recipient.

Arms length pricing is not normally a problem to the IRD because it is more common for transactions between associated residents and non-residents to give rise to more profits to the resident in view of the usually higher tax rates which apply elsewhere.

However there are provisions in Sec. 20 which are designed to counteract the diversion of profits from Hong Kong to a closely connected non-resident person. For this purpose a person is closely connected with another person if the Commissioner, in his complete discretion, considers that such persons are substantially identical or that, the ultimate controlling interest of each is owned directly or indirectly by the same person or persons (Sec. 20(1)(a)). In the case of companies it is necessary to look at the ultimate controlling interests of each, if necessary looking through one company or series of companies that own shares in other companies. Also, nominee holdings must be ignored and the beneficial ownership ascertained (Sec. 20(1)(b)). Accordingly, the Commissioner has wide powers to identify persons as closely connected.

Where a resident person is found to be closely connected with a non-resident person under these rules (and resident is not defined) and they carry on business together in such a manner that the profits which arise in Hong Kong to the resident are either nil or less than might be expected, the provisions of Sec. 20(2) are applicable. It is not as may be expected that the pricing between the parties is adjusted to an arm's length price so that the resident's taxable profit is increased; the counteracting procedure is much more complicated in that the business done by the non-resident in pursuance of his connection with the resident is deemed to be carried on in Hong Kong and the profit derived by the non-resident therefrom is assessed in the name of the resident person as if he was the non-resident's agent.

A point to note is that it is not only underpriced sales proceeds or overpriced purchase costs which are caught but also the position is caught where, because of special arrangements between the parties, the profits do not have a source in Hong Kong. The IRD of course has practical difficulties in identifying circumstances where the provisions apply and it is not commonly enforced other than in blatant avoidance cases.

Example 36

Dodger Ltd. is incorporated in Hong Kong and is owned equally by A, B, C and D. Ripoff S.A. is incorporated in Panama and is also owned equally by A, B, C and D. Dodger sells thingummybobs in Hong Kong at $20 each and, in respect of customers outside Hong Kong, sells to Ripoff at $10 each which in turn sells to the customers at $20 each.

(1) Dodger and Ripoff are sufficiently identical to be regarded as closely connected under Sec. 20(1) and it is therefore a question of whether Dodger is making less profit than might reasonably be expected.

(2) If Ripoff has a sales force which actively seeks out customers, bears shipping costs, deals with letters of credit, takes debt risks etc., the lower sale price may well be no lower than may be expected in the circumstances.

(3) However, if Ripoff does factually nothing other than reinvoice, the position will be challengeable under Sec. 20(2).
   In this event, the profit of $10 per unit earned by Ripoff, less any expenses properly attributable to that profit is deemed to be from a business carried on in Hong Kong and will be assessed in the name of Dodger Ltd. as agent.

(4) It is assumed that Ripoff concludes sales with customers independently of Dodger because if in fact Dodger is concluding the sales and merely booking them in Ripoff, Ripoff would probably be regarded as carrying on business in Hong Kong regardless of Sec. 20(2).

9. Assessment and Payment of Tax

The assessing system for Profits Tax consists of a Provisional Profits Tax assessment in an estimated amount followed, after a return has been made, by a final Profits Tax assessment on the true figure in which the Provisional Profits Tax already paid for the year of assessment is credited. In practice the assessment form is a two part set containing the final Profits Tax assessment for a year of assessment and also the Provisional Profits Tax assessment for the immediately succeeding year of assessment (Sec. 63I(b)). A single Provisional Profits Tax assessment which is usually issued during the year of assessment in which a new business has commenced is however quite valid on its own (Sec. 63I(a)).

The charge to Provisional tax is authorised by Sec. 63G and, when a new business has commenced, the Provisional assessment for the first year of assessment is estimated (Sec. 63H(4)) and the estimate is made from the details supplied by the tax payer in a Provisional Profits Tax return giving date of commencement, first accounting date and estimated profit or loss for the first six months of business in addition to other details of the business. The assessor is also empowered to estimate the Provisional assessment for the second year of assessment which he would do if the first year's true profit had not been ascertained by the time the assessment for the second year was due to be issued. He would base his estimate upon whatever information is available to him. In subsequent years the Provisional assessment is always in the same figure as the immediately preceding Final assessment less any un-relieved losses carried forward from that Final assessment (Sec. 63H(1)). However, any losses which have been deducted from that Final assessment cannot of course be taken into account because they would not be available again (Sec. 63H(2)).

Example 37

Giddy Ltd. has an agreed assessable profit for 1981/82 as follows:—

Assessable profit	$165,000
Losses brought forward under Sec. 19C	($280,000)
Assessable profit	Nil
Losses carried forward under Sec. 19C	$115,000

The Provisional Profits Tax assessment for 1982/83 will be:—

Previous year's assessable profit	$165,000	
Losses brought forward under Sec. 19C	115,000	
Provisional assessment	$ 50,000	@ 16½%

Where a Final assessment is based on an accounting period of more or less than 12 months which could be the case in respect of a year of commencement or a year affected by a change of accounting date (see paragraph 6) it would obviously be inappropriate to base the Provisional assessment for the succeeding year on the same figure and the Assessor therefore is empowered to estimate the Provisional assessment in such circumstances (Sec. 63H(3)). What he in fact normally does is to pro-rate the figures to correspond to a twelve month period.

The Assessor has further powers to estimate where the person is about to leave Hong Kong or it is otherwise expedient to quickly raise a Provisional assessment (Sec. 63H(6)) or in the absence of a return (Sec. 63H(5)).

Once assessed, the Commissioner is empowered to issue a notice of assessment and fix the due dates for payment (Sec. 63H(7)). The dates of payment are entirely at the discretion of the Commissioner but these are normally fixed in a consistent pattern which ensures that there is no element of payment in advance. The normal due date of payment is between November and January but obviously, if an accounting date falls after the normal due date, to ask for full payment of the Provisional tax on the normal due date would call for a part payment in advance and therefore in those circumstances only 75% is demanded on the due date and the balance of 25% about three months later. However, it is now a matter of policy, if the first instalment is in default, the second instalment becomes immediately due. This enables the Commissioner to impose a surcharge on both instalments and enforce collection of both at the earlier date.

Example 38

If Giddy Ltd. had an agreed assessable profit of $165,000 for 1981/82 based on an accounting year ended 30th June 1981 its Provisional Profits Tax liability for 1982/83 would be:—

$165,000 @ 16½% = $27,225 payable November 1982

If however its accounting date had been 31st March 1982, the payment dates would probably have been:—

$20,418	in January 1983
6,807	after 31st March 1983
$27,225	

If Giddy defaults on paying the January instalment, the total tax of $27,225 becomes immediately due together with any surcharges imposed.

When the Final assessment for a year is raised, the Provisional tax already paid for that year is credited against the final liability (Sec. 63K(a)). Any balance of Final liability is added to and payable on the same date as the first instalment of Provisional tax for the following year. Where the Provisional tax paid for a year of assessment exceeds the final liability for that year, the excess is not refunded but is deducted first from the first instalment of Provisional tax for the following year and then from the second instalment (Sec. 63K(b)). Any balance of overpayment still remaining is then repaid. Accordingly an overpayment for a year may not be recoverable until after the final liability for the following year has been ascertained and therefore a taxpayer should pay careful heed to the holdover provisions which are open to him. However, where an excess of Provisional Tax over the final liability is applied against the Provisional Tax for the next year and an opportunity arises to hold over all or part of the Provisional Tax (see following paragraphs) which is frustrated by the fact that it is already paid by the overpayment set-off, it is departmental practice to refund the amount that would otherwise have been held over.

Because of the estimated nature of Provisional tax, there are provisions to enable collection of the tax to be wholly or partly held over in appropriate circumstances. Given the appropriate grounds, the tax payer must apply in writing within at least 14 days before the due date of payment for the holdover to be made (Sec. 63J(1)). If the opportunity is missed in respect of the first instalment, all or part of the second instalment may still be held over. The appropriate grounds in Sec. 63J(2) are:—

(1) Where the assessable profits for the year of assessment assessed to Provisional tax are, or are likely to be, less than 90% of the amount assessed to Provisional tax. This is before taking into account losses brought forward. In the case of a claim under this heading it is normally necessary to submit documentary evidence such as management accounts although these need not be for the whole of the basis period, they can be for as long a period as is practicable in the circumstances and be grossed up to a 12 month period. It is normally not necessary to adjust the projected profit in accordance with Profits Tax principles except where differences are material.

(2) Where a loss brought forward under Sec. 19C has not been taken into account or is incorrect.

(3) Where the tax payer has ceased business or will cease before the end of the year of assessment and the assessable profits for the year of assessment assessed to Provisional tax are, or are likely to be, less than the amount assessed. Similar evidence will be required as in (1).

(4) Where the tax payer has elected for personal assessment (see Chapter 7) or is deemed to have elected and this is likely to reduce his liability for the year of assessment.

(5) Where the Final assessment for the preceding year (upon which the Provisional assessment is of course based) is under objection (see Chapter 10). As will be seen, this is also an occasion for a holdover claim in respect of the Final assessment as well.

Any holdover is entirely at the discretion of the IRD (Sec. 63J(3)) but in practice, where the rules for application have been complied with and the grounds satisfied, the holdover will be given in all but exceptional cases. The holdover does not automatically apply to the whole of the Provisional tax, only to the part which is shown to be affected by the grounds cited. The IRD must in all cases notify their decision in writing (Sec. 63J(4)).

Where the holdover is granted, it will be effective until the Final liability for the year is ascertained and due for payment but in the case of ground (5) above, if the objection against the previous year's assessment is determined or settled earlier, the earlier date will apply (Sec. 63J(1)).

Example 39

Oldit Ltd. has received the following composite assessment after submitting its Profits Tax return based on its accounting year ended 28th February 1982:—

1981/82 Final

Assessable Profits		$275,000
Sec. 19C losses brought forward		55,000
Net chargeable		$220,000
Profit Tax @ 16½%		$ 36,300
Less: Provisional Profits Tax assessed	$42,000	
Less heldover	12,000	30,000
Net due		$ 6,300

1982/83 Provisional

Assessable	$275,000	
Provisional tax @ 16½%		45,375
Total tax payable as follows:—		$ 51,675

	23.01.83	23.04.83
1981/82 Final	$ 6,300	
1982/83 Provisional	34,031	$ 11,344
	$40,331	$ 11,344

The management accounts for the period from 1st March 1982 to 30th November 1982 show a net profit of $161,000 including a capital profit of $20,000. Oldit's tax representatives therefore submit a holdover claim on 6th January 1983 under Sec. 63J(2)(a) showing the following expected profit for the year ended 29th February 1983:—

Profits for 9 months to 30.11.82	$161,000
Less: capital profit	20,000
	$141,000

$$\text{Extended to 12 month period } (x \, \frac{4}{3}) \quad = \quad \$188,000$$

The tax to be held over is therefore ($275,000 − $188,000)

$$= \$87,000 @ 16\tfrac{1}{2}\%$$
$$= \$14,355$$

75% is held over against the first instalment and 25% against the second instalment as follows:—

	23.01.83	23.04.83
Due — Final	$ 6,300	
— Provisional	34,031	$ 11,344
	40,331	11,344
Held over	10,766	3,589
Now payable	$29,565	$ 7,755

Notes:—

(a) If the claim had not been made by 9th January 1983, the whole of the first instalment of $40,331 would have been payable but the whole of the second instalment of $11,344 could have been held over.

(b) If there is default in paying the first instalment of $29,565, both instalments totalling $37,320 become immediately payable together with any surcharges thereon.

(c) No further tax is payable until the Final liability for 1982/83 is established when Provisional tax paid of $37,320 is credited and any balance due will be payable in early 1984.

Apart from the foregoing, the general provisions governing assessments, objections and appeals and payment of tax as contained in Parts X, XI and XII of the IRO respectively, are applicable (see Chapters 9 and 10). See also Departmental Interpretation and Practice Notes Nos. 4A and 12 reproduced in Appendices 4 and 11.

Chapter 6

DEPRECIATION ALLOWANCES

1. Legislation

The law governing Depreciation Allowances is contained in Part VI of the IRO Secs. 34 to 40. Subsidiary legislation covering, primarily, the rates of depreciation is contained in Rule 2 of the IRR.

2. Scope of the Reliefs

Depreciation allowances represent the statutory means of allowing for exhaustion of capital expenditure and in effect replace the depreciation charge in financial accounts by a controlled system of allowances but, as well as regulating the rate at which depreciation may be deducted, there is also a control upon the expenditure which qualifies for allowances. As a result, there are some areas of capital expenditure which do not qualify for depreciation allowances and, because of the provisions of Sec. 17(1)(c), do not qualify for any other deduction.

Primarily, depreciation allowances relate to Profits Tax computations but it must not be overlooked that Sec. 12(1)(b) provides for depreciation allowances on relevant capital expenditure to be deductible for Salaries Tax purposes.

There are broadly three areas of capital expenditure for which separate rules apply in computing depreciation allowances. These are:

      Industrial Buildings

      Commercial Buildings

      Plant and Machinery.

In the case of industrial buildings and plant and machinery, both an initial allowance at the outset and an annual allowance are available and, on the occasion of the disposal of the asset, or certain other specified occasions, a balancing allowance or balancing charge may arise to effectively adjust the total allowances to the actual net cost of the asset over its life. Although this is the theoretical intention, it does not always prove to be the case because of statutory adjustments to the cost or to the disposal proceeds in certain circumstances. With effect from the year of assessment 1980/81 provisions have been introduced which largely avoid the computation of balancing allowances and charges in respect of the disposal of plant and machinery. Commercial buildings attract only a small annual allowance, there is no initial allowance and no balancing allowances or charges.

There are special provisions to cover plant and machinery on hire purchase, basis periods, assets bought from or sold to associated persons at other than market value and assets replaced by similar assets. There are also special provisions to cover the years of assessment 1974/75 and 1975/76 which were affected by the transition from the "old" basis of Profits Tax assessment to the "new" basis. These provisions are ignored in this chapter which concentrates on the law and practice applicable to 1976/77 and subsequent years although all of the material outlined, apart from the basis periods, is applicable to earlier years.

3. Industrial Buildings

Separate rules apply to expenditure incurred on the construction of an industrial building, which is defined. This must not be confused with a commercial building which is also defined and for which the allowances are much less generous. It is also important to isolate expenditure which, although the businessman may consider it as part of the building, may separately qualify as plant and machinery and thereby attract more generous allowances, for example air conditioning and lift machinery.

QUALIFYING EXPENDITURE. In order to qualify for relief a person must incur capital expenditure on the construction of a building or structure which is to be an industrial building occupied for the purposes of a trade (Sec. 34(1)). A number of important pointers emerge from this:—

(1) It must be capital expenditure although naturally one would expect revenue expenditure to be deductible in full against profits and in fact the definition of capital expenditure for this purpose in Sec. 40(1) specifically provides that expenditure which is otherwise deductible must be excluded. Furthermore it provides that grants, subsidies or similar financial assistance must be deducted. Sec. 40(1) does however specifically provide that from 1980/81, capital expenditure includes interest and commitment fees which have been incurred on a loan made for the sole purpose of financing the provision of the asset.

(2) The expenditure need only be incurred by legal obligation in the basis period, there is no requirement that relief depends upon actual payment. (See page 115 for a discussion on when a liability is incurred.)

(3) Expenditure must be on the construction of a building or structure and therefore expenditure not directly related to construction does not qualify. In particular, expenditure on the acquisition of or of rights

in or over land is excluded by Sec. 40(3). Similarly, expenditure on demolition of a previous building does not qualify but site investigation work does (BR 5/79). However, capital expenditure on an existing industrial building or part of a building will qualify even though it does not physically give rise to any additional structure, i.e. improvements. As will be seen there are provisions to provide annual allowances to the purchaser of a completed building from another person but, unless the purchase is from a person whose business comprises property development and sale and who has not used the property, the expenditure which qualifies still relates to the original cost of construction not the purchase price, unless it is less.

(4) It must be an industrial building or structure which is defined in Sec. 40(1) and must be used for the purpose of a trade, but not necessarily by the person who incurs the expenditure. In other words, a property investment company can lease an industrial building to a trading company and it will obtain the industrial buildings allowance so long as the building itself qualifies by virtue of the trader's use of it. The most important criterion is the use to which the building is put because this largely governs whether it falls within the definition of industrial building or not.

The types of use which qualify a structure as an industrial building are laid down in Sec. 40(1) as follows:—

(1) For a trade carried on in a mill, factory or other similar premises. This is of course largely a question of fact but see Ellerker v Union Cold Storage Co. (22 TC 195) wherein it was held that premises used to manufacture and store ice fell within this definition.

(2) For a transport, tunnel, dock, water, gas or electricity undertaking or a public telephone or telegraph service. Thus, the mass transit railway tunnels and stations qualify as industrial buildings as do power stations, telephone exchanges, etc. This definition extends to all forms of transport businesses, for example buildings associated with airline activities and even with taxi businesses although, as will be seen, certain buildings or parts of buildings are specifically excluded even if connected with a qualifying trade.

(3) For a trade consisting of the manufacture of goods or materials or the subjection of any goods or materials to any process. A manufacturing trade is relatively easy to identify but whether or not goods have been subjected to a process is more difficult to determine. The processing must be the nature of the trade and not something which is incidental to a trade consisting primarily of some other activity, e.g. distributing (see CIR v Tai On Machinery Works, HKTC 411). U.K. law in this respect is identical and in Kilmarnock Equitable Co-operative Society v CIR

(42 TC 675) it was held that screening and packaging coal was a process for this purpose. A motor repair workshop is regarded as within the definition although, for example, a workshop where motor cars are polished and tuned before being placed in a showroom may not be.

(4) For a trade which consists of the storage of:−

   (i)   goods or materials to be used in the manufacture of other goods or materials

   (ii) goods or materials which are to be subjected to a process

   (iii) goods or materials on their arrival into Hong Kong.

   Note that the trade must be one of storage. Of course, if the building was to house goods awaiting manufacture or process by the store owner, the building would qualify under (3) above but if the building was for storing goods on their arrival into Hong Kong and the store owner was a retailer or distributor, the building would not qualify because the trade is not one of storage nor is it within (1), (2) or (3) above.

(5) For a farming business

(6) For scientific research business in relation to any type of trade or business. Thus a laboratory attached to a trade or business which did not otherwise qualify would attract the allowances. This should not be confused with the 100% relief given for capital expenditure on scientific research under Sec. 16B because expenditure on buildings is specifically excluded. Otherwise, the definition of scientific research in Sec. 16B(4)(a) probably applies. (See page 123.)

The word "structure" is used and accordingly the expenditure in question must be in connection with building something which amounts to a structure. As this word is not defined in the IRO it must be given its natural meaning which clearly extends beyond what one normally understands as a building. Structure includes:−

   Walls
   Bridges
   Dams (of whatever construction)
   Fish-ponds
   Banks around paddy fields
   Constructed parking grounds
   Roads
   Boreholes and wells
   Sewers
   Water mains and tunnel linings
   Wharves (which are specifically excluded from the definition of plant and machinery by Rule 2(3) of the IRR)

It is not essential that the whole of a building or structure should qualify as an industrial building. If a part qualifies, the relevant proportion of capital expenditure attracts the allowances. However if that part of a building or structure which does not qualify attracts not more than ten percent of the capital expenditure on the whole, the whole is treated as qualifying expenditure.

The following buildings, structures, or any part, do not qualify, regardless of the fact that they may be associated with a qualifying trade:—

> Dwelling house (other than for housing manual workers)
> Retail shop
> Showroom
> Hotel
> Offices

These non qualifying uses are subject to the ten per cent rule mentioned earlier if they represent part of a total building.

However, it is also specifically provided that any building or part of a building which is provided for the welfare of workers in the employment of a trader in one of the qualifying trades (1) to (6) listed earlier, qualifies as an industrial building. This would apply, for example, to a canteen or sporting facilities.

Not every person however constructs his own industrial building, in fact most persons either buy them from a builder or buy a used building from another trader. The IRO lays down what is to constitute cost in these cases but, as will be seen, the principle of "cost of construction" still remains unless the purchase is from a person whose business comprises property development and sale and who has not used the property.

If the claimant purchases a building or structure which is to be used as an industrial building and capital expenditure on its construction was incurred by the vendor who did not however bring it into use as an industrial building, the vendor is entitled to no allowances (Sec. 35B(a)) and the claimant is entitled to allowances based on the lesser of his purchase price or the actual cost of construction to the vendor and he is deemed to have incurred this expenditure on the date when his purchase price became payable (Sec. 35B (b)(ii)) assuming that he brings it into use. If there is a string of sales before it is brought into use, it is only the user who obtains the allowances based on the original cost of construction (Sec. 35B(b) proviso (b)). Where a person purchases an industrial building or structure from a person whose business comprises the development and sale of property and who has not used the property, he is treated as having incurred expenditure on the cost of construction equal to the price actually paid by him (Sec. 35B(b)(i)) assuming that he brings it into use. Where there is a string of sales before it is brought into use, it is only the user who obtains the allowances based on the price paid by the first purchaser from the builder (Sec. 35B(b) proviso (a)).

Example 1

Plastigames Ltd. is expanding rapidly and decides to purchase a new factory in Kwai Chung from the builder, Buildafac Ltd., and does so at a cost of $15 million which includes $6 million for the associated land. The construction work cost Buildafac $7 million. The factory proves insufficient and Plastigames acquires an identical factory on adjacent land from a textile company which constructed the building but reductions in trade prevented it being used. It cost the textile company $7 million to build and Plastigames pays $15 million including $6 million for the land. Under Sec. 35B(b)(i) the allowable cost of the first factory to Plastigames is $9 million, i.e. what it pays but under Sec. 35B(b)(ii) the allowable cost of the second factory is $7 million, i.e. the textile company's cost of construction.

Where a claimant buys an industrial building or structure from a person who has also used it as an industrial building, his allowances are based on the "residue of expenditure" immediately after the purchase (Sec. 34(2)(b)). The "residue" is defined in Sec. 40(1) and is the means by which tax relief is limited to the cost of construction over the life of the property, no matter how many claimants have been involved. A claimant can in effect only claim relief on the balance of any cost of construction not already claimed by a previous claimant but as balancing allowances and charges are taken into account it is often the case that, upon sale, a balancing change, equal to the whole of the allowances granted, arises and therefore the purchaser can claim relief on the whole cost of construction again. The "residue" is quite simply:—

> The historical cost of construction
> Less: Initial, annual and balancing allowances given
> Plus: Balancing charges made.

In computing this "residue" it is necessary to take into account notional annual allowances at the rate of 2% for years of assessment up to 1964/65 and at 4% thereafter for any year of assessment for which a claim was not made on the assumption that Sec. 34 (initial and annual allowances) had been in force at the time.

Example 2

Soldafac Ltd. has owned an industrial building since May 1960 for which the cost of construction was $900,000. It sold the building to Bortafac Ltd. in July 1979 for $8 million which includes the land value of $4 million.

Soldafac had received depreciation allowances of $558,000 but no claim had been made for 1967/68 when the building had been temporarily out of use.

Upon sale, Soldafac has a balancing charge of $558,000 and therefore, immediately after the sale, the "residue of expenditure" is as follows: —

Cost of construction		$900,000
Less: Allowances given	$558,000	
Notional Allowance		
67/68 (4%)	36,000	594,000
		$306,000
Plus: Balancing charge		558,000
Residue of expenditure		$864,000

Bortafac's qualifying expenditure is $864,000.

When the sale proceeds are less than the cost of construction, the qualifying expenditure to the purchaser cannot of course exceed what he pays. This is illustrated as follows: —

Example 3

The same facts as Example 2 except that the sale price is $800,000 for the building.

Soldafac's balancing charge is computed as follows (see page 186): —

Sale proceeds	$800,000
Notional residue	306,000
Balancing Charge	$494,000

The "residue of expenditure" immediately after the sale is: —

Cost of Construction		$900,000
Less: Allowance given	$558,000	
Notional Allowance		
67/68 (4%)	36,000	594,000
		$306,000
Plus: Balancing charge		494,000
		$800,000

Bortafac's qualifying expenditure is therefore equal to its cost of purchase, $800,000.

INITIAL ALLOWANCE. A person who incurs capital expenditure on the construction of a building or structure which is to qualify as an industrial building becomes entitled to an initial allowance for the year of assessment which relates to the basis period in which the expenditure was incurred (Sec. 34(1)). The allowance is available even if the building or structure is not yet in use as an industrial building. Furthermore, expenditure incurred before a trade is commenced is treated as if it was incurred on the day on which trading commences (Sec. 40(2)). However, if, when the building or structure is first brought into use, it does not qualify as an industrial building, any initial allowance already given is withdrawn by additional assessment (Sec. 34(1) proviso (b)).

The initial allowance is twenty per cent of the qualifying expenditure and is only granted to the person who incurs the cost of construction, it is not given on qualifying expenditure obtained by purchase except where under Sec. 35B a purchaser is treated as having incurred the expenditure by virtue of the fact that he purchases the building or structure unused.

ANNUAL ALLOWANCE. In order to qualify for an annual allowance, it is not necessary for a claimant to himself incur expenditure on the cost of construction, he must however have an interest in the building or structure at the end of the basis period for the year of assessment and that interest must be the "relevant interest" in relation to the capital expenditure incurred on the cost of construction. "Relevant interest" is defined by Sec. 40(1) and merely means that the claimant must hold the same legal interest in the property as the person who incurred the original expenditure. In other words, expenditure by an owner entitles the owner and subsequent owners to claim annual allowances in relation to that expenditure and expenditure by a lessee entitles that lessee and his subsequent assignees to claim annual allowances in relation to that expenditure.

Furthermore the building or structure must be in qualifying use at the end of the basis period. The annual allowance in respect of cost of construction incurred by the claimant is four per cent of the qualifying expenditure (Sec. 34(2)(a)). In the case of persons inheriting the residue of the expenditure, the amount of the annual allowance varies according to the formula discussed after Example 4.

Example 4

Constructafac Ltd. built a building in its accounting year ended 31st December 1977 at a cost of $6 million. It could not find a tenant until the year ended 31st December, 1978 when it granted a lease to Yewsafac Ltd. In its year ended 31st May, 1979 Yewsafac incurred additional qualifying expenditure of $800,000 before bringing the factory into use on 15th January, 1979.

Initial allowance depends only on incurring capital expenditure on the cost of construction, therefore both companies qualify for initial allowance as follows:—

Constructafac   20% x $6 million = $1.2 million for 1977/78
Yewsafac   20% x $800,000 = $160,000 for 1979/80

Annual allowance depends upon the "relevant interest" as follows:—

Allowance based on $6 million (or the residue thereof) to the owner at the end of his basis period

Allowance based on $800,000 (or the residue thereof) to the lessee at the end of his basis period.

Accordingly the following allowances arise:—

To Constructafac, 4% x $6 million for 1979/80 and each subsequent year of assessment at the end of the basis period for which it is still the owner. Subsequent owners will receive annual allowances based on $6 million or the residue thereof (Note (a)).

To Yewsafac, 4% x $800,000 for 1979/80 and each subsequent year of assessment at the end of the basis period for which it is still the lessee. Subsequent assignees of Yewsafac's lease will receive annual allowances based on $800,000 or the residue thereof (Note (b)).

Notes:—

(a) Constructafac receives no allowance for 1978/79 because the factory was not in use at 31st December 1978.

(b) There can be any number of sub tenants and each would have a separate "relevant interest". If Yewsafac granted a sub lease it could continue to claim annual allowances based on $800,000. If Constructafac sold its interest as owner, this would not affect Yewsafac's continuing claim based on $800,000.

When the "relevant interest" changes hands, the purchaser inherits the "residue of the expenditure" related to that relevant interest as discussed on page 182. The rate of the purchaser's annual allowance depends upon a formula which takes into account when the building or structure was first used and an assumed depreciable life based on that first date of use. To understand why there are two different formulae dependant upon the date of first use it only needs to be known that until 1964/65 the rate of annual allowance was 2% (i.e. a 50 year assumed life) and from 1965/66 it has been 4% (i.e. a 25 year assumed life).

The annual allowance for a building or structure purchased from a previous user is therefore as follows (Sec. 34(2)(b)):—

(1) First used before the basis period for 1965/66

Residue of Expenditure × $\dfrac{1}{\text{No. of years of assessment from the year the first annual allowance granted to the purchaser to the 50th year after first use.}}$

(2) First used during or after the basis period for 1965/66

Residue of Expenditure × $\dfrac{1}{\text{No. of years of assessment from the year the first annual allowance granted to the purchaser to the 25th year after first use.}}$

Although these formulae and the fixed 4% annual allowance provide a fixed annual allowance year by year the total allowances must not of course, with the initial allowance where applicable, exceed the total allowable expenditure and therefore the final annual allowance is usually a balancing figure (Sec. 34(2)(c)).

As each new expenditure on an existing building constitutes, in effect, another "part" of the building, a purchaser will normally have to make separate computations under the foregoing formulae for each piece of expenditure because the period of depreciable life will run from the date of the expenditure and not the date of first use of the original building.

Example 5

Same facts as in Example 2 and assuming that the companies accounting periods are to 31st December in each case.

The residue of expenditure available to Bortfac has been ascertained at $864,000

The year of assessment of first use was 1961/62 (basis period –y/e 31.12.60 under the discontinued "previous year" basis). The 50th year thereafter in 2010/11.

The year of assessment of first use by Bortafac is 1979/80.

Therefore the annual allowance to Bortafac for 1979/80 et seq. until the residue is used up is:–

$$864,000 \times \frac{2}{1979/80 \text{ to } 2010/11 \text{ inclusive}} = 864,000 \times \frac{2}{32}$$
$$= \underline{\$54,000}$$

Note:–

If Soldafac had incurred further expenditure since first use, there would have to be a separate computation, as in Example 2, of each residue of expenditure and consequently a separate computation as above of each amount of annual allowance in respect of each residue.

BALANCING ALLOWANCE/CHARGE. In order to relate the total depreciation allowances to a claimant over his period of relevant interest in a building or structure to the exhaustion of his qualifying expenditure, balancing allowances are granted or balancing charges made on specified occasions which are related to the cessation of use by the claimant having the relevant interest in the building or structure. The specific occasions identified by Sec. 35(1) are as follows:–

(1) The relevant interest in the building or structure is sold, or

(2) If the relevant interest is a leasehold, the lease comes to an end other than in circumstances where the leaseholder acquires the reversionary

interest. However, notwithstanding the termination of a lease, this is not to apply as an event giving rise to a balancing allowance or charge if either:—

(i) the lessee remains in possession without being granted a new lease in which case the lease is regarded as subsisting so long as he remains in possession (Sec. 35A(a)), or

(ii) a new lease is granted either by re-grant or under the terms of an option in the first lease in which case the original lease is regarding as continuing throughout the life of the new lease (Sec. 35A(b)).

(3) The building or structure is destroyed or demolished or ceases to be used as an industrial building. Demolition would of course normally result in a balancing allowance because there are no disposal proceeds. However a proviso to Sec. 35(1) denies a balancing allowance where the building or structure is demolished for purposes not connected with the business for which allowances have been granted. In other words the allowance can be given where a factory is demolished to build a better one for the same business but not where it is demolished for re-development for resale. If however the building is sold giving rise to a balancing allowance and the new owner demolishes it, the proviso cannot deny the allowance because it is only applicable where demolition is the reason for claiming a balancing allowance.

A balancing allowance equal to the remaining unrelieved qualifying expenditure arises where there are no sale proceeds or insurance, salvage or compensation monies or, if there are any such receipts, is the excess of unrelieved qualifying expenditure over such receipts (Sec. 35(2)). Where the receipts exceed the unrelieved qualifying expenditure, the excess is a balancing charge (Sec. 35(3)). The balancing charge cannot however exceed the aggregate of initial and annual allowances already given on the building or structure (Sec. 35(4)); in other words the balancing charge procedure cannot amount to a capital gains tax. It of course follows that the disposal proceeds of a building or structure must be suitably apportioned where part or parts of the original expenditure did not qualify for relief.

Example 6

Onafac owns a piece of land on which are Factory A and Factory B which it uses for its business and for which the residual value of unrelieved qualifying expenditure after 1977/78 allowances is $278,000 and $1,120,000 respectively. During the accounting year ended 31st December 1978 Factory A is demolished to allow Onafac to build a bigger one on the same site. When it is completed in the year ended 31st December 1979, Factory B and the piece of land on which it stands is sold for $5 million. The original cost of construction of Factory B was $2 million. The annual allowance for 1978/79 on Factory B is $80,000.

Onafac has a balancing allowance of $278,000 for 1978/79 on Factory A but it would not have been allowed if the objective had been to build something on the vacant site for resale. Its total industrial building allowances for 1978/79 are therefore $358,000.

For 1979/80 it has a balancing charge computed as follows:—

Qualifying Expenditure	$2,000,000	
Allowances given to 1978/79	960,000	.... (a)
Residual value	$1,040,000	
Sale Proceeds (Note a)	2,500,000	
Excess	$1,460,000	.... (b)

The balancing charge is the lesser of (a) or (b) and is therefore $960,000.

Notes:—
(a) It is necessary to divide the sale proceeds between the building, or part, which qualifies for industrial building allowances and the land plus any part of the building which does not qualify. In this case 50% is taken as the relevant apportionment which is commonly accepted by the Inland Revenue Department. It is however a question of fact, open to negotiation.
(b) The balancing charge is either deducted from depreciation allowances or added to assessable income, the effect is the same.

See also Departmental Interpretation and Practice Notes No. 2 reproduced in Appendix 2.

4. Commercial Buildings

A very small allowance is available for commercial buildings which should not be confused with industrial buildings for which much more generous allowances are available. It is also important to isolate expenditure which, although the businessman may consider it as part of the building, may separately qualify as plant and machinery and thereby attract even more generous allowances, for example air conditioning and lift machinery.

QUALIFYING EXPENDITURE. In order to qualify for relief, a person must have an interest in a commercial building or structure at the end of the basis period for assessment and that interest must be the relevant interest under which capital expenditure was incurred on the construction of the building or structure (Sec. 36). Some of these points are now examined in more detail:—
(1) It must be capital expenditure. The comments in relation to capital expenditure on industrial buildings on page 178 also apply to commercial buildings.

(2) The claimant does not have to incur the capital expenditure himself, it is sufficient that he holds the relevant interest in relation to which the expenditure was originally incurred. In other words expenditure incurred by an owner is available for allowances to him and subsequent owners and expenditure incurred by a lessee is available for allowance to him and his assigns but a lessee cannot inherit the owner's expenditure.

(3) Expenditure must be on the construction of a building or structure and therefore expenditure not directly related to construction does not qualify. In particular, expenditure on the acquisition of or of rights in or over land is excluded by Sec. 40(3). Similarly, expenditure on demolition of a previous building does not qualify. However, capital expenditure on an existing commercial building or part of a building will qualify even though it does not physically give rise to any additional structure, i.e. improvements.

(4) A commercial building or structure is defined in Sec. 40(1) as any building or structure or part of a building or structure used by the person entitled to the relevant interest on which the expenditure was incurred in his trade, profession or business and which does not qualify as an industrial building or structure. Therefore the comments as to what qualifies as a structure for industrial building allowance purposes on page 180 apply to commercial structures.

ALLOWANCES.   There are no initial allowances or balancing allowances or charges. There is a single allowance for each year of assessment of three quarters of 1% of the qualifying expenditure. In theory therefore it is possible for the aggregate allowances given to ultimately amount to more than the expenditure.

See also Departmental Interpretation and Practice Notes No. 2 reproduced in Appendix 2.

5.   Expenditure Qualifying as Plant and Machinery

Plant and machinery attracts the most generous allowances of all assets qualifying for depreciation allowances. It is therefore important to be able to identify which assets fall within the definition as opposed to being classified as expenditure on buildings, and, as will be seen, the dividing line is often very narrow.

In order to qualify for relief, capital expenditure on the provision of machinery or plant must be incurred by a person carrying on a trade profession or business for the purposes of producing profits chargeable to Profits Tax (Sec. 37(1) and 39B(1)) or by an employee on machinery or plant the use of which is essential to the production of income assessable to

Salaries Tax (Sec. 12(1)(b)). There are therefore a number of essential in-
gredients to qualification for relief and these are:–
(1) The expenditure must be capital expenditure and for further comments
    on this, see page 178 in connection with capital expenditure on industrial
    buildings. However, capital expenditure qualifying as scientific research
    expenditure under Sec. 16B is specifically excluded because it qualifies
    for full deduction under Sec. 16B(1)(b).
(2) The expenditure need only be incurred by legal obligation in the basis
    period, there is no requirement that relief depends upon actual payment
    (see page 115 for a discussion on when a liability is incurred). There are
    however some special provisions dealing with the availability and timing
    of relief in respect of expenditure incurred under a hire purchase agree-
    ment which are dealt with in this chapter.
(3) Ignoring the position of an employee, the claimant must be carrying on a
    business which is subject to Profits Tax and the assets in question must
    be used to earn assessable profits.
(4) The assets must fall within the definition of plant and machinery and this
    is now considered in detail.
    The IRO contains no definition of plant and machinery and it is there-
fore necessary to turn to case law of which there are numerous U.K. decisions
which are accepted authorities in Hong Kong. The IRO does however say in
Sec. 40(1) that capital expenditure on the provision of machinery or plant
includes capital expenditure on alterations to an existing building incidental
to the installation of plant or machinery. As will be seen, it is the case that
certain of the expenditure incurred on and during the construction of a
building will qualify as expenditure on plant and machinery and the provision
in Sec. 40(1) therefore only seems to provide additionally for relief on the
extra expenditure necessitated by having to make the installation in an existing building, such as demolition, making good etc.

As to the judicial interpretation of the meaning of plant and machinery,
the earliest case of importance was the U.K. case of Yarmouth v France which
was not a tax case but which nevertheless identified a general rule which
holds good to this day. It was held that plant includes "whatever apparatus is
used by a businessman for carrying on his business, not his stock-in-trade
which he buys or makes for sale, but all goods and chattels, fixed moveable,
live or dead, which he keeps for permanent employment in his business".
From this and subsequent cases has developed the general principle that
expenditure on plant and machinery may be identified and distinguished
from expenditure on buildings in that the former relates to the "tools" *with
which* business is carried on whereas the latter is the "environment" *in which*
the business is carried on. (See particularly J. Lyons & Co. v AG, which was

not a tax case.) This principle comes to the fore in dealing with expenditure on partitioning within a building. In Jarrold v John Good & Sons (40 TC 681) it was held that partitioning which was moveable and which required to be regularly moved because of the changing nature of the business requirements, qualified as plant and machinery. However, merely being moveable or demountable is not, of itself, sufficient as demonstrated in St. Johns School v Ward (49 TC 524) wherein a portable laboratory and gymnasium were held to be buildings.

It will be seen therefore that it is not only the obvious pieces of machinery that fall within the definition but everything which is used as a "tool" within the business, whether or not it may be fixed to a building. It is difficult in many cases to distinguish those parts of a building which qualify although a certain amount of logic can be applied. Electric lighting, for example is clearly part of the "environment" but special lighting installed in a photographic studio would qualify as equipment, even if wired into the building. Plumbing fixtures such as washbasins and toilets qualify and as they cannot function without piping the plumbing from the equipment to the main should also qualify. This can also extend to special trunking and wiring installed to service a computer. Other parts of a building which come to mind as qualifying include fire extinguishing equipment, air conditioning and lifts. It is solely a question of fact and of logic where the building ends and equipment begins. In the case of IRC v Scottish & Newcastle Breweries (1982 Simons Tax cases 296), pictures, murals and decor in a hotel were regarded as equipment necessary to provide atmosphere and therefore qualifying as plant and machinery.

It has been held in Cooke v Beach Station Caravans (49 TC 514) that a swimming pool provided by a caravan site operator is a "tool" and therefore qualifies. Similarly, the functional nature of a dry dock for ship repairs qualified it as plant and machinery in IRC v Barclay, Curle & Co. (45 TC 221). At one time it was the position that the technical library of a solicitor, or indeed of any other professional person, was not plant and machinery but the earlier decision in Daphne v Shaw (11 TC 256) has been overruled by Munby v Furlong (1976 Simons Tax Cases 72).

Relief is only available for the expenditure incurred on the provision of the plant or machinery which broadly means the expenditure directly incurred in purchasing or constructing it apart from the specific provision in Sec. 40(1) permitting incidental expenditure on altering a building to be included. Accordingly, incidental expenditure such as legal fees, commissions etc. cannot be included. In the Barclay Curle case mentioned earlier, the cost of excavation was allowed as an essential element in the construction of the dock. In Powlson v Ben Odeco (1978 Simons Tax Cases 460) capitalised interest paid on a loan specifically taken out to finance the construction of an oil rig was not regarded as part of the cost of provision of the oil rig, however, Sec. 40 now provides that, from 1980/81, qualifying capital expenditure includes interest and commitment fees which have been incurred on a loan made for the sole purpose of financing the provision of plant and machinery.

Having determined the judicial definition of plant and machinery, the IRR makes some amendments in Rule 2. Firstly in Rule 2(3), wharves are specifically excluded from the definition of plant and machinery and accordingly qualify for industrial building allowances. Secondly, the following items are excluded from plant and machinery and are, instead, deemed to be "implements, utensils and articles":—

Belting
Crockery and cutlery
Kitchen utensils
Linen
Loose tools
Soft furnishings (including curtains and carpets)
Surgical and dental instruments
Tubes for X-ray and infra-red machines.

Accordingly, initial expenditure on these items is disallowed as capital expenditure and no depreciation allowances are available but the cost of replacement of these items is wholly deductible (Sec. 16(1)(f)).

See also Departmental Interpretation and Practice Notes No. 7 reproduced in Appendix 7 where appendices B and C to the Notes give the IRD views on expenditure falling within and outside of the definition respectively. Some of the items in Appendix C might be challenged on the basis of case law.

6. Plant and Machinery Allowances to 1979/80

For the prime purpose of minimising the number of calculations of balancing allowances and charges, the method of computing annual allowances changed with the introduction of the "pooling" system with effect from the year of assessment 1980/81 (Sec. 36A(1)). The pooling system is described from pages 201 to 208. However, even after 1979/80, there are specific circumstances where the pooling system will not apply and the provisions described in the following pages will continue to apply. In particular, the Commissioner is empowered to set aside the pooling provisions and direct that the allowances be computed in the following manner if the pooling provisions appear to him to be impracticable or inequitable in the circumstances (Sec. 36A(2)).

INITIAL ALLOWANCE. An initial allowance equal to 25% (increased to

35% from 1980/81) of the qualifying expenditure is given for the year of assessment relating to the basis period in which the expenditure is incurred (Sec. 37(1) and 37(1A)(b)). It is not necessary for the asset to be brought into use in the basis period, it is sufficient that the expenditure is incurred while a trade, profession or business is carried on. Where a person succeeds to a trade profession or business, including the assets used for that business, other than by way of purchase, although, as will be seen, he can claim annual allowances notwithstanding having incurred no expenditure, he cannot claim an initial allowance (Sec. 37(5)).

Where the plant or machinery is acquired under a hire purchase agreement, the initial allowance is spread over the period during which instalments are paid. The relief is given on the instalments paid in each basis period and is only given on the capital element of the instalments (Sec. 37A(1) and (1A)). The revenue element, being interest, would normally qualify as a revenue expense for the periods in which incurred.

Example 7

Nevanevva Ltd. has entered into a hire purchase agreement on 1st June 1979 to buy some machinery for its Hong Kong manufacturing business. The cash price of the machinery was $240,000 and the Company agreed to pay $312,000 by 24 monthly instalments commencing 1st June 1979. The Company's accounting date is 31st December.

The instalments are $13,000 per month
The capital element is $10,000 per month

Initial Allowance	— **1979/80**	— Instalments to 31.12.79	$ 70,000
		— Initial Allowance (25%)	$ 17,500
	— **1980/81**	— Instalments in year to	
		31.12.80	$120,000
		— Initial Allowance (35%)	$ 42,000
	— **1981/82**	— Instalments in period	
		to 1.5.81	$ 50,000
		— Initial Allowance (35%)	$ 17,500

The interest element of $3,000 per month would be allowed as a revenue expense in the three years of assessment.

Although Sec. 37A refers to a hire purchase agreement, this is not defined and there is no hire purchase law in Hong Kong which could provide guidance as to what such an agreement comprises. It is assumed however to comprise an agreement which has the characteristics of a hire purchase contract as understood in other countries, particularly the U.K. Accordingly an agreement comprising instalments which are calculated to fully recover the cash price plus interest and which contains an ultimate option to purchase for a nominal sum would comprise a hire purchase agreement for this purpose. The main feature which distinguishes a hire purchase agreement from an instalment credit sale is that under the former the title passes to the purchaser at the end of the agreement whereas under the latter the title passes at the outset. It is likely that Sec. 37A would be applied to any agreement where title passes under an ultimate option to purchase, whatever the relationship between the instalments and the amount of the option payment.

ANNUAL ALLOWANCE. An annual allowance is available where, at the end of a basis period for a year of assessment, a person owns and has in use machinery or plant for the purposes of producing profits assessable to Profits Tax (Sec. 37(2)). Note that the two important criteria of "ownership" and "in use" do not apply for initial allowance. Accordingly initial allowance can be claimed on a capital contribution to an asset owned by another person provided that the claimant has the use of the asset but no further allowances and where an asset is acquired but not brought into use for a period of time, the initial allowance is available at the outset but the annual allowances are deferred.

The annual allowances for each basis period are computed on the amount of the qualifying expenditure less:−

(1) the initial allowance given on that expenditure; and
(2) previous annual allowances given

There are also two situations where notional annual allowances have to be deducted in arriving at the net expenditure upon which annual allowances are to be given. These are:−

(1) Where an asset was acquired before the basis period for 1947/48 (there was no Profits Tax or Salaries Tax before 1947) notional annual allowances must be deducted as if such allowances had been available throughout the whole period of ownership of the asset except that where use of the asset was prevented by enemy occupation (1941 to 1945) no notional allowances are to be deducted for the period of deprivation (Sec. 37(2) proviso (a)).

(2) Where an asset was used by the owner for other purposes prior to bringing it into use for the purpose of producing profits chargeable to Profits Tax, notional annual allowances must be deducted as if such allowances had been available since the owner's acquisition of the asset (Sec. 37(2A)).

There is no single rate of annual allowance prescribed by the IRO. The rates are to be as prescribed by the Board of Inland Revenue (Sec. 37(2)). The prescribed rates are laid down in Rule 2 of the IRR and the table is reproduced in Appendix 7. The Commissioner has power to allow a higher

rate than that prescribed by the Board of Inland Revenue but he would need
to be satisfied that this was justified by exceptional circumstances leading to
an unusually short life for the asset in question (Sec. 37(2) proviso (b)).

Example 8

Ben Dover has a toy manufacturing business in Hong Kong and in his
accounting year ended 31st December 1977 he bought a new plastic mould-
ing machine for $280,000. He was however unable to bring the machine into
use until July 1979. He also brought into his Hong Kong factory in
December 1977 a small computer which he had bought in 1975 for
$200,000 and which had been in use in his Taiwan factory.

Extracts from Ben's depreciation allowance schedules are as follows:—

	Plastic Moulder	Computer	Other Plant & Machinery (15%)	Total
Written Down Value 1.1.77			$630,000	
Acquisition	$280,000	$128,000(a)		
1977/78				
Initial Allowance (25%)	70,000	—	—	$ 70,000
	$210,000			
Annual Allowance	— (b)	25,600(c)	94,500	120,100
				$190,100
Written Down Value 1.1.78	210,000	102,400	535,500	
1978/79				
Annual Allowance	— (b)	25,600(c)	80,325	$105,925
Written Down Value 1.1.79	$210,000	$ 76,800	$455,175	
1979/80				
Annual Allowance	52,500(b)	19,200	68,277	$139,977
Written Down Value 1.1.80	$157,500	$ 57,600	$386,898	

Notes:—
(a) Because the computer has been previously used in circumstances not attracting
    depreciation allowances (used in trade outside Hong Kong) it must be notionally
    written down for earlier use as follows:—
    Cost 1975 $200,000

Notional allowance 1975/76 (20%)	40,000	
	$160,000	
Notional allowance 1976/77 (20%)	32,000	
Written Down Value at 1.1.77	$128,000	

There is no requirement to deduct a notional initial allowance.

(b)   No annual allowance can be given for 1977/78 and 1978/79 because the machine was not in use at 31st December 1977 and 1978. There is no requirement in these circumstances to deduct notional allowances.

(c)   The annual allowance for a computer was 20% up to 1977/78 and 25% thereafter. No initial allowance is available because the expenditure was incurred at a time when the asset did not qualify.

If a person acquires a trade, profession or business together with assets used therein, from another person other than by way of purchase e.g. by way of gift or succession on death, the predecessor cannot of course claim depreciation allowances because he no longer carries on the business and the successor would not have a starting figure for annual allowances but for Sec. 37(4) which provides that he continues to claim annual allowances based on the predecessor's written down values at the time of the handover, in other words he stands in the predecessor's shoes.

There are also special provisions relating to annual allowances in respect of an asset purchased under a hire purchase agreement. The aspects of what constitutes a hire purchase agreement have been considered under "Initial Allowance" in this chapter where it was seen that the initial allowance is spread over the period of purchase. There is no such spreading of the annual allowance which, provided the asset is in use at the end of the basis period, is available on the full cash cost (i.e. excluding interest) on the reducing balance basis as already described (Sec. 37A(2) and (3)).

Example 9

The same facts as in Example 7.

Nevanevva's full depreciation allowance schedule for the machine is as follows:−

	Cash Price June 1979	$240,000	
1979/80			
	Initial Allowance (Note (a))	17,500	$17,500
		$222,500	
	Annual Allowance		
	(Say 15%) (Note (b))	33,375	33,375
	Written down value at 1.1.80	189,125	$50,875

1980/81	Initial Allowance	42,000	42,000
		$147,125	
	Annual Allowance (20%)(Note (d))	29,425	29,425
	Written down value at 1.1.81	$117,700	$71,425
1981/82			
	Initial Allowance	17,500	17,500
		$100,200	
	Annual Allowance (20%)	20,040	20,040
	Written down value at 1.1.82	$ 80,160	$37,540

Notes:—

(a) For the calculation of the initial allowance see Example 7.

(b) For the purpose of the example the rate of annual allowance is assumed to be 15%. The actual rate would of course be governed by Rule 2 of the IRR or the Commissioner's power to agree a higher rate.

(c) Although the pooling provisions described on pages 201 to 208 in general apply to 1980/81 et seq., the pooling provisions do not apply to expenditure which is subject to a hire purchase agreement (see page 201).

(d) The 15% rate was increased to 20% from 1980/81.

BALANCING ALLOWANCE/CHARGE.   In order that the total depreciation allowances given to a claimant over his period of ownership of an asset can be related to the exhaustion of his qualifying expenditure, balancing allowances or charges are computed upon certain specified events occurring where an initial or an annual allowance has been given on the asset (Sec. 38(1)). The events are:—

(1) Where the machinery or plant is sold whether while still in use or not (Sec. 38(1)(a)).

(2) Where the machinery or plant is destroyed (Sec. 38(1)(b)).

(3) Where the machinery or plant is permanently put out of use (Sec. 38(1)(c)).

Where one of these events take place while the person is carrying on a trade profession or business or is coincident with him ceasing that trade, profession or business, an allowance or charge is computed and is allowed or assessed for the year of assessment in the basis period for which the event occurs.

Where the sales proceeds or other receipts upon disposal such as insurance or salvage receipts are either nil or are less than the unrelieved qualifying expenditure, the result is a balancing allowance equal to the difference. Where the receipts exceed the unrelieved qualifying expenditure, the result is of course a balancing charge equal to the difference. In the case where the starting cost is ascertained under Sec. 37(2A) in respect of an asset being used for other purposes before being brought into use to produce profits assessable to Profits Tax the ascertained starting cost and not the actual original cost represents the qualifying expenditure for the purpose of the allowance or charge. Also where annual allowances have been given to a successor to a business, other than by purchase, under Sec. 37(4), the inherited written down value is the qualifying expenditure for the purpose of the allowance or charge (Sec. 38(2) and (3)).

Where a person ceases to carry on a trade profession or business and a balancing allowance or charge arises as a result of machinery or plant being put out of use, the disposal receipts to be brought into account is the open market value which the Commissioner considers should be attached to the machinery or plant as at the date of cessation. If however the machinery or plant is sold within 12 months of the date of cessation, the taxpayer may claim to adjust the allowance or charge to the figure which would have been computed if the actual sale proceeds were substituted for the open market value. If the result necessitates a reduction to an assessment which has become final and conclusive, the assessor must make the reduction notwithstanding the provisions to the contrary in Sec. 70 (Sec. 38(4)).

A balancing charge must do no more than recover an initial allowance and annual allowances actually given, it is not a tax on a capital profit (Sec. 38(5)). In cases where the starting point for allowances is lower than the original cost, as already described this position is protected by the lower figure being treated as the qualifying expenditure for balancing charge purposes.

Example 10

Artie Vee inherited a printing business from his deceased father's estate together with the printing machine which had cost his father $350,000. At the date of his father's death, the written down value of the machine was $250,000. Artie used the machine in the business for two years, receiving annual allowances as follows:—

Inherited Cost (Sec. 37(4))	$250,000	
Annual Allowance 15%	37,500	$37,500
	$212,500	
Annual Allowance 15%	31,875	31,875
Written down value at date of sale	$180,625	$69,375

He then sells the machine for $300,000.
His balancing charge will be:—

Sale proceeds	$300,000

Unrelieved qualifying expenditure	180,625	
	$119,375	
But restricted to actual allowances given		$69,375

No part of the allowances claimed by his father can be recovered by the balancing charge. Had his father lived and continued the business, his balancing charge would have been $119,375.

Where a balancing charge arises in respect of the disposal of plant or machinery and that plant or machinery is replaced, tax on the balancing charge can be deferred by making an election to reduce the qualifying expenditure on the replacement asset and thereby reduce future initial and annual allowances (Sec. 39). The election must be made in writing and although no time limit for the election is given, this would have to be before an assessment incorporating the balancing charge became final and conclusive because there is no specific authority to re-open an assessment to admit the election and it is unlikely that failure to make an election could be construed as an error or mistake within the provisions of Sec. 70A (see Chapter 9).

The election is effected as follows:—

(1) Where the balancing charge exceeds the qualifying expenditure on the replacement asset, the following consequences ensue:—

    (i) The balancing charge is restricted to the difference between the original balancing charge and the replacement expenditure.

    (ii) No initial or annual allowances can be given on the replacement expenditure because it effectively becomes nil.

    (iii) When a balancing charge comes to be made on a disposal of the replacement asset, the amount of such charge is the smaller of the sales proceeds or the amount of the replacement expenditure.

Example 11

Assume in the facts in Example 10 that Artie had been able to buy another printing machine for $50,000.

If he made the election under Sec. 39, the following consequences would ensue:—

1) His balancing charge would be restricted to $69,375 − $50,000 = $19,375

2) He could claim no initial or annual allowances on the replacement machine.

3) If in due course he disposes of the replacement machine for, say, $30,000, he would have a balancing charge of $30,000. If he disposed of it for, say $60,000, he would have a balancing charge of

$50,000. In either case he could of course again elect under Sec. 39 if he replaced it again.

(2) Where the balancing charge is less than the qualifying expenditure on the replacement asset, the following circumstances ensue:—
   (i) The balancing charge is completely eliminated.
   (ii) The initial allowance and annual allowances on the replacement asset are to be given on expenditure equal to the difference between the actual qualifying expenditure and the eliminated balancing charge.
   (iii) In computing the balancing allowance or charge on disposal of the replacement asset, the initial allowance under (ii) is deemed to have been increased by the amount of the eliminated balancing charge.

Example 12

Assume in the facts in Example 10 that Artie had bought a replacement printing machine for $100,000.

If he made the election under Sec. 39, the following consequences would ensue:—
   1) His balancing charge would be reduced to nil
   2) Allowances on the replacement asset would proceed as follows:—

Cost	$100,000
Less Balancing charge	69,375
	$ 30,625
Initial Allowance (25%)	7,657
	$ 22,968
Annual Allowance (15%)	3,446
Written down value	$ 19,522 etc.

   3) If the machine is then sold for, say $50,000, the balancing charge calculation proceeds as follows:—

Sale Proceeds	$ 50,000
Written down value	19,522
Balancing charge	$ 30,478

Notes:—
(a) Ordinarily, the balancing charge would be limited to the allowances actually given, namely $11,103, but as the balancing charge of $69,375 which has been set off is deemed to be an initial allowance, the maximum balancing charge on disposal of the replacement is $80,478 and therefore the above calculation is correct.
(b) Artie could of course again elect under Sec. 39 if he replaced it again.

7.   Plant and Machinery Allowances from 1980/81

The "pooling" provisions were introduced with effect from the year of assessment 1980/81, largely to minimise the work and records required for computing balancing allowances and charges. The difference between these provisions and the earlier ones described in paragraph 6 primarily concerns the method of calculating the annual allowances and the substantial elimination of balancing allowances and charges except on certain specified occasions. As will be seen, the provisions involve aggregating single items of expenditure into classes or "pools" which expand and contract with additions and disposals. The computation of initial allowances is unchanged.

However, the pooling system does not apply automatically to all plant and machinery qualifying expenditure from 1980/81. The exceptions are:—

(1) In relation to any qualifying expenditure, the Commissioner can direct that the pre-pooling provisions shall apply if the operation of the pooling provisions would seem to him to be impracticable or inequitable. He can also direct for what period his direction is to apply (Sec. 36A(2)).

(2) Plant and machinery being acquired under a hire purchase agreement is subject to the pre-pooling method of computation (see page 192) until such time as title passes under the agreement to the purchaser, when the unrelieved expenditure is transferred to the pool (Sec. 39C(1)(a) and (2)). Title passes when the option to purchase is exercised, usually at the end of the period of the agreement, and the transfer of the unrelieved expenditure to the pool takes place in the year of assessment following the year of assessment in the basis period for which the transfer of title takes place. See page 193 as to the meaning of a hire purchase agreement.

(3) Where, because the whole of a person's profits or income are not assessable, the depreciation allowances are apportioned and Sec. 39A applies to the computation of residual value (see page 210); it would complicate the calculations if the expenditure was included in the pool. It is therefore excluded from the pool and allowances continue to be calculated under the pre-pooling method (Sec. 39C(2)). Where plant and machinery expenditure has been included in the pool and, during a basis period, is thereafter not used wholly for the purpose of earning assessable profits, the allowances thereafter will require apportionment and so the expenditure must then be excluded from the pool. Sec. 39C(3) requires that an amount equal to the estimated open market value of the relevant items of plant and machinery is to be deducted from the pool for the year of assessment for which the period in which the change of use takes place is the basis period and allowances for that year of assessment commence to be computed under the pre-pooling method.

Example 13

The facts are the same as in Examples 7 and 9. The option to purchase is exercised with the final instalment in May 1981.

Title therefore passes in May 1981 which is in the basis period for 1981/82. Therefore, up to and including 1981/82, the pre-pooling method as described in paragraph 6 continues to apply.

As from 1982/83 the unrelieved expenditure of $104,342 is transferred to and aggregated with the pool of expenditure attracting the 20% annual allowance.

Example 14

The facts are the same as in Example 8 except that on 30th June 1981 the nature of the business changed so that the assets were only used 75% for earning assessable profits. The estimated market values of the plant and machinery at that date were:−

Plastic Moulder	$125,000
Computer	$ 40,000
Other Plant etc.	$300,000

As the change takes place during the basis period for 1981/82, the annual allowances for 1981/82 are computed on the pre-pooling basis starting with the open market values as if they were the amounts of unrelieved expenditure brought forward.

For 1980/81, the unrelieved expenditure brought forward from 1979/80 would be aggregated into pools for each rate of allowance (i.e. a 30% pool and a 20% pool the 15% and 25% rates were increased to 20% and 30% respectively from 1980/81). In 1981/82 the pools would be reduced by the estimated market values.

The calculations would proceed as follows:−

1980/81	30% Pool	20% Pool	Total Allowance
Expenditure Brought Forward	$157,500	$386,898	
	57,600		
	$215,100		
Annual Allowance	64,530	77,379	$141,909
Pool Carried Forward	$150,570	$309,519	
1981/82			
Assets Excluded	165,000	300,000	
Reducing value	(14,430)	9,519 (Note (c))	($ 14,430)
Balancing charge	14,430		

	Plastic Moulder 30%	Computer 30%	Other Plant 20%	
Expenditure per				
Sec. 39C(3)	$125,000	$40,000	$300,000	
Annual Allowance	37,500	12,000	60,000	82,125 (75%)
Written Down Value				
at 1.1.82	$ 87,500	$28,000	$240,000	
				$ 67,695 (Note (c))

Notes:—
(a) For the computation of the pool and balancing charges and allowances see pages 203 to 208.
(b) No initial allowance arises in respect of the transfer from the pools to the pre-pooling system because no expenditure has been incurred in the basis period, Sec. 39C(3) only deems the reducing value of the expenditure to be equal to the market value figures.
(c) There is no provision for a balancing allowance in these circumstances. At the time of writing it is not clear whether annual allowances continue to be claimable on this amount of $28,864 and, if so, whether they have to be apportioned according to non assessable use. If the latter is correct it would of course defeat the point of transferring the expenditure of $300,000 to a computation on the pre-pooling system.

INITIAL ALLOWANCE. Under the the pooling system, the computation of the initial allowance in respect of expenditure incurred is identical to the pre-pooling system except that as from 1981/82 the rate is increased to 55%. See page 192 to 194 (Sec. 39B(1)).

ANNUAL ALLOWANCE. Whereas under the pre-pooling system, that applied in general up to and including 1979/80, annual allowances were computed on an item by item basis and ceased, with respect to any given asset, upon the disposal of that asset with accompanying balancing allowance or charge; under the pooling system annual allowances are computed in a single amount for all assets within a class and there is normally no balancing allowance or charge upon disposal.

The qualifications for annual allowance as regards basis periods and type of expenditure are identical to the pre-pooling system. However, the requirement to be in use at the end of the basis period for the purpose of the trade, profession or business is replaced by a requirement merely to have been in use at some time. This is to permit the fact that, following disposal of an asset, annual allowances continue to be claimed on the residue of expenditure left in the pool. The difference is that the allowance is granted in respect of each "class" of plant or machinery (Sec. 39B(2)). A "class" exists for assets of which the prescribed rate of depreciation is the same (Sec. 40(1)) and the rates are as prescribed by the Board of Inland Revenue and reproduced in Appendix 7 (Sec. 39B(3)). Therefore there is a maximum of three possible classes to accommodate the rates 10%, 20% and 30% and there could be additional classes to accommodate any other rate which may apply by virtue of the Commissioner's discretionary power to allow a higher rate than the 3 prescribed rates. Prior to 1980/81 there were 5 rates of allowance of 5%, 10%, 15%, 25% and 30%. For 1980/81 et. seq. they were increased, where necessary, to the next higher rate. Before exercising that discretion he would need to be satisfied that the higher rate was justified by exceptional circumstances leading to an unusually short life for the class of asset in question (Sec. 39B(11)). A "class" could of course comprise a single asset.

Having identified which assets fall into each class it is necessary to arrive at the reduving value of the class. Reducing value is as follows (Sec. 39B(4)): –

1) Capital expenditure incurred on the provision of the plant and machinery
   LESS: 2) Initial allowances given under either the pooling or pre-pooling systems.

   3) Annual allowances given under either the pooling or pre-pooling systems.

   4) Sale, insurance, salvage or compensation moneys received in respect of any plant or machinery in the class. Such amounts must, if necessary, be limited to the original qualifying expenditure in respect of that plant or machinery which was brought into the class (Sec. 39D(6) & (7)).

   5) The estimated open market value of assets which are to be excluded by virtue of not being wholly used for earning assessable profits but which were previously wholly used. See (3) on page 201.

   6) The written down value of any assets for which a balancing allowance or charge has been computed for 1979/80 or earlier (Sec. 39B(5)).

From a practical point of view the reducing value of each class for 1980/81 is created by classifying and aggregating written down values brought forward from 1979/80. This automatically takes care of 1), 2), 3) and 6) above and of course items within 5) will not be classified because the pre-pooling system will continue to apply to them. From then on additional qualifying expenditure, less initial allowances thereon, will be added and sales proceeds (limited where necessary) deducted. After such adjustments have been made for each year, the relevant percentage is applied to arrive at the annual allowance which is then deducted from the reducing value carried to the next year.

Where however an asset which has been owned for some time is suddenly brought into use for the purpose of earning assessable profits there will of course be no qualifying expenditure to bring into the reducing value. Instead, the original cost, less notional annual (not initial) allowances from the outset computed as if the asset had been in use, is added (Sec. 39B (6)).

If a person acquires a trade, profession or business together with assets used therein, from another person other than by way of purchase, e.g. by way of gift or succession on death, the successor of course has no qualifying expenditure to add to the reducing value of the class. Sec. 39B(7) provides that he is to bring in the predecessor's reducing value, i.e. he stands in the predecessor's shoes. The successor is not entitled to any initial allowance thereon (Sec. 39B(8)).

Although it is a statement of the obvious, if the various deductions from the reducing value have the effect of reducing this to nil or a negative figure, no annual allowance is given on that class for the year (Sec. 39B(9)). In fact, in this situation a balancing charge will arise. See page 207.

Example 15

Puh Ling Limited has carried on a manufacturing business for many years and the following are the written down values of its various assets under Plant & Machinery after 1979/80 depreciation allowances have been granted:—

Computer	Machinery & Moulds	Motors	Air Conditioning	Lifts	Office Machines, Fixtures etc.
(25%)	(25%)	(25%)	(10%)	(10%)	(15%)
$176,500	$319,862	$164,305	$78,262	$92,104	$37,677

During its accounting periods ending 31st December 1980 and 1981 it has the following transactions in its plant and machinery:—

31st December 1980
  Manufacturing machinery sold for $25,000 (cost $75,000)
  Bought Desks and Chairs for $15,000
  Transferred manufacturing machine from Taiwan factory
      (cost $120,000 in 1978)
  Photocopier sold for $35,000 (cost $30,000)

31st December 1981
  Transferred manufacturing machine to Taiwan factory
      (cost $100,000, market value $120,000)
  Sold motor vehicle for $20,000 (cost $40,000)
  Bought motor vehicle for $45,000

The depreciation allowances for 1980/81 et seq. proceed as follows:—

1980/81		30% Class	20% Class	10% Class	Allowances
Reducing Value					
brought forward		$660,667	$37,677	$170,366	
Additions:—					
Desk and Chairs	$15,000				
Initial Allowance					
35%	5,250	5,250		9,750	$ 5,250
Machine from Taiwan					
(note (a))		67,500			
Disposals:—					
Machine		(25,000)			
Photocopier (note (b))			(30,000)		
		703,167	17,427	170,366	
Annual Allowance		210,950	3,485	17,036	231,471
					$236,721
Reducing Value		$492,217	$13,942	$153,330	

1981/82		30% Class	20% Class	10% Class	Allowances
B/F		$492,217	$13,942	$153,330	
Additions:—					
Motor Vehicle	$45,000				
Initial Allowance					
55%	24,750	24,750	20,250		$ 24,750
Disposals:—					
Motor Vehicle		(20,000)			
Machine Transferred					
(note (c))		(120,000)			
		$372,467	$13,942	$153,330	
Annual Allowance		111,740	2,788	15,333	129,861
					$154,611
Reducing Value		$260,727	$11,154	$137,997	

Notes:—

(a) The cost of the machine previously used in circumstances not giving rise to assessable profits must be written down by notional allowances since acquisition (Sec. 39B(6)).

Cost in 1978	$120,000
1978/79 notional annual allowance (@ 25%)	30,000
	$ 90,000
1979/80 notional annual allowance (@ 25%)	22,500
Reducing Value	$ 67,500

No notional initial allowance is to be deducted.

No initial allowance is due for 1980/81.

(b) Sale proceeds of photocopier must be limited to original cost. (Sec. 39D(6)).

(c) Sec. 39C(3) requires the market value to be deducted from the pool with no restriction to cost as for sales. This is an anomaly.

BALANCING ALLOWANCE/CHARGE. It can be seen from the procedure whereby sale, insurance, salvage or compensation proceeds are merely deducted from the reducing value (or pool) brought forward that balancing allowances and charges do not normally arise under the pooling system.

However, a balancing charge can arise in two circumstances and a balancing allowance in only one circumstance.

A balancing charge arises when, at the end of a basis period for a year of assessment, the reducing value of a class of plant and machinery is a negative figure because the deductions from the pool for that period have exceeded the reducing value brought forward plus additions. The negative amount then becomes a balancing charge for the year of assessment related to the basis period and the reducing value carried forward becomes Nil (Sec. 39D(1)).

The occasion when both a balancing charge or a balancing allowance may arise is when a person ceases to carry on a trade, profession or business. At the end of the basis period in which the cessation takes place, the reducing value of each class of plant and machinery is reduced by the sale, insurance, salvage or compensation proceeds from the relevant assets and if there is a positive balance, this becomes a balancing allowance. If there is a negative balance, this becomes a balancing charge (Sec. 39D(2)). However, in arriving at a balancing charge, the amount of sale etc. proceeds deducted must not exceed the original qualifying expenditure in respect of that plant or machinery which was brought into the class (Sec. 39D(6) & (7)).

Where there are no sale etc. proceeds as a result of another person succeeding to the business by way of gift or on death of the owner, there is no balancing allowance or charge (Sec. 39D(3)). The successor inherits the reducing value (see page 205).

Where however there are no sale etc. proceeds but there is no succession to the business by another person, the Commissioner will estimate the open market value of the plant and machinery and deduct this from the relevant class as if it had been sale etc. proceeds received immediately prior to cessation. The balance of each class then becomes the subject of a balancing allowance or charge (Sec. 39D(4)). However, if there is an actual sale within twelve months of the date of cessation, the taxpayer can claim an adjustment to the balancing allowance or charge consequent upon substitution of the sale price for the estimated open market value and the assessment is adjusted, even if it had become final and conclusive (Sec. 39D(5)).

Example 16

The facts are as in Example 15. In the year ended 31st December 1982 there are no purchases of fixed assets and a photocopier is sold for $20,000, having cost $25,000 some years ago. On 10th April 1983 all of the remaining assets except the computer were sold and the business ceased. Sales proceeds were:—

Machinery and moulds	$140,000
Motors	$ 40,000
Air conditioning and Lifts	$100,000
Office machines etc.	$ 5,000

The computer which had an estimated open market value of $60,000 in April 1983 was sold in December 1983 for $50,000.

Depreciation Allowances are:—

	30% Class	20% Class	10% Class	Allowances
Reducing Value				
Brought Forward	$260,727	$11,154	$137,997	
1982/83	**30% Class**	**20% Class**	**10% Class**	**Allowances**
Disposal		20,000		
		(8,846)		
Balancing Charge		8,846		$ (8,846)
		Nil		
Annual Allowance	78,218		13,799	92,017
				$83,171
Reducing Value	$182,509	Nil	$124,198	
1983/84 (Final)				
Sales	180,000	5,000	100,000	
	$ 2,509	(5,000)	$ 24,198	
Market Value of Computer	60,000			
	(57,491)			
Balancing Charges	57,491	5,000		(62,491)
Balancing Allowance			(24,198)	24,198
				($38,293)

Note:—

The 1983/84 assessment being the cessation year is initially settled with a balancing charge of $38,293. When the computer is sold in December 1983 Puh Ling Limited can claim to adjust the assessment, even if it final and conclusive, by amending the balancing charge to $28,293 because of the substitution of sale proceeds of $50,000 for the estimated market value of $60,000.

8. Miscellaneous Points Relating to Depreciation Allowances

There are some provisions which are not related just to one class of depreciation allowances but which cover the application of depreciation allowances in general.

BASIS PERIODS. It is of course necessary to relate depreciation allowances to a year of assessment. This is achieved in the same way as profits or losses are related to a year of assessment in that events which govern the allowances (acquisition, disposal, use, etc.) give rise to adjustments for the year of assessment of which the period in which these events occur is the basis period.

However, this general rule cannot be applied where an event falls into a period which either falls out of account in computing profits or which forms the basis period or part of a basis period for more than one year of assessment. These situations can arise on commencement, cessation of business or change of accounting date (see paragraph 6 in Chapter 5). In these circumstances the rules in Sec. 40(1) are as follows:—

(1) Where 2 basis periods overlap, the period which is common to both is deemed to fall into the first basis period only.

(2) Where there is an interval between the end of a basis period for one year of assessment and the beginning of a basis period for the next year of assessment, the interval is deemed to fall into the second basis period.

Example 17

Because of a change of accounting date from 31st December to 30th June, a Company's Profits Tax assessments for 1979/80 and 1978/79 are based on the following basis periods:—

       1978/79   —   Year ended 31st December 1978

       1979/80   —   12 months to 30th June 1979.

The Company purchased a machine on 31st December 1978 and a lorry on 1st January, 1979.

As the period 1st July 1978 to 31st December, 1978 is common to both 1978/79 and 1979/80, this period is deemed to fall only into the basis period for 1978/79 for depreciation allowance purposes. Accordingly the machine purchased on 31st December 1978 qualifies for initial allowance for 1978/79 and for annual allowances for 1978/79 and 1979/80 but the lorry qualifies only for initial and annual allowances for 1979/80.

Example 18

A company, whose normal accounting date was 31st December and which had been in business for 20 years, ceased business on 15th June, 1978 as a result of which its final Profits Tax assessments were based on the following basis periods:—

| 1977/78 | — | Year ended 31st December 1977 |
| 1978/79 | — | Period 1st April 1978 to 15th June 1978 |

It sold one of its industrial/buildings on 1st January 1978 on which a large balancing allowance arises.

As the period 1st January 1978 to 31st March 1978 falls out of account and does not fall into the basis period for either year of assessment, it is deemed to fall only into the basis period for 1978/79 for depreciation allowance purposes. Accordingly the balancing allowance arising on the sale of the building will fall into 1978/79.

APPORTIONMENT.   When the whole of the profits of a business is not liable to Profits Tax it is necessary to appropriately apportion the expenses and outgoings (see "Apportionments" in Chapter 5). It is equally necessary to apportion depreciation allowances in the same circumstances and the authority for this is the use of the phrase "to the extent to which the relevant assets are used in the production of assessable profits" in Sec. 18F(1). Accordingly, the full depreciation allowances are computed and then apportioned to the amount allowable. It is specifically provided that the calculation is to be made in this way and not by computing a reduced initial and annual allowance before deducting it from the expenditure brought forward (Sec. 39A).

COMMISSIONER'S POWERS TO DETERMINE COST OR VALUE OF ASSET.   There are certain situations where the cost of an asset can be manipulated to obtain a tax advantage or where it is not possible to accurately determine the cost of a single asset. The IRO deals with these circumstances by giving the Commissioner power to determine the position.

Where an asset is acquired together with other assets as a bargain at a single price and it is necessary to determine the individual price of any one or more of these assets for the purpose of computing depreciation allowances, the Commissioner is empowered to allocate a price to each individual asset, having regard to all the circumstances of the transaction (Sec. 38A).

Where an asset which qualifies for depreciation allowances is sold and the purchaser and seller are persons under common control, if the Commissioner considers that the sale price does not represent a true market value at the date of sale, he has the power to substitute his determination of the true market value (Sec. 38B).

In each of these cases, as a matter of practice, the power is delegated to Assessors in the normal course of their duties.

Chapter 7
PERSONAL ASSESSMENT

1. Legislation

The law governing Personal Assessment is contained in Part VII of the IRO Secs. 41 to 43A. Also relevant are the assessing provisions in Part X and provisions covering returns and information in Part IX.

2. The Purpose of Personal Assessment

The taxation system in Hong Kong, unlike most Income Tax systems does not involve a computation of total income upon which tax is charged but consists of four separate taxes, Property Tax, Salaries Tax, Profits Tax and Interest Tax and each is separately assessed, independent of the others. Furthermore, only Salaries Tax carries an entitlement to deduct personal allowances and to be charged at progressive rates of tax; the other taxes are all charged at a fixed single rate of tax with no deductions for personal circumstances.

There are a number of circumstances where assessment under a total income computation would in fact produce a smaller overall tax liability than the separate combined taxes and the Personal Assessment provisions provide an opportunity for an individual to elect for total income assessment involving the personal allowances and progressive tax rates that otherwise apply only to Salaries Tax. In addition, Personal Assessment provides some other deductions that would not be available against any of the separate taxes and also allows business losses to be set against other sources of income. It does not however cause any sources of income to be taxed that would not be taxed under the separate taxes.

The following occasions would give cause to elect for Personal Assessment:—
(1) Having agreed losses for Profits Tax purposes and having a source or sources of income under Salaries Tax, Interest Tax or Property Tax;
(2) Having a source of income under Profits Tax, Interest Tax or Property Tax where the total income does not reach the breakeven point (for break-even point see page 69);

(3) Liable to Salaries Tax at a marginal rate which is lower than the standard rate and having a source of income liable to Profits Tax, Interest Tax or Property Tax;

(4) Having incurred certain interest payments for which a deduction would not otherwise be available; and/or

(5) Where charitable donations are limited to 10% of assessable income under Salaries Tax or Profits Tax and there is a source of income under Interest Tax or Property Tax.

Under each of these circumstances, the tax may be lessened by bringing all assessable income together in a single assessment attracting personal allowances and progressive rates of tax. The Personal Assessment provisions however contain a limitation by which the tax cannot be greater than would be the case under the separate heads bearing in mind that the progressive rates rise to 25% whereas the standard rate for individuals is only 15%.

3. Persons Who Qualify

An election can only be made by an individual who is either a permanent or temporary resident of Hong Kong (Sec. 41(1)). This is one of the few places in the IRO where residence status is significant. The terms permanent resident and temporary resident are defined in Sec. 41(4). "Permanent Resident" means an individual who ordinarily resides in Hong Kong. It does not however define what ordinarily resident means. For this it is probably necessary to look to U.K. case law wherein it will be found that it broadly means resident from year to year. It is then of course necessary to look further into U.K. law to find the meaning of resident where the rules are complicated. See for example Lysaght v CIR (13 TC 511) and Cooper v Cadwalader (5 TC 101). The following will normally establish residence, based on the U.K. law:—

(1) Where a residence is maintained in Hong Kong which is available as a place of abode, an individual is a permanent resident if he visits Hong Kong regularly from year to year and this will even apply to an isolated intervening year in which he does not visit Hong Kong so long as the place of abode is available to him.

(2) In the absence of an available place of abode, visits totalling 183 days or more in a tax year will make him resident for that year. As will be seen, this would in any event qualify him as a temporary resident. An intervening year in these circumstances in which there is no visit would however fail the residence test.

(3) Where there is no available place of abode but visits over a period are "habitual and substantial". Under U.K. law and practice this test is regarded as satisfied where, over a four year period, visits average 90 days per year.

Example 1

1) Barry Munday normally lives in Australia but he owns a flat in Hong Kong which he lets except for one room which is retained as a bed-sitting room for him to use on his visits to Hong Kong. He visits for about one month every year to attend to business matters.
Barry will qualify as a permanent resident.

2) Eileen Dover normally lives in the U.K. but made a number of visits to Hong Kong in the year ended 31st March 1977 totalling 190 days and returned again for a number of visits in the year ended 31st March 1979 totalling 185 days. She stayed in a hotel.
Under U.K. law, Eileen would qualify as resident but not ordinarily resident for 1976/77 and 1978/79. Presumably therefore she would not qualify as a permanent resident in Hong Kong but she would qualify as a temporary resident and could therefore elect for Personal Assessment for 1976/77 and 1978/79.

3) Horst Diel normally lives in Germany but visited Hong Kong in 1974/75, 1975/76, 1976/77 and 1977/78 for 110 days, 80 days, 92 days and 79 days respectively. He stayed in a hotel.
Horst's visits over the four years total 361 days and therefore average over 90 days per year. Under U.K. law and practice he would be regarded as a resident and ordinarily resident for 1978/79 (not for the earlier four years unless it was clear that it was his intention to make regular visits from the outset). Presumably therefore he could, by the same law, elect for Personal Assessment for 1978/79.

"Temporary Resident" means an individual who is in Hong Kong for a period or periods during the tax year amounting to more than 180 days or for more than 300 days over 2 consecutive years one of which is the year for which an election in sought. This is a clear definition involving no necessity to refer to case law. Eileen Dover in Example 1 would clearly qualify as a temporary resident for 1976/77 and 1978/79.

For the purposes of election for Personal Assessment an individual does not include a person under the age of 18 or a wife unless she is living apart from her husband (Sec. 41(4)). A "Wife living apart from her husband" is defined in Sec. 2 as one so living apart:—

(1) Under a Court order or decree;
(2) Under a deed of separation; or

(3) In circumstances which, in the Commissioner's opinion, is likely to be permanent. Intention not geographical separation is the test here.

The definition also applies to a wife who meets the permanent resident test in Sec. 41 and whose husband meets neither the permanent nor the temporary resident test in that Section.

Accordingly, where a wife is not living apart from her husband, only the residence status of the husband will qualify him (them) for Personal Assessment. Where an individual has died, his executor or administrator can make the election in respect of his income, assuming of course that the deceased's residence status so qualified (Sec. 41(2)).

There is a special provision in Sec. 41(2A) in respect of an individual (or his executor or administrator) who has elected for Personal Assessment for the year of assessment in which the death occurred and the individual was a partner in a partnership. If the individual had a share in the partnership profits or losses for a year of assessment following that in which the death occurred, the executor may claim to have his share of assessable profit or loss for that latter year brought back into the year of assessment in which the death occurred.

4. The Election

The election must be made in writing and must be received by the Inland Revenue Department not later than:—
(1) Two years after the end of the year of assessment in respect of which the election is to be made, or
(2) One month after any notice of assessment on any income which will fall into the total income election has become final and conclusive; (in other words within two months after the issue of an assessment against which no objection is registered or within one month after the settlement or withdrawal of any objection or appeal),
whichever is the later (Sec. 41(3)).

The election is in fact made on an official form and there is also a total income return form on which the relevant sources of income are reported. There is a space on the non-corporate Profits Tax return to indicate a desire to elect for Personal Assessment. There is no such similar provision on the Salaries Tax or Interest Tax returns and there is no return for Property Tax.

5. Computation of Total Income

The computation proceeds by aggregating assessable income from the various heads of charge, deducting from that aggregate certain interest payments which are not otherwise deductible and then deducting charitable donations and allowable losses under Profits Tax rules. The net result is the statutory "total income". This total income then figures in the assessment before deduction of allowances (see page 216). Throughout these calculations, income of an individual which is included is only that income to which he is beneficially entitled (Sec. 43A). This provision which was only introduced in 1980/81 is intended to ensure that an individual cannot bring in trust income of which he is trustee although such a specific provision seems hardly necessary both by common sense and law.

More specifically, the total income is the aggregate of the following:—

(1) That part of the net assessable value of property assessable to Property Tax which is equivalent to the portion of the property which is let having regard both to areas of the property let and periods for which let (Sec. 42(1)(a)). If the individual has been exempted from Property Tax because the rental income is brought into his Profits Tax assessment, the net assessable value is excluded from the total income.

(2) Income assessable to Salaries Tax less the expenses, depreciation allowances and charitable donations deductible in the Salaries Tax assessment under Sec. 12 and losses computed under Salaries Tax rules which are deductible under Sec. 12A (Sec. 42(1)(b)).

(3) Income assessable to Profits Tax (Sec. 42(1)(c)). This would be after the deduction of losses brought forward. This may be after deduction of charitable donations although it must be borne in mind that the same donations cannot be deducted both for Salaries Tax and for Profits Tax.

(4) Interest and the interest portion of an annuity received which is chargeable to Interest Tax (Sec. 42(1)(d)).

From the aggregate so obtained, the following are then deductible:—

I   Interest payable on money borrowed for the purpose of producing any of the income under (1) and (4) above so long as that interest has not already been deducted under one of the heads (1) to (4) (Sec. 42(1) proviso). This would particularly include interest on money borrowed to purchase, improve or repair let property which is not deductible for Property Tax, and interest on money borrowed to invest in securities giving rise to taxable interest income. Any money borrowed for a business subject to Profits Tax is likely to have already given rise to allowable interest which will not therefore be deductible again under this head. The total interest which is relievable under this heading is the aggregate of the income under heads (1) and (4) even if the interest was incurred in producing income under only one of those heads.

II The amount of the individual's loss or share of a loss for the year of assessment as computed for Profits Tax purposes (Sec. 42(2)(b)). If the amount of the loss exceeds the total income as computed in (1) to (4) above as reduced by any interest under I above and charitable contributions (see III below) the excess is carried forward to future years of assessment and set off against total income (Sec. 42(5)). Furthermore, the result of carrying forward such an excess to a subsequent year is that the individual is automatically deemed to have elected for Personal Assessment for that subsequent year (Sec. 42(6)). Although it may seem obvious, an individual cannot bring in losses incurred by a trust of which he is trustee (Sec. 43A).

III   Approved charitable donations, so far as they have not already been deducted against income liable to Salaries Tax included under (2) above or against income liable to Profits Tax under (3) above, payable by the individual or his wife (but not a wife living apart from her husband). The donations must aggregate to at least $100 (Sec. 42(2)(a) and (3)). The total of approved charitable donations deductible under this heading and under (2) and (3) above must not exceed 10% of the total income before such deductions but after deduction of any interest under I above (Sec. 42(4)).

In computing the total income of an individual who is a member of a partnership it is appropriate to bring into the computation his share of profits under (3) above and his share of losses under II above. However, if the partnership consists of more than 20 partners, none of the partners can bring his share of profits or losses into a total income computation (Sec. 42(8)). In counting the number of partners in a partnership, it is necessary to include every partner in a partnership which is a partner in the first mentioned partnership (Sec. 42(9)). This does not mean that such a partner cannot elect for Personal Assessment, it is merely that the results of a partnership consisting of more than 20 partners cannot be brought into the calculation, whether a profit or a loss.

Total income as computed here includes the income of a wife not living apart from her husband because it is deemed by Sec. 42A to be the income of the husband.

For an illustration of these principles see Example 3.

6.   Personal Allowances

In computing the charge to tax, personal allowances are deductible from the total income as computed in paragraph 5. The current available personal allowances are as follows: –

PERSONAL ALLOWANCE.   An allowance of $20,500 is available to every individual (Sec. 42B(1)(a)). If the individual is married to a wife at any time in the year of assessment, a further allowance of $20,500 is available

(Sec. 42B(1)(b)). There is no apportionment of the allowance in the years of marriage or death.

If the wife is living apart from the husband (see definition on pages 213 and 214), the further allowance can only be claimed if the husband is maintaining and supporting her (Sec. 42B(1)(b) proviso (i)). Whether or not he is maintaining and supporting her involves a consideration of her own sources of income as well as his contribution towards her maintenance. Where the allowance is granted by virtue of the husband's support and maintenance, the wife is not treated as a 'wife living apart from her husband' in the various places in the Inland Revenue Ordinance where this is mentioned. In other words her income is treated as that of her husband for Salaries Tax, Profits Tax and Personal Assessment and she cannot elect for Personal Assessment on her own account (Sec. 42B(1)(b) proviso (ii)). Because of this a husband may revoke his claim for the allowance at any time within the year of assessment or six years after the end of the year of assessment in which case the wife would be treated as 'living apart' thereby avoiding the aggregation of income (Sec. 42B(1)(b) proviso (iii)).

ADDITIONAL ALLOWANCE.   An individual who is not entitled to an allowance for a wife is entitled to an additional allowance of $7,500 from 1980/81 ($2,500 to 1979/80). Prior to 1979/80, because this was intended to benefit only those with small incomes it was progressively reduced as income increased. In a total income assessment under Personal Assessment it was reduced by a percentage of the amount by which the net total income (as computed on pages 214 to 216) exceeded $12,500 (Sec. 42B(1)(aa)). The percentage reduction was 10% for 1978/79 and 15% for 1976/77 and 1977/78.

In the case of an individual who is entitled to an allowance for a wife, the additional allowance is $15,000 from 1980/81 ($5,000 to 1979/80) and, prior to 1979/80, it was similarly reduced by the relevant percentage of the amount by which the net total income exceeded $25,000 (Sec. 42B(1)(bb)).

CHILD ALLOWANCE.   Allowances are available to an individual who has an unmarried child living within the year of assessment and maintained by him, so long as the child was either under 18 years of age or, if over 18, but under 25, was receiving full time education at a university, college, school or other similar educational establishment or is over 18 but unable to work because of physical or mental disability. The allowances are from 1981/82:—

$8,000 for the 1st child
$5,500 for the 2nd child
$3,000 for the 3rd child
$2,000 each for the 4th, 5th and 6th children
$1,000 each for the 7th, 8th and 9th children

Thus the maximum allowance is $25,500 (Sec. 42B(1)(c)). For the purposes of child allowance, "child" means:—

(1) The child of an individual by his wife or former wife;
(2) In the case of a woman, her own child;
(3) In the case of an Asian, a child by his concubine so long as it is recognized by him and his family as a member of his family;
(4) An adopted child; or
(5) A step child.   (Sec. 43A)

It is of course possible that 2 or more individuals may be entitled to claim for the same child for the same year of assessment. This is most likely to happen in the case of a separated husband and wife. In these circumstances, the Commissioner has the power to divide the allowance between those persons on such basis as he sees fit, having regard to the contributions to the maintenance and education of the child made by each individual (Sec. 42B(1)(c) proviso (ii)).

DEPENDENT PARENT. An allowance of $8,000 is available from 1981/82 to an individual if he, or his wife (so long as she is not treated as living apart from him) maintains a parent of his or his wife's. There are however a number of restrictions and qualifications which are precedent to obtaining the allowance.

Firstly, the parent must be:—
(1) A permanent resident of Hong Kong. Permanent resident is not defined and, although the definition in Sec. 41(4) only refers to the term permanent resident as used for the purposes of the election for Personal Assessment, it is likely that this definition would apply (see page 212); and
(2) Aged 60 or more or, if under 60, must be eligible to claim an allowance under the Government's Disability Allowance scheme.
                                    (Sec. 42B(1)(d))
Secondly, the parent can only be regarded as maintained if:—
(1) The parent resides with the claimant for at least a continuous period of 6 months in the year of assessment and not for a full valuable consideration; or
(2) The claimant or his wife contributes at least $1,200 in money towards the maintenance of the parent in the year of assessment.
                                    (Sec. 42B(2)(a))
Thirdly, a parent means:—
(1) A parent of a marriage which is recognised by the law in Hong Kong and of which the claimant or his wife is a child;
(2) A parent by whom the claimant or his wife was adopted in an adoption recognised by the law in Hong Kong;

(3) A step-parent;

(4) The natural mother of the claimant or his wife; or

(5) A parent of a deceased husband or wife of the claimant.

(Sec. 42B(2)(b))

The allowance can only be given to one person in respect of each parent and so there are provisions to deal with the position where more than one individual is entitled to claim or indeed has claimed. There is no question of apportionment as there is with child allowance.

Where more than one "individual" is entitled to claim, the Commissioner will not consider a claim until the individuals have agreed between themselves which of them will make the claim Sec. 42B(2A)(a)).

Where an allowance has already been granted to more than one individual for the same year of assessment or has been given to one individual and another individual claims in respect of the same parent within 6 months of the allowance having been granted to the first individual, the Commissioner has certain powers. He must invite the individuals who have already been granted the allowance plus those others who appear entitled to claim, to agree amongst themselves who will claim in which case the Commissioner is enpowered to raise any additional assessments to correct the position, subject to the statutory six year time limit in Sec. 60. If the individuals do not agree within a reasonable time, the Commissioner can raise additional assessments as he sees fit (Sec. 42B(2A)(b)).

Claims to these allowances must be made on the form specified by the Board of Inland Revenue and must contain whatever details or proof may be requested (Sec. 42B(3)).

7. The Charge to Tax

The objective of the Personal Assessment election is to bring together all sources of income subject to Hong Kong taxes, to deduct certain permissible deductions and personal allowances and then charge the remainder at the progressive rates of tax with the ultimate objective of achieving a smaller overall liability than the combined standard rate tax on each source. The assessment proceeds as follows:—

(1) Total income as reduced by certain interest, losses and charitable donations as per pages 214 to 216

less

(2) The personal allowances as per page 216

Charged at the following rates of tax:—

$10,000 @ 5%

10,000 @ 10%

10,000 @ 15%

10,000 @ 20%

Remainder @ 25%

(Sec. 43(1))

However, the tax so computed must not exceed the amount ascertained in (1) above charged at the standard rate (Sec. 43(1A)). All tax already paid under the separate heads, whether by deduction at source or by direct assessment is credited against the tax charged under the total income assessment (Sec. 43(2)). It is not always advantageous to elect for Personal Assessment even if there are deductions available for certain interest, losses and additional charitable donations, as is seen in the next Example.

Example 2

Dan Ger is a permanent resident of Hong Kong and has paid the following tax for 1981/82.

Property Tax on flat owned and wholly let	$110,000 @ 15% =	$16,500
Salaries Tax on wife's employment, Earnings	$ 65,000 Tax =	125
Interest Tax by deduction	$ 25,000 @ 15% =	3,750

He has an agreed loss in his business of $10,000 for 1981/82 and has made approved charitable donations of $7,000.

The Personal Assessment computation is as follows: –

Total income –	Property		$110,000
	Salary	$65,000	
Less Donations (10% maximum)		6,500	58,500
	Interest		25,000
			$193,500
	Loss	10,000	
	Donation (Balance)	500	10,500
Net Total Income			$183,000
Personal Allowances –	Self	$20,500	
	Wife	20,500	
	Additional	15,000	56,000
	Taxable		$127,000
Tax chargeable	10,000 @ 5%	$ 500	
(Sec. 43(1))	10,000 @ 10%	1,000	
	10,000 @ 15%	1,500	
	10,000 @ 20%	2,000	
	87,000 @ 25%	21,750	
		$26,750	. . . . (1)
(Sec. 43(1A))	183,000 @ 15%	$27,450	. . . . (2)

Notes:—
The tax chargeable under Personal Assessment is therefore $26,750 whereas, without election he pays only $20,375 therefore Dan would not elect or, if he did, the Inland Revenue would not raise a total income assessment.

The reason for this situation is that the earnings subject to Salaries Tax already attract the full personal allowances of $56,000, and charitable donations $6,500 and these are greater than the additional reliefs of loss $10,000 and charitable donations $500 available under the Sec. 43(1A) calculation.

Ironically, if the earnings subject to Salaries Tax had been, say, $195,000, they would not have attracted the personal allowances and tax chargeable under Sec. 43(1A) would have given a better result so that an election would be worth while.

Any Property Tax which is available for set-off against Profits Tax under Sec. 25, or would have been available for refund because of exemption under Sec. 5(3), or void relief under Sec. 7 but for the reasons laid down in Sec. 43(2A)(b) and (c), is to be set off against tax due on the total income assessment (Sec. 43(2A)). Any tax paid which exceeds the tax payable under the total income assessment is to be repaid (Sec. 43(3)).

Example 3

David Osborne had a number of sources of income liable to tax in Hong Kong. He owned a flat with a net assessable value of $60,000 of which 25% was used by him for storage purposes and the remaining 75% was fully let at a rental of $84,000 per annum. He had a mortgage used to buy the flat on which interest paid during 1981/82 was $40,000.

In 1981/82 he earned interest of $23,170 on a deposit with a Hong Kong finance company. His business in Hong Kong had resulted in an agreed loss of $16,000 for 1981/82. His wife is in employment and earned $65,000 in 1981/82.

He made donations to the Community Chest in 1981/82 of $10,000.

He had a child of 10 years old.

The following taxes were paid in 1981/82
— Property Tax	$ 9,000	
— Interest Tax	$ 2,317	
— Salaries Tax	$ Nil	(Note (e))
	$11,317	

Personal Assessment 1981/82

1)	Wife's Salary	$65,000		
	Less Donation (10% maximum)	6,500	$58,500	(Note (a))
2)	Let Property		45,000	(Note (b))
3)	Interest		23,170	
4)	Business Loss		(16,000)	
			$110,670	

Less Interest Paid		(30,000)	(Note (b))
		$ 80,670	
Less Donations (Balance)		2,217	(Note (c))
Net Total Income		$ 78,453	
Allowances			
– Self	$20,500		
– Wife	20,500		
– Additional	15,000		
– Child	8,000	64,000	
Taxable		$14,453	

10,000 @ 5% :	$ 500	
4,453 @ 10% :	445	
Tax Due	$ 945	(Note (d))
Tax Paid	11,317	
Refund Due	$10,372	

Notes:—

(a) Wife's salary is deemed to be Osborne's income and allowable donations under Sec. 12(1)(c) are limited to a maximum of 10% of salary.

(b) Only the let portion of a property is brought into the total income computation therefore 75% of the net assessable value is included although credit is given for the whole of the Property Tax paid. As the loan was used to buy the property, the interest paid can be said to earn the income so it is deductible but only to the extent of the income included i.e. only 75% of it. Note that the practice would be to permit a maximum deduction of interest paid of $68,170 ($45,000 Property plus $23,170 Interest) even though the loan did not produce the interest income.

(c) Only $6,500 of the donations could be allowed against the salary because of the 10% limitation in Sec. 12(1)(c). The maximum deduction of donations in the Personal Assessment is 10% of net total income before deduction of any donations i.e. 10% of $87,170 = $8,717. Of this, $6,500 has been given under Sec. 12(1)(c), therefore the balance of $2,217 is due against total income.

(d) The maximum tax, which is not applicable in this case, is the net total income charged at standard rate i.e. –
$78,453 @ 15% = $11,767

(e) The Salaries Tax paid is nil because the full allowances and part of the charitable donations have been taken into account as follows:—

Salary		$65,000	
Donations (10%)		6,500	
		$58,500	
Allowances – Self	$20,500		
– Wife	20,500		
– Additional	15,000		
– Child	8,000	64,000	
		Nil	

For further illustrations see Examples 5 and 6 in Chapter 1.

Chapter 8

RETURNS AND INFORMATION TO BE SUPPLIED, PENALTIES

1. Legislation

The law covering returns and information to be provided by taxpayers and others is contained in Part IX of the Inland Revenue Ordinance, Secs. 51 to 58. Penalties in respect of returns, information and other matters are covered by Part XIV Secs. 80 to 84.

2. Returns and Information

Most of the provisions in Part IX dealing with returns and information deal with returns and information in general in respect of all taxes covered by the IRO but there are also specific provisions in Part IX covering Salaries Tax and Profits Tax.

RETURNS — GENERAL. An assessor has the power to issue a return, as specified by the Board of Inland Revenue, to any person and to require him to complete and submit the return within a reasonable time as stated in the notice to him. He can also call upon such particulars to be reported, and in whatever form, as may be specified by the Board of Inland Revenue. This provision applies to returns in respect of each of the four income taxes and also total income returns by individuals who have elected for, or deemed to have elected for, Personal Assessment (Sec. 51(1)).

The form in which the return is to be made is already laid down by the Board of Inland Revenue and if a statement purporting to be a return is submitted which does not conform in every material particular with the required form it will be rejected and the taxpayer will be treated as if he had not made a return. See CIR v Mayland Woven Label Factory (HKTC 627).

In practice, one month is normally allowed for the submission of returns of income and, if such return has not been submitted by the due date specified on the return as per Sec. 51(1) it is in default when penalties become exigible unless the assessor has granted an extension which has the effect of deferring the statutory due date to the new date specified in the extension notice. In the case of Profits Tax returns there is an automatic extension arrangement available to tax representatives provided they submit suitably detailed lists of affected clients when invited to do so. These arrangements recognise the fact that it is not possible for accountants to audit and present all of their clients' accounts by the end of April each year and therefore the period of extension varies with the proximity of the accounting date to the following April. The automatic extensions are as follows:—

(1) Accounting periods ending in December — Extended to 31st July;
(2) Accounting periods ending between 1st January and 31st March — Extended to 31st October.

These can be further extended by individual application specifying good grounds but extension is entirely at the discretion of the assessor. Apart from these arrangements, Profits Tax returns must be submitted within one month of issue which is normally around 1st April following the year of assessment.

Salaries Tax returns may also have their one month time limit extended by specific application. There is however no automatic extension arrangement for Salaries Tax returns.

If the assessor is not satisfied with the extent of information contained in the return, even if it is properly completed within the specification, he can give notice by letter requiring fuller or further information within a reasonable time limit specified in the notice (Sec. 51(3)). There are penalties for failure to comply with this notice (see pages 232 to 235).

It is not sufficient excuse for failure to report taxable income that no return form was received from an assessor. Any person in receipt of taxable income is obliged to inform the Commissioner in writing that he has such income and such notification must be within four months after the end of the basis period for assessment of that income unless he has already received a specified return form when he must of course comply with the due date of that return (Sec. 51(2)).

Similarly, when a person ceases to carry on a trade, profession or business within the charge to Profits Tax or ceases to own a source of income chargeable to Salaries Tax, Profits Tax or Personal Assessment, he must so inform the Commissioner within one month (Sec. 51(6)). There is also a requirement to notify change of address within one month (Sec. 51(8)).

Any person who is chargeable to Salaries Tax, Profits Tax or Personal Assessment who is about to leave Hong Kong for a period which will exceed 1 month must inform the Commissioner in writing at least one month before departure of his expected date of departure and return. This does not however apply to an individual who must leave Hong Kong in the course of his business or employment (Sec. 51(7)). The purpose of this is to enable the Commissioner to protect the Revenue from any loss of tax which could result from the departure of an individual.

PERSONS RESPONSIBLE.   Where anything in the IRO requires a

return, statement or form to be submitted by a person and it is in fact submitted in a manner whereby it purports to have been submitted or authorised by that person, it is deemed to have been so submitted or authorised unless the contrary is proved (Sec. 51(5)).

If however the person who is required to perform any act under the IRO is incapacitated or is non-resident, the obligation falls upon the trustee of the incapacitated person or upon the Hong Kong agent of the non-resident person (Sec. 53). An agent for this purpose is defined by Sec. 2 as the agent attorney, factor, receiver or manager in Hong Kong or any person in Hong Kong through whom the non-resident receives any income or profits arising in Hong Kong.

Similarly, the obligations of a deceased person fall upon his executor who is also competent to be assessed to tax in respect of income accruing to the deceased before his death. However, no proceedings or penalty imposed under Part XIV or the IRO other than under Sec. 82A (see pages 235 to 237) can be imposed upon the executor in respect of any act of the deceased. Furthermore, the ability to raise an assessment in respect of income accrued prior to the date of death is restricted to a period of one year from the date of death or one year from the date of filing the Estate Duty Affidavit, whichever is the later (Sec. 54).

Where a partnership incurs an obligation under the IRO the person answerable is the precedent partner and as to which partner this is, is of course a question of fact. Any person who has received any notice addressed to him as precedent partner cannot deny that he is responsible unless he can prove that he is either not a partner or that another person is the precedent partner (Sec. 56(1)). Where persons are not in partnership but act jointly, they are jointly and severally responsible for obligations under the IRO (Sec. 56(2)).

Where a corporation incurs an obligation under the IRO, the person answerable can be the Secretary, a manager, director or liquidator of the corporation or, in the case of a body of persons, the principal officer. If there is no such person who is ordinarily resident in Hong Kong, the corporation or body of persons must inform the Commissioner of the name and address of an individual who is ordinarily resident in Hong Kong and who will be responsible for the obligations of the corporation or body of persons under the IRO (Sec. 57). If a corporation purports to submit a return which has been signed by an individual other than one authorised under Sec. 57, the return will be invalid.

RETURNS BY EMPLOYERS. Employers have a number of obligations under the IRO to report information about the commencement and cessation of employees and of their remuneration in order to ensure effective policing and collection of Salaries Tax.

When an employee commences employment in Hong Kong and is likely to be liable to Salaries Tax, the employer is obliged by Sec. 52(4) to report such commencement within 3 months giving the name and address of the individual, the date of commencement and the terms of his employment. Accordingly if an employer takes on an employee who will wholly work outside Hong Kong, he will not be liable to Salaries Tax and there will therefore be no obligation to report his commencement. Similarly there is an obligation to report the cessation of employment of an employee at least one month before the cessation (Sec. 52(5)). The Commissioner is however empowered to accept a shorter period of notice and this is to accommodate the position where the employer is not aware of the date of cessation at least one month before it occurs.

Furthermore, in addition to reporting the cessation of employment, the employer must report when an employee is about to leave Hong Kong for a period in excess of one month and he must report at least one month before the intended departure. This does not however apply to an employee who is required to travel outside Hong Kong frequently in the course of his employment (Sec. 52(6)). Where, as commonly occurs, the cessation of employment is also accompanied by the employee leaving Hong Kong, the employer can make a report on both events on a single form which the Inland Revenue Department supplies for the purpose.

There is also a further provision to protect the Revenue where an employee is about to leave Hong Kong and may owe some Salaries Tax. When an employer has reported the impending departure of an employee in accordance with Sec. 52(6) he must not pay to or on behalf of the employee any money or money's worth, without the Commissioner's written consent, within one month of having given the notice (Sec. 52(7)). This provision gives the employer a valid defence in any action brought by the employee against the employer for non payment. There is of course nothing to prevent the employer making the payment on the day before giving the notice under Sec. 52(6) provided such notice is given within the required time limit.

Apart from these returns giving the movement of employees, an employer is obliged to make a return at the end of the tax year giving details of taxable remuneration paid to each employee plus other specified details (Sec. 52(2)). It is not usually required to report details of employees earning less than $15,000 per annum unless they are in part time employment because a single person is exempt from Salaries Tax up to that amount.

For all of the above purposes, in order that there can be no doubt, Sec. 52(3) provides that a company director or individual engaged in the management of the company is to be regarded as an employee.

INFORMATION.   The IRD has wide powers to obtain information and as will be seen, it is not restricted to obtaining it from the taxpayer himself.

The main provisions are contained in Sec. 51(4) which is drawn in extremely broad terms in that it provides for the obtaining of full information from *any* person:—

> in respect of *any* matter
> which may affect *any* liability or obligation
> of *any* person

Where an assessor or an inspector believes that any person has possession of information that would be useful to the IRD, he can give him notice to report such information, within a reasonable time which must be stated in the notice, which may include not only reporting of facts or figures but also production of any relevant documents. A solicitor is not however required to produce the actual account which he has with a client of his, it is sufficient for him to produce a copy certified as correct by him (Sec. 51(4)(a)). This privilege does not extend to any other person, professional or otherwise.

Where the IRD requires a person to attend an interview at which such information will be sought the notice giving the time and place must be sent by an assistant commissioner if it is to be valid (Sec. 51(4)(b)). At such an interview, the person under examination must answer all questions truthfully and there are penalties if he fails to comply (see pages 232 to 235).

It is important to appreciate that the person receiving these notices may be the taxpayer where he has been slow in providing information and the Section provides a means of enforcing a reply within a specified period under threat of penalty, or it may commonly be any other person who knows something about a taxpayer which could affect his liabilities, responsibilities or obligations.

Sec. 51(4A) expands upon what persons can be called upon to provide information and also what information can be demanded from them. It also makes a further important point that the existence of privilege between the person under enquiry and the person from whom information about him is sought is not a valid defence except in the case of a solicitor or counsel in possession of privileged information which has been communicated to him in that capacity. In other words a solicitor can be forced to divulge information in his possession about a partner or a next door neighbour but not about a client. A bank cannot for example plead a bank secrecy agreement with customers when information is sought about a customer's bank account.

It should be noted that a fundamental feature of these provisions is that the person from whom the information is sought must be in possession of the information before he can be forced to make it available. This gives rise to considerable doubt and practical difficulties where for example information is sought from the Hong Kong branch of a bank with a head office elsewhere in respect of a customer's account with a branch outside Hong Kong. The Hong Kong branch manager is not personally in possession of the information but the bank, as a legal person, is in possession of the information although the bank staff who are actually in possession of the information concerning the account will probably plead secrecy regulations in their own country and that they are outside the jurisdiction of the IRO. For a discussion on what constitutes "possession" and the fact that it is not limited to physical possession see CIR v Mui Y.F. (HKTC 632).

The Commissioner can also call upon any Government employee or any employee of a public body to provide any information which is in his possession except that this does not apply if the person is under a statutory oath of secrecy (Sec. 52). There is no reciprocal obligation because Sec. 4 imposes a secrecy obligation upon employees of the IRD.

STATEMENT OF ASSETS AND LIABILITIES. Where the IRD suspects that a person has filed an incorrect return which has omitted or understated taxable income, one of the methods of detecting undisclosed sources of income is to prepare an annual statement of assets and liabilities when the increase in net assets over a given period should equal the income for that period less outgoings. The taxpayer can then be called upon to explain any discrepancy and, in the absence of a suitable explanation, may be assumed to have been in receipt of undisclosed taxable income (see Departmental Interpretation and Practice Notes No. 11 dealing with "Elements of a Tax Investigation" reproduced in Appendix 10). The IRD is therefore given power by Sec. 51A to demand from a person, a statement of assets and liabilities but the following constraints upon the Department's ability to demand such a statement apply:—

(1) The Commissioner or Deputy Commissioner must be personally of the opinion that the person has filed an incorrect return or other false information.

(2) The Commissioner or Deputy Commissioner must personally consider that the act was not the result of an innocent mistake and that the person does not have a reasonable excuse for it.

(3) The Commissioner must have the consent of the Board of Review (see comment below).

(4) The Commissioner must give written notice requiring the statement within the time stated in the notice which cannot be less than 30 days from the date of service of the notice.

(5) The notice cannot demand a statement in respect of any period earlier than 7 years before the commencement of the year of assessment in which the notice is given (Sec. 51A(2)). (See comment below.)

As regards point (3), there is a laid down procedure for application to the

Board of Review for such consent. The application must be addressed by the Commissioner to the Clerk to the Board in writing and be accompanied by details of why the Commissioner wishes to exercise his power (Sec. 51A(3)). A board of 3 members including a Chairman or Deputy Chairman (it is 4 members for a tax appeal, see Chapter 10) considers the application and the Commissioner, or his delegate, may attend but not the person under investigation or his representative (Sec. 51A(4) and (5)). The person under investigation does not of course know that such an application has taken place and indeed the name of the person concerned is not disclosed to the Board (Sec. 51A(6)). The Board will merely consider whether, on the facts, the Commissioner is entitled to hold the views in (1) and (2) above and their decision will be final (Sec. 51A(8)). The person who receives the notice can request the Commissioner to product a certificate from the Board of Review to the effect that the Board has given consent and in those circumstances, it is of course necessary for the Commissioner to disclose the person's name to the Board (Sec. 51A(7)).

As regards point (5) it is perhaps surprising that only 7 years information can be requested in view of the extended time limit by which an assessment can be raised in cases of fraud or wilful evasion (see Chapter 9). If for example, a notice is sent out in December 1979 it can only demand information back to 1st April 1972 which would enable assessments under Profits Tax or Salaries Tax to be raised for 1973/74 et seq. which is the normal 6 year time limit. However, in the case of fraud or wilful evasion, assessments for 1969/70 et seq. could be raised but the statement would not of course reveal the required information for the early assessment which would be required back to 1st April 1968.

The statement of assets and liabilities must reveal the following information (Sec. 51A(1)):—

(1) All assets in the person's possession in Hong Kong including the relevant proportion of those assets which are shared jointly or severally with some other person.

(2) All liabilities to which the person was subject in Hong Kong including the relevant proportion of those liabilities which are shared jointly or severally with some other person.

(3) All expenditure and disbursements out of funds in Hong Kong by the person. This will detect funds transferred out of Hong Kong.

(4) All sums whether by way of gift or remittance from overseas funds received in Hong Kong by the person.

SEARCH WARRANTS.   In the case of fraud or wilful evasion, a notice requiring a statement of assets and liabilities may not achieve the desired information particularly where there is a possibility that records will be removed, altered or even destroyed if the person under investigation becomes aware that an enquiry has commenced. For this and whatever other reason may be appropriate, the IRO gives the IRD the power of entry and search and the ability to take away relevant documents (Sec. 51B).

The powers can only be granted by a magistrate and only then if he is satisfied by a statement on oath from the Commissioner or other officer authorised in writing by the Commissioner, who is a Chief Assessor or higher, that:—

(1) There are reasonable grounds to suspect that the person has made an incorrect return or otherwise supplied false information so that his assessable income has been understated and that he does not have a reasonable excuse for his action and that it was not an innocent omission; or

(2) the person has failed to comply with a Court order to complete a tax return or provide the further information requested by an assessor under Sec. 51(3).

It will be noticed that the cause outlined in (1) is the same as that which gives the Commissioner power to demand a statement of assets and liabilities. He therefore has, in effect, an option in these cases, the exercising of which would be governed by his judgement as to whether the more usual course of demanding an assets statement would produce the desired result.

Once the warrant has been obtained, the Commissioner or his authorised officer may exercise the following powers:—

(1) Power of entry to any premises where it is suspected that there may be any books, records or other information which would be helpful in assessing the liability to tax of the person under investigation and to search for and then examine those books, records, etc.

(2) Power to take possession of and retain any books, records, etc. of the person under investigation and to make copies of any parts of books, records, etc. of any other person, so long as any such information may assist in assessing the liability to tax of the person under investigation.

In the case of any records retained for more than 14 days, the person may apply in writing to the Board of Review for an order for their return. Following hearing at which the person and the Commissioner may be represented, the Board may make any order, with or without condition, as they see fit.

In carrying out these powers, the Commissioner or authorised officer may enlist the assistance of any other IRD officer (Sec. 51B(1A)) but must produce his warrant to search if required to do so (Sec. 51B(2)).

The person whose books have been retained may examine them and take extracts is accordance with whatever conditions the Commissioner may attach to such rights (Sec. 51B(3)).

Although the power of entry is not confined to premises of the person under investigation, it is important to note that the right to take and retain books, records, etc. relates only to those of the person under investigation. Only copies may be taken of other person's property. In this connection it is interesting to note the U.K. proceedings in Commissioners of Inland Revenue v Rossminster Ltd. and Others (not yet published) wherein during the course of an authorised search by tax officials in the U.K. the amount of documents was so considerable that all was taken and it was discovered that the property taken included a child's school report. Upon application to the Courts, the Court of Appeal held that the search had been invalidly carried out and the whole of the property was ordered to be returned. The House of Lords however ultimately reversed the decision of the Court of Appeal but nevertheless the proceedings are of interest in considering how these powers of search and entry may be carried out.

The Commissioner is not required to give notice of his intention to enter and, in fact, this would of course not be in his interests to do so.

BUSINESS RECORDS.   There would of course be practical problems in enforcing most of the information and return provisions without some form of statutory obligation concerning the keeping of business records. This is contained in Sec. 51C and requires every person carrying on a trade profession or business to keep sufficient records, either in English or Chinese language, of his income and expenditure to enable his assessable profits to be readily ascertained. Furthermore, there is an obligation to retain such records for at least 7 years after the transactions to which they relate, subject only to the following exceptions:—

(1) When a corporation has been dissolved all records may be destroyed.
(2) Records may be destroyed in any other case where the Commissioner gives his consent.

3.   Service of Notices

In view of the fact that there are time limits within which returns and information must be provided and the fact that there are penalties for failure to comply, it is essential that the law be precise as to the form of notices and the manner of their delivery.

Every notice must bear the name of the Commissioner or other officer authorised by the IRO to deliver the notice and it is sufficient that his name be merely printed or stamped on the notice (Sec. 58(1)). A notice can be served personally or be sent by post to the person's last known address whether private or business address or to any address at which he was, during the year to which the notice relates, employed or carrying on business. However a notice of assessment, other than a Property Tax notice of assessment which follows the rules already described, must be served either personally or by registered post (Sec. 58(2)). Where a notice is sent by post, regardless of when it is actually received, it is deemed to have been received in the ordinary course of the post (Sec. 58(3)). However, it is difficult to predict what day that might be in view of the inconsistencies in delivery of post in different parts of Hong Kong. In the case of Charles C.Y. Cheng v CIR (HKTC 1087), the taxpayer claimed that a penalty assessment sent to his last known private address in Hong Kong should be invalid because he had told the assessor that he had intended to emigrate to the U.S.A. and had done so by the time the notices were delivered although he had not advised his actual change of address to the Commissioner. The court held that the notices were valid.

If the IRD is called upon to prove that a notice was posted within the requirements of the IRO it is sufficient to bring evidence that the notice was duly addressed and posted, it is not necessary to prove that it was delivered because of the presumption of delivery in Sec. 58(3) (Sec. 58(4)). It is important to realise however that the time limit for objection against a notice of assessment (see Chapter 10) is measured in relation to the date of the assessment, not the date on which it is received or deemed to be received.

Any time limit stated in a notice can be extended by the Commissioner or authorised officer at his discretion (Sec. 58(6)). This is normally done where a good reason is shown. This general power to extend however only applies to a time limit set by the IRD and stated in the notice. It does not apply to statutory time limits such as the time within which an objection against an assessment must be lodged.

4. Penalties

The sanctions for failure to observe obligations imposed by the IRO are primarily fiscal penalties but also involve Court orders to do things where there has been a failure to do so. The penalties for fraud are naturally more serious and can and do involve imprisonment. Where there is no question of fraud or wilful evasion, the IRO imposes penalties where some act has been done or, alternatively, has not been done and where there is no "reasonable excuse". There is not and could not be any statutory definition of "reasonable excuse" and this must be a fact which depends upon the circumstances of each case. The Hong Kong Courts have not had occasion to consider the meaning of "reasonable excuse" but reference to legal decisions in other countries as to what constitutes a reasonable course of conduct for various purposes adduces the fact that the person would have to show that he had acted reasonably and in good faith in doing what he did and that a reasonable man would regard this as an excuse consistent with a reasonable standard of conduct. In BR 80/76 an individual was held to have had a reasonable excuse for omitting a source of income from his return because he had been professionally advised that the income was not taxable although it subsequently proved to be taxable. It was however held in BR 7/79 that it was not a reasonable excuse for understating a personal Salaries Tax return to say that the amount in question was correctly reported in the employer's return.

OMISSIONS, FAILURE TO MAKE RETURNS ETC.   A person is guilty of an offence under Sec. 80(1) if, without reasonable excuse, he:—

(1)   Fails to supply the further information requested by an Assessor under Sec. 51(3);
(2)   Fails to supply a statement of assets and liabilities under Sec. 51 A;
(3)   Fails to supply information under Sec. 52(1);
(4)   Fails to supply an Employer's return of employees' remuneration under Sec. 52(2);
(5)   Fails to supply information under Sec. 64(2) in connection with an objection against an assessment;
(6)   Fails to attend following a summons under Sec. 64(2) to answer questions in connection with an objection against an assessment or attends but fails to answer questions;
(7)   Fails to attend following a summons under Sec. 68(6) to provide evidence at a hearing of the Board of Review or attends but fails to answer questions;
(8)   Is a corporation exempt from Property Tax and fails to notify change of ownership of property under Sec. 5(2)(c);
(9)   Is an owner occupier of property and fails to notify cessation of his occupation of property for which he has obtained exemption from Property Tax under Sec. 5(4);
(10) Is a payer of interest who has deducted Interest Tax and fails to supply a certificate under Sec. 29(2)(a) or (b);
(11) Fails to notify under Sec. 51(6) cessation of business or cessation of a source of income chargeable to Salaries Tax, Profits Tax or Personal Assessment;
(12) Is a person chargeable to Salaries Tax, Profits Tax or Personal Assessment and fails to notify departure from Hong Kong under Sec. 51(7) or change of address under Sec. 51(8);
(13) Fails to keep or retain proper business records under Sec. 51C;
(14) Is an employer who fails to notify the commencement of an employee under Sec. 52(4), cessation of an employee under Sec. 52(5) or departure of an employee from Hong Kong under Sec. 52(6) or fails to retain monies owing to the employee in accordance with Sec. 52(7); or
(15) Is a person receiving a notice under Sec. 76 to pay over to the Com-

missioner sums held to the credit of a tax defaulter and fails to notify inability to comply under Sec. 76(3).

Not all of these offences involves the person in the receipt of a notice before he commits a default. Every person should therefore be aware of his obligations without prompting and it is doubtful whether ignorance of the obligation comprises a "reasonable excuse".

In the case of the foregoing offences, the maximum fine is $2,000 but the Commissioner may, and commonly does, compound this penalty to a smaller figure (Sec. 80(5)). In addition to the fine, the matter may be put before the Court when the Court may order the person to do the thing which he has failed to do and may specify a time within which he must do it. If he further fails to do the act within the specified time he is subject to a further maximum fine of $5,000 (Sec. 80(2B)). A prosecution cannot however be brought without the sanction of the Commissioner (Sec. 84).

The position of a person who fails to supply information when requested under Sec. 51(4)(a) or to attend after receiving a summons to do so under Sec. 51(4)(b) or attends but fails to answer questions, is not dealt with under Sec. 80. However, similar provisions are contained in Sec. 51(4B) whereby, failing a reasonable excuse, the maximum fine is $2,000 and again, if brought before the Court, he may be ordered to provide the information. Note that these are civil and not criminal proceedings. There are also similar provisions to enable the Commissioner to compound the penalty.

All of the foregoing relate to the failure of a person to do some act although failure to submit a return of his income or notify liability to tax is not included. Sec. 80(2) deals with these and with the position where some incorrect statement has been made and the penalties in these cases are more serious. More specifically, where a person without reasonable excuse has committed any of the following acts, he is guilty of an offence under Sec. 80(2).

(1) Made an incorrect return by omitting or understating something.
(2) Made an incorrect statement when claiming a deduction or an allowance.
(3) Supplied incorrect information in respect of his own or any other person's tax liability.
(4) Failed to submit a return by the due date.
(5) Failed to notify the Commissioner under Sec. 51(2) of chargeability to tax.

In these cases, the penalty is a fine of $2,000 plus treble the amount of the tax that was either underpaid as a result of the omission, understatement or failure or would have been underpaid had the information been taken as correct or the offence been undetected. However, like the penalties under Sec. 80(1), the Commissioner can, and commonly does, compound the penalty to a smaller sum.

The authority of the Court may be invoked to enforce the failure under (4) and the Court may order the return to be submitted within whatever period may be ordered (Sec. 80(2A)). Failure to comply with an order of the Court to submit a return amounts to a further offence for which the fine is $5,000 (Sec. 80(2B)).

None of the foregoing penalties are limited to the person actually committing the offence. They equally apply to any other person who aids, abets or incites the person in committing the act and this can of course include professional advisers (Sec. 80(4)).

There is a time limit within which these penalties may be invoked and this is within six years after the end of the year of assessment for which the offence took place (Sec. 80(3)).

PENALTY ASSESSMENTS (ADDITIONAL TAX). For the five offences under Sec. 80(2), there is an alternative penalty under Sec. 82A which involves an assessment to so-called additional tax which is not however additional tax as it is normally understood but is merely a fiscal penalty imposed in addition to the actual tax liability (Sec. 82A(2)). The provisions of Sec. 82A are only applicable if the penalty provisions under Sec. 80(2) itself have not been imposed and the person has not been prosecuted for fraud or wilful evasion (see pages 237 to 238) and once an assessment has been made under Sec. 82A, the person cannot be further prosecuted under Secs. 80(2) or 82(1) for the same offence (Sec. 82A(7)).

The "additional tax" assessable is in fact merely a constituent of the penalty that would have been imposed under Sec. 80(2) in that it can be up to three times the amount of the tax that was either underpaid as a result of the omission, understatement or failure or would have been underpaid had the information been taken as correct or the offence been undetected (Sec. 82A(1)). There is no need for the Commissioner to have separate power to compound the penalty because the additional tax can be any figure which he chooses up to a maximum of three times the tax. The assessment must however be made by the Commissioner or the Deputy Commissioner personally (Sec. 82A(3)).

Before an assessment can be made, there is a specific procedure to be followed and this involves the sending of a notice by the Commissioner or the Deputy Commissioner personally to the person concerned. The notice must:—

(1) Specify the offence in respect of which the additional tax is to be assessed;
(2) Inform the person of his right to submit written representations; and
(3) Specify a date by which the representations must be received. This date must not be sooner than 21 days from the service of the notice (Sec.

82A(4)(a)).

The notice can only be dispensed with in limited circumstances and this is where the person concerned is about to leave Hong Kong. As delay may result in an inability to collect the tax, the Commissioner or Deputy Commissioner is empowered to issue an assessment immediately without inviting any representations (Sec. 82A(4A)).

Where however the notice is issued, the Commissioner or Deputy Commissioner will give due consideration to any representations made by the person, or on his behalf, before raising the assessment (Sec. 82A(4)(a)). Representations would normally give reasons why it was considered the person concerned had a reasonable excuse for the omission, understatement or failure or would otherwise admit culpability but request the Commissioner's clemency. His views on the representations made are reflected in the amount of the assessment that he finally issues.

The form and manner in which a notice under Sec. 82A(4) is issued must conform to the same rules as for any notice of assessment (see pages 244 to 245) (Sec. 82A(5)). An assessment to additional tax under Sec. 82A is still competent upon the executor of a deceased person (Sec. 82A(6)).

A person assessed to additional tax under Sec. 82A may appeal to the Board of Review against the assessment on any of the following grounds:–

(1) He has a reasonable excuse and is not therefore liable for additional tax. A discussion of what may constitute a reasonable excuse is contained on page 232.

(2) The additional tax exceeds the amount for which he is chargeable. In other words it is more than three times the amount of tax affected by the omission, understatement or failure. In this connection see CIR v Kwok Siu-Tong (HKTC 1012).

(3) Although the tax is validly chargeable, it is excessive having regard to the circumstances. The Board of Review would merely make an independent judgement of whether the amount of the tax is reasonable in the circumstances (see BR 23/75) (Sec. 82B(2)).

In the case of Charles C.Y. Cheng v CIR (HKTC 1087) the taxpayer appealed to the Board of Review on the ground that he had been prevented by duress from appealing against the original assessments on which the Sec. 82A assessments were based, the duress being that he was about to emigrate, had confided this to the assessor and did not want to delay his departure. The Sec. 82A assessments were reduced by the Board of Review but re-instated by the court.

It is also important to note that the charge can only be imposed upon a person which is specifically defined by Sec. 2 (see page 83). In BR 3/79, a Sec. 82A assessment had been raised upon the personal representative of a deceased's estate in respect of incorrect returns relating to the estate submitted by the personal representative. The assessment was held to be invalid because an estate cannot be a person but, in passing, that an assessment on the personal representative in a personal capacity would have been competent.

An appeal to the Board of Review must be made in writing within one month of the receipt of the notice of assessment and must include the following:—

(1) A copy of the notice of assessment;
(2) A statement of the grounds of appeal; and
(3) A copy of the notice issued by the Commissioner under Sec. 82A(4), if any, together with a copy of the representations submitted to him (Sec. 82B(1)).

Various but not all of the provisions applicable to appeals against assessments contained in Part XI of the IRO are applicable to an appeal against additional tax under Sec. 82A, particularly the right to take the appeal further to the High Court and beyond (Sec. 82B(3)).

FRAUD AND WILFUL EVASION.   This is of course the most severe of the penalty provisions and involves imprisonment in addition to the usual fines. The level of the fine and imprisonment which can be imposed depends upon the level at which the prosecution is brought. It must not be assumed that every detected case of fraud or wilful evasion brings imprisonment because, the Commissioner cannot impose a prison sentence and it is his decision whether or not to bring a case before the Courts because the IRO gives him specific power to compound any offence and settle for a monetary penalty (Sec. 82(2)). Many such cases are settled in this way. Of course, where the Commissioner has a doubt as to whether he could prove fraud or wilful default, he would opt for penalties under Sec. 82A or Sec. 80 as described on pages 232 to 235.

However, the serious provisions of Sec. 82 will apply to any person who commits any of the following acts with the deliberate objective of evading tax or assisting someone else to do so; again therefore it can apply to professional advisers:—

(1) An omission from a return.
(2) A false entry or statement in a return.
(3) A false statement in a claim for a deduction or allowance.
(4) Signing a statement or return without reasonable grounds to believe that it is true.
(5) A false reply to any question whether orally or in writing.
(6) Preparing, maintaining or authorising false books and records.
(7) Making use of or authorising any fraud, art or contrivance. This should not apply to contrived tax avoidance schemes which use legal loopholes

although the wording of Sec. 82(1)(g) must leave some doubt and certain other countries are known to treat such schemes as an offence subject to prosecution.

Any person caught by any of those provisions is guilty of a misdemeanour with the following maximum penalties:—

On summary conviction — Fine of $2,000.
                         — Additional fine of three times the tax which was or would have been underpaid.
                         — Imprisonment of 6 months.
On indictment   — Fine of $10,000.
                         — Additional fine of three times the tax which was or would have been underpaid.
                         — Imprisonment of 3 years.

No prosecution can be brought without this being at the instance or with the sanction of the Commissioner. Northing can however prevent the Attorney-General from bringing criminal prosecutions (Sec. 84).

An act of omission or understatement of a single item for one year would of course amount to more than one misdemeanour under Sec. 82 because the omission or understatement would amount to an offence under (1) or (2) and signing the return with the false entry in it would amount to an offence under (4). Also if it was a Profits Tax return prepared from falsified records, even though the return was in agreement with the records, the result would be a further offence under (6). The result could therefore be multiple fines and certainly so when more than one year is involved. However, it is usually the multiplicity of offences and the amount of tax involved that influences the Commissioner in his decision as to the level of prosecution or, if he decides to compound the offences, the extent of fine which he would impose.

See the Inland Revenue Department statement on "Elements of a Tax Investigation" reproduced in Appendix 10.

FAILURE TO DEDUCT OR PAY INTEREST TAX. An offence is committed by a person who pays interest which is subject to Interest Tax if he either:—

(1) Fails to deduct Interest Tax, either wholly or in part, without a reasonable excuse; or

(2) Fails to pay the tax to the Government within the 30 days prescribed under Sec. 29(1).

For the offence there is a maximum fine of $2,000 but the Commissioner has power to compound this to a smaller sum (Sec. 80A(1) and (4)).

In deciding whether there has been a failure to pay within the prescribed time, Interest Tax is deemed to have been deducted if an amount of interest has been paid which is subject to Interest Tax whether or not the tax was actually deducted (Sec. 80A(2)). However the Court will not convict an offender if he has ultimately paid the tax and can show that his failure to pay it within the prescribed 30 days was due to accident, illness or other cause beyond his control (Sec. 80A(3)). Presumably, if the Commissioner was aware of such circumstances he would not seek to penalise the offence in the first instance.

What is perhaps puzzling is how an offence under (1) above could ever arise if a payer is deemed, under Sec. 80A(2), to have deducted tax on every occasion where there is a payment of interest subject to Interest Tax.

MISCELLANEOUS.   All employees of the IRD, in fact anybody who has to perform duties under the IRO are subject to the secrecy provisions of Sec. 4 and in fact must sign an oath of secrecy under Sec. 4(2). Any such person who acts in contravention of those secrecy provisions or who aids, abets or incites any other person to do so is subject to a fine of $50,000 under Sec. 81. This cannot be compounded to any smaller sum.

Although the IRO may impose severe penalty provisions, including imprisonment, for tax offences, the imposition and suffering of such a penalty does not absolve the person from being assessed in respect of the tax in question which he must still pay as well as suffering the penalty (Sec. 83).

Chapter 9
ASSESSMENTS AND PAYMENT OF TAX

1. Legislation

As the provisions for the assessment and payment of tax affect all four income taxes, the legislation covering this is contained in various parts of the IRO. However, the legislation dealing with the matters specifically covered in this Chapter is contained in Part X in respect of the powers to assess and the form and validity of notices, in Part XII in respect of the payment of tax and enforcement of collection and Part XIII in respect of tax refunds. Provisional Salaries Tax and Provisional Profits Tax are covered in Parts XA and XB respectively but a discussion of the legislation in those Parts is dealt with in Chapters 3 and 5 respectively.

2. The Power to Assess

The power to raise assessments covers more than the obvious authority to raise assessments upon taxpayers but must deal with the timing of assessments, authority to estimate where necessary, special arrangements concerning persons who elect personal assessment and powers and time limits relating to additional assessments for prior years. All of these points are dealt with independently in the following pages.

GENERAL. There is a general power for an assessor to raise an assessment upon any person who, in his opinion, is liable to tax under the IRO. However, he cannot raise an assessment at any time, he is limited to raising an assessment only after the time limit for submitting a return for that year of assessment has expired. In other words he cannot raise an assessment for a year of assessment until a month after the issue of a return for that year or after the date to which the time limit may have been extended (see Chapter 8). However, in order to protect the IRD's ability to collect tax where a person is departing from Hong Kong, there is a power to assess at any time when a person is about to leave Hong Kong or when it is otherwise expedient to urgently raise an assessment such as in the case of impending liquidation or bankruptcy (Sec. 59(1)).

This power must not be confused with the powers to raise Provisional

Salaries Tax and Provisional Profits Tax assessments which must of course be raised long before a return is issued. The rules governing these Provisional assessments are dealt with in Chapters 3 and 5. Where a return is submitted and the assessor accepts the figure on the returns he merely raises an assessment accordingly (Sec. 59(2)(a)). Where he does not accept the figure reported or the return is not submitted by the due date, he has additional powers which are dealt with below.

ESTIMATED ASSESSMENTS.   There are three specific circumstances in which an assessor can raise an estimated assessment and, again, this should not be confused with Provisional Profits Tax or Provisional Salaries Tax assessments which are necessarily estimates. The difference between Provisional assessments and estimated final assessments are that the former are always adjusted to the final figure for the year when known whereas the latter can only be adjusted under the formal objection and appeal procedure (see Chapter 10).

The three specific circumstances under which the assessor may estimate the final assessment are:—

(1) Where he does not accept the figure reported on the return (Sec. 59(2)(b)). This may only be because he disagrees with an amount claimed as a deduction or with an amount treated as not taxable. In these circumstances his estimate will probably be the return figure plus the amount in dispute. There is nothing however to prevent him raising an estimate which has no bearing upon the returned figure and this is done in cases of fundamental disagreement.

(2) Where a return has not been submitted (Sec. 59(3)). Such an assessment is not valid if the return has been lodged with the IRD, even if it is overdue. This occasionally happens when an assessor raises an estimated assessment before he is aware that the return has been received by the Department. In these circumstances the assessment is cancelled and no formal objection is required.

(3) Where the accounts of a trade or business have not been kept in a satisfactory form so that the return is unreliable (Sec. 59(4)). In these cases, the estimate takes the form of the application of the usual rate of profit for that type of trade or business to the turnover for the relevant period. The Board of Inland Revenue is empowered to prescribe the usual rates of profit. Note that this provision does not seem to apply to the profits of a profession. However, it is understood that, in practice, Sec. 59(4) has never been invoked.

In each of these cases, the taxpayer is entitled to object against the assessments but in the case of assessments under (2) he has more difficulty in substantiating a valid objection because not only must he object within the prescribed time limit, he must also submit a valid return within the prescribed period (see Chapter 10). When assessments are made under any of these three provisions, the actual Section of the IRO under which it is raised is stated on the assessment otherwise the person assessed will not know what objection rights or obligations he has.

Except in the case of assessments under (1), which are based on the return figure, the estimates are necessarily arbitrary and considerable assessments may be raised where, in reality, there is a much smaller profit or indeed there may be a loss. Notwithstanding this fact, the estimate will become final and conclusive and the tax payable unless a valid objection is submitted.

PERSONAL ASSESSMENT. Because Property Tax and Profits Tax assessments are made at a fixed standard rate with no regard for personal allowances, an election for Personal Assessment may result in a total or partial refund. Accordingly, in order to limit the administration, the assessor is empowered to refrain from raising assessments in certain cases where an election for Personal Assessment would result in a total refund. If only a partial refund would be made then the full assessment is made and the refund procedure applied.

The specific cases identified are:—

(1) All Property Tax assessments where a Personal Assessment election would result in a total refund (Sec. 59(1A)).

(2) An individual eligible for Personal Assessment or his wife has income from a trade, profession or business carried on by him (her) as a sole proprietor of not more than $10,000 and neither he nor his wife have any other sources of income liable to tax under the IRO (Sec. 59(1B)). There would of course be a total refund because the profits would be covered by the personal allowance. In view of the additional allowance introduced in recent years this limit could be raised to $28,000 and for married persons could be $56,000 and even higher for those with children and/or dependent parents but these circumstances are covered by the next case.

(3) An individual eligible for Personal Assessment or his wife has income from a trade, profession or business either carried on solely or in partnership with other persons and has no other sources of income liable to tax under the IRO and the profits, or share of profits, are such that they would be covered by the allowances to which the individual would be entitled under Personal Assessment, and, furthermore, if the assessor has already raised an assessment on the individual or a partnership of which he is a partner, he is empowered to cancel the individual assessment or reduce the partnership assessment by the individual's share, notwithstanding that it may have become final and conclusive (Sec. 59(1C)).

ADDITIONAL ASSESSMENTS. Additional assessments comprise not only further assessments for a year for which a person has been under-assessed but also original assessments for a year for which no assessment has yet been raised.

The assessor is empowered to raise an additional assessment at any time within 6 years after the end of the year of assessment which he proposes to assess if he is of the opinion that a person has been underassessed for that year (Sec. 60(1)). In the case of fraud or wilful evasion the time limit for additional assessment is increased to 10 years after the end of the year of assessment (proviso (b) to Sec. 60(1)). There is no necessity for the additional assessment to be an accurate figure, it can, if necessary, be an estimate (Mok Tsze Fung v CIR (HKTC 166)).

Where the taxpayer has died, the time limit for additional assessment upon the executor in respect of periods up to the date of death is 1 year from the date of death or 1 year from the date of filing the Estate Duty affidavit, whichever is the later (Sec. 54).

Where a repayment of tax has been made and it appears to the assessor that the repayment was made as the result of a mistake in law or in fact, he may make an additional assessment within the 6 year time limit to correct the mistake (Sec. 60(2)). This power is however negated in two circumstances:—

(1) Where the repayment was made as a result of the determination of an assessment by objection or appeal (Sec. 60(2)).

(2) Where the repayment was made as a result of a practice generally prevailing at the time when the repayment was made (Sec. 60(3)). In other words if a subsequent legal decision changes, in favour of the IRD, what was generally thought to be the position previously, and a repayment had been made in an earlier year on that previous understanding, an additional assessment cannot be made on the basis of the subsequent legal decision.

Note that these two restrictions do not apply to the power to raise additional assessments in other than repayment cases.

The full rights of objection and appeal apply to all additional assessments (see Chapter 10).

3. Notices of Assessment

An assessment of course involves the sending of a notice to the person assessed and the form of such notice is laid down by the IRO. Every notice must separately state the amount assessed and the tax charged and must state the due date or dates of payment as fixed by the Commissioner (Sec. 62(1)).

If the law changes after an assessment has been validly made so as to affect the amount of tax charged in the assessment, the Commissioner can make the necessary amendments and send a notification to the person assessed in which case the notification is treated as a notice of assessment so far as the changed details are concerned (Sec. 62(3)). Therefore an objection can be given against the details in the notification as if it was an assessment.

Although an assessment may contain mistakes or omissions in describing the person assessed or other detail, this does not have the effect of rendering the assessment invalid so long as the assessment is clearly in accordance with the intent and meaning under which it was issued (Sec. 63).

The regulations governing delivery of notices of assessment are dealt with under "Service of Notices" on page 231.

4. Payment of Tax

Once the amount of tax has been fixed by an assessment, the Commissioner, in his complete discretion, decides upon the due date of payment. In the case of Provisional Salaries Tax and Provisional Profits Tax, in certain circumstances the tax is fixed to be paid in two instalments. Detailed comments on fixing of dates for payment of Provisional Tax are contained in Chapters 3 and 5.

When the due date has been fixed by the Commissioner and stated in the notice, it is accordingly due for payment on or before that date, subject to any agreed holdover or instalment payment plan, and if it is not so paid is deemed to be in default. The defaulter is the person named in the assessment, and, in the case of a partnership, each partner is a defaulter (Sec. 71(1)).

Where tax is in default, a surcharge is added to the tax and is then recoverable in the same way as the tax. Although a 5% surcharge is added, in fact any amount up to but not exceeding 5% can be charged (Sec. 71(5)). Furthermore, if tax remains in default for six months or more a further surcharge is added. Whilst again it is usual to charge the maximum of 10%, the surcharge can in fact be any amount not exceeding 10% of the tax in default plus any surcharge imposed for earlier default (Sec. 71(5A)).

Notwithstanding a due date stated on a notice of assessment, the Commissioner is empowered to accept payment by instalments (Sec. 71(6)). Payment by instalments is not granted unless the taxpayer can show hardship or other good reason why he could not pay on the specified due date. Furthermore, upon agreeing to payment by instalments, it is usual for the surcharge to be added.

There are provisions to enable tax in dispute in an assessment under objection or appeal to be held over pending determination of the objection or appeal. It is however entirely within the discretion of the Commissioner whether or not to hold over any of the tax, there is no automatic right of holdover with an objection or appeal (Sec. 71(2)). It is however usual for the IRD to grant a holdover except where:—

(1) The objection is considered to be of a frivolous nature or to have little merit; or

(2) Withholding collection of tax could cause difficulties in ultimately collecting any tax found to be due. This could be, for example, where an individual leaves Hong Kong before the objection is determined.

These policies are explained in Departmental Interpretation and Practice Notes No. 6 reproduced in Appendix 6.

Where the Commissioner has granted a holdover and subsequently, before determination of the objection or appeal, discovers that the tax is likely to become irrecoverable or that the person assessed is unreasonably delaying settlement of his objection or appeal, the Commissioner can rescind the holdover and make such other order as he sees fit (Sec. 71(3)).

If the Commissioner rescinds a holdover order or, if tax previously held over becomes payable, either in the same, a lesser or a greater amount, the Commissioner must send a notice specifying a new date of payment and any tax not paid by that date is deemed to be in default (Sec. 71(4)).

5. Recovery of Tax

Apart from surcharges which may be added to tax which is in default there must of course be statutory provisions to enable collection of tax to be enforced. In all of the enforcement provisions discussed in the following pages, the tax collectible includes the surcharges and also any fines, penalties, fees or costs incurred in enforcement (Sec. 72).

DISTRICT COURT PROCEDURE. The Commissioner can take action to recover tax in default through a civil debt action in the District Court (Sec. 75). Although there is normally a limit on the amounts which can be recovered in a District Court action, there is no such limit to an action by the Commissioner.

As evidence of the debt upon which the Court can give judgement it is sufficient authority for the Commissioner to sign a certificate giving the address of the defaulter and particulars of the tax which he owes. The taxpayer cannot plead that the tax is excessive because there are sufficient options open to him under the IRO, i.e. the objection and appeal procedure, and the Court is only concerned with the enforcement of debts not the accuracy of them. However, in the case of a penalty under Sec. 51(4B)(a) which is referred to the Court, because it is the Court's function to determine the quantum of penalties as opposed to debts, the Court may give judgement in a smaller amount.

Where the Court has given judgement on tax in default, collection of course proceeds in accordance with those avenues of the law which apply to the enforcement of judgement debts.

RECOVERY OF TAX FROM WIFE. If an individual has been charged to Salaries Tax in respect of income earned by his wife or has had his wife's income included in a total income assessment under the Personal Assessment procedure and the tax is in default, it, or a relevant proportion may be collected from the wife as if it had been her liability, notwithstanding that no assessment has been raised upon her (Sec. 75A). Where the tax in default relates to both income of the husband and the wife, the tax is apportioned in the same ratio as the income and the part attributable to the wife's income is collectible from her. If the wife has died, the tax is still collectible from her executor. Note that this provision is not applicable to Profits Tax assessed on a husband in respect of his wife's business.

COLLECTION FROM DEBTOR OF TAXPAYER. Where tax is in default or the taxpayer has left Hong Kong or is likely to leave Hong Kong without paying his tax, there is a procedure for recovering tax from any third party who:—
(1) owes or is about to pay money to the defaulter; or
(2) holds money for or on account of the defaulter; or
(3) holds money on account of some other person for payment to the defaulter; or
(4) has authority from some other person to pay money to the defaulter.

The Commissioner may commence recovery by issuing a notice to the third party, with a copy to the defaulter, requiring him to pay over to the IRD either the sum which he owes, holds, etc. or the amount of the tax in question if it is less (Sec. 76(1)). The requirement relates to all such monies in his possession or due from him at the date of the notice or at any time within 30 days after its issue.

Where a third party pays over such money to the IRD, he is indemnified by Sec. 76(2) in respect of any action brought by any person entitled to that money.

When a person receives such a notice he must either pay over the required sum or, if he is unable to comply with the notice because he is not holding or owing any money, he must notify the Commissioner of such inability in writing within 14 days after the expiry of the 30 days period from the date of the notice (Sec. 76(3)). If he fails to notify such inability there are penalty provisions under Sec. 80(1) (see Chapter 8). Alternatively, if he could have complied but failed to do so within 14 days after the 30 day period, he is personally liable for the tax which he should have paid and this may be recovered from him as if he was a tax defaulter (Sec. 76(4)).

These provisions most commonly apply to Salaries Tax when the notice is sent to the employer or ex employer. This ties in with the information provision in Sec. 52(6) under which an employer must notify when an employee is about to leave Hong Kong and with Sec. 52(7) under which after giving such notice the employer must retain mones due to an employee.

DETENTION OF DEFAULTERS LEAVING HONG KONG. Whilst there is no formal tax clearance procedure in Hong Kong there is nevertheless full authority for preventing defaulters from leaving. If the Commissioner has reason to believe that a person is likely to leave Hong Kong without paying his tax he can issue a certificate, containing details of the outstanding tax and his name and last known private or business address, to a District Judge. The District Judge will then direct the Commissioner of Police to take such action as is necessary, including force, to prevent the person leaving Hong Kong without paying the tax or providing security for payment (Sec. 77(1)).

The District Judge will inform the person owing the tax of this action at his last known private or business address (Sec. 77(2)). The person can renew his ability to leave Hong Kong by satisfying the Commissioner by paying the tax or providing security for payment. The Commissioner will then sign a certificate to this effect which will be the person's authority to leave (Sec. 77(3)).

If a person who has had such a 'stop' notice issued against him and who has been so informed, attempts to leave Hong Kong without paying the tax or providing security, he has committed an offence. For the offence he is subject to arrest by a police officer or immigration officer and liable to a fine of $2,000 and imprisonment for six months (Sec. 77(4)). No proceedings can be brought against any officials carrying out their duties under these provisions (Sec. 77(5)). The IRD should be alerted to a person leaving Hong Kong by the notification which an employer must send under Sec. 52(6) or which persons subject to Profits Tax or Personal Assessment must send under Sec. 51(7).

IMPOUNDING SHIPS OR AIRCRAFT. Apart from all of the other means of collection and enforcement, an owner or charterer of ships or aircraft who is in default in respect of his Profits Tax on the profits from the operating of such ships or aircraft is liable to have the ships or aircraft impounded by the Director of Marine or Director of Civil Aviation (Sec. 77A(1)). The Commissioner must obtain the approval of the Colonial

Secretary before he may issue the necessary certificates to the relevant authorities. The ships and aircraft of course remain impounded until the tax is paid or security for payment is furnished (Sec. 77A(2)). The fact that a ship or aircraft is detained against the owner's or charterer's will is not a valid defence against paying the harbour or airport dues. Furthermore, no action can be brought against any of the authorities for carrying out their duties under these provisions (Sec. 77A(3)).

6. Repayment of Tax

There are specific provisions in Sec. 79 to enable repayments of tax to be made where payment has been made in excess of the amount for which a person is properly chargeable. It is perhaps surprising that statutory authority should be needed because it ought to follow that any sum paid beyond the legal liability of the payer should rightfully be returned to the payer without specific authority. The Section does not operate to re-open assessments which are final and conclusive and in no way extends the time limits for objection or appeal (proviso to Sec. 79(1)). Accordingly, repayments will arise in the following cases:—

(1) Excessive payments made in error;
(2) Paid assessments validly reduced or cancelled either by objection or appeal or by statutory options or Personal Assessment;
(3) Assessments found to be invalid;
(4) Assessments re-opened by the error or omission procedure under Sec. 70A (see pages 250 to 251);
(5) Property Tax which is to be applied against Profits Tax liability (Sec. 25); and
(6) Interest Tax deducted from interest liable to Profits Tax (see pages 84 to 85).

The claim to repayment must be made within 6 years after the end of the year of assessment affected or within 6 months after the notice of assessment was served whichever is the later. In the case of a revised assessment issued following the settlement of an objection or appeal, the 6 month time limit would apply to the date of the service of the revised notice not of the original assessment. In the case of item (6), the claim must be made within 90 days of receipt of the certificate of deduction (see Chapter 4).

The same rights to repayment arise to an executor, trustee or receiver for the benefit of an incapacitated, deceased or bankrupt person (Sec. 79(2)).

If an assessment in respect of a non-resident person has been raised upon and paid by an agent, either the non-resident or the agent may claim the repayment and where the repayment has been made to the agent, the IRD is indemnified in respect of a claim by the non-resident (Sec. 79(3)).

7. Assessments Final and Conclusive

When considering the legal authorities for recovering tax assessed, it is essential to know when an assessment becomes final and conclusive and the tax thereby legally due, whether or not the assessment may be in accordance with the taxpayer's actual income. Sec. 70 determines when an assessment is final and conclusive and defines the circumstances as follows:—
(1) Where no valid objection or appeal has been lodged; or
(2) Where an objection or appeal has been withdrawn or an appeal has been dismissed; or
(3) Where an assessment under objection has been agreed; or
(4) Where an assessment is determined upon objection or appeal and no appeal or higher appeal is given.

The fact that an assessment is final and conclusive does not prevent an assessor from raising an additional assessment so long as it does not involve re-opening any question which has been determined on objection or appeal (proviso to Sec. 70).

A taxpayer cannot re-open a final and conclusive assessment except:—
(1) Where he has statutory options e.g. the right to amend the basis of assessment of a life insurance company to the actuarial basis; or
(2) When he makes an error or omission claim.

ERROR OR OMISSION CLAIM. An assessment which is otherwise final and conclusive can be re-opened within six years after the end of the year of assessment or within six months after the service of the notice of assessment, whichever is the later, if it can be shown that the assessment is excessive by virtue of:—
(1) An error or omission in a return or statement submitted; or
(2) An arithmetical error or omission in the calculation of the assessable profit or the tax charged (Sec. 70A(1)).

The assessment cannot be re-opened for an error or omission in a return or statement where that return or statement was made on the basis of a prevailing practice (proviso to Sec. 70A(1)). It is of course a question of fact as to what is a prevailing practice but where a legal decision is made in favour of a taxpayer it is not possible to apply that decision to re-open assessments which became final and conclusive prior to that decision because following the law as it was previously understood is a prevailing practice. The second area of claim mentioned above really provides for arithmetical errors or omissions by the assessor in transferring the figures from the return to the assessment which should of course be picked up in the time permitted for objection and settled by objection. The Sec. 70A procedure however allows for spotting assessor's mistakes, and correcting errors in one's return, after the objection time limit has expired. The typical errors which might be the subject of a claim are:—

(1) A taxpayer (or his representative):—

> Fails to exclude income which is not assessable;
>
> Fails to deduct a relief which is available;
>
> Mistakenly adds back an item which is deductible;
>
> Submits a computation on an incorrect basis; and
>
> Makes an arithmetical error in a return, schedule or computation.

(2) The assessor:—

> Makes an arithmetical error in adjusting the return or transmitting the figures to the assessment; and
>
> Mistakenly omits a deduction that has been claimed.

Where a claim has been made to reduce an assessment in accordance with Sec. 70A(1) and, for whatever reason, the assessor refuses to correct the assessment, he must send a written notice of refusal to the claimant who is then entitled to treat the notice as if it was a notice of assessment and accordingly the objection and appeal procedure is open to him (Sec. 70A(2)).

For the objection and appeal procedures see Chapter 10.

Note that Sec. 70A(1) does not apply if the assessor treats as taxable something which is not shown as taxable in the return or changes the basis of assessment or indeed does anything which does not amount to an omission or an arithmetical error. In all these circumstances the dispute must be the subject of the objection procedure (see Chapter 10).

Chapter 10

OBJECTIONS AND APPEALS

1. Legislation

The legislation covering objections and appeals is contained in Part XI of the IRO, Sections 64 to 69A.

2. Objections

An objection is the initial means by which a taxpayer statutorily disputes an assessment made upon him and the IRO lays down the strict form in which and the timing within which an objection must be made for it to be valid. Furthermore the IRO also lays down how an objection is to be determined.

THE FORM OF AN OBJECTION. To be valid, an objection against an assessment must satisfy the rules in Sec. 64(1) which are as follows:—

(1) It must be in writing addressed to the Commissioner. In practice, notices addressed to the Assessor are treated as satisfying this requirement.

(2) It must state precisely the grounds for the objection. It is insufficient merely to state that the assessment is disputed, the objection must state why.

(3) It must be received by the Commissioner within 1 month after the date of the notice of assessment. The Commissioner has discretionary power to extend the permitted period of 1 month in cases where he is satisfied that, because of absence from Hong Kong, or sickness, or other reasonable cause, the person submitting the objection was prevented from giving the notice within 1 month. This discretion is exercised only sparingly and not where the taxpayer has been ignorant of his rights, busy etc. In the case of Lam Ying Bor Investment Co. Ltd. v CIR (HKTC 1098), it was claimed on behalf of the company that the Commissioner should have exercised his discretion and accepted a late notice on the grounds that, of the three directors of the company who were responsible, one was sick, one was too old and the other was too busy. It was held that the Commissioner had not acted unreasonably.

(4) There is a further constraint in the case of estimated assessments made

under Sec. 59(3), i.e. estimated in the absence of a return. In these cases it is not sufficient just to object in accordance with (1), (2) and (3) that the "assessment is estimated and may prove to be excessive" (which is a satisfactory ground for an estimated assessment). For the objection to be validated, a valid return of income must be submitted within 1 month from the date of the notice of assessment or such extended period as the Commissioner in his absolute discretion may allow. It is not essential that the objection and the return be submitted together, it is usually desirable to submit the objection immediately and then to submit the return, if possible, within the required month or, if not possible, seek a reasonable extension of time to submit the return. It is essential to realise that, failing the causes mentioned in (3) it is not possible to extend the time for objection but, given a good reason, a reasonable extension for sub-mission of the return will usually be given. If however the return is not submitted by the time limit given, the objection is not valid and the estimated assessment becomes final and conclusive.

If the assessment comprises a re-assessment which either increases or reduces the person's liability to tax, and such a re-assessment would normally result from an objection against the original assessment, no new right of objection arises except in relation to any new or additional liability imposed by the re-assessment (proviso (c) to Sec. 64(1)).

Also, an objection against a total income assessment under the Personal Assessment procedure can only be against the composition of that assessment from agreed amounts of income under the four income taxes. It cannot have the effect of re-opening any existing assessment under any of the four income taxes which is already final and conclusive. The objection can however be effective in respect of the allocation to the individual of his share of the agreed profits of a partnership of which he is a partner (Sec. 64(7)). However, any objection by an individual involving the allocation of the profits of a partnership is treated as an objection by all of the partners so that they are all bound by its determination (Sec. 64(8)).

NEGOTIATION OF OBJECTION.   Upon receiving a valid objection the assessor will consider it and after receiving the answers to any further questions he may raise he may decrease, cancel or even increase the assess-ment assuming of course that the taxpayer agrees to the increase. This is strictly a function of the Commissioner but the Assessor has delegated power to make the adjustments. He may of course not agree to make any adjust-ment at all when either the objection is withdrawn by the person giving it or it proceeds to the Commissioner's determination.

In order to ensure progress of an objection the Commissioner is em-powered to give written notice of further information required including production of any relevant books or documents. He may also give notice to any person to attend and give oral evidence in connection with the objection. An authorised representative can of course act in supplying the information or attending the interview (Sec. 64(2)).

It is usual for the negotiation of an objection to proceed in the ordinary course of correspondence and for a revised assessment to be based upon an agreement reached between the assessor (delegated power) and the taxpayer. Upon the assessment being adjusted in accordance with the agreement it becomes final and conclusive (Sec. 64(3)). It is the exception for a formal notice to be issued for information under Sec. 64(2) but such a notice will contain a date by which the information is required and if that date is not met, a fine may result (see pages 232 to 235).

If the assessor does not agree to make any adjustment or does not agree to make the adjustments sought by the taxpayer, he will submit the case to the Commissioner for determination.

For the purposes of negotiating an objection, the Commissioner is granted certain of the powers under the Commissions of Inquiry Ordinance (Sec. 64(5)).

COMMISSIONER'S DETERMINATION.   When the assessor cannot reach agreement with the taxpayer or his representative on the determination of an objection the appeal must be formally determined by the Commissioner. In practice, determinations are made by the Commissioner, the Deputy Commissioner or by the Assistant Commissioner, Headquarters Unit in respect of Property Tax cases. The Commissioner can determine the assessment in any amount which he can justify but it will of course be an amount with which the taxpayer does not agree because otherwise the objection could be determined by agreement under Sec. 64(3). Once the Commissioner has made his determination he must, within 1 month, send a written notice of his determination to the person who lodged the objection and such notice must contain a statement of the facts upon which the determination is based and also the reasoning behind the determination (Sec. 64(4)).

In practice, the assessor will prepare the statement of facts beforehand and he usually sends them to the person who lodges the objection for his agreement or observations. Although the assessor has no statutory obligation to present the facts for prior agreement it is obviously in the interests of all parties to do so in the event of the case proceeding to hearing before the Board of Review because the statement is submitted to the Board of Review in an appeal. However the Commissioner does not regard himself as bound by the statement of facts submitted to him. He may exclude facts which he may deem to be irrelevant to the point at issue and may include facts which have emerged from correspondence which he considers should be included.

If the person does not appeal against the Commissioner's determination, the assessment as determined becomes final and conclusive.

3. Appeals

An appeal is different from an objection in that it is presented to an impartial arbitrator for determination. There are a number of levels of appeal beginning with a semi-formal hearing before the Board of Review and, if appealed further, proceeding through the High Court to the Privy Council.

BOARD OF REVIEW. If a person does not agree with the Commissioner's determination of his objection he has the right of appeal to the Board of Review.

To constitute a valid appeal, Sec. 66 lays down the following requirements:—

(1) Notice must be given to the Clerk to the Board of Review in writing by the taxpayer or his authorised representative.

(2) It must be within 1 month of the transmission to the taxpayer of the Commissioner's determination. The Board may extend the 1 month time limit to whatever period it considers fit in the event that the appellant was prevented by illness, absence from Hong Kong or other reasonable cause from giving the notice within 1 month (Sec. 66(1) and (1A)).

(3) It must be accompanied by a copy of the Commissioner's determination, the statement of facts upon which the determination is based and a statement of the grounds of appeal (Sec. 66(1)).

(4) A copy of the notice of appeal including the grounds of appeal must be sent to the Commissioner (Sec. 66(2)).

Whilst the grounds of appeal do not have to agree with the grounds for the original objection, no grounds can be relied upon at the Board's hearing of the appeal other than those contained in the notice of appeal, except with the specific consent of the Board (Sec. 66(3)).

The Board of Review is an independent body of persons appointed by the Governor and the constitution and powers of its members are laid down by Sec. 65. At a hearing of an appeal there are usually four members constituting the panel of which the chairman has legal training and experience. The other members of the panel may or may not have legal experience but, if not, will otherwise be members of the community selected for the experience and knowledge which they can bring to the panel.

The hearing of the appeal is an informal matter or at least lacks the strict formality of a Court hearing. The hearing is in private but selected cases are published for information purposes in a manner which does not reveal the identity of the appellant (Sec. 68(5)). Either the appellant in person or his authorised representative can, and commonly does, conduct his case although from time to time Counsel is briefed to conduct the hearing on behalf of the appellant. Also from time to time Counsel is briefed to conduct the Commissioner's case although it is more usual for an officer of the IRD to conduct the case.

Despite the lack of formality, Sec. 68 sets down a number of regulations concerning the hearing of appeals by the Board. First of all it is provided that, unless the appeal has been transferred for direct hearing by the High Court (see pages 259 to 261) the Clerk to the Board of Review is charged with the responsibility of fixing the time and place of the hearing as soon as possible and giving at least 14 days, notice to the appellant and the Commissioner. The hearing cannot be fixed however for a time before the expiry of the time limits within which the appeal can be set down for direct hearing by the High Court (Sec. 68(1)). In practice, the hearings are at the Board of Review offices and are usually held in the evening, the number of evenings depending upon the complexity of the case. There is also presently a considerable delay before cases are heard, due to the number of cases listed. The appellant can withdraw his appeal by notice in writing at any time before the hearing (Sec. 68(2A)).

The appellant or his authorised representative must attend the hearing in person (Sec. 68(2)) but if either fails to appear at the appointed time the Board have the option of:—

(1) Postponing or adjourning the hearing if they are satisfied that the absence is due to sickness or other reasonable cause; or
(2) Hearing the appeal; or
(3) Dismissing the appeal. (Sec. 68(2B))

If the appeal is dismissed, the appellant has the chance, within 30 days after the order, to request the Board of Review to reconsider their decision in the light of facts which he may bring to show that due to sickness or other reasonable cause an appearance was not possible. If satisfied they will amend their order and hear the appeal (Sec. 68(2C)).

The Board may, in any event, hear an appeal in the absence of the appellant upon the application of the appellant if he will be absent from Hong Kong when the appeal is to be heard (Sec. 68(2D)). In these circumstances the Board may consider the appellant's written submissions (Sec. 68(2E)). An officer of the IRD must attend the hearing and there is no provision for his absence (Sec. 68(3)).

At the hearing, the facts as contained in the Commissioner's statement of facts are accepted unless challenged by the appellant. Also any additional facts sought to be introduced will be accepted if such facts have been agreed between the Commissioner and the appellant but if not agreed will have to be proved by oral or documentary evidence (Sec. 68(7)). At the hearing, additional facts can be adduced by both the taxpayer and the Commissioner. In hearing evidence the Board has power to summon witnesses as necessary and pay their reasonable expenses (Sec. 68(6)). It is usual for the Board to hear the appellant's case first and then to allow the Commissioner's representative to question any witnesses brought by the appellant, then to hear the Commissioner's case, allowing the appellant or his representative to question any witnesses, and finally to permit the appellant's final comments.

Following the hearing the members of the Board will meet and reach their decision which will be to confirm, reduce, increase or cancel the assessment or they may remit the assessment back to the Commissioner to make whatever adjustments are necessary consequent upon their decision (Sec. 68(8)). If the assessment is not cancelled or reduced, the Board is empowered to impose costs of not more than $100 (Sec. 68(9)) but this is not commonly done. The intention of this provision is to deter vexatious or trivial appeals but is not an effective deterrent.

At the hearing of an appeal, Sec. 68(4) states that the onus is upon the appellant to prove that the assessment is excessive or incorrect. However there are a number of legal authorities which state that the appeal is to be determined upon the balance of probability and that there is no automatic assumption that the Commissioner is correct until proved otherwise. This view has also been reached in a number of decisions of the Board of Review, see for example the comments in BR 20/71.

The decision together with the reasons therefor is notified later to the appellant in writing, his authorised representative if there is one, and the Commissioner. The chairman usually prepares the written determination and therefore the delay between the hearing and the written determination depends upon how busy the chairman is.

Penalty assessments under Sec. 82A are also subject to the appeal procedure (see Chapter 8). As such assessments have to be made by the Commissioner or the Deputy Commissioner personally, disputes proceed direct to the Board of Review because the objection procedure would be a mere formality.

The loser, whether it be the appellant or the Commissioner is entitled to address an appeal to the High Court but, in the absence of such further appeal, the assessment becomes final and conclusive in accordance with the Board's decision.

HIGH COURT.   If either the appellant or the Commissioner disagrees with the decision of the Board of Review he may apply in writing to the Clerk to the Board requiring the Board to state a case for the opinion of the High Court. The application must be made within 1 month of the date on which the Board's determination is notified to him and be accompanied by a fee of $50 (Sec. 69(1)). The opinion of the High Court can only be obtained on a point of law as the Board of Review is the last arbiter on questions of fact. See page 18 of the judgement in CIR v Karsten Larssen & Co. (HK) Ltd. (HKTC 11) for a discussion on the question of the difference between a point of law and fact.

The stated case must contain the facts upon which the Board reached their decision and the decision and reasons therefor. The person requiring the case must transmit it to the High Court within 14 days of receiving it (Sec. 69(2)). Furthermore, he must send a copy to the other party at or before the time of transmitting it to the High Court and must notify the other party that it was obtained upon his application (Sec. 69(3)).

Upon receipt by the High Court, any judge may return the stated case for amendment (Sec. 69(4)). Otherwise a judge of the High Court hears the case in accordance with the formalities applicable to Court hearings and reaches a decision on a point of law which may result in an increase or reduction or cancellation of the assessment. Alternatively the judge may remit the assessment back to the Board of Review to make whatever factual adjustments may be necessary consequent upon his opinion (Sec. 69(5)).

The Court may also make any order which it sees fit in connection with the costs of the case and the $50 fee paid to the Clerk to the Board (Sec. 69(6)). If the loser disagrees with the decision he may appeal to the Court of Appeal and then to the Privy Council subject to the Supreme Court Ordinance, the Rules of the Supreme Court and the Orders and Rules governing appeals to the Privy Council (Sec. 69(7)).

The cost of a Court hearing is inevitably high because of the necessity to employ legal representatives and this plus the thought that the Commissioner's costs may have to be borne by the taxpayer if he loses the case are a sufficient deterrent to most taxpayers from taking their case beyond the Board of Review.

DIRECT APPEAL TO COURT OF APPEAL.   Where a case has been determined by the Board of Review, either the appellant or the Commissioner may appeal direct to the Court of Appeal, thereby by-passing the High Court, provided that the Court of Appeal grants leave for such an application (Sec. 69A(1)). The Court of Appeal will take into account whether such a short cut is desirable by virtue of a substantial amount of tax being involved, or that the point at issue is a matter of public importance or is of a complex nature or for some other good reason (Sec. 69A(2)).

The procedure for submitting a case direct to the Court of Appeal is identical to that for a case submitted to the High Court except of course that where action is required by a judge, the reference is to a judge of the Court of Appeal (Sec. 69A(3)). Obviously, if the matter is of such importance that the loser would appeal from the High Court to the Court of Appeal, it makes sense from a cost and timing point of view to cut out the High Court. This provision was however not introduced until 1979.

DIRECT APPEAL TO HIGH COURT.   There are provisions whereby the Board of Review procedure can be by-passed and the Commissioner's determination of an objection submitted directly for the opinion of the High

Court. This would not of course be a cost-saving measure but where a point of considerable importance is at issue it is obviously desirable to obtain a Court opinion as soon as possible and the provisions of Sec. 67 therefore provide the opportunity. However, more to protect the taxpayer than the Commissioner, a case cannot be referred direct to the High Court by either party without the consent of the other party. This is because the case may not have proceeded further than the Board of Review and therefore reference directly to the Court introduces a substantial cost element.

The procedure can only be commenced after a notice of appeal has been given to the Board of Review. Within 21 days after the date that the notice of appeal has been received by the Clerk to the Board of Review, either the appellant or the Commissioner can give notice in writing to the other party that he desires to transfer the appeal to the High Court. At the same time he must copy the notice to the Board of Review (Sec. 67(1) & (2)).

If the party who receives the notice agrees to it, he must give his consent in writing to the Board of Review within 21 days of receiving the notice and send a copy of his consent to the other party. Obviously, if the party receiving the notice does not reply, the consent is not given and the appeal is not therefore transmitted to the High Court. Upon receipt of a notice of consent the Clerk to the Board of Review transmits the appeal to the High Court together with all documents submitted to the Board with the appeal (Sec. 67(3)). So far as the Court is concerned the case is then heard and determined in the same way as an appeal from a determination of the Board of Review (Sec. 67(4)). The difference however is that the Court becomes the fact finding body as well as giving an opinion on points of law. The matter could in fact be entirely factual with no point of law involved at all. Also, unlike an appeal to the Board of Review, once referred to the High Court, there is no automatic right of withdrawal of the appeal before the hearing, this can only be done with specific consent of the Court and subject to such costs as the Court may determine (Sec. 67(6)).

The following further rules apply to the appeal (Sec. 67(5)):–

(1) The Court must give at least 14 days' notice to the parties of the date of the hearing, and may adjourn the hearing.

(2) The Commissioner is entitled to be heard at the hearing.

(3) As in an appeal to the Board of Review, the appellant cannot rely upon any grounds of appeal other than those contained in the notice of appeal, except with the leave of, and subject to the conditions of the Court.

(4) It is stated that the onus is upon the taxpayer to prove that the assessment is excessive or incorrect. However, there is authority in numerous U.K. cases, where there is a similar provision, for the view that the appeal is to be determined upon the balance of probability and that there is no automatic acceptance of the Commissioner's assessment until proved wrong.

(5) The Court may summon and examine any relevant witnesses.

In determining the appeal the Court can increase, reduce or cancel the assessment or remit the case to the Commissioner to make appropriate adjustments. Also the Court can make whatever order as regards costs which it sees fit (Sec. 67(7)).

See also Departmental Interpretation and Practice Notes No. 6 reproduced in Appendix 6.

Chapter 11
MISCELLANEOUS MATTERS

1. Double Taxation Relief

GENERAL. Double taxation arises where the taxation jurisdictions of two or more countries overlap and the same item of income or profit is subjected to tax in each country. The amount of the income or profit chargeable to tax in each country may be different and the rates of tax and basis of assessment may be different but nevertheless double taxation occurs. Some relief is usually given by one or more of the following means:—

(1) By exemption in one country where the income is taxed in another country.
(2) By allowing foreign tax to be deducted as an expense by the home country.
(3) By unilateral tax credit relief (i.e. allowing a measure of foreign tax to be actually deducted from the home country tax).
(4) By tax credit and/or other arrangements under Double Taxation Treaties.

In order to limit the possibility of, or complications of, relief arising in each country it is quite common for the relief to be limited to the country in which the person is resident although the definition of resident varies from country to country. Double Taxation Treaties always obviate these problems by specific provisions.

Hong Kong is in a special position in that by virtue of the principle whereby only Hong Kong source income is subject to tax, there is not normally any necessity to consider double taxation, for example if a Hong Kong company has a branch in the U.K. or U.S.A., the profits of that branch will be subject to U.K. or U.S. tax but not Hong Kong tax therefore, in fact, relief by (1) above applies in Hong Kong but being taxed in another country is not essential to freedom from Hong Kong tax. If a company with a head office elsewhere has a branch in Hong Kong which is subject to Profits Tax and is also subject to tax in the country of the head office it is up to that other country to consider what relief to give for the Profits Tax paid.

However double taxation does occur in Hong Kong where Hong Kong source rules conflict with other tax jurisdictions. When this occurs the amount of relief available in Hong Kong is very limited and, in many cases, no relief is available at all.

Generally, relief is not available as an expense as indicated in (2) above and in fact it is available in Hong Kong in only one specific case and that is where a "financial institution" is charged to Profits Tax on interest derived from an offshore source (see pages 156 to 159). Because the interest in these cases would be likely to have suffered a withholding tax elsewhere, taxing it in Hong Kong without recognition of this in some way would be anomalous and therefore Sec. 16(1)(c) was introduced to allow the foreign tax which had been suffered by deduction or otherwise to be deducted as an expense against the taxable income. It is not allowed as a tax credit. Furthermore the relief is limited to financial institutions which are managed and controlled in Hong Kong (effectively the residence test). A Hong Kong branch of a financial institution with a head office elsewhere therefore cannot claim the relief but in those circumstances it would be usual for relief to be given for the Profits Tax against tax charged by the country of the head office. Also, relief is not available as an expense if relief is available under the relief provisions for Commonwealth income tax which are the only provisions under which a limited measure of tax credit relief is available (see below).

Hong Kong has not entered into any Double Taxation Treaties with other countries although the IRD contains full powers in Sec. 49 for the Governor in Council to enter into such agreements. In the event that an agreement was entered into, the detailed provisions for granting tax credits in accordance with such agreements are contained in Sec. 50. Until such time, Sec. 50 is ineffective. If ever such a Treaty is signed and Sec. 50 becomes applicable in respect of tax paid in another country, the Commonwealth income tax relief available under Sec. 45 will not be available in respect of the same tax. Similarly, relief by deduction as an expense under Sec. 16(1)(c) would also not be available (Sec. 49(3)).

Claiming double taxation relief often involves obtaining detailed information from the country imposing the tax. The Hong Kong IRD could not disclose any information to authorities of other countries because of the secrecy provisions in Sec. 4. However, notwithstanding Sec. 4, it is provided that in order that relief can be properly claimed under the IRO or under the law in another Commonwealth country in respect of tax paid under the IRO, the IRD can disclose relevant information to properly authorised officers of the Government of that Commonwealth country (Sec. 46). Wider powers to disclose information to other countries under a Double Taxation Treaty with that country are contained in Sec. 49(5) but these are of course presently ineffective.

COMMONWEALTH INCOME TAX RELIEF.   Relief is available where tax is payable under any of the four income taxes covered by the IRO and Commonwealth income tax has been paid, by deduction or otherwise, on the same income (Sec. 45(1)). For this purpose, Commonwealth income tax means a tax imposed under the law in a Commonwealth country except for the U.K. and Hong Kong itself provided that the Commonwealth country has a system of double taxation relief under which relief for Hong Kong taxes would be given in similar circumstances (Sec. 45(3)). In other words, the other country must have a system of unilateral tax credit relief. The countries to which this relief currently applies are:—

Bahamas	Lesotho	Swaziland
Bangladesh	Malawi	Tanzania
Botswana	Malaysia	The Gambia
Cyprus	Nauru	Tonga
Ghana	Nigeria	Uganda
Guyana	Sierra Leone	Western Samoa
India	Sri Lanka	Zambia
Kenya	Singapore	

The amount of the relief is different depending upon whether the claimant is resident or not resident in Hong Kong. Unfortunately, residence is not defined in the IRO and it is necessary to look to case law of other countries, particularly the U.K., for assistance. As regards the residence status of an individual, the U.K. rules would probably be applicable and a discussion of this is contained on pages 212 to 213. As regards corporations, residence would probably be determined by the place at which the central management and control is exercised. For this purpose, central management and control means the control exercised by the directors and is therefore the place where the directors normally meet and decide policy matters. (See De Beers Consolidated Mines v Howe (5 TC 211)). The place of incorporation and the residence status of shareholders is not relevant in determining the residence status of a corporation.

Similarly, the residence status of a partnership is determined by the place at which it is managed and controlled, in other words where the partners meet to decide policy.

Where, because of conflicting residence rules, a person is a resident of Hong Kong and of a Commonwealth country, that person is to be treated, for the purposes of this relief, as resident in the country in which he resides the longest (Sec. 45(5)). This is obvious enough in the case of an individual but it is doubtful as to how this can be determined in the case of a company or a partnership although presumably the decision would be based upon numbers of Board or partners' meetings. This problem could in fact arise in respect of companies quite often as it is relatively common to find that the residence status of a company is determined elsewhere by the place of incorporation.

The relief is given by deducting from the Hong Kong tax payable a tax credit computed by applying the applicable rate of credit to the doubly taxed

income. The rate of credit is decided as follows:—
(1) For resident persons, the rate of relief is the smaller of:—
    (i)   The foreign effective rate of tax, or
    (ii) One half of the effective rate of applicable Hong Kong tax. (Sec. 45(1))
(2) For non-resident persons, the rate of relief depends upon whether or not the effective foreign rate is greater or not greater than the effective Hong Kong rate:—
    (i)   If the foreign effective rate is greater than the effective Hong Kong rate, the rate of relief is the amount by which the Hong Kong effective rate exceeds one half of the foreign effective rate. Accordingly, if the foreign rate is at least twice the Hong Kong rate, no relief is available.
    (ii) In other cases, the rate of relief is one half of the effective foreign rate (Sec. 45(2)).

The effective rates governing this relief are not necessarily the rates fixed by the relevant governments but are found by dividing the tax payable by the taxable income and therefore take account of reliefs deductible from taxable income (except double taxation relief) and have the effect of averaging progressive rates of tax (Sec. 45(4)).

Example 1

A Hong Kong resident company has a source of income on which it is subject to Profits Tax and on which tax is also payable in a Commonwealth country. For the year in question its taxable income is $125,000 on which the following taxes are payable:—

    Profits Tax $20,625
    Commonwealth Tax 35,000

The effective rates are therefore:—

$$\text{Hong Kong} \qquad \frac{20,625}{125,000} \times 100\% \quad = \quad 16.5\%$$

$$\text{Foreign} \qquad \frac{35,000}{125,000} \times 100\% \quad = \quad 28\%$$

When relief is claimed, therefore, the Profits Tax payable is:—

    $125,000 @ 16½%   = $20,625
    Less $125,000 @ 8¼% =   10,312
    Tax Payable $10,313

Example 2

As for Example 1 except that the Company is not resident in Hong Kong.
The Profits Tax payable when relief is claimed is:—

$125,000 @ 16½%   = $20,625
Less: $125,000 @ 2½%   =   3,125 (Note)

Tax Payable $17,500

Note:—
Because the effective foreign rate is greater than the effective Hong Kong rate, the rate of relief is the Hong Kong rate (16½%) less half the foreign rate (½ x 28%).

2. Exemptions

The IRO contains specific exemptions from each of the four taxes in the relevant Parts, for example Sec. 5(2) & (3) contains exemptions from Property Tax, Sec. 8(2) the exemptions from Salaries Tax, Secs. 26 and 26A the exemptions from Profits Tax and Sec. 28(1) the exemptions from Interest Tax. Apart from these, there are two other general exemption provisions in Part XV of the IRO.

Sec. 87 gives the Governor in Council a general power to exempt any person, office or institution from all or any part of the taxes imposed under the IRO and this is done by making an order to that effect. Any person or body may of course petition the Governor for exemption for some specific person or class of income or persons. For example, the following exemption orders have been issued under the powers in Sec. 87:—

(1) There is an exemption from Interest Tax in respect of interest derived from an account or fund in the name of:—

  The Registrar, Supreme Court

  Official Administrator

  Master in Lunacy.

 so long as the interest does not exceed $1,000 for the year of assessment.

(2) There is an exemption from Salaries Tax in respect of pensions received under Section 31 of the Pensions Regulations by virtue of permanent injuries received in the Second World War.

The second general exemption is granted under Sec. 88 to charitable institutions or trusts of a public character. It is therefore important to be able to identify that which qualifies as a charity. For this, it is necessary to refer to Pemsel's case (3 TC 53) which laid down the basic tests of charitable purpose as follows:—

  The relief of poverty

  The advancement of religion

  The furtherance of education

When the charitable status has been proved to the satisfaction of the Commissioner, the body is exempt from all taxes under the IRO except that, in the case of profits from a trade or business carried on by the charitable body, there are additional qualifications to the exemption from the Profits Tax thereon. The exemption only applies to such Profits Tax if:—

(1) The profits are applied solely for charitable purposes, and

(2) They are not expended substantially outside Hong Kong.

and either:—

(1) The trade or business is exercised in the course of carrying out the objects of the charity as for example the operation of a school; or

(2) The work in connection with the trade or business is mainly performed by persons who are the beneficiaries of the charity as for example goods manufactured by disabled persons, the proceeds going to relief for the disabled.

3. Retirement Schemes

An employer can set up a scheme, which in Hong Kong usually takes the form of a provident fund, to provide for his employees upon their retirement. Furthermore, the employer can seek the Commissioner's approval to the terms of such fund under Sec. 87A.

Sec. 87A requires the application to be made in the form laid down by the Board of Inland Revenue and the Board has, under the authority of Sec. 85, made the Inland Revenue (Retirement Scheme) Rules which govern applications. A Schedule to the Rules sets out the requirements of the scheme which must be satisfied in order to gain approval. If the terms or conditions of the scheme are changed after approval has been given, the approval is deemed to have been withdrawn as at the effective date of the change. However, if an application is made to the Commissioner not later than one month after the date of the alteration and the facts given to him, provided that the changes are within the requirements laid down in the Schedule to the Retirement Scheme Rules, the original approval will stand.

The consequences of obtaining approval are:—

For the employee: Any benefits received by way of a lump sum are free of Salaries Tax whereas such benefits from a non-approved scheme are subject to Salaries Tax.

Benefits received by way of a regular pension payment are subject to Salaries Tax whether the scheme is approved or not. Similarly the employee's contribution, if any, is not tax deductible to him whether the scheme is approved or not.

For the employer: An initial contribution to set up an approved scheme is deductible for Profits Tax purposes, spread over 5 years, whereas such a contribution to a non-approved scheme is not deductible at all.

On the other hand, any subsequent contribution which is other than an ordinary annual contribution is also deductible over 5 years if it is for an approved scheme whereas such a contribution to a non approved scheme may be wholly deductible in the year in which it is paid subject only to the usual rule that it must be incurred for the purposes of earning assessable profits. An ordinary annual contribution is deductible whether the scheme is approved or not. However in the case of an approved scheme, the allowable contribution is limited to 15% of each employee's remuneration.

4. Other Miscellaneous Matters

BOARD OF INLAND REVENUE. The constitution of the Board of Inland Revenue under the IRO has been dealt with in Chapter 1. One of the prime functions of the Board is its power under Sec. 85(1) to make the Inland Revenue Rules. It can make any such rules for carrying out the provisions of the IRO and for the ascertainment and determination of any income or profits assessable under the IRO. It is not however a unilateral power because all such rules must be submitted to the Governor and be subject to the approval of the Legislative Council (Sec. 85(4)).

Apart from the general purposes for which the rules may be made by the Board, Sec. 85(2) and (3) lays down some specific purposes which are:—
(1) The procedures to be followed on application for refunds and relief.
(2) Provide for any matter which the IRO requires to be prescribed.
(3) Prescribe what is to be included in the definitions of "Plant or Machinery" and "Implement, Utensil or Article".
(4) Prescribe fines on summary conviction not exceeding $200 in each case.

Once any rule has been made and approved by the Legislative Council it becomes, in effect, a part of the IRO and is enforceable as such.

The Board also has specific power to fix the specification of any forms necessary for the administration of the IRO (Sec. 86) and in fact meets at least once annually for this purpose. Where the Board has fixed the specification of a form of application or return, such application or return is invalid unless made strictly in the prescribed form (see CIR v Mayland Woven Labels Factory HKTC 627).

ANTI-AVOIDANCE LEGISLATION. The policies and objectives which govern the construction of the Hong Kong tax system have been discussed in Chapter 1 and arising out of the basic principle of simplicity is the fact that the IRO contains very little strict anti-avoidance legislation because such legislation is necessarily detailed, complicated and difficult to administer; which would clearly conflict with the policy of simplicity.

Many of the sections of the IRO contain sub-sections which limit the available loopholes but these are no more than can be reasonably expected in a relatively sophisticated tax system but do not really amount to anti-avoidance legislation as understood in countries with much more sophisticated legislation. There is an inter-company pricing provision in Sec. 20 but this is severely limited in its effect compared to its sophisticated equivalent in the U.K. and U.S.A. Sec. 20 is discussed from pages 170 to 171. Also, the provisions which extend the Profits Tax liability of shipowners (Secs. 23B and 23C) and financial institutions (Sec. 15(1)(i)) are not really anti-avoidance provisions but are deeming provisions to extend the tax base.

The only true anti-avoidance provision is, ironically enough, a potentially wide ranging provision but somewhat limited in its practical application by the IRD and also having been limited in its scope by some legal decisions. This is Sec. 61 which states that if an assessor is of the opinion that any transaction which either reduces, or would reduce the amount of tax payable by any person is either: artificial, or fictitious, or a disposition not given effect to, the assessor may disregard any such transaction or disposition and raise an assessment accordingly.

The difficult area of interpretation is of course as to what is meant by artificial or fictitious and this has been examined in a number of cases both in and outside Hong Kong as a result of which the application of the provisions is a lot more limited than might at first be expected. Earlier decisions however tended to give Sec. 61 a wide application. In CIR v Rico Internationale Ltd. (HKTC 229), certain payments were regarded as artificial because they were motivated by non-commercial reasons, not documented or evidenced, and fixed in retrospect. However, part of the payments was allowed representing the part which had been properly incurred for the purposes of earning assessable profits. In effect, therefore, Sec. 61 was used as a substitute for Sec. 20 although the Judge observed that, strictly, if the assessor has regarded the transaction as artificial, Sec. 61 gave him authority to disregard the *whole* of the transaction.

In the later case of Kum Hing Land Investment Co. v CIR (HKTC 301), a payment to another company was actually made and properly evidenced but it was held that payment is only a part of a transaction and that all surrounding circumstances, particularly the motives, must be considered and as the payment was not one which a businessman could reasonably be expected to make in the circumstances it was held to be both artificial and fictitious. A similar decision, although in connection with different legislation, can be found in Petrotim Securities v Ayres (41 TC 389).

The comment in the Kum Hing case that the transaction was fictitious as well as artificial is somewhat surprising in that a transaction cannot be fictitious if it actually takes place and as that case would have gone against the taxpayer in any event on the grounds that the transaction was artificial it is doubtful whether any weight can be put on the point. In fact, in the much later case of CIR v Douglas Henry Howe (HKTC 936) a careful distinction was drawn between artificial and fictitious based on the authority of a decision of the Privy Council on an anti-avoidance provision in Jamaican tax law which is almost identical to Sec. 61, the case being Seramco Ltd. Superannuation Fund Trustees v Income Tax Commissioner. As this established that a fictitious transaction is one which "the parties to it never intended should be carried out", Howe's case was pursued by the Commissioner before the Court only on the grounds that the transaction was artificial. Furthermore the Court in Howe's case held that the transaction was not artificial because a transfer of a business by an individual to a company wholly owned by him, albeit for tax reasons, was not an unreasonable or unrealistic thing to do.

Howe's case therefore substantially cuts down the application of Sec. 61 and certainly prevents its application solely on the basis that a transaction was motivated by tax reasons. The Judge in fact underlined the general principle in the Duke of Westminster case (19 TC 510) that every person is entitled to arrange his affairs as he sees fit, in order to minimise his taxes. That case and many subsequent cases have established the principle, which holds good in Hong Kong, that the form in which a transaction is carried through is not to be ignored for tax purposes by virtue of the "substance" or underlying intent of the transaction.

U.K. ASSESSMENT AGENT. Because of Hong Kong's special relationship with the U.K. it is possible for the Governor to appoint an agent in the U.K. to carry out certain obligations under Hong Kong law. In order to assist the administrative machinery in raising assessments upon U.K. residents, Sec. 63A provides for the Governor to appoint an agent in the U.K. who, solely in connection with the affairs of U.K. residents, may exercise any of the powers conferred upon an assistant commissioner by the IRO. This is, however, only upon the specific application of the U.K. resident. The rights of objection and appeal are unaffected by assessments made in this manner.

The function was carried out by the overseas territories income tax office in the U.K. until its abolition. The work has since been done wholly in Hong Kong and the provisions of Sec. 63A are not therefore currently in use.

TAX RESERVE CERTIFICATES. These are a means by which a taxpayer can provide for future payment of income taxes and at the same time earn interest thereon.

The certificates can be purchased direct from the Inland Revenue Department or through a number of banks in Hong Kong and are sold in multiples of $50. The interest, which is currently paid at a rate of 10.8% is only credited where the certificate is used in payment of tax and not when it is encashed, but it is exempt from Interest Tax and Profits Tax. The interest is computed from the date of the certificate up to the due date of payment of the tax, even if presented in advance of that due date.

Where certificates presented in payment of tax, with interest, exceed the tax due, the IRD will issue a balance certificate or refund in cash, as required. Where only part of a certificate is required to pay tax, it is the usual practice of the IRD to compute interest on an amount of principal equal to the nearest $50 in excess of the tax due, i.e. if tax of $2,775 is payable and a certificate for $5,000 is tendered, interest will be computed on $2,800 and the balance refunded as appropriate.

TRUSTEES AND DECEASED ESTATES. The IRO does not separately identify the tax position of a trustee or of an executor of a deceased estate and it is necessary therefore to look to the law as it stands to see whether and how they are chargeable. There are however a number of provisions in the IRO affecting the powers and liabilities of executors, for example:—

(1) An executor can be assessed in respect of income or profits arising to the deceased but no assessment can be raised on him more than one year after the date of death or one year after the date of filing the Estate Duty affidavit if later (Sec. 54). Note that BR 3/79 held that a penalty assessment under Sec. 82A cannot be raised against an estate because it is not a person. An assessment under Sec. 82A can however be raised against the personal representative personally if he has committed an indescretion.

(2) An executor cannot claim Personal Assessment in respect of income arising to the estate after the date of death except that a share of partnership profits arising to an individual after his death can be related back to a Personal Assessment for the year of death and the executor can make the election (Sec. 41(2) and (2A)).

(3) An executor can claim repayment of tax due to a deceased (Sec. 79(2)).

The question of assessment of a trustee to tax is more difficult because the IRO does not specifically authorise assessments upon trustees. A trustee will be liable to Interest Tax because Part V of the IRO provides for liability upon a recipient which would include all manner and class of recipients. Similarly Property Tax is upon an owner of property. However, in regard to Profits Tax, this is chargeable on a "person" and, although the definition of person in Sec. 2 includes, from 1st April 1980, a trustee whether incorporated or unincorporated there is doubt as to whether a trustee can be assessed upon income or profits which are not beneficially his but which he receives in a fiduciary capacity. It would only put the matter beyond doubt if the definition of person included a trust rather than a trustee and then provided that assessments could be raised upon the trustee as agent for the trust. This is important in connection with the assessment of unit trusts which is a current controversial area. On the assumption that a trustee can be assessed to Profits Tax, the IRO provides in Sec. 19C(6)(e) from 1980/81 that losses incurred in a trade carried on by a trustee for the benefit of a trust can only be set against profits from that trade carried on by that trust. This provision seems to have been born out of the confusion created by including trustee instead of trust in the definition of person in that it may be theoretically possible for the somewhat unlikely proposition that this enables a trustee to bring together the assessable incomes and allowable losses of all trusts that he administers. The position of trusts, trustees and Profits Tax seems destined to remain confused for some time yet.

APPENDIX 1

Departmental Interpretation & Practice Notes
No. 1

Part A: Valuation Of Stock-In-Trade And Work-In-Progress
Part B: Ascertainment Of Profit And The Valuation
Of Work-In-Progress
In

BUILDING AND ENGINEERING CONTRACTS
PROPERTY DEVELOPMENT, AND
PROPERTY INVESTMENT CASES
PART A

Valuation of Stock-in-Trade and Work-in-Progress

It is essential for the proper computation of taxable profits for a given period that opening and closing stock-in-trade be correctly valued. The argument sometimes encountered that the matter corrects itself if the stock is correctly valued in subsequent years cannot be accepted.

2. These notes, which do not relate to professional work-in-progress, are intended to explain the bases of valuation that are acceptable for tax purposes as such valuations may not always be the same as those used by auditors for the purpose of commercial accounting.

3. As there are no statutory provisions relating to stock valuation for tax purposes other than Section 15C, which relates to cessation of business, ordinary commercial principles and practice have first to be looked at. Further guidance can be found in decided cases.

4. The basic rule, whether for accounting purposes or taxation purposes, is that stock should be valued at the lower of cost or market value (*WHIMSTER v C.I.R., 12 TC 813*). As these terms are in themselves not sufficiently precise, it is necessary to state what the Revenue understands by them.

Meaning of "Cost" or "Market Value"

5. The basic Revenue view is that "cost" means the actual or historical cost. As set out in the recommendations made to the Accountancy Profession, to which reference is made in paragraph 7, this includes all expenditure incurred directly on the purchase or manufacture of the stock and the bringing of it to its existing condition and location, together with such part, if any, of the overhead expenditure as is appropriately carried forward in the circumstances of the business instead of being charged against the revenue of the period in which it was incurred.

The term "market value" is subject to various interpretations, however the Revenue generally would require this to mean realizable value, again as defined in the recommendation made to the Accountancy Profession.

Court Decisions

6. The Courts have ruled on certain methods of valuation —

(i) In the case of *AHMEDABAD NEW COTTON MILLS LTD. v. BOMBAY COMMISSIONERS OF INCOME TAX, 8 A.T.C. 575,* it was held that where opening and closing stocks have been undervalued, the true profits can only be established by raising both valuations.

(ii) *C.I.R. v COCK RUSSELL & CO. LTD., 29 TC 387,* established the right to apply cost or lower market value to individual items of stock.

(iii) In *MINISTER OF NATIONAL REVENUE v. ANACONDA AMERICAN BRASS LTD., 34 A.T.C. 330,* the L.I.F.O. method of determining cost was rejected by the Privy Council.

(iv) In *PATRICK v BROADSTONE, 35 TC 44,* the base stock method was rejected, even though it was accepted as sound commercial practice in the cotton spinning trade.

(v) In *DUPLE MOTOR BODIES LTD. v OSTIME, 39 TC 537,* consistency in the basis of valuation of stock and work-in-progress was stressed. The Courts, however, in refusing to decide between the rival claims of direct cost and oncost methods of valuation as a broad principle, found that the direct cost method, which had been consistently applied in the past, was one of the methods recognised as sound accountancy practice and saw no reason in the circumstances of that case, to compel a change to the oncost basis.

(vi) In *FREEMAN, HARDY & WILLIS v RIDGEWAY, 47 TC 519,* it was held that for tax purposes replacement value is not acceptable.

Acceptable Accountancy Practice

7. Guidance as to the best accountancy practice has been given by the "Statement of Standard Accounting Practice" (S.S.A.P.) which tax representatives will no doubt already have and to which reference is made in the following paragraphs. This statement is approved by the recognised accountancy bodies in the United Kingdom. The basic recommendations in the S.S.A.P. follow closely those made in "Recommendation No. 22" published in November 1960 by the Institute of Chartered Accountants in England and Wales, to which reference was made in the previous issue of these notes, so that a basis of valuation that has been accepted by the Revenue as conforming to the recommendations given in "Recommendation No. 22" will continue to be acceptable.

8. The recommendations contained in the S.S.A.P. are broadly acceptable to the Inland Revenue Department. Any reservation the Revenue has on
certain of the recommendations are referred to in later paragraphs of these
notes, and Part B of these notes deals with the question of valuation of
work-in-progress on long-term contracts.

Adjusted Selling Price

9. It is accepted that there may be practical difficulties in arriving at
actual or historical cost, and for that reason some other method may have to
be used. Where the adjusted selling price method has been adopted, the
Revenue should be made aware as to the reasons for desiring to continue on
this basis and information given as to –

   (*a*) the nature and amount of expenses deducted as necessary to bring
         the goods to their saleable condition and location (such as com-
         mission, transportation and other selling expenses); and

   (*b*) the deduction for the estimated margin of profit.

Again, in the case of slow moving stocks, e.g. spare parts or books, it is not
sufficient that an arbitrary reduction be made from original cost.

10. Where stock is valued at current selling price less the normal gross
profit margin, in the circumstances described in the S.S.A.P. paragraph 4 of
Part I, the valuation will be accepted for revenue purposes only if the further
test set out in paragraph 14 of Appendix I of the Statement is clearly
satisfied. It is considered that the selling price to be used for the purpose of
discounting should normally be the original price fixed for the article determined by operating the normal mark-up on the original cost price, otherwise,
for goods marked at a "sale price", the deduction of the normal gross profit
margin would bring the valuation to below cost.

Net Realisable Value

11. To arrive at a valuation acceptable for revenue purposes based on net
realisable value, the expression "less all costs to be incurred in marketing,
selling and distributing directly related to the items in question", would not
include general selling costs. In practice, specific identifiable items of
expenditure directly related to the stock in question, including provision for
commission and brokerage which would have been incurred on sale, would be
allowed.

Replacement Cost

12. Reference is made in (vi) of paragraph 6 of these notes to the
decision in the case of *FREEMAN, HARDY & WILLIS v. RIDGEWAY*. The
objection by the Revenue to a valuation on the basis of replacement cost is
that it could be less than actual cost where no loss is expected. However, it is
the Revenue practice to accept replacement cost as being equivalent to

realisable value in the case of raw materials awaiting processing that are on hand in excess of that required to carry out firm orders.

Basis of Valuation Used

13. If the present practice for valuations to be stated as having been made at "market value" or "at or under cost" is continued to be used by traders and auditors, then because more than one interpretation can be placed on such expressions, the Assessor should be made aware as to exactly what basis of valuation has been used. In addition, where the basis adopted for the valuation of stock and work-in-progress is one that is clearly not acceptable for tax purposes, the adjustment that is considered necessary should be made in the figure of profit returned for assessment and the basis on which the adjustment is made brought to the notice of the Assessor.

14. Once a satisfactory basis of valuation has been agreed, the Revenue in subsequent years will normally only require the information to be given in the annual form of return as to any change in the basis of valuation from that previously adopted.

Shares and Securities held as Trading Stock

15. The Revenue does not regard as obligatory the valuation of shares and securities held as trading stock to be at the lower of cost or market value. Either a valuation on a consistent basis of cost or a consistent basis of the lower of cost or market value would be regarded as a valid basis and acceptable by the Revenue. A change from one valid basis to another would not be admitted unless good reasons, other than tax advantages, are given for the change. For example, if accounting changes are forced upon the taxpayer by circumstances beyond his control, e.g. absorption by a group or a change in the nature of the trade, the Revenue would be prepared to consider the computation of future profits by regard to the changed basis of valuation. The Revenue would, however, have regard to whether or not the changed basis gives rise to, or will give rise to, a distortion in the true and fair profits, as shown by the tax computations for the years in which the shares were held, the true and fair profit being on the eventual disposal, the difference between the cost and sale prices.

16. If the shares and/or securities relate to a holding that is composed of purchases made at varying dates with possibly rights issues and/or bonus issues, it may not be possible to identify the individual parcels of stock sold. Valuation of remaining shares and/or securities on hand in these circumstances should, it is considered, be made on average cost or lower of average cost and realisable value, dependent on whichever of the two valid bases has been adopted.

Work-in-Progress

17. The S.S.A.P. recommends that work-in-progress should include all related production overheads. It is already general practice for overheads to be so included but the Revenue has been required to accept as valid a valuation consistently adopted based on direct cost only, i.e. cost of material plus wages. This followed from the decision in the case of DUPLE MOTOR BODIES (referred to at paragraph 6(v)). The Revenue will not admit a change from a valid basis unless good reasons are given for the change, other than tax advantages, and the general comments in paragraph 15 above relating to a change from such a valid basis are relevant. Part B of these notes refer to the valuation of work-in-progress on long-term contracts.

Post-Balance Sheet date events

18. The S.S.A.P. (e.g. paragraph 19) recommends that events occurring between the Balance Sheet date and the date of the completion of the accounts be considered in determining the market value of stock. There are, from an accounting point of view, sound reasons for this recommendation, e.g. this is something the directors would wish to take into account when recommending a dividend; however, it is the Revenue view that for tax purposes the quantum of profits of an accounting period must be determined without reference to events which took place after that period.

Undervaluations

It is recognised that many small concerns may not have adequate costing records and the Department has no desire to impose requirements which will require an increase in staff or costs. However, if accounts are submitted in which there has been a clear undervaluation for tax purposes of stock and work-in-progress, the Revenue will need to look at past liabilities at the time when the question is considered as to what the valuation figure should be if made on a valid basis. Should there have been deliberate or wilfully misleading irregularities, the Revenue would also consider the question of penalties on the under-payment of tax that resulted.

PART B

Ascertainment of Profit and the Valuation of Work-in-Progress in Building and Engineering Contracts, Property Development and Property Investment Cases

1. These notes deal with the above subjects as one, because there are aspects which are inter-related although at the same time there are special features of each.

2. With the low rate of tax in Hong Kong and the fact that the standard rate applies in most cases, there are many instances where there is very little or no difference in the ultimate tax position even though there may not have been a strict application of proper taxation principles in the ascertainment of profit or in the valuation of work-in-progress. In these cases of course there would be no purpose in requiring a strict application of those principles.

3. Nevertheless, there are cases where the application of proper principles will have an appreciable bearing on the ultimate tax position. For this reason it is desirable that these principles be stated, together with an indication as to what is the departmental policy and practice.

BUILDING AND ENGINEERING CONTRACTS

4. It has been found that the accounting treatment of profits (or losses) from these types of contracts has varied. Strictly, the profit arising on the contract would not arise for tax purposes until the contract is completed. However, where the accounting methods adopted have the effect of accounting for some profit or loss at various stages of the contract, then if these methods follow a normally acceptable practice, consistently followed, the tax computation may be based on those accounts. The Revenue would expect, however, that a consistent accounting method be applied to all contracts being carried out.

5. The recommendations contained in the S.S.A.P. as to the treatment of work-in-progress on long-term contracts would in general be admitted by the Revenue as an acceptable practice, but the Revenue would not be able to allow for tax purposes the whole of the provisions for loss referred to in paragraph 9 of Part I of the S.S.A.P.

6. Thus, where a loss on a contract as a whole is foreseen, a proportion of the overall loss, calculated either by reference to time, normally up to the due completion date under the terms of the contract, or to expenditure incurred may be taken into account year by year during the remainder of the contract period so long as all contracts, profitable or otherwise, are dealt with similarly. This is the practice of the Revenue as given in paragraph 4 above. It would follow that a provision for an expected future loss would be disallowed.

Change in Basis of Valuation

7. Where there is a change in the basis for treatment of long-term contracts, the opening figure in the year of change must, for taxation purposes, be the same as the closing figure for the preceding year.

8. The Inland Revenue will not accept a claim for a tax-free uplift based on the grounds that the opening and closing figures in the year of

change must be on the same basis. Alternatively, the Inland Revenue would accept the continuance of the existing basis for long term contracts current at the beginning of the year of change, with the new basis being applied only to contracts entered into in or after the year of change.

9. Except as herein indicated no treatment other than that outlined in paragraph 4 will be accepted. In the case of Hong Kong contracts awarded to non-resident contractors, if the profit is to be spread over the life of the contract but cannot be quantified until it is completed, the method of spread to be adopted must be agreed at the start of the contract. Arrangements should then be made for the sub-mission of annual returns of estimated profit or loss so that corresponding assessments can be raised. Objections should be made to keep the assessments open until the final account is available.

10. Where the profit is not spread, care must be taken that there is no undue understatement of profit on the completed contracts in any one accounting period, because of incorrect apportionment of overheads to the uncompleted contracts at any stage. The overhead expenditure to be included in cost of work-in-progress, when appropriate, should include all direct and variable expenses attributable to the contract. These would also include expenses of the site office and the cost of preparation of any plans, estimates and tenders for the job.

11. As was stated in "Recommendation No. 22" (see paragraph 7 of Part A of these notes). —

"In businesses which undertake contracts extending over a period of years the normal tendency is to include overhead expenditure in work-in-progress except where it is considered to be irrecoverable. If overheads are not included in work-in-progress on such contracts the accounts for the early years may indicate losses followed by unduly large profits in the years when the contracts are completed. This would be a wholly unrealistic presentation in relation to a contract showing a normal profit."

This principle has been accepted by the S.S.A.P. by the recommendations made as to the basis on which work-in-progress should be valued.

Retention money and maintenance period

12. Where the terms of a contract provide for the retention of a percentage of the contract price until the end of the maintenance period this will not involve either

(a) an extension of the date of completion of the contract, or

(b) the exclusion of the retention moneys from the profits brought into computation at that stage.

13. The contract is regarded as being completed when a final certificate is issued by the supervising architect or consulting engineers. The retention

moneys are a delayed payment for the work done to that stage and are withheld as security for the making good of any defects that may appear during the maintenance period. If nothing occurs during the maintenance period it cannot be said that any portion of the profit was derived during that period. It is necessary, however, to see that any expenditure, including a due proportion of overhead, incurred during that period is allowed in such a way as not to produce an inequitable result. This can be done by either

(a) allowing it in the period in which it was actually incurred as a deduction against profits of subsequent activities, or

(b) if there are no or insufficient subsequent profits, bringing it in as if it had been incurred at the date of completion of the contract.

14. If the circumstances are such as to warrant the adoption of alternative (b) then it is agreed that earlier assessments may be reopened.

15. A person would of course, be regarded as still carrying on business during the maintenance period, even if there were no other activities or no maintenance expenditure.

PROPERTY DEVELOPMENT

16. This has become a major activity in Hong Kong over recent years and appears certain to continue for some time. For the purposes of these notes, "property development" is treated as being development for profit by sale; development for an income return from leasing or letting or otherwise by use in a trade or business is treated as "property investment."

17. It is common practice for agreements for sale of the developed property by flats or units to be entered into before or during construction. These normally provide for payment of a deposit and instalments, with a provision that failure to meet any payments due under the agreement will result in the forfeiture of all payments made.

Date of Commencement

18. Where a person first enters into a property development project, he is regarded as having commenced business for the purposes of Section 18C of the Inland Revenue Ordinance when he takes the first clear step towards that end. This may be the date of acquisition of the site, or if the land has been held for some time, when some definite move is made towards development.

Ascertainment of Profit – Deduction for cost

19. If a property has been held for some time and it is established that it was not acquired with the intention of development or re-sale, then the practice is not to restrict the deduction for the cost of the property to the

amount actually paid at the time of original purchase (plus any additions), but to admit the valuation of the property as at the date there was a clear indication of the change of intention in regard to the property. [This so-called "practice" in fact has the authority of case law. — Author]

When is profit brought in

20. Notwithstanding that agreements of sale are entered into and payments are received prior to the completion of the building, the profit on sale is regarded normally as arising when the contract is capable of completion by performance and the purchaser can be given possession. The sale is therefore regarded as taking place when the Occupation Permit is issued by the Building Authority.

21. If the sales are in either cash or extended terms, the amount of proceeds in either case to be brought in at this stage in determining the profit is based on the cash price only. Instalments are treated as including an element of interest (which is only assessable when paid or credited) representing a proportion of the excess of all payments over the cash price.

22. In the case of C.I.R. v. Montana Lands Ltd., H.K.T.C. 334, the contracts for sale provided for payment by instalments over a period of 100 months, with assignment of the property deferred until payment of the final instalment. The company's accounts brought in only the portion of the profit that was represented by the instalments received. The Supreme Court held that the company's method was in accordance with established accountancy principles, and should be followed for tax purposes. In similar circumstances, therefore, similar methods may be adopted. Taxpayers may, however, follow the method indicated in paragraphs 20 and 21 if they so desire, provided that this method is followed consistently.

Overhead Expenditure

23. In many cases the period covered by a development project will extend over two or more years of assessment. The same considerations will apply as to when and if so to what extent, overhead expenditure should be included for tax purposes in cost of work-in-progress, as in the case of building contractors. Here again it may not be the general practice to carry forward any of the overhead expenses in the developer's accounts or to treat only some as in the nature of oncost. This may be accepted when there is relatively little effect on the over-all tax position, but the Revenue must reserve the right to examine the position more closely where circumstances so require.

24. Where it is appropriate that overhead expenditure should be carried forward, this may include expenses of arranging and providing finance, including interest up to the date the property is available for sale.

PROPERTY INVESTMENT

25. Where a person incurs expenditure on the acquisition and construction of a property which is to be used for the purposes of his trade or business, or for the production of income by way of rents, it is of primary importance that all expenditure in the nature of capital expenditure is correctly treated for taxation purposes.

26. In such cases therefore, it is always necessary that there be a strict application of proper principles in distinguishing between revenue and capital expenditure.

27. Where the person is carrying on business and there is already an established organization, it is necessary to see that all overhead expenditure, including administration expenses, correctly attributable to the acquisition of the site and the construction of the property, is properly capitalized. These will include finance expenses up to the date when the property is capable of being used for the production of profits. This will usually be the date of the Occupation Permit or the date from which rent is first receivable. After that date interest is correctly a revenue charge.

28. The remuneration of employees and staff directly engaged on the planning, construction and fitting up of the property should also be included in the expenses charged to the cost of the property.

CONCLUSION

29. The practice of the Department is not to insist upon a strict application of the full requirements and principles in small cases, or where there can be little or no effect on the ultimate over-all tax position.

30. It is realized that the level of expenditure in Hong Kong on detailed costing and accounting is not relatively high and that detailed allocation of oncosts may not be made throughout the year.

31. Where the method of accounting in use results in a distortion of the true and fair profits for tax purposes, then it is expected that necessary adjustments will be made in the returns and computations. Where detailed costing records are not available and the cost of work-in-progress is based solely on direct costs, then a reasonable estimate should be made of the indirect expenses and general overhead properly attributable to the cost of production and work-in-progress.

JULY 1976

APPENDIX 2

Departmental Interpretation & Practice Notes
No. 2 (Revised 1974)

PROFITS TAX
Part A — Industrial Buildings Allowances
Part B — Rebuilding Allowances — Commercial Buildings

(1) Whereas Section 17(1)(c) of the Inland Revenue Ordinance prohibits the deduction for Profits Tax purposes of any expenditure of a capital nature, Part VI provides for the granting of capital allowances in respect of (a) Industrial Buildings, (b) Commercial Buildings and (c) Machinery and Plant. [Other than Machinery and Plant a deduction for which has been allowed under Section 16B(1)(b) as expenditure relating to scientific research — See D.I. & P.N. No. 5].

(2) This paper is a summary of the Departmental practice and interpretation of the provisions relating to (A) Industrial Buildings and (B) Commercial Buildings.

PART A — INDUSTRIAL BUILDINGS ALLOWANCES

(3) *Trades which Qualify*

An industrial building or structure is defined in Section 40 as meaning "a building or structure or part of any building or structure used—

(a) for the purposes of a trade carried on in a mill, factory or other similar premises; or

(b) for the purposes of a transport, tunnel, dock, water gas or electricity undertaking or a public telephonic or public telegraphic service; or

(c) for the purposes of a trade which consists of the manufacture of goods or materials or the subjection of goods or materials to any process; or

(d) for the purposes of a trade which consists in the storage —

    (i) of goods or materials which are to be used in the manufacture of other goods or materials; or

    (ii) of goods or materials which are to be subjected in the course of a trade to any process; or

    (iii) of goods or materials on their arrival into the Colony; or

(e) for the purposes of the business of farming; or

(f) for the purposes of scientific research in relation to any trade or business."

Except for (e) and (f), it is only *trades* which qualify. Of the trades specified, the type most frequently met with is "(c) for the purposes of a trade which consists in the manufacture of goods or materials or the subjection of goods or materials to any process." This is wider than "(a) a trade carried on in a mill, factory or other similar premises." It should not be thought that in order to qualify, a trade must involve a manufacturing process. For example, a motor-repair workshop has been held to qualify, as the trade involved the subjection of goods or materials to a process by the application of machines and hand tools. Similarly, an explosives shed used in the trade of quarrying and mining has been held to be a building to which the allowances apply; and again buildings used in the trade of motion picture producers qualify.

In order to come within (d) of the definition, it should be noted that the trade itself must be one of storage. Godowns or warehouses for the storage of goods or materials for sale or for use in the trade or business of the storer, which does not itself qualify, would not rank for allowances.

In a case heard by the Supreme Court of Hong Kong in 1969 (Tai On Machinery Works Ltd. v. C.I.R.), allowances were refused to a retail distributor of goods who claimed to have subjected the goods to a process, it being held that the alleged processing was at best a part of the trade and not the trade itself.

(4) *Buildings which Qualify*

The allowances apply to all buildings and structures *used in qualifying trades* other than the stated exceptions, which will be dealt with later.

The words "buildings and structures" are not defined, so they must be given their ordinary meaning. In practice the term "structure" is interpreted as covering artificial works that are not commonly regarded as buildings, such as walls, bridges, dams, roads, dry docks, bore holes and wells, sewers, water mains and tunnel linings. In addition, the practice is to regard boundary walls, railway sidings and other works forming part of the premises as qualifying for the allowances.

Any buildings or structures provided for and in use for the welfare of workers, or for the housing of manual workers, employed in the specified trades, will also rank for allowances.

The term "industrial building or structure" includes part of a building or structure. When additions are made to an existing building, therefore, the expenditure incurred will rank for separate allowances.

(5) *Buildings excluded*

Excluded from the allowances are any buildings or structures in so far as they are in use as a —

(i)   dwelling house (other than for housing manual workers),
(ii) retail shop,
(iii) showroom,
(iv) hotel, or
(v)   office.

Where a building is partly an industrial building and partly not and where the cost of construction of the part of the building which is excluded does not exceed 10% of the total cost of the building, the whole building is regarded as qualifying. Otherwise an apportionment is made so as to bring in only the cost of the part which does qualify.

(6) Expenditure which Qualifies

The allowances granted are based on the "capital expenditure incurred on the construction of the building or structure." This will not include the cost of the site or the preparation and levelling of the land. There may be included, however, the expenditure on the ordinary work done preparatory to laying foundations, and the cost of laying drains, sewers and water-mains to serve the building.

The allowable expenditure does not include anything that is reimbursed by any grant, subsidy, or similar assistance.

(7) Persons entitled to the Allowance

Allowances are granted to any person who is entitled to an interest in an industrial building or structure, where that interest is the relevant interest in relation to the capital expenditure incurred on the construction of that building or structure.

It is not necessary for the building to be used for a qualifying purpose by the owner himself, so that where a building is leased and used by the occupant for a qualifying purpose, the landlord, being the person having the relevant interest in the capital expenditure incurred on construction is entitled to the allowances.

No allowances are due to a lessee who merely pays rent and/or a premium for the lease of a building and who has not himself incurred capital expenditure on construction or acquired the relevant interest of a person who did incur such expenditure but a tenant who incurs expenditure on a building which he occupies for the purposes of a qualifying trade or business will have a relevant interest for the purposes of the allowances.

(8) Relevant Interest

"Relevant Interest" is determined at the time when the capital expenditure is incurred. It is defined in Section 40 as meaning —

"in relation to any expenditure incurred on the construction of a building or structure the interest in that building or structure to which the person who incurred the expenditure was entitled when he incurred it."

A relevant interest can be acquired where the person who incurred the expenditure sells the whole of his interest, not just part. For example, A holds a lease of land from the Crown for 99 years. He gives B a lease for 50 years and B erects an industrial building thereon at a cost of $100,000. After some time B assigns the balance of his lease to C, who acquires the relevant interest which B had in the capital expenditure incurred on the construction of the building. C is entitled to annual allowances calculated under Section 34(2)(b), and also to balancing allowances at the expiration of the lease under Section 35(1)(b). If, however, B merely sub-let the premises to C for a term of years, the relevant interest would not pass and C would not be entitled to any industrial building allowances. B, however, having retained the relevant interest would continue to be entitled to the allowances, provided C is carrying on a qualifying trade.

(9) Buildings and Structures bought unused

Where capital expenditure is incurred on the construction of a building and before it is used the relevant interest therein is sold, (a) no allowances may be claimed on that expenditure and any initial allowance given is withdrawn, (b) the person who buys that interest is treated as having incurred on the date on which the purchase price is payable, capital expenditure on construction of an amount equal to the lesser of the net price paid by him or the actual cost of construction. [This has now been modified (see page 181). — Author]

Should the building change ownership more than once before it is used (b) above applies only in relation to the last change.

(10) The Allowances

(i) Initial Allowance

With effect from the year of assessment 1965/66 an initial allowance of one-fifth of the capital expenditure on the construction of an industrial building is granted to the person who incurs the expenditure. The allowance is given to the person who incurs the expenditure and is made in the year of assessment in the basis period of which the expenditure is incurred.

Initial allowance is granted as expenditure is incurred and there is no requirement that the building must be in use. Where, however, on the first occasion that the building comes to be used it is not an industrial building any initial allowance previously given is withdrawn and appropriate additional assessments made.

No initial allowance is given for expenditure relating to the eight years of assessment commencing on 1st April 1957 and ending on 31st March 1965. For years of assessment prior to 1st April 1957 an initial allowance of one-tenth was granted on qualifying expenditure.

(ii) *Annual Allowances*

Prior to 1965/66 an annual allowance of 2% of the capital expenditure on the construction of the building was granted to the person having the relevant interest and carrying on a qualifying trade. However, commencing with the year of assessment 1965/66 annual allowances are computed as laid down in paragraphs (a) and (b) of Section 34(2) of the main Ordinance, as amended by Clause 17(c) and (d) of the amending Ordinance of 1965. Depending on the circumstances, the allowances are either –

(a) 4% of the capital expenditure on the construction of the building, or

(b) if the relevant interest in the capital expenditure has been sold while the building was an industrial building, then, depending on whether the building was first used before or after the commencement of the basis period for the year of assessment 1965/66 –

1. [if used *before* the 1965/66 basis period] the fraction of the "residue of expenditure after the sale" the numerator of which is two and the denominator of which is the number of years in the period from the first year of assessment in which the buyer is entitled to an annual allowance to the fiftieth year after the year in which the building was first used.

2. [if used after the commencement of the 1965/66 basis period] the fraction of the "residue of the expenditure after the sale" the numerator of which is one and the denominator of which is the number of years in the period from the first year of assessment in which the buyer is entitled to an annual allowance to the twenty-fifth year after the year in which the building was first used.

Two conditions must be fulfilled before a person is entitled to annual allowances for any year of assessment:—

(1) The building must be in use as an industrial building at the end of his basis period of assessment;

(2) He must be entitled to an interest in the building at the end of the basis period for that year of assessment; and that interest must be the relevant interest in relation to the capital expenditure for which allowances are claimed.

(11) *"Residue of Expenditure"*

This term is defined in Section 40, as the original cost of the building reduced by any initial, annual and balancing allowances actually made and as increased by any balancing charges. A notional allowance is deemed to have been made for any year in which no annual allowance could be made.

(12) *Balancing Allowances and Charges*

Where any of the following events occur:—

(a) the relevant interest in the building is sold,

(b) the claimant's interest in the building was leasehold and the lease comes to an end other than by reason of the claimant acquiring the superior interest or the happening of the events referred to in paragraph 13,

(c) the building is demolished, destroyed or it ceases altogether to be used,

a balance is struck between the residue of expenditure immediately before the event and the sale price, insurance, salvage or compensation moneys (if any). If the residue exceeds the sale price or other moneys the difference is allowed as a balancing allowance. If the difference is the other way, it forms a balancing charge.

No charge or allowance falls to be made unless the building was an industrial building at the time of the event giving rise to the charge or allowance. Further, with effect from the year of assessment 1965/66, no balancing allowance is given where the building is demolished for purposes unconnected with the trade or business for which the building was used. Thus, for example, where the land is ripe for re-development, and the building is demolished to enable the land to be sold unencumbered no balancing allowance is given, even though the building was in use as an industrial building immediately prior to demolition.

(13) *Termination of Leasehold Interests*

If a lessee has incurred capital expenditure on the building which he has leased, a balancing allowance or charge does not arise when the lease comes to an end if the lessee remains in possession with the consent of the lessor without a new lease being granted. His leasehold interest is to be treated as continuing. If a new lease is granted to him or if the old lease is extended by reason of an option available to him, the second lease is to be treated as a continuation of the first lease.

(14) *Examples*

Two examples of the operation of the allowances are shown as an Appendix to these notes.

PART B – REBUILDING ALLOWANCES –
COMMERCIAL BUILDINGS OR STRUCTURES

(15) *Buildings which Qualify*

For the purposes of Section 36 a commercial building or structure is any building or structure or part of any building or structure used by the person entitled to the relevant interest for the purposes of his trade, profession or business, other than an industrial building or structure.

For "relevant interest", refer to para. (8) in Part A above.

As in the case of industrial buildings, part of a building can qualify separately.

(16) *Rebuilding Allowance*

A rebuilding allowance of ¾% of the capital expenditure on the cost of construction is granted for each year of assessment while the building or part of the building is so used at the end of the basis period of the year of assessment.

As with industrial buildings, the allowance is based on the capital expenditure incurred on the construction – see para. 6 in Part A above.

The allowance is an annual allowance and there is no special initial allowance or any balancing allowance or charge.

(17) *Persons entitled to the Allowance*

The allowance is deducted in ascertaining the profits of the person entitled to the relevant interest, in the same way as Industrial Buildings Allowance.

Before 1969/70, the allowance was restricted to the *owner* of the building.

From 1969/70, however, the tenant may be able to claim in respect of capital expenditure on additions to the building which he has incurred himself, or for which he otherwise has the relevant interest.

JULY 1974

Example (1)

XYZ Ltd., textile manufacturers, prepares accounts annually to 31st December. The company incurred capit

		Building No. 1	*Buildi*
(a)	Year in which expenditure incurred	1962	19
(b)	Cost of construction	$50,000	$50
(c)	Initial Allowance	Nil	l
(d)	Annual Allowance –		
	(i) First granted in year of assessment	1963/64	196
	(ii) At 2% for years of assessment prior to 1965/66	$1,000 (1963/64 and 1964/65)	$1, (196
	(iii) At 4% for years of assessment 1965/66 et. seq.	$2,000 (from 1965/66)	$2 (from 1
	(iv) If building continues in use final allowance will be granted in year of assessment	1988/89 (i.e. $\frac{100 - (2 \times 2)}{4}$ years from 1965/66)	19 (i.e. $\frac{100 - (2 \times 1)}{4}$

(e) In fact, actual disposal of the buildings was as follows – .....

Building No. 1:
Destroyed by fire on
1st May 1967 –
Insurance proceeds
$35,000

Building No. 2:
Sold to A
31st Octo
Sale p
$4

(f) Balancing Allowance/Charge ....

Building No. 1:

Cost		$50,000
Allowances:–		
2 years at 2%		
3 years at 4%		8,000
		42,000
Insurance proceeds		35,000
Balancing Allowance 1968/69		$ 7,000

Building No. 2:

Cost	
Allowances:–	
1 year at 2%	
4 years at 4%	
Sale proceeds ...	
Balancing Charge 1969/70	

NDIX

al expenditure on construction of industrial buildings as follows:—

g No. 2	Building No. 3	Building No. 4
63	1964	1965
000	$50,000	$50,000
il	$10,000 (in 1965/66)	$10,000 (in 1966/67)
4/65	1965/66	1966/67
000 4/65)	–	–
,000 965/66)	$2,000 (from 1965/66)	$2,000 (from 1966/67)
9/90 ears from 1965/66)	1984/85 (i.e. $\dfrac{100-20}{4}$ years from 1965/66)	1985/86 (i.e. $\dfrac{100-20}{4}$ years from 1966/67)

| BC Ltd. on ber 1968 – roceeds ,000 | Sold to ABC Ltd. on 31st July 1970 – Sales proceeds $55,000 | Demolished for re-development unconnected with the trade on 31st December 1971. |

Building No. 3:

Cost	$50,000
Allowances:–	
Initial	10,000
	40,000
Annual	
6 years at 4%	12,000
	28,000
Sale proceeds	55,000
Balance	$27,000

Balancing Charge 1971/72 –
restricted to allowances granted
i.e. $10,000 + $12,000 = $22,000
[Section 35(4) applies].

Building No. 2 (cut off):

....	$50,000
....	9,000
	41,000
....	42,000
....	$ 1,000

Building No. 4:

No Balancing Allowance to be granted – proviso to Section 35(1) applies. Final annual allowance granted in 1971/72.

Example (2)

ABC Ltd., who acquired Buildings Nos. 2 and 3 from XYZ Ltd., also carries on a qualifying trade and us
March. The company will therefore be entitled to annual allowances, calculated in accordance with Secti

		Building No. 2
(a)	Date of purchase	31st October 1968.
(b)	Residue of expenditure	$42,000

(c) Annual Allowance—

    (i) First granted to ABC Ltd. in year of assessment — 1969/70

    (ii) Amount of allowance . . . .

$$\$42{,}000 \times \frac{2}{1969/70 \text{ to } (1964/55 + 49)}$$

$$= \$42{,}000 \times \frac{2}{45}$$

$$= \$1{,}867 \text{ per annum.}$$

    (iii) If building continues in use a final allowance will be granted in year of assessment . . . . — 1991/92 ($926) s the buildings for industrial purposes and prepares accounts annually to 31st

n 34(2)(b) as follows:—

Building No. 3

31st July 1970.

$50,000

$$\$50,000 \times \frac{\overset{\displaystyle 1971/72}{1}}{1971/72 \text{ to } (1965/66 + 24) \text{ years}}$$

ears

$$= \ \$50,000 \times \frac{1}{19}$$

$$= \ \$2,632 \text{ per annum.}$$

1989/90
($2,624)

APPENDIX 3

Departmental Interpretation & Practice Notes
No. 3 (Revised 1974)

PROFITS TAX
Apportionment of Expenses

(1) Section 16(1) of the Inland Revenue Ordinance provides that in ascertaining the assessable profits of any year there shall be deducted outgoings and expenses to the extent to which they are incurred in the production of the profits chargeable to tax.

2. The following rules adopted in practice are largely based on Rules 2A, 2B and 2C of the Inland Revenue Rules:—

(a) If a concern is deriving trading profits partly within the Colony and partly outside the Colony—

Expenses directly attributable to the profits arising outside the Colony are to be disallowed and an apportionment made of such expenses as are partly one and partly the other. The basis of such apportionment may be on turnover or sales or such basis as is most appropriate to the activities of the business.

(b) If a concern is deriving profits from trading and also from investments in the form of dividends, two questions arise—

(i) Has there been any charge for interest on money borrowed and used for the purpose of acquiring the investments? If so, the interest charge is not allowable.

(ii) What proportion of the activities of the concern is involved in the management and supervision of the investment portfolio and the collection of dividends? Unless this is likely to be relatively appreciable no attempt will be made to treat any proportion of the administration and general expenses as applicable to the receipt of the non-taxable dividends.

(c) If a concern, apart from any other profit-earning activities is engaged in share-dealing, then—

(i) No attempt is made to split any interest paid in respect of the investments and the whole sum is allowed as against the profits arising from the buying and selling of stocks and shares and no portion treated as applicable to the earning of the non-taxable profits from dividends.

(ii) In these cases there is usually a large portfolio which would involve time and expense in supervision and management. Only a small fraction of such expenses however will normally be disallowed as applicable to the earning of the non-taxable dividends.

(d) Where there is a substantial investment portfolio, which would involve a degree of supervision and management, as well as clerical and accounting records it is a question of ascertaining the direct expenses and of allocating a proportion of the management, clerical and general expenses properly attributable to those activities. Unless a more practical and suitable basis is available, the proportion of the expenses to be disallowed will be based on the total cost of the investments and securities comprising the investment portfolio and will not exceed ½% or 1/8th% for the concern that is engaged in share dealing and holds the portfolio, therefore, not solely for investment purposes.

JULY 1974

APPENDIX 4

Departmental Interpretation & Practice Notes
No. 4A (Revised 1978)

PROFIT TAX

Business Receipts — Lease Premiums
Unreturnable Deposits
Key Money
Construction Fees Etc. Etc.

1. Taxpayers or their representatives are sometimes inclined to assume that receipts of the nature indicated above are capital receipts, and consequently fail to show them separately in their accounts or computations. Such an assumption should not be made, because these receipts, by virtue of the nature of the trade or business carried on, can often be and more frequently are revenue receipts.

2. By the definition of "business" in Section 2, corporations letting property are carrying on a business, and so are other persons sub-letting property held by them under a lease other than from the Crown. Persons dealing in property are carrying on a trade.

3. It is therefore important that all persons letting or dealing in property should give full information concerning such receipts in their accounts supporting Returns to this Department.

4. Representatives if they claim such receipts to be capital receipts are asked to ascertain and report the precise facts and the exact legal relationship between the parties occasioned by the agreements under which such items were received and paid.

5. Appeals to determine whether such receipts are capital or income have not reached the Hong Kong Courts but the Departmental view as to the income nature of such receipts where a trade or business is carried on is supported by the East African Tax Case No. 37 — A.L. et al v. The Commissioner of Income Tax E.A.T.C. Vol 2 at page 148. It dealt with the question "premium for lease of premises — whether premium a capital or income receipt — whether premium should be spread over term of lease". It went to the Court of Appeal for Eastern Africa and it was held:—

   (i) That the premiums were received for the user of a capital asset and not for its realization and that they were therefore income receipts and taxable.

   (ii) That the premiums were taxable in the year of receipt and that in the absence of express power spreading over is not permissible.

It is considered that the reasons or grounds for this judicial decision are acceptable reasons for establishing these receipts as income of property owning and dealing businesses and so included in the computation of assessable profits in accordance with the provisions of Part IV, Hong Kong Inland Revenue Ordinance.

The Department's copy of East African Tax Cases is open to study by representatives upon application to the Librarian.

JULY 1978

APPENDIX 5

Departmental Interpretation & Practice Notes
No. 5 (Revised 1977)

PROFITS TAX

Deductions for Expenditure on —
(A) Scientific Research
(B) Technical Education

INTRODUCTORY

The Inland Revenue (Amendment) Ordinance, No. 35 of 1965, which introduced two new Sections — Section 16B relating to Scientific Research and Section 16C relating to Technical Education — marked an important change from the normal principles of what are allowable deductions. It is a canon of taxation that capital expenditure is not normally an allowable deduction in ascertaining the assessable profits of any trade or business. The basis of granting any deduction for capital expenditure is usually by way of capital allowances based on the wear and tear or depreciation of the assets in the course of producing profits.

By the provisions of Sections 16B and 16C, expenditure on Scientific Research (except capital expenditure on land and buildings) and expenditure on Technical Education may qualify as a full deduction for the year of assessment in the basis period of which such expenditure was incurred.

(A) SCIENTIFIC RESEARCH — SECTION 16B

1. Any person carrying on a trade or business is allowed as a deduction —

(*a*) any payments to —
   (i) an approved research institute for scientific research related to that trade or business, or
   (ii) an approved research institute, the object of which is the undertaking of scientific research related to the *class* of trade or business to which that trade or business belongs, and

(*b*) expenditure on scientific research related to that trade or business, *including capital expenditure* except to the extent that it is expenditure on land or buildings or on alterations, additions or extensions to buildings.

MEANING OF "SCIENTIFIC RESEARCH"

2. "Scientific research" is defined as "any activities in the fields of natural or applied science for the extension of knowledge".

3. It is only expenditure by a trader for scientific research *related to his trade or class of trade or business* that qualifies as a tax deduction, whether the research is undertaken or to be undertaken by an approved research institute or by the trader himself.

4. Scientific research is to be treated as related to a trade if it may lead to or facilitate an extension, or an improvement in the technical efficiency, of that trade or business, or if it is medical research which has a special relation to the welfare of workers employed in that trade or class of trade.

5. Thus scientific research undertaken by a trader with the object of branching out into a new line of business or of improving the technical efficiency of his existing business will be treated as related to the trade; and expenditure by a trader on research into an occupational disease peculiar to his industry would be treated as expenditure on research related to his trade.

SCIENTIFIC RESEARCH UNDERTAKEN
BY A RESEARCH INSTITUTE

PAYMENTS TO AN APPROVED RESEARCH INSTITUTE

6. "An approved research institute" is defined as meaning "any university, college, institute, association or organization which is approved in writing for the purposes of this section by the Director of Education as an institute, association or organization for undertaking scientific research which is or may prove to be of value to the Colony". The approval of the Director of Education may be sought at any time by the institute or any other person by way of application through the Commissioner of Inland Revenue.

7. Payments to an approved research institute will be allowable where they are —

   (i) for scientific research directly related to the particular trade or business of the claimant, or

   (ii) to an institute which undertakes scientific research related generally to the class of trade or business to which the claimant's trade or business belongs.

8. Thus a deduction may be allowed for payments made to an approved research institute for specific research in connection with the claimant's own trade or business, or for gifts or donations for general research related to the claimant's class of trade or business. The deduction does not

extend to gifts or donations to a research institute for research not related to the donor's trade or class of trade.

9. The deductions are allowable whether the payments are to be used by the institute for capital or revenue purposes. Thus payments for establishing or extending an approved research institute are allowable the same as contributions towards the administration of the institute or the actual carrying out of scientific research.

SCIENTIFIC RESEARCH UNDERTAKEN BY A TRADER

10. All expenditure on scientific research undertaken by the trader in relation to his trade or business is allowable, except capital expenditure on land or buildings and unless there is a restriction necessary as regards expenditure incurred outside the Colony — see paragraphs 20 and 21.

CAPITAL EXPENDITURE – PLANT AND MACHINERY

11. Capital expenditure on plant and machinery purchased for scientific research related to the trade is allowed in full as a deduction for the period when incurred. If the expenditure is incurred before the trade begins it is treated as incurred in the first basis period.

12. Where an allowance has been granted of the cost of any plant or machinery and that plant or machinery ceases to be used for scientific research, then the proceeds of any subsequent sale of that plant or machinery are treated as a trading receipt occurring at the time of the sale (or, where the sale takes place after the trade has ceased, in the final accounting period of the trade).

13. A similar situation arises if the plant or machinery is destroyed and insurance or compensation money is received.

14. If plant or machinery for which an allowance has been granted under Section 16B is diverted to some other use, no adjustment arises at that stage, but any subsequent sale or disposal will give rise to the consequences mentioned above.

CAPITAL EXPENDITURE – LAND AND BUILDINGS

15. No deduction is allowable under Section 16B in respect of any capital expenditure on land or buildings or on alterations, additions or extensions to buildings.

16. Where, however, such expenditure results in a relevant interest in a building or structure then allowances will be granted under Section 34 and

the building will be regarded as an "industrial building or structure" irrespective of the nature of the trade carried on. This is provided for by an amendment to the definition of an "industrial building or structure" in Section 40, so as to include any building or structure used for the purposes of scientific research in relation to any trade or business.

17. The allowances due under Section 34 are 20% initial allowance, plus an annual allowance of 4% of the capital expenditure. The initial allowance is given only on capital expenditure incurred on construction by the claimant in the basis period of the year of assessment: the annual allowance is computed on expenditure on the cost of the construction of the building, whether or not incurred by the claimant.

SUBSIDIES AND GRANTS – SECTION 16B(6)(a)

18. Where a trader incurs expenditure on scientific research and part of the cost is met by a contribution from the Crown, or a public or local authority, or any person other than the trader himself, only the net amount qualifies for allowances.

RIGHTS ARISING OUT OF SCIENTIFIC RESEARCH – SECTION 16B(5)(a)

19. It is specifically provided that no deduction is allowable for any expenditure incurred in acquiring rights in or arising out of scientific research. This applies whether or not the rights are patented in the Colony or elsewhere.

EXPENDITURE OUTSIDE THE COLONY – SECTION 16B(2)

20. Where any payment or expenditure which qualifies under these provisions is made or incurred outside the Colony it is necessary to consider whether or not it is allowable in full. If the trade or business to which it relates is carried on solely in the Colony then the full amount of the scientific research expenditure is allowed as a deduction in arriving at the chargeable profits.

21. Where the trade or business is carried on partly in and partly out of the Colony, it is necessary to consider the whole of the activities of the trade or business to arrive at the reasonable proportion of such expenditure as relates to the production of profits chargeable to tax. This is a question to be determined in the light of the circumstances of each case.

(B) TECHNICAL EDUCATION – SECTION 16C

22. Any person carrying on trade or business in the Colony is allowed a tax deduction for "any payment to be used for the purpose of technical education related to that trade or business at any university, university college, technical college or other similar institution which is approved for this purpose by the Director of Education". – Section 16C(1).

23. Applications for the approval of the Director of Education may be made at any time through the Commissioner of Inland Revenue and shall operate from whatever date is specified in the approval. This may be before or after the date of approval.

24. Technical education is deemed to be related to a trade or business only if it is of a kind specially requisite for persons employed in that class of trade or business.

25. The right of deduction extends to any payment to an approved institution to be used for the purposes of technical education related to a particular trade or business and provided it is of a kind specially requisite for persons employed in that class of trade or business, it does not have to be directly for the education of any person or persons actually employed in the particular business at that time. The right to deduction would extend to a payment to establish a unit or for the general maintenance of a unit at an approved institution so as to provide technical education of a kind specially suited or requisite to a particular class of trade or business.

26. Where payments are made for the technical education of particular persons, the payment may be made to either the student or the institution.

27. The intention of Section 16C is to broaden and not to restrict what would ordinarily be allowable deductions, so expenditure by an employer on the technical training or education of any of his employees may still be allowable even though the training or education is not through an approved institution. For example, expenditure on technical education or training provided in the employer's own business establishment would still qualify under the general authority of Section 16(1).

SEPTEMBER 1977

APPENDIX 6

Departmental Interpretation & Practice Notes
No. 6 (Revised 1977)
Inland Revenue Ordinance — Provisions As To
(A) Objections To The Commissioner
(B) Appeals To The Board Of Review
(C) Appeals To The Courts

_____

(A) OBJECTIONS TO THE COMMISSIONER

Objections by Taxpayers

1. A taxpayer who disputes an assessment must, under Section 64, give notice of objection within one month of the date of the notice of assessment.

2. Provision is retained whereby the Commissioner may extend such period where he is satisfied that a person was prevented from giving notice within that period by reason of absence from the Colony, sickness or other reasonable cause.

Requirements for a Valid Objection

3. No objection is valid unless the following requirements are fulfilled:—

   (*a*) The notice of objection is received by the Commissioner within the prescribed period or such extended period as he may consider reasonable in the circumstances mentioned in paras. 1 and 2 above. It should be noted that the prescribed period of *one month* runs from the *date* of the notice of assessment to the *receipt* of the notice of objection.

   (*b*) The notice must be in writing and must state precisely the grounds of objection to the assessment. The word "precisely" precludes any vague claim such as "the assessment is not agreed". The grounds need not be stated in legal form, they can be expressed in ordinary language, but they should be sufficiently explicit to direct the attention of the Commissioner to the particular respects which the taxpayer contends are erroneous.

   (*c*) If the assessment objected to has been made under Section 59(3) in the absence of a prescribed return, less precise grounds of objection would be accepted in the first instance; but in addition to the notice of objection being given within the prescribed period [sub-para. (*a*)] , the required return, properly completed, must also be lodged within such period, or within such further period as the Commissioner may approve for the making of such return. Before granting any further period for lodging a return, the Commissioner will usually need to be satisfied that definite steps are being taken for the preparation of the return.

(*d*) Claims for relief against Property Tax, by owner-occupiers [Section 5(3)] , and in respect of vacancy [Section 7] , are to be made within 90 days of the end of the relevant year of assessment (or within 90 days of the date of the Notice of Assessment, if later), but the Commissioner may extend such period if he is satisfied that a person was prevented from giving notice within that period by reason of absence from the Colony, sickness or other reasonable cause. These claims are treated as objections under Section 64.

4. Where there is a reassessment of tax, either increasing or reducing the liability, the person assessed shall have no further right of objection than he would have had if the reassessment had not been made, except to the extent to which a fresh liability in respect of any particular is imposed, or an existing liability is increased or reduced.

Departmental Action on Objections

5. It is, of course, impossible for the Commissioner personally to proceed to deal fully with each and every objection from the moment it is received. The preliminary stages must be delegated to the Assistant Commissioners and through them to the Assessors. The Departmental procedure is aimed at avoiding, as far as possible, any delay in dealing with objections. This can only be achieved if there is firstly a proper presentation of the objection by the taxpayer or his representative, followed by a prompt reply to any further information requested by the Assessor or Assistant Commissioner on behalf of the Commissioner. With co-operation all round it is hoped that objections can be speedily considered with a view to reaching an early agreement, and where that is not possible within four months, preparations will then be made to have the case referred to the Commissioner for his determination.

6. A proper presentation of the objection will involve not only a statement of the precise grounds of objection [para. 3(*b*) above] but also the furnishing of evidence and arguments in support of the contention that the assessment is erroneous. As there is no formal hearing of the objection before the Commissioner, any arguments advanced in support of the grounds of objection should quote the reference to any relevant authorities or decided cases.

7. Upon receipt of an objection it will firstly be examined to see whether it fulfils the requirements for a valid objection. If not, the taxpayer and his representative will be informed promptly by an Assistant Commissioner of any defects and advised of any action which could make it a valid objection.

8. Where an objection is valid, it will be acknowledged by an Assistant Commissioner who will also advise whether or not any of the tax has been stood-over under Section 71(2) pending the result of the objection or appeal. Tax will not be stood-over where the objection is considered at that stage to be frivolous or to have little merit, or if there are circumstances which may, with delay, create doubts as to ultimate collection or recovery of the tax. Where there is some real merit or substance in the objection, then only the amount of tax in dispute will be stood-over and any balance must be paid by the due date.

9. There will be cases where, by reason of the information and evidence given in support of a properly prepared objection, the Commissioner may be able to admit promptly the taxpayer's claim. In that event the taxpayer and his representative will be so informed by an Assessor on behalf of the Commissioner and a revised notice of assessment will then be issued, with an advice of any refund due.

10. In many cases further information or facts may be required before the Commissioner can determine the objection. These will be asked for as soon as possible after receipt of the notice of objection. The prompt submission of this information will enable the objection to be dealt with expeditiously. Undue delay by a taxpayer or his representative may result in the withdrawal of any stand-over of tax or if the delay is prolonged, in the objection having to be determined forthwith.

11. Attempts will be made to see if further explanation of the assessment or of the provisions of the law, can remove misunderstandings and bring about agreement to the original assessment. In other cases, after consideration of the fresh and further information a revision of the assessment may be proposed which may not be entirely on the lines of the objection. If agreement can be reached as to the assessment, the objection can be withdrawn and any necessary adjustment of the assessment can be made in accordance with Section 64(3).

12. In the process of attempting to reach agreement or of finally determining the objection, the Commissioner may by notice in writing require the taxpayer to furnish such particulars as may be deemed necessary in connexion with the assessment. He may require the production of all books or other documents, and may summon any person, who in his opinion is able to give evidence respecting the assessment, to attend before him and may examine such person on oath or otherwise — Section 64(2).

13. Where the Commissioner proposes to examine any person *on oath* he is required to give prior notice in writing so as to afford the taxpayer or his authorized representative a reasonable opportunity to be present at such examination.

14. In cases where no agreement is possible (or if there is undue delay in furnishing further facts or particulars which have been sought) the taxpayer and his representative will be notified that it is proposed to refer the objection to the Commissioner for his determination in accordance with Section 64(4). In most cases this position should be reached within not more than four months of the receipt of the notice of objection; in many cases it can be less; but any cases carrying over that period will be kept under constant review. There would, of course, be no point for either party to deal with objections based upon questions of law which may still be sub-judice and pending clarification in other appeals already before the Board of Review or the Court.

15. With the advice that a case is to be referred for the Commissioner's determination, there will be sent out a copy of what are considered to be the facts as ascertained from information available to the Department. The taxpayer and his representative will be asked whether there are any further facts, documentary evidence, representations or arguments which they may wish to bring forward. In the absence of any comment within two weeks the Commissioner will then proceed to this determination.

Determination of an Objection by the Commissioner

16. There is no formal hearing and the taxpayer or his representative will not appear before the Commissioner unless the Commissioner so requires or they specifically so request and the Commissioner is of the opinion that granting the request could assist in the determination. They will, of course, be given an opportunity to be present if the Commissioner proposes to examine any person on oath.

17. If the Commissioner requires any person to attend before him in connexion with the determination of an objection, he may allow any such person, other than the taxpayer or his authorized representative, any reasonable expenses necessarily incurred by him in so attending.

18. The Commissioner may authorize the Deputy Commissioner or an Assistant Commissioner to determine any objection and the Deputy Commissioner or the Assistant Commissioner then has all the powers and functions of the Commissioner.

19. The Commissioner is required to consider every valid objection and within a reasonable time may confirm, reduce, increase or annual the assessment. Within one month after the determination he will transmit his deter-

mination in writing to the person objecting to the assessment, together with his reasons for such determination. There will also be given a statement of the facts which the Commissioner has considered in arriving at his determination. A determination is not necessary where agreement as to the amount of the assessment is reached between the taxpayer and the Commissioner or an Assessor acting on behalf of the Commissioner.

20. In determining an objection, the Commissioner acts in an administrative, not a judicial capacity. He is not a tribunal deciding an issue between the Assessor and the objecting taxpayer. His function is purely an administrative one in which he puts himself in the place of the Assessor and determines what according to his view the assessment ought to be, subject to the right of appeal to the Board of Review.

(B) APPEALS TO THE BOARD OF REVIEW

21. An appeal against the determination of the Commissioner on any valid objection may be made to the Board of Review.

22. The Board of Review is an independent tribunal consisting of persons drawn from various walks of life and activity. There is a panel consisting of a chairman and two deputy chairmen, all qualified and experienced legal men, and not more than 75 other members, all of whom are appointed by the Governor. For the purpose of hearing appeals, three or more members, including the chairman or a deputy chairman, are nominated by the Colonial Secretary, as may be necessary from time to time. Decisions are based on a majority vote, with the chairman or deputy chairman having, if necessary, a second or casting vote.

Requirements of a Valid Appeal

23. For an appeal to be valid, it must —

(a) be made in writing to the Clerk to the Board of Review within one month of the transmission of the Commissioner's written determination, or within such further period as the Board may allow if satisfied that the appellant was prevented by illness or other reasonable cause from giving the notice within one month,

(b) be accompanied by a copy of the Commissioner's written determination, and the reasons therefor and of the statement of facts, with all appendices,

(c) contain a statement of the grounds of appeal (see para. 30),

(d) the Commissioner must at the same time be served with a copy of the notice of appeal and of the statement of the grounds of appeal.

Hearing and Disposal of Appeals

24. A time and date for the hearing of an appeal is fixed as soon as possible after the receipt of a notice of appeal. Fourteen clear days' notice is given to both the appellant and the Commissioner. Appeals will usually be heard at On Hing Building, 5/F, 1-4 On Hing Terrace, Hong Kong. Sittings are held generally from about 5 p.m. to 7 p.m. However, at any time before the hearing the appellant may give notice in writing to the Clerk to the Board withdrawing the appeal.

25. An appellant shall attend each meeting of the Board at which his appeal is heard either in person or by an authorized representative. (An "authorized representative" is a person authorized in writing by a person to act on his behalf for the purpose of the Inland Revenue Ordinance).

26. If there is no attendance the Board may either (i) dismiss the appeal or (ii) proceed with the appeal or (iii) postpone or adjourn the hearing if satisfied that non-attendance was due to sickness or other reasonable cause. If the appeal is dismissed, (i) above, the appellant is given 30 days in which to ask for a review and should the Board be satisfied that non-attendance was due to sickness or other reasonable cause, set aside the order for dismissal and hear the appeal.

27. If the appellant is outside the Colony and is unlikely to be in the Colony within a period considered reasonable by the Board, the Board, provided the appellant has made an application that has been received by the Board at least seven days before the day fixed for the hearing, may hear the appeal in the absence of the appellant or authorized representative, taking into consideration any written representations made to them by the appellant.

28. The Assessor who made the assessment appealed against or some other person authorized by the Commissioner attends each meeting of the Board in support of the assessment.

29. All appeals are heard in camera, but official publication of the hearings may be made in such a manner that the identity of the appellant is not disclosed.

30. The onus of proving that the assessment appealed against is excessive or incorrect is on the appellant. Failure to discharge this onus can be fatal to the appeal. [There is substantial legal authority for the view that such a requirement is invalid and that appeals are to be determined on the balance of probability, see BR 20/71. — Author]

31. An appellant may not at a hearing rely on any grounds other than the grounds contained in his statement of grounds of appeal unless the Board so consents.

32. As soon as possible before the date fixed for the hearing of an appeal the Assessor or other person representing the Commissioner at the appeal will notify the Clerk to the Board of Review and also the taxpayer of his representative, of the references to authorities or decided cases which will be cited during the appeal. It will assist the Board if the taxpayer or his representative will do likewise with a copy to the Commissioner.

33. The Board has power to summon any person to attend as a witness at any meeting if it considers such person may be able to give evidence affecting the appeal. A witness may be examined on oath or otherwise and may be allowed any reasonable expenses for so attending. For the purposes of appeals the Board has the powers granted under paras. (d), (e), (f) and (g) of Section 4 of the Commissions of Inquiry Ordinance.

34. The Board may admit or reject any evidence adduced, whether oral or documentary and the provisions of the Evidence Ordinance, relating to the admissibility of evidence do not apply. This gives the Board greater freedom of action in ascertaining or reaching a conclusion as to the facts on which to base a decision.

35. In so far as the facts are not agreed by the parties when the case was dealt with by the Commissioner, the Board is the fact-finding body. If certain facts are not agreed, the onus of introducing evidence before the Board, in the first instance, lies upon the appellant. If he gives no evidence the Board will deal with the case on the material before it. If all the facts are agreed, then only points of law are involved in deciding the issue.

36. The Board sits as a judicial tribunal with the duty firstly of ascertaining the primary facts. Where these are agreed by the parties, the Board may accept them without further proof. If they are in issue in any respect, then the Board must resolve this issue judicially. Having ascertained the primary facts, they then draw any inferences which may reasonably be drawn from the primary facts; and finally they come to a conclusion on whether the facts so found by them bring the case within the provisions of the Ordinance.

37. After hearing the appeal the Board may confirm, reduce, increase or annul the assessment appealed against or may remit the case to the Commissioner with the opinion of the Board thereon. The Commissioner shall then revise the assessment in accordance with the opinion of the Board. If necessary, the Commissioner may go back to the Board for direction as to how to give effect to that opinion.

38. Where the Board does not reduce or annul the assessment, the appellant may be ordered to pay as costs to the Board a sum not exceeding $100.

39. There is no provision for the awarding of costs to either the appellant or the Commissioner on an appeal to the Board of Review.

40. A decision of the Board of Review is final, subject to the rights of appeal to the Supreme Court as explained below.

(C) APPEALS TO THE COURTS

41. If either the appellant or the Commissioner is dissatisfied with a decision of a Board of Review they may make an application requiring the Board to state a case on a question of law for the opinion of the High Court.

42. Such application must be made in writing delivered to the Clerk to the Board, within one month of the date of the Board's decision or the date of the communication by which the decision is notified in writing. A fee of $50 must accompany the application for a case stated.

43. A question of law will include a question of mixed fact and law. There is no appeal on a question purely of fact and the Courts will only interfere with a finding of the Board of Review if on the primary facts and evidence no person acting judiciously and properly instructed as to relevant law could have come to the determination under appeal. (See Commissioner of Inland Revenue v Rico International Ltd. H.K.T.C. pages 269-271).

44. A judge of the High Court may hear and determine any question of law on a stated case and may confirm, reduce, increase or annul the assessment determined by the Board of Review, or may remit the case to the Board with the opinion of the court thereon. In that event the Board will revise the assessment in accordance with the opinion of the Court.

45. The Court may make such order as to costs as may seem fit.

46. Appeals from decisions of the High Court to the Full Court or to the Privy Council are governed by the provisions of the Supreme Court Ordinance, the Rules of the Supreme Court, and the Orders and Rules governing appeals to the Privy Council.

[Since this practice note was written, the law has been changed to permit appeals to bypass the Board of Review or to bypass the Lower Court in appropriate circumstances (see page 261). – Author]

OCTOBER 1977

APPENDIX 7

Departmental Interpretation & Practice Notes
No. 7

INDEX

MACHINERY OR PLANT –
DEPRECIATION ALLOWANCES

Part I – INTRODUCTION

1. The Inland Revenue (Amendment) (No. 4) Ordinance 1980 introduced changes in the system of granting depreciation allowances in respect of machinery or plant. The new system, known as the "Pooling" System, applies for years of assessment 1980/81 et seq, and is dealt with in Sections 39B, 39C and 39D of the Inland Revenue Ordinance. The old system, comprised in Sections 37, 37A, 38 and 39, applies for years of assessment up to and including 1979/80; in certain circumstances, referred to in paras. 20 and 23, the Old Scheme may also apply for subsequent years.

2. **Persons entitled to the allowances**

Unlike the provisions relating to industrial buildings allowances, [Departmental Interpretation and Practice Notes No. 2 refer], which limit those allowances to certain specified trades or businesses, depreciation allowances in respect of machinery or plant are available to all persons who carry on a "trade, profession or business", without placing any limitation on the meaning of those words. Accordingly, the allowances, under Sections 37 and 39B extend to all persons carrying on all types of trades, professions or businesses in respect of which they are chargeable to Profits Tax under Part IV of the Ordinance. They may also be extended to employees where the use of machinery or plant is essential for the production of income assessable to Salaries Tax – Section 12(1)(b).

3. **Expenditure which Qualifies**

The expenditure in respect of which the allowances are to be granted is "capital expenditure". "Capital expenditure" does not include expenditure which is reimbursed by way of or is attributable to any grant, subsidy or similar financial assistance and in relation to the person incurring the expenditure does not include any expenditure which is allowed to be deducted in ascertaining for Profits Tax the profits of a trade or business carried on by that person. [Section 40(1)]

Both Sections 37 and 39B refer to "capital expenditure on the provision of machinery or plant" and subsection (2) of Section 37 refers to "the cost of the asset". Both phrases are construed as meaning the net cost of acquisition of the asset to the owner for the time being who is claiming the allowances, the net cost of acquisition being the supplier's price for the item, plus any charges relating to freight, insurance, delivery, import duties etc., and less any discounts, rebates, subsidies etc. accorded to the purchaser. The decision in

C.I.R. v. Hong Kong Bottlers Ltd. (H.K.T.C. 497) was that cost is to be taken as meaning the same as capital expenditure incurred by the person claiming the allowance but see paragraph 13 below as to plant and machinery which is acquired other than by purchase.

Hire purchase interest charges do not form part of the qualifying expenditure (see para. 12 of this pamphlet).

4.   Capital expenditure on the provision of machinery or plant for the purposes of scientific research does not qualify for depreciation allowances under Part VI if a deduction in respect of such expenditure has been allowed under Section 16B (see D.I. & P.N. No. 5).

5.   "Machinery or Plant" Defined

The Ordinance contains no exhaustive definition of "machinery or plant". However, Section 40 of the Ordinance and Rule 2 of the Inland Revenue Rules do assist in determining what is "machinery or plant" for the purposes of the allowances.

(i)   Section 40(1) provides, inter alia, that "capital expenditure on the provision of machinery or plant" — "includes capital expenditure on alterations to an existing building incidental to the installation of that machinery or plant for the purposes of the trade, profession or business".

(ii)   Rule 2 of the Inland Revenue Rules provides, inter alia, that the expression "machinery or plant" — "shall include or be deemed to include the items specified in the second column of the First Part of the Table annexed to this rule". The Table (see Appendix A(i)) lists specific items which are "machinery or plant". Furthermore, the Second Part of the Table (see Appendix A(ii)) lists specific items which are to be treated as "implements, utensils and articles". — These include such items as loose tools, crockery, linen, etc. which are normally dealt with on the "replacements basis" under Section 16(1)(f) and are not, by virtue of paragraph (1) of Rule 2, "machinery or plant" in respect of which depreciation allowances are to be granted. Finally, paragraph (3) of Rule 2 provides that wharves shall not be or be deemed to be "plant or machinery".

6.   None the less, as stated above "machinery or plant" is not exhaustively defined and for the purposes of the allowances the Table annexed to Rule 2 lists as the last of the items "machinery or plant not specified in items 1–32". Where, therefore, allowances are claimed in respect of expenditure on an item not particularly specified in the list it is still necessary to consider whether the item falls into the general description "machinery or plant".

7.   The meaning of the phrase "machinery and plant" has been

considered in a number of Cases by the Courts in the United Kingdom and Commonwealth Countries. On the principles established, the Department has ruled on a number of items which are not covered by those listed in Appendix A. Such items are listed in Appendices B and C.

8. Capital Expenditure incurred prior to Commencement of Business

(i) Under the provisions of Section 40(2) of the Ordinance, where a person incurs capital expenditure preparatory to the commencement of his trade or business, etc. such expenditure will, for the purposes of the allowances under Part VI, be deemed to have been incurred on the day that business commences. The provision applies to all expenditure ranking for allowances under Part VI, namely on machinery or plant and on buildings.

(ii) In this connexion it should be noted that where a person carries on a trade or business and incurs capital expenditure on the provision of assets to be used in a *new* trade about to be commenced, the provisions of Section 40(2) apply and no allowances in respect of the expenditure thus incurred can be granted until commencement of the new business, i.e. the allowances cannot be granted against the profits of the *existing* business.

(iii) Section 40(2) only applies for the purposes of expenditure affected by Part VI. The practice as to other expenditure incurred prior to the commencement of business is broadly to treat this the same way as it would be if it had been incurred after the commencement of business. So any capital expenditure on plant or machinery which represented expenditure on scientific research and which was incurred prior to the commencement of business, would be allowed under Section 16B as a deduction for the first basis period.

9. Changes in Partnerships — Treatment of Allowances under Part VI

(N.B. — It should be noted that the following remarks apply to Industrial Buildings and Commercial Buildings, as well as to Machinery and Plant.)

For the years 1975/76 onwards, where there is a change in the constitution of a partnership, assessable profits are to be computed as if no such change had occurred. Depreciation Allowances are therefore given in calculating assessable profits without regard to the partnership change and no balancing adjustments arise on the change.

Part II — THE "OLD SCHEME" (Years of Assessment up to and including 1979/80)

10. The Allowances

(i) *Initial Allowance*

Section 37(1) provides for the granting of an initial allowance of one-fourth of the capital expenditure incurred on the provision of machinery or plant. The allowance is given for the year of assessment in the basis period for which the expenditure was incurred. There is no requirement that the asset must be in use in the basis period but the allowance is subject to the asset eventually being acquired and used in the trade carried on. It is the Departmental view that the mere payment of a deposit or advance is not expenditure on the provision of machinery or plant unless it is irrecoverable under a binding contract for the purchase of the asset. It is to be noted that the allowance is granted in respect of capital expenditure "incurred", so that the allowance is not limited only to sums actually paid. Where there is a definite contractual obligation existing, the due date for payment of deposits, instalments, etc. will be regarded as the date when the expenditure is incurred, even if actual payment occurs later. A mere contingency does not, however, give rise to expenditure incurred, and following the decisions in the courts elsewhere, no allowance is granted in respect of a contingent liability only. In the absence of a contract, the date of delivery of the asset is normally taken to be the date on which the expenditure is incurred.

In connexion with the Initial Allowance it is important to note that the statutory definition of "basis period" contained in Section 2 of the Ordinance is qualified for the purposes of the allowances under Part VI by the further definition contained in Section 40; so that (a) where two basis periods overlap the period common to both is deemed to fall into the first basis period only and (b) where there is an interval between the end of the basis period for one year of assessment and the beginning of the basis period for the next succeeding year of assessment the interval is deemed to fall in the second basis period. The amended definition thus ensures that, on the one hand, initial allowance is granted only once in respect of expenditure falling into two basis periods (as could happen when the Commissioner determines the basis periods on a change of accounting date) and on the other hand ensures that initial allowance on expenditure is not lost by reason of its having been incurred in a period that is not part of a basis period for any year of assessment (as, for example, on the cessation of a trade assessed under Section 18D(2) plant may have been purchased during the gap between the end of the basis period of the penultimate year and the commencement of the basis period for the final year on 1st April following).

(ii) *Annual Allowances*

Section 37(2) provides for the granting of an annual allowance in respect of each year of assessment at the end of the basis period for which the person carrying on the trade, etc. owns and has in use machinery or plant for the purpose of his trade, etc. It is important to note that whereas the initial allowance is granted simply when capital expenditure has been incurred by a person carrying on trade, etc. the annual allowance is available only to the person who owns the asset and has it in use at the end of the basis period. It is the Departmental view that "in use at the end of the basis period" ought not to be too strictly construed. Thus, where the last day of the basis period falls on a public holiday resulting in assets being temporarily out of use on that day, the allowance is none the less granted. Again, where a machine is temporarily idle during the last few days of the basis period, e.g. awaiting commencement of a new production run, the machine is considered to be "in use" for the purposes of the allowance. In regard to spare engines, e.g. reserve engines for taxis, the Department's attitude is that where these are "on the bench" ready for installation and use they store for issue or are held crated as received from the supplier they are not considered to be "in use" for the purposes of the allowance. Where a person ceases one trade and transfers the plant and machinery to another trade which is carried on by him, it is not considered that he is entitled to claim more than one annual allowance on that plant and machinery for any one year of assessment as the allowance is granted to the "person" and not to the "trade" or "business".

(iii) *Rate of the Annual Allowance*

The section provides that the annual allowance shall be calculated at the rates prescribed by the Board of Inland Revenue and the rates prescribed by the Board are set out in the third column of the First Part of the Table annexed to Rule 2 of the Inland Revenue Rules. The Table — (see Appendix A(i)), (a) gives the rates of depreciation for certain classifications of machinery or plant, and (b) for machinery or plant not specifically itemized, lays down a general rate of 15% per annum. (The Commissioner has power to allow a higher rate where appropriate (see para. 28)).

(iv) *Calculation of the Allowances*

The section provides that the annual allowance is to be calculated upon the "reducing value of the asset". This is defined as the "cost of the asset" (see para. 3 above) reduced by any initial allowance given in respect of the asset, and by any annual allowances computed under the section.

(v) The following example illustrates points mentioned in the above sub-paragraphs —

Example 1

PQR Co. Ltd., which has been trading for some years as textile manufacturer, incurred the following expenditure on the purchase and installation of machinery for use in its factory:—

1st August 1978 — Cost of looms	$100,000
30th September 1978 — Alterations to factory building in connexion with machinery installation	16,000

17th April 1979 — Cost of major
modification to adapt looms for use
with new synthetic fibre thread   10,000
                                                                  $126,000

Owing to the decision by the directors to modify the machine it was not put into use until completion of the modification work in April 1979. The allowances due to PQR Co. Ltd. would be as follows, assuming that accounts are prepared annually to 31st March:—

		Allowances granted
Year ended 31st March 1979 Cost	$116,000	
Initial Allowance — 1978/79	29,000	$29,000
	$ 87,000	
Annual Allowance — 1978/79	—	Nil (asset not in use)
	$ 87,000	
Year ended 31st March 1980 — cost of modification	10,000	
	$ 97,000	
Initial Allowance — 1979/80	2,500	$ 2,500
	$ 94,500	
Annual Allowance — 1979/80 (at 25%)	23,625	
Carry forward to 1980/81 W.D.V.	$ 70,875	

11. Balancing Allowances and Balancing Charges

(i) Section 38 provides for the granting of balancing allowances or the imposition of balancing charges in respect of machinery or plant, (for which initial and/or annual allowances have been granted for any year of assessment), which is either —

(a) sold (whether still in use or not), or

(b) destroyed, or

(c) put out of use (as being worn out, obsolete, or otherwise useless or no longer required).

An allowance or charge will arise if the happening of one of these events occurs either whilst the taxpayer is carrying on his trade, etc., or at the time he ceases to do so, and the allowance will be granted or the charge imposed for the year of assessment in the basis period for which the event occurs.

(ii) *Calculation of Balancing Allowance or Charge*

The allowance or charge is computed by reference to the amount of "expenditure still unallowed" — that is to say on the cost of the asset, less any initial and annual allowances granted in respect of the asset. The resultant figure is compared with the total proceeds of disposal (if any) by way of sale, insurance, salvage or compensation monies. Where these are less than the amount of the expenditure unallowed a balancing allowance arises in respect of the difference and where these exceed the amount of expenditure unallowed a balancing charge falls to be made in the amount of the excess.

(iii) *Limitation on Balancing Charges*

Subsection (5) of Section 38 provides that, in any event, any balancing charge which falls to be made in respect of machinery or plant shall be restricted to the total of (a) any initial allowance granted in respect of the asset and (b) any annual allowances granted in respect of the asset, including allowances computed, at a higher rate than laid down in Rule 2, under the Commissioner's discretionary powers (see para. 28).

(iv) The following examples demonstrate the operation of the balancing allowances or balancing charges provision:—

Example 2

X and Y Co., that had been trading for some years, purchased printing machinery on 1st October 1977 at a cost of $100,000. The machinery was put into immediate use and remained in use until 30th November 1979 when it was destroyed in a fire at the firm's business premises. The firm received $25,000 by way of insurance proceeds for the total loss of the machinery. Accounts are prepared annually to 31st December. A balancing allowance would be granted for the year of assessment 1979/80 as follows:—

			Printing Machinery
Cost — 1st October 1977			$100,000
1977/78	Initial Allowance 25%	$25,000	
	Annual Allowance 15%	11,250	36,250
			$ 63,750
1978/79	Annual Allowance 15%		9,563
			$ 54,187
Insurance proceeds — 30th November 1979			25,000
Balancing Allowance — 1979/80			$ 29,187

Example 3

L. & M. Co. Ltd. with an old established trade, purchased the following assets:—

Cost

1st June 1977	New motor van (No. BY1234)	$36,000
	New motor van (No. BY1235)	36,000
	Second hand motor van (No. AR4321)	16,000

Accounts are prepared annually to 30th June.

As a result of group reorganization, the company on 31st July 1979, transferred to its Parent Company, Hold-All Ltd., the motor van BY1234 for $4,000. On 1st July 1979 a new van was purchased from Excelsior Car Dealing Co. Ltd., the vans BY1235 and AR4321 being taken in part exchange. $23,000 was allowed as the value of the vans traded in. In regard to the vans traded in, the Commissioner under Section 38A, (see para. 24) on the basis of further information given allocated the part exchange value as to BY1235 $18,000 and AR4321 $5,000. The sale of the van BY1234 was a sale between a seller and a buyer having control over the seller. If under the provisions of Section 38B (see para. 25) the Commissioner decided that the Market Value was $17,000, the following balancing allowances and charges would result:—

Motor Van 25%

	BY1234	BY1235	AR4321
Cost June 1977	$36,000	$36,000	$16,000
1977/78 Initial Allowance	9,000	9,000	4,000
	$27,000	$27,000	$12,000
Annual Allowance	6,750	6,750	3,000
W.D.V.	$20,250	$20,250	$ 9,000
1978/79 Annual Allowance	5,063	5,063	2,250
W.D.V.	$15,187	$15,187	$ 6,750
Sale and Part Exchange	17,000(S.38B)	18,000(S.38A)	5,000(S.38A)
1979/80 Balancing Charge	$ 1,813	$ 2,813	—
Balancing Allowance			$ 1,750

12. **Machinery or Plant acquired under a Hire Purchase Agreement**

(i) Special provisions are contained in Section 37A for the granting of allowances in respect of machinery or plant purchased under a hire purchase agreement. The section provides for the granting of the initial allowance of one-fourth in respect of each instalment paid during the basis period for the year of assessment and for the granting of annual allowances based on the cost of the asset for each year of assessment at the end of the basis period for which the asset is in use. In computing the allowances only the capital portion of instalments and of the total price is to be brought in. (The interest portion would qualify as an outgoing or expense deductible subject to the provisions of Section 16(1)).

(ii) The following example demonstrates the application of Section 37A:—

Example 4

X, who has been in business for some years as a stock-broker, acquires on hire purchase an electric typewriter. The hire purchase agreement, which is entered into on 1st December 1975 states the cash price of the typewriter to be $4,000 and the total price including interest $4,800. The agreement provides for an initial deposit of $400, payable on execution of the agreement and the balance (interest and capital), to be paid by twenty monthly instalments of $220, the first instalment payable 1st January 1976 and the remaining nineteen instalments on the 1st day of each succeeding calendar month. The instalments are expressed to be as to capital $200 and as to interest $20. X prepares his accounts annually to 30th June. Allowances under Part VI would fall to be granted as follows:—

	Capital Instalments	Electric Typewriter (15%)
Year ended 30.6.76 (Deposit + 6 instalments)	$1,600	$4,400 (Total "Cash Price")
1976/77 Initial Allowance 1,600 × ¼		400
		$4,000
Annual Allowance		600
		$3,400
Year ended 30.6.77 (12 instalments)	$2,400	
1977/78 Initial Allowance 2,400 × ¼		600
		$2,800
Annual Allowance		420
		$2,380
Year ended 30.6.78 (2 instalments)	$ 400	
1978/79 Initial Allowance 400 × ¼		100
		$2,280
Annual Allowance		342
		$1,938
1979/80 Annual Allowance		291
W.D.V. C/F.		$1,647

13. Machinery or Plant passing without being sold

Paragraph 9 should be referred to as regards the treatment in the case of partnership changes.

Section 37(4) refers to cases of succession to a trade etc. where an asset passes from the old proprietor to the new, and without having been sold continues to be used in the trade. In such cases the reduced value still unallowed to the old proprietor is to be taken as the reduced value for the purpose of allowances to the successor. No initial allowance is due [Section 37(5)]. When the asset is subsequently disposed of, Section 38(2) provides that the reduced value taken over is treated as the capital expenditure incurred by the successor, for the purpose of computing balancing allowances and/or balancing charges.

Section 37(4) does not apply where there is no succession to the trade etc. so that strictly no allowances are due to an individual who acquires an asset otherwise than by purchase; for example where the individual does not succeed to a trade but becomes possessed of an asset by inheritance or by gift. In practice however, the Revenue will grant annual allowances to the recipient and will compute the subsequent balancing allowance or balancing charge, on the basis of treating the cost of acquisition as the written down value at the date of acquisition, the written down value being computer in the case of an asset which had been used for private purposes by the donor, by writing off notional allowances (see para. 27) for the period of such use.

In this type of disposal no balancing allowance or balancing charge arises in respect of the testator or donor, as a devolution of property in such circumstances is not within the events specified in Section 38(1) [see para. 11].

14. Replacement of Machinery or Plant

(i) Section 39 of the Ordinance offers a measure of relief against a balancing charge arising under Section 38 where the machinery or plant in respect of which the charge arises is replaced by the owner. The relief is given by setting off the balancing charge on the old machinery or plant against the capital expenditure incurred on the new machinery. The treatment of balancing charges under this section is at the option of the taxpayer and the section is implemented only where notice in writing is given to the Commissioner election for the provisions of Section 39 to apply to a particular item of machinery or plant.

(ii) The effect of an election will depend upon whether the balancing charge on the old machinery or plant exceeds the cost of the replacement machinery or vice versa:—

A. Where the balancing charge exceeds the cost of the replacement asset the balancing charge to be included in the chargeable profits will be the difference between the original balancing charge and the cost of the new asset. Further, no initial or annual allowances are granted on the new asset and, in the event of its subsequent disposal, etc., no balancing allowance is given. On the other hand, upon disposal of the new asset, there may arise a balancing charge and for this purpose the balancing charge set off in respect of the old asset is deemed to have been an initial allowance granted in respect of the replacement asset to the extent of the cost of the replacement asset.

Example 5

(a) An asset that is sold for $14,000 has a written down value of $5,000 (i.e. cost $20,000 less the total of allowances given $15,000).

A replacement cost $8,000: an election is made under Section 39 with the result that:—

Balancing Charge on asset sold ($14,000 less W.D.V. $5,000)	$9,000
Less offset against cost of replacement	8,000
Net Balancing Charge to be included in assessable profits	$1,000

Replacement cost $8,000 less balancing charge offset $8,000.
Balance on which depreciation allowances due – nil.
(b) If in a later year: the replacement machine was destroyed.
(i)   there being no insurance recovery, no balancing allowance would be due;
(ii) if the insurance recovery was $8,500 the balancing charge would be limited to $8,000, the amount of the deemed initial allowance given under the provisions of Section 39.

B. Where, however, the balancing charge arising on the disposal of the old machinery or plant is less than the capital expenditure incurred on the replacement asset the effect of an election is that –
(a) No balancing charge is made in respect of the old asset.
(b) Initial and annual allowances are granted in respect of the replacement asset on the difference between the cost thereof and the amount of the balancing charge on the asset.
(c) In the event of the disposal, etc. of the replacement asset any resultant balancing allowance or charge is to be calculated as though the balancing charge on the old asset had been an initial allowance granted on the new asset.

Example 6

(a) If in example 5 the replacement machine, on which annual allowance is due at the rate of 15%, had cost $18,000, the treatment under Part VI will be:—

Machine Cost		$18,000
Less Balancing Charge offset (Sec. 39)	$ 9,000	$9,000
Initial Allowance		2,250
		$6,750
Annual Allowance		1,013
W.D.V. C/F.		$5,737

(b) If in the following year this machine is sold for $12,000 not replaced, a balancing charge of $6,263 will be made i.e. sale price $12,000 less the written down value $5,737. [This charge of $6,263 is less than the total allowances given — see (c) above.]

Part III — THE "NEW SCHEME" (1980/81 Onwards)

15. Outline

The new scheme for granting Depreciation Allowances was introduced by the Inland Revenue (Amendment) (No. 4) Ordinance 1980 and is effective for the years of assessment 1980/81 et seq. The new system does not make any fundamental changes to the allowances given or charges made; the intention is merely to dispense with frequent balancing adjustments having to be made on the disposal of assets and to save the time and expense involved in maintaining detailed records of the written down values of individual items of machinery or plant. The scheme seeks to achieve these objectives by creating a "pool" of expenditure on machinery or plant which qualifies for an annual allowance at the same rate. The annual allowance is given at the appropriate rate on the residue of expenditure remaining in the pool after deducting the sale, etc., proceeds of any items included in the pool. A balancing charge will arise only when disposal proceeds exceed the residue of expenditure in the pool and a balancing allowance can be given only on the cessation of the trade, profession or business.

16. The Allowances

(i) *Initial Allowance*

Section 39B(1) provides for the granting of an initial allowance equal to one quarter of the capital expenditure incurred by the person carrying on a trade, profession or business on the provision of machinery and plant for the purpose of producing profits chargeable to Profits Tax. The Sub-Section uses the same terms as Section 37(1) so that the allowance continues to be due for the year of assessment in the basis period for which the expenditure is incurred and there is again no pre-requirement as to ownership or to the asset being in use. The Departmental views on the meaning of expenditure incurred and basis periods remain as set out in paragraph 10(i) above.

(ii) *Annual Allowances*

Section 39B(2) provides for an annual allowance to be given for each year of assessment. This is calculated at the appropriate rate on the reducing value of each class of machinery or plant. A class of machinery or plant is made up of all items carrying the same rate of depreciation. There is no requirement that the asset must be owned and in use at the end of the basis period. Section 39B(2) requires only that the machinery and plant is owned or has been owned at some time during the basis period or during an earlier one; similarly it needs only to have been used at some time for the production of profits for it to qualify for an annual allowance. The reducing value of a class of machinery or plant on which the annual allowance is given is calculated by *aggregating* (as applicable) —

(a) the reducing value remaining in the "pool" brought forward after giving the Annual Allowance due for the previous year;

(b) qualifying capital expenditure incurred in the basis period for the current year on machinery and plant of the same class less any initial allowance given in respect of that expenditure;

(c) the residue of expenditure unallowed after Initial and Annual Allowances given in previous years on machinery and plant purchased under a hire-purchase agreement where such machinery or plant passed into the ownership of the trader during the basis period for the previous year of assessment (see para. 19);

(d) the cost less notional annual allowances of machinery and plant previously used for other purposes prior to being brought into use in the trade during the basis period (see para. 27);

(e) the reducing value taken over in respect of any asset acquired without being purchased (see para. 22);

— and *deducting* (as applicable) —

(f) the aggregate of any sale, insurance, salvage or compensation money received in respect of any item of machinery or plant belonging to that class disposed of during the basis period (see para. 18);

(g) the reducing value (determined by the Commissioner) of any machinery or plant previously used wholly and exclusively in the production of profits which ceased to be so used during the basis period (see para. 21).

The following examples illustrate the operation of the pooling system:—

Example 7

A.B. Ltd., a textile manufacturing company, makes up its accounts to 31st December. Written Down Values for depreciation allowance purposes brought forward to 1980/81 are as follows:

Motor Vehicles (25%)	$42,670
Sewing Machine (25%)	$38,572
Office Furniture (15%)	$ 8,228
Room Air-conditioning Units (15%)	$ 5,430

During the year to 31st December 1980 a van was damaged beyond repair in an accident. The Insurance Company paid $9,362 and $500 was obtained from a scrap dealer for the wreck. A new van was purchased for $36,000.

Some old office furniture was disposed of for $1,300 (i.e. less than its cost price). A new air-conditioning unit for the manager's office cost $3,000; the old one was sold to the member of the staff for $500.

1980/81 The machinery and plant within the same class (bearing the same rate of depreciation allowance) is "pooled".

Machinery & Plant (25%)

W.D.V.s b/f		$ 81,242
($42,670 + $38,572)		
Additions Van	$36,000	
Less Initial Allowance	9,000	27,000
		$108,242
Less Disposals —		
Van ($9,362 + $500)		9,862
		$ 98,380
Annual Allowance		24,595
"Pool" c/f		$ 73,785

Machinery & Plant (15%)

W.D.V.s b/f		$ 13,658
($8,228 + $5,430)		
New Unit	$ 3,000	
Less Initial Allownace	750	2,250
		$ 15,908
Less Disposals —		
Furniture & Air Conditioning		1,800
($1,300 + $500)		
		$ 14,108
Annual Allowance		2,117
"Pool" c/f		$ 11,991

1980/81 Total allowances due $36,462 ($9,000 + $750 + $24,595 + $2,117).

[The 15% and 25% rates no longer exist and the rate of initial allowance for 1980/81 is 35%. — Author]

Example 8

Mr. C carries on a trade of car hire. Accounts are made up to 30th June each year.

Pool (25%) brought forward after 1980/81 allowances is $36,482. During the year to 30th June 1981 a vehicle which had cost $38,000 is sold for $40,000. A car purchased in July 1978 for $32,000 was introduced into the business on 1st September 1980.

1981/82 "Pool" b/f	$36,482	Car Introduced: Cost	$32,000
+ New Expenditure			
(Car introduced)	18,000	*Less* "Notional" allowances	
	$54,482	for years of non-business	
Less Disposal		use (two complete years)	
(restricted to cost)	38,000	1979/80 allowance	8,000
	$16,482		$24,000
Annual Allowance	4,121	1980/81 Allowance	6,000
"Pool" c/f	$12,361	"Cost" for business	
		purposes (S.39B(6))	$18,000

Notes:—
(I) No initial allowance is due on the car introduced as no capital expenditure was incurred during the basis period (see para. 27).
(ii) Any new expenditure has to be added to the pool *before* disposal proceeds are deducted. To do otherwise would be to create a Balancing Charge, which would be against the provisions of Section 39D(1); a balancing charge can arise only where at the end of the basis period for a year of assessment aggregate reductions exceed aggregate capital expenditure on the class of machinery or plant.
[The 25% rate no longer exists. — Author]

17. Balancing Allowances and Balancing Charges

Section 39D(2) provides that where a person ceases to trade and the sale, etc., money received for the machinery or plant are less than the reducing value in the pool a balancing allowance equal to the difference is to be made. This is the only situation in which a balancing allowance can be given since any sums received on the disposal of assets at any other time are simply deducted from the value of the pool. A balancing charge can, however, arise whenever disposal proceeds of one or more assets exceed the reducing value of the pool as well as on the disposal of the whole class of machinery or plant on the cessation of trading. However, no balancing charge or balancing allowance can arise where on cessation machinery or plant passes to a successor to whom the Reducing Value of the machinery or plant is transferred under Section 39B(7).

Example 9

Suppose Mr. C in Example 8 owned three vehicles at 30th June 1981. During the year to 30th June 1982 he sold one for $13,000 without replacing it and during the year to 30th June 1983 he sold another for $6,000 without replacement.

1982/83	R.V. of Pool b/f		$12,361
	Less Disposal		13,000
	Balancing Charge (S.39D(1))		$ 639
	R.V. of Pool c/f		Nil
	1983/84 Disposal		$ 6,000
	Balancing Charge (S.39D(1))		$ 6,000
	R.V. of Pool c/f		Nil

Example 10

Mr. J. a toy manufacturer, commencing trading in 1976. His accounts are made up to 30th September each year. On 30th September 1981 he ceases trading. During the final year he purchased machinery costing $18,000 which qualified at the 15% rate. Pools brought forward after 1980/81 allowances are − (15% rate) $13,462; (25% rate) $21,437. On cessation machinery and plant was sold for $46,989; it was agreed that this should be divided between the 15% and 25% pools in the proportion $24,341 : $22,648.

1981/82	(15%) Pool b/f		$13,462	(25%) Pool b/f	$21,437
	New Expenditure	$18,000			
	Less Initial				
	Allowance	4,500	13,500	New Expenditure	−
			$26,962		$21,437
	Disposal Proceeds		24,341	Disposal Proceeds	22,648
	Balancing Allowance		$ 2,621	Balancing Charge	$ 1,211
	(S.39D(2))			(S.39D(2))	

Note:−

There is no annual allowance for the year of cessation, but Initial Allowance is due on capital expenditure incurred during the final basis period. [This calculation is out of date, the 1981/82 initial allowance is now 55% and the 15% and 25% rates no longer exist. − Author]

18. Proceeds of Machinery or Plant disposed of

Section 39D makes it clear that it is the aggregate of the sums received for any items of machinery or plant disposed of which is to be deducted both in calculating the reducing value of the pool and in calculating a balancing adjustment. Thus if machinery or plant is destroyed the sum to be deducted is the total of any insurance, salvage or compensation received. The total amount is not, however, to exceed the "cost" of that particular item for depreciation allowance purposes. Cost is normally the capital sum expended on the provision of that machinery or plant; where the asset was introduced into the business after non-business use, however, cost will be the deemed cost to the business, i.e. after the deduction of notional allowances for years of non-business use.

19. Assets acquired under a Hire Purchase Agreement

The initial and annual allowances due in respect of expenditure incurred on the provision of machinery or plant under a hire purchase agreement must be calculated separately from the pool in the same way as under the Old Scheme (see para. 12). This ensures that the initial allowance is given on the capital element of the instalment payments as each amount of expenditure is incurred. When the instalment payments are completed however and no further initial allowance is due the reducing value of the asset is added to the appropriate pool, i.e. in the year following that in the basis period for which the machinery or plant passes into ownership of the taxpayer (Section 39C(2)).

Example 11

If in Example 4 (para. 12) the typewriter had been purchased on the same terms three years later, i.e., on 1st December 1978, and the first instalment had been payable on 1st January 1979, the last year for which any initial allowance would be due would be 1981/82 as the typewriter would pass into ownership of the taxpayer on payment of the last instalment on 1st August 1980 (Accounts year to 30th June 1981). The reducing value of the asset after 1981/82 allowances, $1,938 would be added to the 15% pool in calculating 1982/83 allowances. [The 15% rate no longer exists − Author]

20. Machinery and Plant used for non-business purposes

An asset which is not used wholly for business purposes can never be included in the pool. The allowances due in respect of any such asset need to be separately calculated (as if the asset were in a separate pool of its own) so that the appropriate restriction for non-business use can be made. Even if non-business use ceases and the asset becomes used wholly for trade purposes, it is necessary to continue making a separate calculation because any balancing charge on disposal of the asset will need to be apportioned to take account of the earlier private use. Thus Section 39C provides that pooling does not apply to assets which are not used wholly for producing profits and the calculation of allowances due on each such asset should continue to be made as under the Old Scheme (see para. 26).

21. Assets removed from pool for non-business use

Where machinery or plant which has been used wholly and exclusively in the production of profits ceases to be so used, e.g. when it becomes used wholly or partly for private purposes, its reducing value must be taken out of pool for the year of assessment during the basis period for which this change occurs. The reducing value of the machinery or plant is the amount which the Commissioner considers it would have realised if sold in the open market at the time it ceased to be wholly and exclusively used for business purposes (Section 39C(3)). If the machinery or plant continues to be used partly for business purposes after this event depreciation allowances will be separately calculated for the year of change and subsequent years until disposal in the same way as for any other asset involving non-business use (see para. 26).

22. Succession to a trade

The provisions of Section 39B(7) are similar to Section 37(4) relating to the old scheme. Thus if on succession to a trade, ownership of machinery or plant passes to the successor without being sold to him, the reducing value of each pool of expenditure unallowed to the old proprietor is taken over by the new proprietor. The successor will be entitled to an annual allowance under Section 39B(2) once machinery or plant has been in use in his trade. No Initial Allowance is however due on the transfer (Sub-section 8). For the purpose of calculating any subsequent reduction from the pool or balancing charge on disposal, the cost of the asset acquired by the successor in this way will be deemed to be equal to the reducing value of the pool taken over.

23. Commissioner's power to direct that Old Scheme should apply

Section 36A(2) gives the Commissioner power to direct that the provisions of the Old Scheme should continue to apply for any year from 1980/81 onwards whenever he is satisfied that the application of the new provisions to particular machinery or plant would be impracticable or inequitable. It is not anticipated that the Commissioner will need to exercise this authority very frequently but there may be situations in which the strict application of the new provisions could produce an inequitable result.

Part IV – MISCELLANEOUS Provisions (Applying to both schemes)

24. Assets sold together

Particularly where cessation occurs, it is not uncommon to find that assets are sold together for one price and without specifying in detail the consideration in respect of each individual asset sold. Where this occurs the Commissioner is empowered by virtue of the provisions of Section 38A to allocate a price to each individual asset sold (see Example 3).

25. Assets sold to/by Persons under Common Control

Section 38B provides that where an asset is sold in circumstances where it would appear that the transaction was not "at arms length" viz. the buyer is a person over whom the seller has control, or vice versa, or both seller and buyer are persons over both of whom some other person has control, the Commissioner, if he is of the opinion that the sale price does not represent its true market value, shall determine the true market value of the asset transferred. The value so determined by the Commissioner is then deemed to be the sale price for the purposes of calculating any allowances or charges under Part VI of the Ordinance (see Example 3).

26. Machinery or Plant used partly for the purposes of the Trade, etc.

Whereas the allowances under Part VI are granted in respect of capital expenditure incurred in the provision of assets "for the purposes of the trade, etc. "Section 18F and 39A of the Ordinance envisage that such assets will from time to time be used partly for purposes other than for the purpose of the production of profits in respect of which the person is chargeable to tax. In such circumstances it is provided that the allowances under Part VI are to be calculated in the first instance in the full amount, and then apportioned as appropriate in relation to the extent to which the assets are or have been used (a) in the production of the chargeable profits and (b) for other purposes. Any charges under Part VI are to be similarly apportioned. This treatment will apply whether the asset was acquired under the old or the new scheme, as machinery or plant used partly for private purposes is excluded from the pooling system (see para. 20).

By way of illustration, the following example shows the method of calculating the allowances and balancing charge where the proportion on non-business use has not been constant:—

Example 12

A, a sole trader commences to trade on 1st June 1977 on which date he purchased a motor vehicle for $28,000. This vehicle was used wholly for the business until 31st March 1978. As from 1st April 1978, having sold his private motor car, the business vehicle was used for private purposes, the estimated private use being 50% of the total annual mileage. Twelve months later he acquired a new motor car that is used wholly for private purposes by himself and his family but he continued to use the business vehicle for private purposes but now estimated the private use to be only 1/3. In April 1980 the business vehicle was sold for $10,000. His accounts are made up each year to 31st March.

		Allowances granted against business profits	Disallowed in respect of private use
Vehicle Cost 1.6.1977		$28,000	
1977/78 Initial Allowance		7,000 $7,000 (100%)	
		$21,000	
Annual Allowance		5,250 5,250 (100%)	
		$15,750	
1978/79 Annual Allowance		3,938 1,969 (50%)	$1,969 (50%)
		$11,812	
1979/80 Annual Allowance		2,953 1,969 ($66\frac{2}{3}$%)	984 ($33\frac{1}{3}$%)
W.D.V.		$ 8,859 $16,188	$2,953
Sale Proceeds		10,000	
Excess over W.D.V.		$ 1,141	

In 1980/81 the balancing charge will be —

$$\text{Excess } 1,141 \times \frac{16,188}{16,188 + 2,953} = \$965$$

27. Assets brought into the business after non-business use

Under both old and new schemes Notional Allowances are to be computed if there is other use of the asset before it is brought into the trade. Where a person owns an asset and uses it for some other purpose before bringing it into use in his trade, profession, business or employment, the "cost of the asset" for the purpose of Annual Allowances is taken to be the actual cost less notional allowances. These notional allowances are the Annual Allowances that would have been due if the owner had used the asset for his trade etc. ever since he acquired it. [Section 37(2A) and Section 39B(6)]. There is no provision for deducting a notional initial allowance.

No initial allowance is due at the date of introduction into the business, because there has been no capital expenditure at that date on the provision of machinery or plant for the purpose of producing profits chargeable to Profits Tax, or in the case of employment, the income liable to Salaries Tax.

Example 13

A person who has been trading for some years, purchased a car for $30,000 for private use on 10th May 1978. It was transferred to business use on 12th August 1980. Accounts are made up to 31st March each year.

Cost	$30,000
1978/79 Notional Allowance 25%	7,500

	$22,500
1979/80 Notional Allowance 25%	5,625
Deemed cost of asset	$16,875

For the purposes of the 25% Pool for 1980/81 onwards the car is to be treated as if it had been bought on 12th August 1980 for $16,875. [Except that the 25% has been increased to 30% from 1980/81.— Author]

28. Commissioner's Discretion — Rates of Annual Allowance

Both proviso (b) to Section 37(2) and Section 39(B)(11) empower the Commissioner in his discretion to allow a higher rate for annual allowance than that prescribed by the Board of Inland Revenue. Factors which are considered upon receipt of an application for increased rates of allowance include:—

(a) Estimated working life of the asset.

(b) Anticipated disposal/scrap value at end of its working life.

(c) Where excessive wear and tear is claimed in respect of the use of an asset on a specific project, the possibility of rehabilitation and further use in the business on completion of the project.

At the present time the rates of initial and annual allowances are such that the Commissioner considers it is unlikely that any claim for a higher annual allowance could be justified.

29. Assets put out of use upon Cessation of Trade

Both Section 38(4) and 39D(4) and (5) contain similar rules to the effect that where machinery or plant is put out of use upon the cessation of trade, etc. by the taxpayer, such machinery or plant shall be deemed to have been sold immediately prior to the cessation, the sale price to be taken being such amount as the Commissioner may consider the asset would have realized if sold in the open market. However, if within twelve months of the date of cessation the taxpayer sells the asset he may claim for the actual sale price to be substituted for the Commissioner's valuation for the purposes of a balancing allowance or charge. The sections provide for this adjustment to be made, notwithstanding that the assessment has become final and conclusive under the provisions of Section 70. These Sections are not considered to apply where upon the cessation of one business, any machinery or plant used therein is transferred to another trade or business carried on by the same person, whether or not there is an interval of time.

Example 14

On 17th February 1979 the trade carried on by DEF & Co. ceased. The plant and machinery, on which depreciation allowances had been given, was sold on that date for $80,000. The original cost of the plant and machinery was $75,000 and immediately prior to the date of sale the amount still unallowed was $35,000. The office furniture that had cost $20,000 had not been sold when the accounts for the final period of trading were submitted to the Inland Revenue Department, the Expenditure unallowed at the date of cessation being $8,000. The Commissioner placed an open market value of $8,500 on the furniture and on 9th July 1979 a Notice of Assessment was issued to the firm advising the assessable profits under Section 18D for the final year of assessment of the business i.e. 1978/79. No objection was lodged but on 1st November 1979 the firm wrote advising that the furniture had been sold for $6,300, claiming adjustment to the assessment in accordance with the proviso to Section 38(4).

Balancing charges would have been included in the original assessment as follows:—

	Plant/ Machinery	Office Furniture
Expenditure unallowed (i.e. after allowances given for years to 1977/78)	$35,000	$8,000
Sale price	80,000	8,500 (S.38(4))
	$45,000	
Balancing Charge	$40,000 (restricted to allowances granted S.38(5))	$ 500

Upon receipt of the claim under the proviso to Section 38(4) a revised assessment would be issued to give effect to a reduction of $2,200 made up as follows:—

	Office Furniture
Expenditure unallowed	$8,000
Sale proceeds	6,300
Balancing Allowance	$1,700
Add Balancing Charge now withdrawn	500
Reduction in assessment	$2,200

MARCH 1981

APPENDIX A(I)

Rates of Depreciation (Effective from 1978/79), as
Prescribed by the Board of Inland Revenue

TABLE

Item	First Part	Rate	*
1.	Air-conditioning plant excluding room air conditioning units `....	10%	
2.	Aircraft (including engines)	30%	
3.	Bank safe deposit boxes, doors and grills	10%	
4.	Bar syphon apparatus	25%	30%
5.	Bicycles	25%	30%
6.	Bleaching and finishing machinery and plant	25%	30%
7.	Broadcasting transmitters	10%	
8.	Cables (electric)	5%	10%
9.	Concrete pipe moulds	25%	30%
10.	Domestic appliances	15%	20%
11.	Electric cookers and kettles	25%	30%
12.	Electronic data processing equipment	25%	30%
13.	Electronics manufacturing machinery and plant	25%	30%
14.	Furniture (excluding soft furnishings)	15%	20%
15.	Lamp standards (street) − gas or electric	5%	10%
16.	Lifts and escalators (electric)	10%	
17.	Mains (gas or water)	5%	10%
18.	Motor vehicles	25%	30%
19.	Oil tanks	5%	10%
20.	Plastic manufacturing machinery and plant including moulds	25%	30%
21.	Room air-conditioning units	15%	20%
22.	Shipping − Ships, junks and sampans	10%	
	Launches and ferry vessels	15%	20%
	Outboard motors	25%	30%
	Lighters	10%	
	Tugs	10%	
	Hydrofoils	15%	20%
23.	Silk manufacturing machinery and plant	25%	30%
24.	Sprinklers	10%	
25.	Sulphuric and nitric acid plant	25%	30%
26.	Tank lorries	30%	
27.	Taxi meters	15%	20%
28.	Textile and clothing manufacturing machinery and plant	25%	30%
29.	Tractors − bull dozers and graders	25%	30%
30.	Type and blocks (if not dealt with on renewals basis)	15%	20%
31.	Weaving, spinning, knitting and sewing machinery	25%	30%
32.	Machinery or plant, not specified in items 1 to 31, and used for the purposes of a transport, tunnel, dock, water, gas or electricity undertaking or a public telephone or public telegraphic service ...	10%	
33.	Any other machinery or plant, not specified in items 1 to 32	15%	20%

* [Rate effective from 1980/81. − Author]

APPENDIX A(II)

"Implements, Utensils and Articles", as Prescribed
by Board of Inland Revenue

TABLE

Item   *Second Part*

1.   Belting.
2.   Crockery and cutlery.
3.   Kitchen utensils.
4.   Linen.
5.   Loose tools.
6.   Soft furnishings (including curtains and carpets).
7.   Surgical and dental instruments.
8.   Tubes for X-ray and infra-red machines.

APPENDIX B

Items which Qualify as Machinery or Plant

In addition to the items specified in the First Part of the Table annexed to Rule 2 of the Inland Revenue Rules, the following items have been held to qualify as "machinery of plant" (in the case of (iii) and (v) as "capital expenditure on the provision of machinery or plant") for the purposes of the depreciation allowances:—

(i)   Design and process plans (for the construction of a machine to be used in the production of the saleable product of the taxpayer).
(ii)   Display platforms.
(iii)   First Registration Tax (paid on acquisition of a new motor vehicle).
(iv)   Iron gates (where not an integral part of a building or structure).
(v)   Office partitioning (where not an integral part of a building or structure).
(vi)   Poster-boards (advertisement hoardings).
(vii)   Sign-boards.
(viii) Computer software.

APPENDIX C

Items which Do Not Qualify as Machinery or Plant

 (i) Accoustic tile ceilings (installed as an integral part of a building).
 (ii) Ceiling lighting points.
(iii) Cocklofts.
 (iv) Fish ponds.
  (v) Formica wall panelling (installed as an integral part of a building).
 (vi) Telephone cable and wiring (installed as an integral part of a building).*
(vii) Wiring and electrical fixtures and fittings (installed as an integral part of a building).*

* [Challengeable; being built into the building does not of itself disqualify the expenditure, it depends upon what it is used for. — Author]

APPENDIX 8

Departmental Interpretation & Practice Notes
No. 9

EXPENSES DEDUCTIBLE FOR SALARIES TAX

INDEX

1. **Expenses which may be claimed.**

The Inland Revenue Ordinance (Cap. 112) provides under Section 12 that a deduction may be claimed from income assessable to Salaries Tax of:—

"all outgoings and expenses, other than expenses of a domestic or private nature and capital expenditure, wholly, exclusively and necessarily incurred in the production of such assessable income."

In order to qualify for deduction, therefore, the expenditure must satisfy each of the following tests in addition to not being expenditure of a domestic or private nature or expenditure of a capital nature e.g. expenditure to acquire an asset:—

(a) it must have been "incurred".

(b) it must have arisen "wholly and exclusively" in "the production of the income".

(c) it must have been "necessary" for the production of the income. These terms are discussed in paragraphs 4 to 7.

2. How expenses are to be claimed.

The Salaries Tax return provides for entries to be made of outgoings and expenses claimed, any claim to be supported by documentary evidence where possible.

3. Nature of evidence to be supplied.

The onus of establishing the claim is on the claimant. If the Assessor does not accept the claim as made, the Ordinance provides that it is for the appellant to prove that the assessment is excessive or incorrect. If, therefore, the appellant has neglected to keep records or vouchers to show that his claim to certain expenses is justified, then, in law he must accept the consequences of his own omission.

A taxpayer who incurs outgoings and expenses which are claimed as deductions for Salaries Tax is strongly advised to keep *contemporaneous records* so that if called upon he will be able to provide with reasonable precision, details of expenditure claimed to be deductible together with vouchers or other evidence of payment.

Latter paragraphs deal with specific types of expenditure and incorporate statements as to the nature of the evidence which the Department would expect to be available in support of claims made.

4. "Incurred"

The word "incurred" has been judicially considered on a number of occasions and the authorities are generally agreed that for an expenditure to have been incurred it must be an established liability or a definite commitment which arose in the year of assessment in which it is sought to claim a deduction. Actual payment during the year in question is not necessary, but where payment has not been made before the end of that year no deduction can be allowed unless there is existing on the last day of that year an actual and known liability or obligation of *ascertainable amount.* A mere contingent liability or an anticipated future outgoing will not therefore generally rank for deduction.

5. "Wholly" and "Exclusively"

The words are not to be construed too narrowly. Where expenditure is incurred for more than one purpose (e.g. running expenses of a car used partly for private purposes), such expenditure would be apportioned (usually on a mileage basis), and the part attributable to the employment allowed provided the other tests are satisfied.

6. "Necessarily"

The word necessarily is to be construed as meaning essential to the conduct of the employment. It is not sufficient that the expenditure is related to the production of the income and possibly facilitate and aid the production of income: the expenditure must be necessarily incurred. The basic test is whether the expenditure is vital to the employment to the extent that it would not be possible for the taxpayer to produce the income from the employment without incurring that expenditure. If the duties imposed by the employer require the expenditure to be incurred then unless in the contract of employment the employee is required to bear expenses out of his remuneration, it could not be said that the employee has necessarily incurred the expenditure. However, it does not follow that because the employer has required the expenditure to be incurred by the employee that such expenditure is admissible: the test is "not whether the employer imposes the expense but whether the duties do, in the sense that, irrespective of what the employer may prescribe, the duties cannot be performed without incurring that particular outlay". [The words quoted are from the United Kingdom Tax Case of Brown v. Bullock: reference is made in paragraph 7 as to the relevance of United Kingdom Case Law in the interpretation of the wording of the Hong Kong Ordinance].

7. In the "Production of the Assessable Income"

The meaning of this phrase was considered in the Supreme Court of Hong Kong [Commissioner of Inland Revenue v. Humphrey] when the judgement referred to the wording of the United Kingdom Taxing Act "in the performance of the duties" and to the wording of the Australian Taxing Act "in gaining or producing the assessable income". Legal authority in Australia was quoted as "The relevant provisions of the English Income Tax Acts are not in the same terms as those of the Australian Law, but the whole course of English authority involves a like conclusion. To escape from the course of reasoning on which they proceed requires the taking of refined and rather insubstantial distinctions."

The judgement in the Supreme Court was made on the basis that as far as the appeal in that case was concerned (a claim for travelling expenses) the difference in phraseology between the Taxing Acts, the Hong Kong provision having a certain affinity to the wording of the Australian Taxing Act, was immaterial.

Expenditure is not incurred "in the performance of the duties" if it is incurred to enable the duties to be performed e.g. travelling to and from the place of employment: expenditure to acquire an employment or appointment: the cost of further education: the cost of membership to a social or sports club whether or not required by the employer. It will be noted that certain of the items mentioned would also fail to qualify for allowance under the other tests referred to in the preceding paragraphs.

8. **Expenses Allowances from Employer**

Allowances which are reasonable in amount and do no more than cover the cost to the employee of subsistence, travelling and accommodation when, on his employer's business, he is working away from his usual base or place of residence, would not be brought into charge as assessable income. Any claim for expenses in excess of the employer's reimbursement would be expected to fail the test "necessarily" incurred.

A reimbursement from an employer to cover expenses incurred by an employee in connection with his employment is, however, assessable to Salaries Tax to the extent to which it is a reimbursement of expenses which would not be allowable as a deduction for Salaries Tax on the principles referred to in the preceding paragraphs.

9. **Flat Rate Allowances for Expenses**

These are given to employees in the following employments in order to save the examination of numerous claims where the amounts involved are not large. The allowances are intended to cover the small allowable expenditure incurred by employees but a claim may be made by an employee for an increased deduction if evidence can be produced to justify such a claim.

    (a) Members of (i)   the Royal Hong Kong Regiment,

                  (ii)   the Auxiliary Police Force,

                  (iii) the Auxiliary Fire Services,

                  (iv) the Auxiliary Medical Service,

                  (v)   the Civil Aid Services,

                  (vi) the Royal Hong Kong Auxiliary Air Force,

                  (vii) Uniformed members of the Royal Hong Kong Police Force:—

Flat rate allowance of $50 to cover the maintenance of equipment, etc.

    (b) Seafarers, airline pilots and crews:—

Flat rate allowance of $250 to cover the cost of uniforms, instruments, charts, etc.

10. **Specific Items of Expenditure**

    (a) *Clothing.* The cost, if borne by the employee, of the replacement of special clothes required by the nature of the employment would be allowable (e.g. overalls). Otherwise the test "wholly and exclusively" would not be expected to be complied with.

    (b) *Commissions: Payments for Services.* Employees whose remuneration in part depends upon commission may claim that they are required to pay commission or to make payments in order to obtain contracts or to make sales. It is important with this type of claim that full information should be given to the Revenue not only to justify the claim but to enable the recipient of the commissions etc. to be identified.

[The Revenue is entitled under Section 51(4)(a) to call for a statement of such payments and failure to comply can give rise to a penalty of $2,000 (Section 51(4B)(a))].

If claimants omit to keep records showing to whom the payments have been made, the amounts paid together with other evidence such as receipts duly stamped, in order to show that the payments properly fall within the wording of the Ordinance, the Revenue practice will be to resist any claim for a deduction from the gross income assessable to Salaries Tax, but in addition the Revenue will take action under Section 51(4)(a) in any case where action is considered justified.

It should be noted that payments referred to above would include payments in kind or gifts.

(c) *Entertainment.* The claimant is expected to be able to show that any expenditure claimed was necessarily incurred, that it would not have been possible to have produced the income from the employment without incurring such expenditure. Mere social entertaining would be debarred as not being "wholly and exclusively incurred": any entertaining must be shown to have been necessarily incurred directly as part of business negotiations and records kept should not only give details of the cost and the names of the persons entertained but the nature of the business in question.

If the employee is given a round sum allowance by the employer to cover entertaining, the excess over the part of the allowance which the employee can justify as admissible under the tests detailed in paragraph 1 is assessable as income from the office or employment.

(d) *Payments to Assistants.* In general such an expense would not be "necessarily" incurred. However, in any case for example in which an employee is remunerated on a commission basis a claim for such payments would be admitted provided that the necessity can clearly be shown for the need of assistance e.g. having regard to the volume of business transacted, and the amounts paid can be shown to be reasonable for the work done.

(e) *Subscriptions to Professional Societies etc.* Although it is considered that such subscriptions are in general not allowable under a strict interpretation of the wording of the Ordinance, in practice an allowance is admitted where the holding of a professional qualification is a prerequisite of employment and where the retention of membership and the keeping abreast of current developments in the particular profession are of regular use and benefit in the performance of the duties.

Subscriptions and fees paid to Trade Unions would not qualify.

(f) *Travelling Expenses.* Reasonable expenses of travel from one place of employment to another would be admitted.

Allowable expenses are restricted to those necessarily incurred in the performance of the duties. If for example motor car expenses are claimed regard would be had as to whether the amount claimed is reasonable having regard to the availability of public transport and taxis.

If the nature of the employment is such that use of a car is necessary to the carrying out of the duties, the claim should include information as to the basis on which the employer reimburses expenditure incurred, and the extent to which the car is used for purposes other than for the employment. The cost of repairs and running expenses would be apportioned as between private use and use for the employment: only an exceptional item such as an insurance surcharge premium in respect of carriage of goods solely for the purposes of the employment would be allowable in full.

(g) *Use of Residential Premises.* A claim would not in general come within the tests listed in paragraph 1 but where it is necessary for the employee to do work at home i.e. where the employee is required by the terms and nature of his employment to work outside the employer's premises, the employer not providing office facilities, any expense would be limited to the additional cost of heating, lighting etc. unless the nature of the office or employment is such that it is necessary for a distinct and separate part of the residence to be used solely for the purposes of the employment, in which event the Department would agree to an appropriate proportion of the total expenses incurred on rent rates etc. No allowance will be admissible for part of the expenses of the residence on a claim that there is occasional use for business entertainment.

11. Allowances for Capital Expenditure

The Inland Revenue Ordinance also provides in Section 12 for "allowances calculated in accordance with the Provisions of Part VI of the Ordinance in respect of capital expenditure on machinery and plant the use of which is essential to the production of such assessable income".

Claims under this provision would not arise other than in an employment in which the employer does not reimburse the employee for the use of the machinery or plant (the most common example would be a motor car) and where the employee can show that the use of the plant or machinery is essential to the performance of the duties giving rise to the assessable income.

Information as to the computation of allowances under this provision is contained in the pamphlet Departmental Interpretation and Practice Notes No. 7. (See Appendix 7)

12. False Claims

The wilful submission of an incorrect return or the making of a false statement in connection with a claim for any deduction or allowance renders the person or the person who has assisted any other person to evade tax, to a fine on summary conviction of two thousand dollars and a further fine of treble the amount of tax which has been undercharged in consequence of the offence or which would have been undercharged if the offence had not been detected, and to imprisonment for six months, and on indictment a fine of ten thousand dollars and a further fine of treble the amount of tax so undercharged or which would have been so undercharged and to imprisonment for three years.

JUNE 1976

APPENDIX 9

Departmental Interpretation & Practice Notes
No. 10

THE CHARGE TO SALARIES TAX

(I) *BASIC CHARGE – EMPLOYMENTS*

The basic charge to Salaries Tax, i.e. "income arising in or derived from the Colony", is imposed by Section 8(1). No general rules are given in the Ordinance for determining whether income "arises in or is derived from" the Colony. As the issue is largely a matter of fact, the Hong Kong Board of Review in appeals relating to *employment* has taken the view that it is the *totality* of the facts of each particular case which determines whether income arises in or is derived from the Colony. The Board rejected attempts to decide this problem by reference to a single determining factor, such as the place where the contract of employment was signed or the place at or the currency in which the salary was paid. Factors which the Board did however take into account in reaching their decisions and which the Department consequently has also taken into account are:—

(1) the place where the contract, whether verbal or written, is enforceable;

(2) the exact nature of the taxpayer's duties and identification of what he is remunerated for;

(3) whether the taxpayer serves or holds office in, or has employment with, a Hong Kong company, organisation or establishment in Hong Kong of a non-resident business;

(4) who remunerates the taxpayer — where the cost of this remuneration or of his service is ultimately borne;

(5) whether the remuneration or cost forms ultimately or directly part of the expenses or cost of a Hong Kong company or establishment;

(6) whether the duties performed by the taxpayer during temporary absences from the Colony were incidental to his employment or office in the Colony or completely distinguishable from that role.

(II) *EXTENSION OF CHARGE – EMPLOYMENTS*

If the income from employment does not come within the basic charge, because it does not "arise in" or "derive from" a source in the Colony, then consideration will need to be given as to whether liability arises under the extension to the basic charge by the provisions of Section 8(1A). Sub-section (a) of Section 8(1A) does not in any way limit the charge in Section 8(1); it extends the charge by specifically *including* as income arising in or derived from the Colony, all income derived from *services rendered* in the Colony including leave pay attributable to such services. It should be noted that this Sub-section relates only to employments; it does not apply to offices of profit [see paragraph (IV) below].

For the purposes of quantifying the amount of income derived from services rendered in the Colony, the Department will usually look at the number of days an employee spent in the Colony and apportion his remuneration including leave pay accordingly. The application of this formula is however not invariable because circumstances may arise in which an employee, whilst only spending a small proportion of his time in Hong Kong may nevertheless render the major part of his services in Hong Kong. In this event a different approach may be appropriate. In order to arrive at the amount of income which is derived from services rendered in the Colony, it should be noted that an employee should include in his Salaries Tax Returns, apart from remuneration received locally, all other payments which are related to his employment and received by him, for example, from his overseas parent company or head office.

(III) *EXCLUSION FROM CHARGE – EMPLOYMENTS*

Sub-section (b) of Section 8(1A) excludes from the charge to Salaries Tax income from services rendered by persons (other than Government employees and ship and air crews) who render all their services outside the Colony. For the purposes of this exclusion, services rendered during *visits* to the Colony not exceeding a total of 60 days in the basis period for the year of assessment are ignored [Section 8(1B)] so that a person visiting the Colony for less than 60 days in such period will be regarded as rendering all services outside the Colony.

The exclusion applies to all *employment* income irrespective of whether liability arises under Section 8(1) or under the extended charge in Section 8(1A)(a). Thus an employee, who is deriving income from the Colony and who is posted to say, Taipei or Tokyo to represent his firm and renders all his services there will in effect be wholly exempt from Salaries Tax. The position will not be affected if he visits the Colony for not more than 60 days in the basis period; if he visits the Colony for 61 days or more, he will be liable on the *whole* amount of his income for the basis period. Similarly an employee who is not deriving income from the Colony within the context of Section 8(1), will not be liable if he is here to carry out short assignments during visits to the Colony, provided that such visits do not exceed a total of 60 days in the basis period; if his visits exceed 60 days he will be liable on the appropriate fraction of his income which is derived from the services rendered in the Colony under the extended charge of Section 8(1A)(a).

The exclusion under Section 8(1A)(b) only refers to *visits* e.g. a person may be chargeable even though he spent 60 days or less in the basis period in the Colony if this is the start of a longer period of residence in the Colony or his presence does not constitute a "visit".

(IV) *DIRECTORS FEES*

It is to be noted that fees paid to persons who hold the office of director of a corporation, the control and management of which is exercised in the Colony, are chargeable to Salaries Tax under the basic charge of Section 8(1) wheresoever the director resides. In appeals relating to remuneration accruing to a director, the Board of Review has accepted that the decision in *McMillan v Guest 24 TC 190* applies, namely the office of director of a corporation is located where the control and management of the corporation is exercised, which consequently determines where the income therefrom "arises". The extension to the basic charge under Section 8(1A) does not therefore require to be considered as regards the income from an office; in any event Section 8(1A) only refers to employments. Similarly the exclusion from charge provided in Section 8(1A)(b) applies only in relation to services in connexion with employments.

(V) *SHIP AND AIRCRAFT PERSONNEL*

The liability of ship and aircraft personnel is determined under Section 8(1) and the extension under Section 8(1A)(a) in the first instance in the same way as other employees [see paragraphs (I) and (II) above]. Thereafter there are important exemptions to be considered under Sub-section 8(2)(j). Under this Sub-section income from services rendered by a person who present in the Colony on not more than 60 days in the basis period and a total of 120 days falling partly in each of the basis periods for two consecutive years of assessment, one of which is the year of assessment being considered, is *excluded* from charge. The broad effect of this exclusion is to exempt from charge all seamen and airmen other than those who spend a substantial portion of their time in Hong Kong (including territorial waters).

JANUARY 1982

APPENDIX 10

Departmental Interpretation & Practice Notes
No. 11
ELEMENTS OF A TAX INVESTIGATION

Introduction

With the passing of the Inland Revenue (Amendment) (No. 4) Ordinance 1975 the penalties for evasion of tax have been increased. The Ordinance came into effect on the 4th July 1975 and the revised scale of penalties relate to offences committed on or after that date. Offences committed before that date will continue to be governed by the provisions of the Ordinance before amendment. The reasons for the changes in the law were given in the Financial Secretary's Speech introducing the seconding reading of the Bill in the Legislative Council on 2nd April, 1975. He said:—

"The other amendment which merits elaboration is the increase in the penalties which the Courts may impose from $2,000 plus a fine equal to the amount of tax undercharged, to $2,000 plus *treble* the amount of the tax undercharged. This is provided for in Clause 6 and it should also be noted that by Clause 7 the Commissioner is empowered, subject to a right of appeal by the taxpayer, to impose an administrative penalty known as "Additional Tax". These amendments also bring into the net for the first time, the case where the taxpayer just sits back and fails to submit a return at all.

Clearly the amendments are intended as a deterrent and also as a punishment to the guilty. It will be evident from the figures I have already given to honourable Members that the existing penalty is not sufficient as a deterrent. As regards punishment, it will be readily appreciated that, because of high interest rates and inflation, even where the maximum penalty of 100 per cent is imposed in the worst type of case, the taxpayer is often no worse off than if he had paid the tax when he should have. Furthermore, it must be remembered that with a standard rate of 15 per cent, except for corporations where the rate is now 16½ per cent, the worst that can happen to an offender if he is caught is to pay tax at 30 or 33 per cent — to put it at its lowest level it is worth taking a sporting chance, although let me say at once that I consider there is nothing sporting about the tax evader. His action, if undetected, simply shifts the burden of the tax on to whose who are honest enough to contribute according to law. He deserves no sympathy from this Council. I would also remind honourable Members that, in some neighbouring countries, the penalties when added to the tax are confiscatory in that in some cases they can exceed the amount of income on which they are levied. Even the maximum 300 per cent penalty will still not be anywhere near confiscatory in Hong Kong.

An additional motive behind the increase in the penalty is to give the Commissioner a greater degree of flexibility in fixing the amount of penalty. At present, as I have already indicated, if one does no more than recover what should have been paid to the Exchequer in the first instance, the penalty would very often have to be close to the 100 per cent margin. There is very little therefore that the Commissioner can offer by way of inducement to a taxpayer to make a clean breast of things and submit corrected returns. Furthermore, it has been the Commissioner's experience that once having been caught out, the taxpayer often sits back and leaves it to the Department's officers to build up the necessary statements from which his true profits can be ascertained. This is a laborious, painstaking task and it is ironic that this should be done at Government's expense when the fault lies entirely with the taxpayer. There is however an insufficient range of penalties for the Commissioner to hold out some inducement to the taxpayer at this stage to pay his own accountant to do this work.

In this connection, I should like to place on record what the Commissioner's practice in relation to the *full* voluntary disclosure of tax evasion is. This is as follows: where offences under the Inland Revenue Ordinance have been committed, the Commissioner may institute prosecution under Part XIV of the Inland Revenue Ordinance. He is, however, also given power to compound these offences, i.e., to accept a monetary settlement instead of sanctioning the institution of a prosecution. Alternatively, he is given the power to impose Additional Tax in lieu of prosecution. Although no undertaking can be given as to whether or not the Commissioner will refrain from prosecution in the case of any particular person, it is the practice of the Commissioner to be influenced by the fact that a person has made a full confession of any offence to which he has been a party and has given full facilities for investigation and has provided corrected returns accommpanied by detailed statements in support of these returns. These facts will also have a favourable bearing on the amount of the penalty or where applicable, Additional Tax, in settlement."

The Department is committed to a strenuous pursuit of evasion and one possible result of the new provisions is that persons guilty of evasion will find it advantageous to obtain professional assistance to put their tax affairs in order.

The production of revised income statements in a back duty case involves the preparation of accounts from incomplete records which is the subject of

Statement No. 107 of the Hong Kong Society of Accountants. The Department's experience has been that in the vast majority of back duty cases, because of the inadequacy or complete absence of records, construction of revised accounts prepared on conventional lines presents great difficulties so that reassessments may have to be based on Assets Betterment Statements (the "capital computation method of estimating profits" mentioned in paragraph 27 of Statement No. 107) which necessarily involve consideration of the taxpayers' private financial situation.

Cases will however be encountered when the omissions are readily identifiable and can easily be quantified e.g. the omission of profit on the sale of property, the omission of salary from part-time employment, simple understatements of the value of stock in trade, and in these cases a simple statement showing the rate and extent of the omissions will suffice, and the paragraphs which follow will not be applicable.

There is so much variety in the circumstances of each case that it is not practicable to lay down any master plan applicable to all types of investigation. The method of evasion may vary from, for example, a simple undervaluation of stock to the creation of false entries supported by faked vouchers. What follows must, therefore, be regarded as a general outline of the process of investigation which might require adaptation to the needs of particular cases. It represents minimum requirements and does not purport to be exhaustive.

1. OBJECT OF THE INVESTIGATION

It is assumed that the taxpayer has made an admission in general terms that his Tax Returns have been incorrect and has instructed the accountant to act on his behalf. The taxpayer desires to put himself right with the Inland Revenue Department by making a revised statement of his true income which he will certify as his full disclosure. The statement will be carefully examined by the Inland Revenue Department, which has to be satisfied that it is complete.

2. PRELIMINARY STAGE

(a) The Accountant should have unambiguous instructions from his client that this is what he has to do and that he should investigate and report to the Inland Revenue Department. He will make it clear to the client that he must have complete information on all financial transactions and full access to all bank accounts and other financial records. He will require explanations from his client and he must receive the client's full cooperation.

(b) At the outset the client will say in what directions his Tax Returns have been incorrect and what method of concealment or omission has been adopted. The investigation cannot, however, be limited to these particular points. The client may not have covered all his irregular practices either because of forgetfulness or because he is still reluctant to reveal the full extent of his misdeeds. If the latter is the case the client must be protected from the results of his own foolishness by a clear explanation of the serious view the Department will take of a deliberate incomplete disclosure, and the accountant must endeavour to see that the disclosure is complete.

(c) The accountant should at the outset make:—
(i) A list of the business books.
(ii) A list of bank accounts in operation both business and private.
(iii) A list of property, investments and other assets including such items acquired in the name of other persons.
He will also, at the earliest possible stage, require bank accounts which have been closed, and particulars of property invest-ments, etc. which have been sold during the period covered by the investigation.
(iv) A copy and a summary of all Tax Returns which have been submitted and of the assessments made.
(v) A list of the names of all members of the family.

3. *BUSINESS BOOKS*

The extent to which these require scrutiny depends very much on the circumstances of each case. If the accountant has previously audited the books he may still require to re-examine them, viewing them now from the different angle that they are admittedly wrong or incomplete. If the accountant has been newly engaged for the investigation he will wish to know what ground the auditor covered and to examine the books more closely. A full statement of the method of handling and recording business receipts and expenditure, and the individuals by whom it is done, may be useful. It may be appropriate to prepare revised Profit and Loss Accounts and Balance Sheets in accordance with the books.

A complete extract is required of the Drawings Account of each in-dividual concerned, or, in the case of a company director, of his Current Account and also of any Loan Accounts. These accounts will need to be analysed, as described in a later paragraph, and the extract might well be made direct into the analysis form.

Note should be taken of any Loan, Debtor or Creditor Accounts in the names of members of the family.

4. *PERSONAL FINANCES*

(a) The foundation of the investigation of the client's personal affairs is the analysis of his Drawings Account or company Current Account,

Loan Accounts and of all his Bank Accounts or other places where money has been deposited or withdrawn. The Bank Accounts of immediate members of the family such as the taxpayer's wife and dependent children will come into review. The analysis should, of course, cover every item and be in date order. The closing date should of course, correspond with the business accounting date. Suggested headings follow:

Lodgements

Transfers (with note of origin, e.g. from another bank account).

Capital Receipts (with brief note of origin, e.g. sale of property).

Income Receipts (with note of source).

Other Identified Receipts (with brief description).

Unidentified Receipts — specific cheques.

Unidentified Receipts — cash.

Withdrawals

Transfers (with note of destination).

Capital Payments (with brief description, e.g. Purchase of Shares).

Personal Payments (with note of nature, e.g. School Fees, Household).

Other Identified Payments (with brief description).

Unidentified Payments — specific cheques.

Unidentified Payments — cash.

(b) It will be obvious that, on the first analysis there may be numbers of unidentified items, but many of these will be cleared as further accounts are analysed or further information is obtained: the total of all the analysis sheets can be embodied in a summary.

(c) Concurrently with this analysis work it is useful to prepare three schedules — (i) a skeleton annual Assets Statement which can be completed as the items emerge, (ii) a skeleton statement of personal and living expenditure on which identified items can be entered as they emerge, (iii) a skeleton statement of income to be completed as each item is identified.

(d) The Assets Statement would, in the case of an individual proprietor, include all his business and private assets and liabilities.

(e) In the case of a partner, the Statement will contain only the balance of his capital account in the partnership and in the case of a director it will include his shares and the balance of his current and loan accounts.

(f) At this stage, it is desirable to set out an Assets Betterment Statements to which the results from the Schedules described in (c) above can be transferred as they emerge, thus:—

	Year I	Year II
Assets:— Business		
Private		
Total Assets (A)		
Liabilities:—		
Business		
Private		
Total Liabilities (B)		
Net Assets (A) − (B)		
Increase in Net Assets		C
Add:— Disallowable Items in accounts		
Tax Paid		
Capital Loss on sale of assets		
Funds remitted overseas		
Gifts		
Household Expenditure		
Other Private Expenditure		
Unidentified Withdrawals		
		D
Deduct:— Gain on sale of assets		
Income other than business		
		E
Betterment Income/Profits		
(C) + (D) − (E)		
Income Returned		

Discrepancy (Additional Income/Profits)

(g) Before going further, it is essential for the accountant to ask himself the following questions:—

  (i) Have I done everything possible to trace the origin of all money which has been lodged or has appeared in banks or elsewhere?

  (ii) Have I done everything possible to find the destination or purpose of all money which has been withdrawn from banks or elsewhere?

  (iii) Have I found all assets from which income has been received?

  (iv) Have I found the full cost of all known assets and how it was paid?

(v) Have I found what was done with all the proceeds of all the assets which are known to have been sold?

(vi) Have I found what was done with all income known to have been received?

(vii) Have I found all the income from known assets which should have been productive of income?

(viii) Have I traced all known items of expenditure normally paid by cheque, e.g. tax, life assurance, school fees, electricity, gas, rates, etc.?

Examination of these points may further dispose of unidentified items, or lead to other bank accounts necessitating revision of the draft Assets Betterment Statement.

(h) It should now be considered whether the amounts brought out by the analyses are adequate for personal and household expenditure. Any untraced items in (g)(viii) above will have to be brought into account and also exceptional items of expenditure, e.g. holidays, doctors' bills, gifts, etc. What domestic expenditure has normally been paid by cheque, e.g. grocer? Are there regular cheques for these, or have some been paid in cash? What other domestic and personal expenditure is paid in cash? Do the figures reveal an amount of cash available adequate to cover these items? If not, there is a sum to be explained representing this deficiency.

(i) Finally there comes up for consideration the question of the character and treatment of the unidentified lodgements and the unidentified withdrawals. Are these omitted business receipts, unrecorded business payments or personal expenditure: what else could they be? This can only be determined by consideration of the details in each case, by examination of the client, by relation to the type of business, the method of accounting on which the original accounts were based, etc. A decision must be taken on all the available material.

5. FINALISING THE INVESTIGATION

When the matters referred to in paragraphs 4(h) and (i) have been resolved, the draft Assets Betterment Statement will receive its final amendments and the overall result can be examined in the light of probabilities concerning, for example, known profit trends.

6. THE INVESTIGATION REPORT

(a) The accountant can now make his report to the Inland Revenue Department, which should set out briefly what materials he has had, what he has done in regard to business books, and on personal finances, to what extent he has failed to obtain verification in any direction, and what treatment he has adopted in regard to unidentified or doubtful items.

(*b*) His report will be supplemented by the schedules of Assets Statement, Personal and Living Expenditure and Statements of Income, together with any supplementary statements the particular case requires. His detailed analyses and workings need not be copied but should be made available, if required, for examination by the Inland Revenue Department.

7. *CERTIFICATE BY CLIENT*

A certificate by the client should accompany the Report and should be on the following lines:—

CERTIFICATE

I have read the Report dated .... which was explained to me by Mr. .... and I certify that to the best of my knowledge and belief it constitutes a full disclosure of all my income/profits chargeable to tax under the Inland Revenue Ordinance for the period ....
.... to ....

8. *PENALTY*

The Commissioner's practice in relation to the *full* voluntary disclosure of tax evasion is contained in the Financial Secretary's Speech referred to above. However when making an additional assessment under Section 82A the Commissioner may take into account, amongst other factors, the length of time during which the taxpayer has had the use of tax which should have properly been paid to the Hong Kong Government. Finalisation of a case may take a long time and occasionally complaints are made that this part of a penalty has been increased either through no fault of the taxpayer or through procrastination on the part of the Department. Whilst the latter complaint is seldom ever justified, the situation can be avoided if a deposit on account of the estimated final tax liability is made with the Department. Further details may be obtained from a particular Assessor handling the case.

I would also like to take the opportunity to remind practitioners that the law requires that Additional Tax under 82A be assessed by the Commissioner or the Deputy Commissioner personally. For this reason it is regretted that it would not be possible for the Assessor handling the case to indicate the likely level of penalties and the instruction given to Assessors is that at no time should they suggest that agreed assessments made under Section 59 and 60 represent anything other than basic liability exclusive of penalties. Representatives acting on behalf of taxpayers should make this point clear when handling back duty cases so that there can be no possibility of an Assessor being accused of trapping taxpayers into accepting assessments which they regard as excessive.

FEBRUARY 1979

APPENDIX 11

Departmental Interpretation & Practice Notes
No. 12

COMMISSIONS, REBATES AND DISCOUNTS
PAYMENT OF ILLEGAL COMMISSIONS

I think the time is opportune to remind practitioners that the appended circular letters issued by my predecessors are still in force. Following recent prosecutions by the Independent Commission Against Corruption, it has become clear that certain auditors have failed to detect by proper audit procedure, what can at best be described as a failure to distinguish these payments in the accounts and tax computations and at worst a deliberate attempt to mislead the Revenue by misdescribing the payments. In addition, these cases very often involve the submission by the company of what are incorrect Employer's Returns of Remuneration, as details of commissions to persons other than employees are called for in these returns. The loss to Government revenue is in some cases substantial.

2. You are invited to consider whether there are any cases where clients should be advised to take advantage of the statement of practice relating to voluntary disclosures contained in Departmental Interpretation & Practice Notes No. 11 (Elements of a Tax Investigation). Taxpayers who do not, run a grave risk of prosecution under the Inland Revenue Ordinance when, as a result of Departmental enquiries, evidence of concealed illegal commissions is obtained. In addition, the auditor responsible may also be liable to prosecution under Sections 80 and 82 of the Ordinance.

R. V. Giddy,
Commissioner of Inland Revenue.

14th June, 1976.

INLAND REVENUE DEPARTMENT.

15th November, 1960.

To: ALL AUTHORISED REPRESENTATIVES.

Sirs,

RE: COMMISSIONS, REBATES & DISCOUNTS

It has long been known to me that a considerable amount of business in Hong Kong is transacted with the aid of commissions, rebates or discounts (commonly known as "squeeze") usually paid to persons, who for obvious reasons, prefer to remain anonymous.

The consequences of these transactions on the revenue is obvious and it has recently been most forcibly brought to my notice when a firm in Hong Kong was unable to return the names and addresses of recipients of such payments, but were prepared instead to pay tax on them so that the revenue would be protected. This arrangement does not provide a satisfactory or complete answer to the problem but is accepted as a compromise more convenient to the business concerned. Neither does this arrangement relieve the recipient of these payments from his responsibility to return the amount for tax purposes.

In order that all businesses be treated in a like manner instructions have now been issued to Assessors in this Department to add to the chargeable income all such commissions, rebates and discounts. You are therefore asked in future to make the necessary adjustments in respect of such payments in your computations and inform your clients accordingly.

In all cases where in the past it may have been customary for you to show the gross income after deduction of such payments this should cease. The gross income should be returned and such payments should be clearly indicated in your accounts submitted in support of profits returns.

The only exceptions to this rule which the Assessor will accept are:—

(i)   Commissions, rebates and discounts allowed in the ordinary course of trade on a principal to principal basis where it is expected that such commissions, rebates or discounts would be reflected in the accounts of each party to the transaction.

(ii) Commissions, rebates and discounts paid to any individual who is an employee or otherwise of either principal and the separate amounts are disclosed under the name and address of the recipient on the statutory B.I.R. Form No. 56 (Employer's Return).

So that any doubt on this matter will be reduced the Assessors will in future expect that any amounts paid by way of commissions, rebates and discounts will be shown in the accounts and they will add it back for tax purposes where the sum, or any part of it, is not properly vouched as having been received by an individual and returned on the Employer's Return.

Any dispute as to whether such payments are correctly deductible as being wholly and exclusively incurred in the production of profits will continue to be open to the appeal provisions of the Inland Revenue Ordinance, (Cap. 112).

Yours faithfully,

W. J. DRYSDALE,
Commissioner of Inland Revenue.

INLAND REVENUE DEPARTMENT.

27th February, 1967.

Ref. No. HQ 52/225/16

To: ALL AUTHORISED REPRESENTATIVES.

Sirs,

RE: COMMISSIONS, REBATES & DISCOUNTS

Further to the letter sent to all authorised representatives on 15th November 1960, I wish to point out that where there has been an acceptance of the adding back of commissions in cases where the payer is unable to disclose the names and addresses of the recipients, such arrangement is by way of compromise only and is only applicable where the revenue is protected by this action and tax paid accordingly.

2.   This is certainly not the case where a loss is involved or if the basis period were to drop out for assessment purposes. In these circumstances, I consider the payer of commissions must either accept an assessment as agent of the recipients of commissions etc. without the benefit of Section 18B(2), or, disclose the information necessary for assessments to be raised. Failure to accept this basis would be followed by action under Section 51(4)(a) to obtain the necessary information.

Yours faithfully,

A. D. DUFFY,
Commissioner of Inland Revenue.

APPENDIX 12

Departmental Interpretation & Practice Notes
No. 13

INTEREST TAX AND PROFITS TAX ON INTEREST

In view of the enactment of the Inland Revenue (Amendment) (No. 3) Ordinance No. 73/78, it is considered appropriate to restate the departmental view on the taxation of interest and, at the same time, to outline the effect of the amendment. These notes replace the departmental circular of 16 August 1973.

Tax on Interest – the position generally

Interest Tax was first introduced to the Colony in 1947 as one of the various taxes making up the Earnings & Profits Taxes and is levied at the standard rate (currently 15%). The charge to Interest Tax is contained in the provisions of section 28(1) of the Inland Revenue Ordinance, Chapter 112 of the Revised Edition 1975. This section provides, *inter alia,* that –

"28. (1) Interest tax shall, subject to the provisions of this Ordinance, be charged for each year of assessment at the standard rate on the recipient of any sum paid or credited to him in that year being –

(a) interest arising in or derived from the Colony on any debenture, mortgage, bill of sale, deposit, loan, advance or other indebtedness whether evidenced in writing or not;

(b) that part of an annuity payable in the Colony computed and deemed to be interest chargeable to interest tax under the provisions of rule 6 of the Inland Revenue Rules:

Provided that there shall be exempt from interest tax –

(a) any interest paid or payable by Government, a bank licensed under the Banking Ordinance, or a public utility company specified in the Third Schedule which accrues at such rate or rates, not exceeding *5 per cent per annum as the Financial Secretary may specify by notice in the Gazette, in respect of all or any of the above classes;

(b) any interest paid or payable to a bank licensed under the Banking Ordinance or to a corporation carrying on trade or business in the Colony or to the Government;

(c) any interest paid or payable on a Tax Reserve Certificate issued by the Commissioner;

* currently 2½% in the case of banks. [This rate varies regularly. For current rate, see the financial press. – Author]

(*d*) any interest paid or payable to any person carrying on business in the Colony as a pawnbroker within the meaning of, and licensed in accordance with the provisions of, the Pawnbrokers Ordinance or as a money-lender within the meaning of, and registered in accordance with the provisions of, the Money-Lenders Ordinance where such interest is paid or payable to him in the ordinary course of his business as a pawnbroker or money-lender."

The collection procedure is set out in section 29(1) and (2). Assessments are normally made on, and collection effected from the borrower by means of what is generally described as a system of withholding tax. The tax withheld (15%) from interest paid must be remitted to this department within 30 days. Normally, the person making the deduction is obliged to issue the recipient a certificate in the specified form containing an acknowledgment by the Commissioner of the receipt of the deduction, however, a licensed bank or a corporation specified by notice in the Government Gazette need only issue a certificate (in a form approved by the Commissioner) on request of the recipient showing the details of the interest and tax deducted.

It is only interest arising in or derived from the Colony which, subject to the exemptions listed, is subject to Interest Tax (or, for that matter, Profits Tax — however, see the separate section on interest received by financial institutions).

The department takes the view that for the purpose of determining where interest arises in or is derived from, it is the originating cause which almost invariably determines the source, i.e., the provision of credit to the borrower. This view is based on decisions in the following three cases —

COMMISSIONER OR INLAND REVENUE (N.Z.) v. N.V. PHILIPS GLOEILAMPENFABRIEKEN, 10 ATD 435,

C.I.R. v. LEVER BROTHERS & UNILIVER LTD. (1946), 14 SATC 1, AND

COMMISSIONER-GENERAL OF INCOME TAX v. ESSO STANDARD EASTERN INC. (COURT OF APPEAL FOR EAST AFRICA).

If the originating cause is in the Colony, the source of the interest is in the Colony irrespective of the currency in which the loan is denominated, the place of residence of the debtor or the place in which the debtor employs the capital. It should also be noted that whilst the emphasis is on the provision of credit, in some cases such as a mortgage, the originating cause might be the mortgage itself.

In addition, in some cases, the interest may be part and parcel of a trading transaction carried out in Hong Kong, for example, where a Hong Kong manufacturer sells his goods to an overseas buyer on extended credit terms. In this case the interest, just as much as the trading profit, arises in

Hong Kong (see Board of Review Case No. 20/75 and *Studebaker Corporation of Australia Ltd. v. C.O.T., 29 CLR 225*). Where interest, arising in or derived from Hong Kong, is exempt from Interest Tax by virtue of proviso (*b*) to section 28(1), it is charged to Profits Tax by section 15(1)(*f*).

Profits Tax on Interest earned by financial institutions

With effect from the year of assessment 1978-79, the provisions of the Inland Revenue (Amendment) (No. 3) Ordinance No. 73/78, which are set out in full as an Appendix to these Notes, (omitted — Author) will materially affect the position in relation to financial institutions by deeming certain interest to arise in or be derived from Hong Kong from a trade, profession or business carried on in Hong Kong. This will be in addition to interest already charged under section 15(1)(*f*).

The main features of the new deeming subsection are as follows —

(1) The subsection only refers to financial institutions. These are defined as a bank licensed under the Banking Ordinance, a registered deposit-taking company registered under the Deposit-taking Companies Ordinance and an associated company of such bank or deposit-taking company. An associated company is, in turn, defined and is further confined to companies which would themselves have been liable to register as a deposit-taking company had it not been for the exemptions in section 3(2)(*a*) and (*b*) of the Deposit-taking Companies Ordinance. In this connection, reference should be made to section 2(1) of the Deposit-taking Companies Ordinance (Cap. 328) which defines "deposit-taking company" as "a company which carries on a business of taking deposits";

and a "deposit" as —

"a loan of money at interest or repayable at a premium or repayable with any consideration in money or money's worth, but does not include a loan of money upon terms involving the issue of debentures of other securities in respect of which a prospectus has been registered under the Companies Ordinance; and references to the taking of a deposit shall be construed accordingly."

The material part of section 3(2) reads as follows —

"3. This Ordinance shall not apply to the taking of any deposit from —

(*a*) a licensed bank;

(*b*) a registered deposit-taking company:

............"

(2) The subsection only charges interest which arises through or from the carrying on of the business in the Colony.

(3) The provision of the credit outside Hong Kong will no longer in itself take the interest outside the ambit of the charge to Hong Kong Profits Tax.

What is, and what is not, interest arising from the carrying on of business in Hong Kong by the financial institution will be a question of fact based on the totality of the circumstances of each case. Modern international banking is highly complex and as practice will vary from company to company it is not possible for me to lay down anything like a comprehensive formula. At the one end of the spectrum will be the bank which carries on business in Hong Kong and nowhere else and which, having accepted deposits over its counters in Hong Kong, uses part of the proceeds to purchase either foreign interest-bearing securities or to lend to overseas borrowers. Clearly all its profits arise from business carried on in Hong Kong. At the other end of the spectrum will be the case where the operations in Hong Kong are confined to entering the transactions in the books of account. Equally clearly, it could not be claimed that in these circumstances the profit arises from the carrying on of business in Hong Kong. Conversely, if the operations relating to the profit were carried out in Hong Kong the deeming charge would not be frustrated if the transactions were to be entered in the books of an overseas branch of the Hong Kong bank.

Cases will obviously arise which will fall between these two extremes, where it could be said that the profits arise partly from business carried on in Hong Kong and partly from business carried on overseas (e.g., there may have been substantial intervention by an overseas branch) and, in such cases, a reasonable apportionment of the profits would be appropriate.

It is appreciated that financial institutions will wish to know their liability, if any, under the new deeming provision as soon as possible and will no doubt be taking professional advice on the matter, however, I regret that I cannot give anything in the nature of advance tax rulings. The Profits Tax returns for 1978-79 will, of course, be processed in the normal way and normal assessment and objection procedures will apply, nevertheless, I will endeavour to ensure that the processing of the returns is completed as speedily as possible and to this end will be making special staffing arrangements. I am sure, however, that it will be appreciated that it will inevitably take some time for all the cases to be processed.

Financial institutions and their representatives can be of considerable help both to this department and themselves by anticipating requests from the Assessors for the kind of information needed to compute the chargeable profits. In some cases the company accounts (or where appropriate the branch accounts) may have been prepared in such a way, and banking operations conducted in such a way that the total profits disclosed would be subject to Hong Kong tax. Where, however, they are not, and the company is of the opinion that certain of the profits are not chargeable to tax, it will be advisable to furnish information on the operations connected with both the borrowing and the subsequent lending of the funds giving rise to the interest. It cannot be stressed too much that a bank's business does not consist solely of lending money; its business involves borrowing more cheaply than it lends. Material factors will include the place where the money was borrowed, the location of the staff engaged in canvassing and accepting the deposits, the place where the money was lent, the location of the staff engaged in arranging and approving the loans, the place where the interest is receivable; also, although of lesser importance, the currency of the transactions and the place where the transaction was entered in the company's books. It must not however be assumed from this that it is only profit entered in the financial institution's local branch accounts that will be subject to tax. The onus will still be on the company to make a full return of profits chargeable to tax.

Where the bank or the deposit-taking company has been registered under the appropriate Ordinance for only part of the basis period for the year of assessment, the deeming charge will only apply to those profits for that part of the basis period. Similarly, in the case of associated companies (as defined), these companies will only be charged in respect of profits for the basis periods during which the bank or deposit-taking company with which it was associated, was registered under the relevant Ordinances.

The amendment provides for a limited form of relief from double taxation to resident companies. This is by way of deduction from profits brought to charge. It is only available to resident companies, i.e., companies managed and controlled in Hong Kong. Should the company wish to claim relief, the computation should be accompanied by a statement on the place of management and control. Tax of "substantially the same nature as tax imposed under this Ordinance" (see section $16(1)(c)$) includes withholding tax. Apart from payment of foreign tax, the normal rules relating to the deduction of expenses will apply when computing the profits chargeable to tax.

SEPTEMBER 1978

APPENDIX 13

Inland Revenue Departmental Practice

25th August, 1971

Gentlemen,

HONG KONG PROFITS TAX
– LOCALITY OF PROFITS

1. As you may know, in the recent case of Commissioner of Inland Revenue v. International Wood Products Ltd. (Supreme Court of Hong Kong, Appellate Jurisdiction, Inland Revenue Appeal No. 2 of 1971), the Court decided against the Revenue on a question involving the locality of profits derived from commissions received by a Hong Kong company in connection with sales ex-Hong Kong by associated concerns. The Court rejected the mere existence of a business in Hong Kong as indicative of the locality of profits and considered that activities of certain sub-agents, ex-Hong Kong, amounted to operations which in substance gave rise to the Hong Kong company's profits.

2. It has been decided not to challenge the Court's decision and in consequence it has been necessary for me to instruct Assessors that effective from the date of the judgement (16th July, 1971) there is to be a change in Departmental practice in that profits, arising from the following types of operations, will not henceforth be charged to Hong Kong Profits Tax, so long as the profits tax charging section remains unchanged –

    (i) TYPE I Hong Kong registered company holding the "Far East Area" sales representation for a product or group of products sold into the area by principals who are associated concerns, the Hong Kong company and the associates being members of a group under the control of a common Parent Organisation. The Hong Kong company is appointed selling agent for the area, either by formally executed agreements or by a directive from the Parent Organisation and is remunerated by a "commission" on all sales and/or deliveries into the area. The Hong Kong company may either –

        (a) actively solicit orders ex-Hong Kong, on behalf of its principals (i) by sending employee sales representatives overseas for the purpose or (ii) by employing sub-agents overseas; or

        (b) factually do nothing whatsoever, either itself or through sub-agents.

    (ii) TYPE II A similar organisational set-up to Type I, but in this case the Hong Kong company is given sales responsibility for Group products in the "Far East Area" as a principal. Factually, the Hong Kong company is unable to handle all (or possibly any!) of the Group range of products and sales into the area are therefore made and/or delivered by associated concerns. The Hong Kong company receives an "infringement commission" for which it does nothing (except possibly the rendering of some "sales service" ex-Hong Kong).

(iii) TYPE III   A similar organisational set-up to Type I. The Hong Kong company sells Group products in the Colony (profits thereon are, of course, subject to Hong Kong Profits Tax) and in addition receives "commissions" on sales by associated concerns into the "Far East Area". These commissions are paid in pursuance of a Parent Organisation directive. The Hong Kong company has no formal function or contractual position in relation to the associates' sales to the Far East Area i.e. it has no "area responsibility" either as principal, agent or sales representative and renders no service in respect of the commission it receives.

(iv) TYPE IV   A similar organisational set-up to Type I. The Hong Kong company receives service fees for the provision to an overseas affiliate of manufacturing "know-how". The Hong Kong company in fact has no proprietorial rights in the know-how and the information is provided direct to the affiliate by the Parent Organisation overseas. The Hong Kong company renders no other services in respect of the fee it receives.

(v) TYPE V   A similar organisation set-up to Type I. The Hong Kong company buys as principal group products from overseas associates and maintains a stock-of-goods in the Colony. An associate company ex-Hong Kong negotiates and concludes contracts and accepts orders on behalf of the Hong Kong company. The Hong Kong company does not receive or solicit orders directly from customers but fulfils orders from stocks upon receipt of advices from the overseas associate. Sale proceeds are received by the Hong Kong company in Hong Kong.

3. It will be observed that, in the case of each of the above types, the operations which give rise to the profits now to be excluded from charge are essentially operations outside the Colony. Where, however, commissions, fees, profits on sales, etc. relate to sales to, or services rendered to, Hong Kong customers the resultant profits/losses will continue to be brought to charge to Hong Kong Profits Tax.

4. It will be appreciated that as a result of the decision to cease assessing profits from operations ex-Hong Kong falling within the above categories

it will be necessary for Assessors to institute searching enquiries in a number of cases in order to establish whether they fall into one of the types now considered not liable to Hong Kong Profits Tax. I feel sure that I can rely upon your co-operation in dealing expeditiously with Assessors' questions.

5. Section 70A Claims

As I have said the decision to discontinue assessing transactions falling within the abovementioned types represents a change in Departmental practice. You will understand therefore that where such transactions have previously been assessed and the assessments made were, at 16th July, 1971, final and conclusive pursuant to Section 70 of the Ordinance, Assessors will not now be prepared to entertain claims that there has been an excessive charge to tax by reason of an error in terms of Section 70A.

Yours faithfully,

A.D. DUFFY,
Commissioner of Inland Revenue.

ADD/VAL/dt

INDEX

*Examples used in this text are listed under "Examples"
and arranged by subject.*